MW01708887

A PART OF THE PEACE

CANADA AMONG NATIONS 1994

A PART OF THE PEACE

Maureen Appel Molot
and
Harald von Riekhoff
Editors

THE NORMAN PATERSON SCHOOL
OF INTERNATIONAL AFFAIRS

Carleton University Press
Ottawa
1994

©Carleton University Press Inc. 1994

Carleton Public Policy Series # 14

Printed and bound in Canada

Canadian Cataloguing in Publication Data

Canada among nations
1984–
Annual.
1994 ed.: A part of the peace
Each vol. also has a distinctive title.
Produced by the Norman Paterson School of International Affairs of Carleton University.
Includes bibliographical references.
ISSN 0832-0683

ISBN 0-88629-226-3 (1994 ed., bound)
ISBN 0-88629-227-1 (1994 ed., pbk)

1. Canada–Foreign relations–1945– –Periodicals. 2. Canada–Politics and government–1984– –Periodicals. 3. Canada–Politics and government–1980–84–Periodicals. I. Norman Paterson School of International Affairs.
FC242.C345 327.71 C86-031285-2
F1034.2.C36

Carleton University Press
160 Paterson Hall
Carleton University
1125 Colonel By Drive
Ottawa, Ontario
K1S 5B6

Distributed in Canada by
Oxford University Press Canada,
70 Wynford Drive,
Don Mills, Ontario,
Canada. M3C 1J9
(416) 441-2941

Cover design: Aerographics Ottawa
Typeset by: Carleton Production Centre, Nepean

Acknowledgements

Carleton University Press acknowledges the support extended to its publishing programme by the Canada Council and the Ontario Arts Council.

The Press would also like to thank the Department of Canadian Heritage, Government of Canada, and the Government of Ontario through the Ministry of Culture, Tourism and Recreation, for their assistance.

Table of Contents

Civil Strife and Efforts to Restore Peace

List of Tables and Charts

List of Contributors

Alan S. Alexandroff is a research associate in the Centre for International Studies, University of Toronto.

Jocelyn Coulon is international affairs editor for *Le Devoir*.

John M. Curtis is in the Department of Foreign Affairs and International Trade, and The Norman Paterson School of International Affairs, Carleton University, Ottawa.

Wendy Dobson is a professor and director, Centre for International Business at the University of Toronto.

Charles Doran is the Andrew W. Mellon Professor of International Relations in the School for Advanced International Studies, Johns Hopkins University.

John M. Fraser is a University Visitor in the School of Canadian Studies, Carleton University

Nancy Gordon is Director of Communications at CARE.

Tom Keating is an associate professor and chair in the Department of Political Science, University of Alberta.

W. Andrew Knight is a lecturer in the Department of Political Science, Bishop's University.

Jeanne Kirk Laux is a professor in the Department of Political Science, University of Ottawa.

David Long is an assistant professor in The Norman Paterson School of International Affairs, Carleton University.

Alexander Moens is an assistant professor in the Department of Political Science, Simon Fraser University.

Maureen Appel Molot is a professor in the Department of Political Science and a professor and director of The Norman Paterson School of International Affairs, Carleton University.

Teresa Rakowska-Harmstone is a professor in the Department of Political Science, Carleton University.

Harald von Riekhoff is a professor in the Department of Political Science, Carleton University.

Robert Wolfe is in the Department of Foreign Affairs and International Trade, and Centre for International Relations, Queen's University.

Glossary

Acronyms for *Canada Among Nations 1994*:

ACC	Administrative Committee on Co-ordination (UN)
AD	Anti-dumping
AEC	Atomic Energy Commission (UN)
AMS	Aggregate Measure of Support (GATT)
APEC	Asia Pacific Economic Cooperation Forum
ARRC	Allied Command Europe Rapid Reaction Corps (NATO)
ASEAN	Association of South East Asian Nations
ASG	Assistant Secretary General (UN)
BIS	Bank for International Settlements
CAP	Common Agricultural Policy (EU)
CCIC	Canadian Council for International Co-operation
CEE	Central and Eastern Europe
CFE	Conventional Forces in Europe Treaty
CFSP	Common Foreign and Security Policy (EU)
CIDA	Canadian International Development Agency
CIS	Commonwealth of Independent States
CNR	Committee on Natural Resources
CPC	Committee on Program and Coordination (UN)
CRT	Constant Readiness Troops (Russia)
CSCE	Conference on Security and Cooperation in Europe
CSO	Committee of Senior Officials
CSTD	Centre for Science and Technology for Development (UN)
CTC	Centre on Transnational Corporations
CUSO	Canadian University Service Overseas
CVD	Countervailing Duty
DAC	Development Assistance Committee (OECD)
DEMOS	Democratic United Opposition of Slovenia
DFAIT	Department of Foreign Affairs and International Trade
DIEC	Development and International Economic Cooperation (UN)
DIESA	Department of International Economic and Social Affairs (UN)

DPI	Department for Public Information (UN)
DPSCA	Department of Political and Security Council Affairs (UN)
DRAM	Dynamic Random Access Memory
DTCD	Department for Technical Cooperation for Development (UN)
EBRD	European Bank for Reconstruction and Development
EC	European Community
ECJ	European Court of Justice
ECOSOC	Economic and Social Council (UN)
ECU	European Currency Unit
EDI	European Defence Identity
EFTA	European Free Trade Area
EIB	European Investment Bank
EMI	European Monetary Institute
EMS	European Monetary System
EMU	Economic and Monetary Union
EPC	European Political Cooperation
EPZ	Export Processing Zone
ERM	Exchange Rate Mechanism
EU	European Union
FDI	Foreign Direct Investment
FSU	Former Soviet Union
FTA	Free Trade Agreement (Canada-U.S.)
FTZ	Free Trade Zone
GA	General Assembly (UN)
GATS	General Agreement on Trade in Services
GATT	General Agreement on Tariffs and Trade
GDP	Gross Domestic Product
GEMS	Global Environmental Monitoring System (UN)
G-7	Group of Seven
G-24	Group of Twenty-Four (UN)
G-77	Group of Seventy-Seven (UN)
HDZ	Croatian Democratic Alliance
IAEA	International Atomic Energy Agency (UN)
IBRD	International Bank for Reconstruction and Development
ICSC	International Civil Service Commission (UN)

IDA	International Development Agency (UN)
IDRC	International Development Research Centre
IFIs	International Financial Institutions
IMF	International Monetary Fund
IRPTC	International Register of Potentially Toxic Chemicals (UN)
IRTM	Investment-related trade measures
ITO	International Trade Organization
JNA	Yugoslav National Army
LCY	League of Communists (Yugoslavia)
LDP	Liberal Democratic Party (Russia)
LIUP	Local Industry Upgrading Program
MFA	Multi-Fibre Agreement (GATT)
MFN	Most Favoured Nation
MINURSO	UN Mission for the Referendum in Western Sahara
NACC	North Atlantic Cooperation Council (NATO)
NAFTA	North American Free Trade Agreement
NAM	Non-Aligned Movement (UN)
NATO	North Atlantic Treaty Organization
NGOs	Non-Governmental Organizations
NIEs	Newly Industrializing Economies
NIEO	New International Economic Order
NIST	National Institute of Standards and Technology (U.S.)
NKAO	Nagorno-Karabakh Autonomous Province
NPT	Non-Proliferation Treaty
OAS	Organization of American States
ODA	Official Development Assistance
ODF	Official Development Financing
OECD	Organization for Economic Cooperation and Development
OMA	Orderly Market Arrangement
ONUC	UN Operation in the Congo
ONUCA	UN Observer Group in Central America
ONUSAL	UN Observer Mission in El Salvador
ORCI	Office for Research and Collection of Information (UN)
PAFTA	Pacific Free Trade Area

PHARE	Poland and Hungary Assistance for Restructuring Economies
PPBB	Programming, Planning and Budgeting Board (UN)
PPBES	UN Planning, Programming, Budgeting and Evaluative System
R&D	Research and Development
RDF	Rapid Deployment Forces
REE	Renaissance Eastern Europe
SACEUR	Supreme Allied Command in Europe
SAF	Soviet Armed Forces
SALs	Structural Adjustment Loans
SEA	Single European Act
SEMATECH	Semiconductor Manufacturing Consortium (U.S.)
SHAPE	Supreme Headquarters Allied Powers Europe
SMEs	Small and Medium-sized Enterprises
SRF	Strategic Rocket Forces (Russia)
STA	Semiconductor Trade Agreement (U.S.-Japan)
START	Strategic Arms Reduction Talks
TRIMs	Trade-Related Investment Measures
TRIPs	Trade-Related Intellectual Property Rights
UN	United Nations
UNAMIC	UN Advance Mission in Cambodia
UNAVEM	UN Angola Verification Mission
UNCED	UN Conference on the Environment and Development
UNCLOS	UN Conference on the Law of the Sea
UNCTAD	UN Conference on Trade and Development
UNCTC	UN Centre on Transnational Corporations
UNDOF	UN Disengagement Observer Force (Golan Heights)
UNDP	United Nations Development Program
UNEF	UN Emergency Force (Sinai)
UNEP	UN Environmental Programme
UNFPA	UN Fund for Population Activities
UNHCR	United Nations High Commissioner for Refugees
UNIDO	United Nations Industrial Development Organization
UNIFIL	UN Interim Force in Lebanon
UNIIMOG	UN Iran-Iraq Military Observer Group

UNIKOM	UN Iraq-Kuwait Observation Mission
UNITAF	Unified Task Force (Somalia)
UNOSOM	UN Operation in Somalia
UNPROFOR	United Nations Protection Force (ex-Yugoslavia)
UNSCEAR	UN Scientific Committee on the Effects of Atomic Radiation
UNTAC	UN Transition Authority in Cambodia
UNTAG	UN Transition Assistance Group (Namibia)
USG	Under-Secretary General (UN)
USITC	United States International Trade Commission
VERs	Voluntary Export Restraints
VIE	Voluntary Import Expansion
WCF	Working Capital Fund (UN)
WEU	Western European Union
WHO	World Health Organization
WTO	World Trade Organization

Preface

This is the tenth volume on Canada in international affairs produced by The Norman Paterson School of International Affairs. The chapters in this book analyze and assess different aspects of Canada's external relations and the setting that shapes Canadian policy formulation, focusing on the period since the beginning of 1993. Our purpose is to stimulate debate about appropriate choices for Canada, a task particularly timely as the Liberal government embarks on a multifaceted review of foreign and defence policies.

The theme of this year's edition is "A Part of the Peace," a vantage point which captures both the tensions of the current global environment and the financial realities which are increasingly constraining Canada's options for participation in international affairs. The articles touch on specific conflicts—those in Bosnia, Somalia, Cambodia, and the former Soviet Union—and their impact on Canada, the strengths and weaknesses of multilateral and regional institutions such as the United Nations, the General Agreement on Tariffs and Trade, and the European Union, and Canada's role in and relationship to them, and the economic challenges facing Canada in terms of its own economic recovery, its ties to various trading partners, and its assistance to Eastern Europe.

Financial support for this volume has been provided by the Cooperative Security Program of the Department of Foreign Affairs and International Trade, the Social Sciences and Humanities Research Council of Canada, and The Norman Paterson School of International Affairs.

Brenda Sutherland has performed her now-legendary role of supervising the initial editing of the manuscript. Her assistance has been invaluable and the editors are happy to acknowledge their debt to her. Janet Doherty organized the authors' workshop and maintained continuous liaison with the authors. Our thanks to her for her willingness to help with the project from its inception to its conclusion. Carleton University Press is again publishing *Canada Among Nations* and we are pleased by our continuing association with the Press. Michael Penner provided research assistance and help with the glossary. In addition to the volume's listed contributors, Gerald Wright was an active participant in the workshop discussions. The editors are indebted to him for sharing his special insights on the policy process and his overall expertise on the Mulroney government's foreign policy priorities. We are pleased to acknowledge the editoral and production assistance of Anne Winship, David Lawrence and Diane Mew. We would also like to thank Pauline Adams for assistance with the final manuscript.

Our hope is that *A Part of the Peace* contributes to the important current debate over future directions for Canadian foreign policies.

Maureen Appel Molot
Harald von Riekhoff
Ottawa, March 1994

Introduction and Overview

1 Introduction: A Part of the Peace

Harald von Riekhoff
Maureen Appel Molot

A PART OF THE PEACE, the title of this year's edition of *Canada Among Nations,* is an inversion of the title of Joseph Nye's well-known book, *Peace in Parts,* which dealt with regional integration in Western Europe and other parts of the world.[1] Writing at the end of the 1960s, Nye recognized the sharp dichotomy between the global East-West confrontation and other forms of international conflict, on the one hand, and the emergence of islands of regional peace and cooperation, where Karl Deutsch's concept of a security community seemed to have taken firm root, on the other. Our title deconstructs Nye's original one in order to emphasize the distinction that we see in today's world: what Nye identified was effective integration in a given region; what we see is partial, albeit often tenuous, success in multilateral efforts to promote peace (e.g., Namibia, Cambodia, and growing cooperation between the North Atlantic Treaty Organization [NATO] and former Warsaw Pact members); to protect basic human rights (e.g., Central America and Somalia); and to promote economic prosperity (e.g., the North American Free Trade Agreement [NAFTA] and the conclusion of the Uruguay Round).

The success in these various spheres has, at best, been partial. Continuing uncertainty and complexity mark the post-Cold War environment. The tragic and brutal civil war in Bosnia continues and there is evidence of growing conflict within and between republics of the former Soviet Union. While human conditions have improved in Somalia as the result of the United Nations (UN) humanitarian enforcement action, as Nancy Gordon's chapter discusses, no comprehensive political settlement has been achieved and anarchy continues. In view of the obvious failure to create an effective European security structure after the Cold War, Alexander Moens, one of the book's contributors, has suggested that "A False Start to the Peace," rather than *A Part of the Peace,* might be a more appropriate title for this volume.

A Part of the Peace can be conceptualized in at least four different ways. First, it can be viewed as a partial or fragmented peace in the sense of an abatement of conflict which falls short of a comprehensive peace settlement. The current situation in Cambodia following the 1993 elections may qualify as a partial peace, although assessments on the prospects of ending inter-faction violence in Cambodia vary sharply. Second, a part of the peace can refer to significant progress in a prolonged peace process short of reaching its ultimate goal. The symbolic handshake between Prime Minister Rabin of Israel and Chairman Arafat of the Palestine Liberation Organization (PLO) on the steps of the White House on September 13, 1993, coupled with an understanding on limited self-rule for Palestinians in Gaza and Jericho, may denote such an instalment in the agonizingly tortuous and difficult process of peace-building between Israelis and Palestinians.

Third, a part of the peace can be defined in functional terms as a cooperative arrangement which makes some progress in some areas but fails to resolve problems in others. The successful conclusion of the Uruguay Round of multilateral trade negotiations in December 1993 will safeguard the survival of a liberal multilateral trade regime and holds considerable promise for easing the strain on the economies of several advanced industrial states; however, it does little to redress the fundamental economic imbalance between members of the First and Third World and thus holds no olive branch for North-South relations. Similarly, as is noted in David Long's chapter, the European Union (EU) after Maastricht is at best a partial peace, as the ultimate realization of monetary union and of a common European foreign and security policy is very much left in doubt. Finally, and from our perspective, critical, a part of the peace describes Canada's part—that is to say its stake and involvement—in various multilateral institutions and cooperative arrangements after the end of the Cold War.

The questions addressed in this year's volume of *Canada Among Nations* are fourfold:

- what shape might the post-Cold War political settlement take?
- what progress has been made at either the global or the regional level in resolving economic conflict?
- what are the principal threats to peace and how are they being addressed?

– in how much of the peace will Canada be able to afford to participate?

The purpose of this introduction is to review briefly the range of the challenges to global peace and to alert the reader to the way in which these issues are reflected in the specific chapters of *A Part of the Peace*. Common to each of the chapters is a consideration of the implications of the events discussed for Canada and the role played by Canada during 1993 in addressing these challenges to peace. The topics discussed in *A Part of the Peace* will be among those discussed during the Liberal government's foreign policy and defence reviews which are now under way. Prominent during the review will be the need to consider the limits that real budgetary constraints will impose on future Canadian foreign policy choices and activities.

The Nature of Peace After The Cold War

The international security order that emerged after World War Two was, at best, a partial one; moreover, it was not a peace achieved by great power policing under UN auspices, as envisaged by those who drafted the UN Charter at San Francisco. The principal sources of the long peace, to use John Gaddis's much-cited term, were bipolarity, nuclear weapons, and attendant deterrence.[2] Following the potentially catastrophic Cuban missile crisis, efforts were made by both sides to stabilize deterrence by adding some forms of reassurance in terms of arms control measures and improved East-West communication and crisis management procedures.[3] In comparison with its intended role, the United Nations was a distinct under-achiever with respect to preserving international peace and security during the Cold War era, operating more as a handmaiden than a principal actor. Despite this shortcoming, the UN played a useful and often behind the scenes part in preventive diplomacy and conflict resolution/settlement in line with Chapter VI of the UN Charter. As well, the UN invented peacekeeping as a means of insulating local wars, most of them in the Third World, to prevent super-power entanglement and consequent globalization of the conflict.

With the demise of the Cold War, the new international system is less *bipolar* than *bizonal*, without the functional parallelism and relative power balance inherent in a bipolar system. Seasoned analysts have very different views on whether the world's democracies have a responsibility for, or will be able to have much impact on, the wide array of global challenges. Canada will obviously be directly implicated by the decisions of the major actors and will have to determine its own position on the issues. Echoing Charles Dickens, Max Singer and Aaron Wildavsky speak of "a tale of two worlds."[4] On the one end of the scale, there are zones of peace, encompassing the prosperous democracies of West Europe, North America, Japan, and the Antipodes, which collectively represent no more than 15 percent of the world's population. The dominating characteristic of the peace zones, or zone of civility as Kal Holsti styles it in the context of post-Cold War European security,[5] is that its members "will not go to war with one another and that each country's safety and bargaining power will not depend on its military forces or its position in a delicate balance of power."[6] In sharp contrast to the former there exist the much more populous zones of turmoil, which encompass the states of the former Soviet Union, the Balkans, and most of the developing countries of the Third World. Members of the zones of turmoil are characterized by lower levels of economic prosperity, fragile or non-existent democratic regimes, and a distinctly greater potential for large-scale domestic violence and inter-state war than exists for occupants of the peace zones. Singer and Wildavsky, who look at the world in starkly dichotomous terms, take a rather negative perspective on whether the United States and other democracies can adopt effective policies that will reduce the instability and potential for civil and inter-state war in the zones of turmoil.

Zbigniew Brzezinski's analysis of the current global system reviews the rise and demise of totalitarianism in the twentieth century and then focuses on the changes wrought by technology.[7] The world has become more intimate at the same time as it has become more congested. Political awareness is rising but it is "emerging in the context of continued, and in some respects, even widening socioeconomic disparities."[8] In contrast to Singer and Wildavsky, Brzezinski contends that the United States and other democracies have a responsibility to cooperate to promote the emergence of a common global community and improve the quality of life in those parts of the world where people are suffering. He argues passionately, however, that unless all of the developed market economies, but particularly the United States, address the moral decay within their own societies, they, and most certainly the United States, will not be able to exercise credible leadership.

Elements of the bizonal division of the world, as sketched here, existed prior to the demise of the Cold War. But conflicts in the zones of turmoil were overshadowed and suppressed by the superordinate conflict between the two super-powers; moreover, to most Western observers, the Soviet Union appeared as a pillar of stability and permanence. Its slide into the zone of turmoil began with the unravelling of Gorbachev's reform program. It is not without irony that so soon after the end of the Cold War, the cleavage between the zone of civility and the zone of turmoil threatens to create a new division in Europe. The new fault-line may not be politically as rigid as in the days of the Cold War, nor does it geographically replicate the former Iron Curtain as it has moved eastward. Western Europe and Scandinavia form the core of the zone of peace. In all probability Central European states such as the Czech Republic, Hungary, Poland, and Slovakia, and perhaps the Baltic States, will join the zone of peace once they observe the principles "of sovereign equality, non-use or threat of force, consultations, reciprocity, and the peaceful settlement of disputes—all key norms promoting civility between nations."[9] Jeanne Kirk Laux's chapter in this volume outlines the economic commitment Canada and other Organization for Economic Cooperation and Development (OECD) members have made to enhance the likelihood that the states of Central and Eastern Europe will make the successful transition to Europe's zone of stability.

The situation facing the successor states of the Soviet Union and the Balkans appears to be substantially different from that of the Central European ones. The former show a higher propensity for traditional territorial and border disputes (e.g., the dispute over the status of Crimea between Russia and Ukraine) and have less well-developed procedures to resolve them; there is a greater potential for inter-ethnic strife and conflicts between different religious, cultural, and linguistic identity groups; and the severe economic dislocations following the collapse of communism threaten social upheaval. Given all of these factors of instability, one may risk the generalization of designating this area as Europe's zone of turmoil.

Intermittent wars in several republics of the former Soviet Union and the protracted and brutal civil war in Bosnia-Herzegovina, now in its second year, have made painfully evident the failure of Europe as a whole to evolve into an integral zone of peace as was originally anticipated during the brief spell of post-Cold War euphoria and codified in the 1990 Conference on Security and Cooperation in Europe (CSCE) Paris Charter. In his post-Cold War survey of Europe, Van Evera identifies nine potential border disputes in Europe and thirteen ethnic groups (not counting the former Yugoslavia) which may seek independence or be claimed by others.[10] Given the current preoccupation with finding a post-Cold War security order for Europe, it appears altogether appropriate that almost half of the chapters in this volume concentrate on the European security problematique or at least raise it obliquely in discussing other international issues.

As Teresa Rakowska-Harmstone argues in her chapter, the disintegration of the Soviet Union has left a complex legacy of instability. All of the Soviet successor states have large minorities. The newly created states are pursuing a vigorous strategy of nation-building to cement their formal status as sovereign and independent states. This strategy of nation-building threatens the national and civil rights of minorities and consequently undermines their loyalty to the new state authorities and encourages secessionist movements. The Russian Federation, in turn, regards these successor states—collectively styled the "near abroad"—as an historically legitimate and exclusive Russian sphere of interest. The need to promote specific Russian national interests in the "near abroad," to prevent destabilization in those regions and to preclude any interference from third parties, has given rise to the Russian equivalent of the Monroe Doctrine. Since the break-up of the Soviet Union, Russia has intervened militarily in a number of ethnic conflicts beyond its proper boundaries. Even though these self-styled Russian "peacekeeping" missions on its periphery were not conducted under a mandate from the United Nations or the CSCE, they enjoyed a degree of international support because they were seen as promoting stability in a zone of turmoil where other international organizations feared to tread.

The European Security Architecture

There exist numerous drafts for a European security architecture, but no convincing master plan has yet emerged from this intellectual growth industry. A few proposals from this rich menu of offerings might be mentioned briefly: the creation of a pan-European collective security system; the expansion of NATO to include all of Central and Eastern Europe in an unprecedented metamorphosis from an alliance to a collective security system; and the organization of diverse partnerships for "Eurokeeping," as discussed in Alexander Moens' chapter, that might involve various combinations and permutations of willing and/or able participants such as NATO, the twinned European Union/West European Union (EU/WEU), the Conference on Security and Co-operation in Europe, and the United Nations. Finally, there is the neo-realist version of a European security order based on a world of nuclear plenty, with Germany and Ukraine figuring as the "logical" candidates for nuclear weapons.[11] To some analysts, this last proposal suggests a blueprint for disaster rather than a plan for a stable European security order. In the face of a plethora of competing security proposals, the bewildered reader may sympathize with Emperor Franz Josef who at the end of his life complained that he had been spared nothing.

Post-Cold War Europe has seen the emergence of a multiplicity of security organizations with imprecisely defined mandates, overlapping and in some cases competing tasks, and, with the exception of NATO, insufficient military capability to discharge their ambitious roles. It appears highly probable that institutional pluralism will continue to be the prevailing norm of European security for the near future. For all the ambiguity and uncertainty which this will create, preserving a pluralism of security institutions may be the safest response to a highly diffuse and shifting security situation in Europe. In this connection, it is interesting to note Kratochwil's criticism of the League of Nations because it provided only a single institutional framework for international security rather than several alternative arrangements.[12]

The current winners in this security sweepstake are NATO, the EU/WEU, the CSCE, and the UN. The UN and the CSCE bear considerable resemblance to each other insofar as they are the most representative of the relevant security institutions, enjoy the greatest legitimacy, and have the most encompassing agenda linking security with human rights and economic well-being. Their greatest shortcomings in terms of the new European security environment are their lack of a stand-by military enforcement capacity, shortage of financial resources, and in the case of the CSCE an inappropriate decision-making structure. Until these deficiencies are remedied, the UN and the CSCE will probably have to rely on partnerships with other organizations or on "renting" military forces from willing supplier states in order to discharge their mandate.

None of the more serious European security plans has argued for the abolition of NATO. Speculation of its death, like that of Mark Twain, seems somewhat premature. Unlike the other candidates, NATO has military forces in being, command and communication structures, plans, and the ability to launch military enforcement actions at a moment's notice. Charles Glaser argues that NATO is still the best security organization to deal with three possible types of security threat facing Europe: the possibility of a renewed threat from a militant nationalist Russia; the militarized inter-border disputes in Central and Eastern Europe; and concerns about a disproportionately powerful Germany.[13] Significantly, Glaser does not include ethnic conflicts in Eastern Europe. As Holsti cautions, NATO's "capacity to deal with ethnic violence, secessionist movements, and potential armed conflicts in Europe's peripheries remains to be seen."[14]

Despite the obvious downsizing of NATO's military capacity after the Cold War, in the short run at least, NATO can register two windfall gains that may enhance its continued *raison d'être*. First, is its attractiveness to countries in Central and Eastern Europe that have expressed the desire to join. Rather than agree to a widened membership, NATO has so far only provided some meagre compensation in the form of bilateral cooperation between NATO and former Warsaw Pact members under the North Atlantic Cooperative Council (NACC) and the Partnership for Peace, the latter allowing for direct military consultation, joint manoeuvres, training, and peacekeeping. The second windfall was the development, in 1993, of an unprecedented partnership between the UN and NATO for peacekeeping in the former Yugoslavia. John Fraser's chapter describes in detail the steps by which this unusual partnership emerged. The UN Security Council resolutions provide the underlying legitimacy for the operation, and the UN maintains blue-helmeted peacekeepers on the ground. In turn, NATO supports the operation with a stand-by enforcement capability. Since April 1993 NATO has promised air coverage for endangered UN peacekeepers; it has agreed to enforce the UN no-fly zone over Bosnia; and it has threatened air strikes for the protection of the civilian population in the designated safety zones. Since the middle of February 1994 it seemed as if all three types of NATO enforcement actions might be executed simultaneously. The no-fly zone was actively enforced on February 28, when four Serbian light bombers, after flying a bombing raid on Bosnian targets, were shot down by U.S. F-16 fighters. This event marked the first time in its history that NATO had actually engaged in direct military combat. The ultimatum to the Bosnian Serbs to withdraw their heavy artillery from the immediate perimeter of Sarajevo was complied with, thus removing the immediate necessity for air strikes. On April 10 and the week following, NATO aircraft conducted limited bombing raids on ground targets to protect UN peacekeepers who had come under direct fire and to halt the advance of the Bosnian Serb forces on the designated UN "safe area" of Gorazde.

The final assessment of the utility of making NATO an active partner in peacekeeping will, no doubt, depend heavily on the success or failure of peacekeeping/peacemaking in Bosnia. As Moens notes in his chapter, after all the frustrating debates about NATO's out-of-area role, it arrived quietly through the back door as the result of the joint peacekeeping enterprise. To many analysts and politicians, NATO's involvement in the conflict in the former Yugoslavia seemed far more natural than the financially insolvent, over-extended and under-equipped UN launching a complex European peacekeeping mission at the doorstep of the world's most advanced military organization. But peacekeeping missions conducted solely under NATO auspices would lack the legitimacy of a UN-sanctioned operation; moreover, they would be subject to criticism for being neither universal in membership nor politically neutral. With respect to the importance of neutrality, we should take note of Jocelyn Coulon's chapter on Cambodia, which argues that several UN national contingents were seen to be openly partial to one or other of the four Cambodian factions, thus drawing attention to the fragile nature of UN neutrality.

The EU/WEU has the material prerequisites to become a viable substitute for NATO. One cannot be as categorical in making predictions about the ability of EU members to muster the political will and to create the necessary decision-making structures to make the WEU an effective military instrument. David Long's chapter on Europe after Maastricht focuses with great precision on the ambiguities and divisions on the formulation of a common European foreign and security policy. In his chapter on a new security strategy for Europe, Alexander Moens favours institutional pluralism and cautions against a hyper-UN strategy in Europe that would place all our security eggs in the UN basket. Moens calls for a pragmatic division of military resources between NATO and the WEU in giving substance to the so-called stability pact which French Prime Minister Balladur announced in 1993. The essence of the Balladur Plan is a meaningful trade-off between credible boundary guarantees and proper protection for national minorities. In this trade-off, the Western powers from the zone of peace would cooperate in arrangements that would make all European boundaries inviolable. In exchange, the states of Central and Eastern Europe would offer effective guarantees for the rights of minorities within their territorial jurisdiction.

The Balladur Plan is not without appeal as it combines the two central security issues in Eastern Europe: the protection of boundaries and of minorities, both of which are part of the ongoing CSCE mandate. What promises to make the Balladur Plan different from CSCE endeavours is its formalization and the use of concrete guarantees in place of declarations of good intentions. The prospects of creatively implementing the Balladur Plan appear, to say the least, very daunting. Even if NATO and the WEU were prepared to act in unison in giving substance to the plan, one must question whether NATO, which has so far refused to extend its membership eastward, would commit itself to guarantee the territorial status quo in Eastern Europe, all the more as a guarantee under the stability pact might also commit the NATO/WEU members to intervene militarily to uphold minority treaties that had been violated. It is very doubtful that members of the zone of peace would undertake such a massive and open-ended commitment. Not only would the West shy away from such unprecedented commitment, but the governments of the East European states might also not be in a position to give viable guarantees for the protection of minorities, even if they should so desire, in the face of the explosive ethnic tensions and violence which may defy control by governments.

Multilateralism After The Cold War

The framers of the international order after World War Two were committed to applying the principle of multilateralism to both international security and economic relations as a means to avoid the tragic repetition of competitive bilateralism which had marked the period between the two world wars. In the security sphere, this led to the creation of a modified system of collective security under the United Nations. When this failed to materialize, some nations improvised a fall-back solution by establishing multilateral defence arrangements on a regional basis like NATO. In the economic sphere, the principle of multilateralism guided the formation of international financial and trading institutions such as the World Bank, the International Monetary Fund (IMF), and the General Agreement on Tariffs and Trade (GATT).

The multilateralism which evolved after 1945, "was constructed according to the principles of indivisibility, generalized norms binding upon all members, and diffuse reciprocity."[15] Multilateralism in practice limits the power of discrimination and discretion normally available to statecraft. At a minimum, multilateralism means that the interests of other members of the institution or regime are taken into consideration before any action is taken that might impact on others. In the economic sphere, as Keohane suggests, multilateral institutions are "designed to support, supplement, or supplant a world market economy."[16]

In analyzing multilateralism after the Cold War, Robert Cox draws attention to the widening cleavage between economic multilateralism, perceived as support for a liberal economic order that is located primarily in institutions such as the World Bank and the IMF, and political multilateralism centred in a reform-minded UN General Assembly which is numerically dominated by developing countries.[17] Within the United Nations system, multilateralism may have reached crisis dimensions. During the Reagan administration, American opposition to the policies and aspirations of the majority of UN members prompted a form of financial boycott of the entire UN system and outright withdrawal from specific agencies such as UNESCO. This had a crippling impact on UN morale and operations, including peacekeeping. During the Bush administration, particularly during the Gulf crisis and war, the United States moved from a position of bypassing or paralysing the organization to one of dominating it by making it an instrument of U.S. policies. In light of this recent experience, Cox questions how the principle of multilateralism might be reconciled with the national interests of the great powers. Multilateralism could be weakened either by its rejection by the most powerful states or by its unrestricted instrumental use by them.

Two chapters in this volume, in particular, focus on the role of the UN in post-Cold War multilateralism. Tom Keating discusses the growing demands on the UN system for more assertive and interventionist activity to deal with sources of conflict, human rights abuses, and environmental degradation. Andrew Knight's contribution, in turn, assesses the ability of the UN to initiate the necessary administrative and budgetary reforms to cope with increased demands. Knight provides an exhaustive analysis of the past record of UN reforms. He distinguishes between the reflexive process of change by which the UN adapts creatively to exogenous pressures, and the process of purposive change which involves conscious and deliberate efforts by the UN to reform the operations of the organization from within. Knight regards a synthesis between the reflexive and purposive approaches as the best method for finding creative solutions to the UN's cascading problems. But if such a synthesis were to be achieved, it is difficult to escape the pessimistic impression that even the most judicious form of UN reform will be unable to redress the institution's central dilemma—that is, downsizing its establishment through administrative and managerial reform precisely at a time when the UN is asked to expand its operations in the spheres of peacekeeping/peacemaking, human rights, and the environment.

The UN's direct supervision of the disarmament of Iraq following the Gulf War and its involvement in a massive humanitarian enforcement action in Somalia, which is the focus of Nancy Gordon's chapter, are only two examples cited by Keating as evidence that the international community is moving toward a more intrusive and assertive form of multilateralism which places less emphasis on the traditional concern for state sovereignty and more weight on norms such as the protection of human rights, promotion of democracy, and preservation of the ecology.

The assertive multilateralism currently practised by the United Nations and its dynamic secretary general, Boutros Boutros-Ghali, is in sharp contrast with the more timid and introspective orientation of NATO after the end of the Cold War. But, as Keating warns, assertive multilateralism is not without inherent risks. One is the risk of over-extension as the UN is sent to deal with the world's most intractable problems woefully underequipped, understaffed, underfinanced, and unprepared. Another is the risk of failure. In 1993 the unresolved war in Bosnia, the continuing anarchy in Somalia, and the aborted UN mission to Haiti have all prompted a critical reaction in many quarters, including Washington, to the consequences of a more action-prone United Nations. Such critical reassessment has worried countries such as Canada that have had a traditional commitment to the principle of multilateralism and have supported its more assertive application in international practice. Representatives of some African and Asian countries have also questioned the UN's authority to intervene in the sovereign affairs of member states by organizing intrusive operations such as the ones mounted in Iraq after the 1991 ceasefire and in Somalia. In the former UN operation, consent of the host government was gained by military coercion; in the latter it was absent altogether. Finally, some have criticized assertive multilateralism for tackling issues of international peace, human rights, and democracy while relegating the UN to a peripheral role with respect to decisions affecting economic relations between developed and developing countries.

The successful conclusion in December 1993, literally as the deadline under the American fast-track procedure was about to expire, of the Uruguay Round of the General Agreement on Tariffs and Trade epitomizes a more positive aspect of multilateralism. As the chapters by Alexandroff and Curtis and Wolfe outline, the Uruguay Round was long and complicated and addressed a series of issues — among them agriculture, textiles, trade in services, and the enhancement of the institutional capacity of the GATT — that desperately required concerted international agreement. The creation of the World Trade Organization (WTO), which was a Canadian proposal, strengthens the liberal trading regime because it provides a forum for regular dialogue on multilateral trade issues which the GATT lacked. That 117 states accepted the GATT package makes it a very significant agreement. Interestingly, as

Curtis and Wolfe note, the less developed countries were prepared to accept the Uruguay Round package and its implications long before the United States, the members of the European Union, and Japan; the major dispute—over agriculture—was transatlantic. Canada was intimately involved throughout the Uruguay Round, as a member of formal groups such as the Cairns Group (on agriculture) and the Quadrilateral Group of Trade Ministers (European Union, United States, Japan, and Canada), and as informal interlocutor on north-south questions.

The global trading system is not without its tensions. A heavily trade-dependent economy such as Canada's must recognize changing patterns of economic activity and adapt to them. The completion of the Uruguay Round demonstrates broad global support for multilateralism. At the same time, regional trading arrangements have become increasingly attractive because they facilitate greater liberalization of trade and investment among a small number of states.

The chapters in *A Part of the Peace* by Doran and Dobson, and to a lesser degree that by Alexandroff, discuss the relationship between multilateralism and regionalism and its implications for Canada. Dobson contends that Asian fears that NAFTA will turn into a trade bloc are misplaced, while Doran suggests that globalism and regionalism reinforce each other. Alexandroff notes that participation in a regional trading arrangement, the Canada-U.S. Free Trade Agreement, has not protected Canada from American trade actions. Doran's chapter examines changes in the pattern of trade and investment that made NAFTA feasible and highlights the challenges to national authority that economic, not security, considerations are generating. In his view, globalization renders national states less relevant in economic terms and promotes subnational centres of economic development. Dobson reviews the rapid growth of many of the East Asian economies, with particular emphasis on China, and suggests that Canada has been slow in recognizing the challenges that these fast-growing Asian markets present. Both the Canadian government and Canadian firms have to appreciate the characteristics of Asian business practices and find ways to adapt to them, including increased Canadian investment in the East Asian economies.

Canadian Response to International Challenges

Since World War Two, Canada has been an enthusiastic and perhaps even a compulsive multilateralist. Initially, Atlanticism provided the principal axis for Canadian multilateralism. But with the shift of Canadian trade and immigration patterns and the gradually diminishing importance of NATO, Canada's multilateral associations and commitments have acquired truly global dimensions. One of the central aims of Canadian multilateralism is to facilitate Canada's management of its relations with the United States by also involving Europe and, more recently, the Pacific Rim.

Canada has generally favoured an assertive multilateralism, as Keating styles it, on issues such as protection of human rights, promotion of democracy, and preservation of the environment. Canada has been emphatic on the need to limit the principle of national sovereignty to achieve these ends. The strategy of assertive multilateralism has been pursued in the UN as well as in the CSCE and the Organization of American States (OAS), where Canada has participated in adopting principles that favour collective intervention measures to strengthen human rights and democratic institutions.

The question naturally arises, what international strategies and tactics should Canada adopt after the demise of the Cold War in order to promote an effective multilateralism? One possible approach might be to develop the habit of treating multilateralism in terms of its potential to address pressing global needs rather than defining it in relation to specific Canadian national interests. Several contributors to this volume have suggested ways in which Canada might help strengthen multilateralism in the post-Cold War era. One might recall Trudeau's method of proceeding unilaterally, as with Arctic environmental protection in 1970, and subsequently using the Law of the Sea Conference to build a multilateral consensus for this action. But to do so requires both diplomatic skill and considerable international leverage which will not always be available.

Another method of strengthening multilateralism might be for Canada to make its own contribution to a multilateral activity explicitly dependent on certain conditions being met or certain reforms being undertaken. For example, Canadian participation in a proposed UN peacekeeping/peacemaking/humanitarian enforcement action could be refused if it is to be undertaken on the basis of muddling through. But participation could be accepted on the explicit condition that the proposed mission be properly financed, have the consent of all parties concerned, and follow an agreed timetable. Canada's prized role as a peacekeeper might give it sufficient leverage to produce a better planned and more precisely formulated mandate, in contrast to the haphazard and hastily improvised ones that have launched so many past UN peacekeeping missions on their inconclusive outcomes.

Andrew Knight's chapter recommends that Canada pursue a long-term, rather than an immediate, UN reform agenda, one that focuses on the needs of international society and how the UN can be adjusted to respond to them. This is in line with the 1993 Liberal party campaign booklet, the much-cited but less widely read so-called Red Book, which called for a new "Agenda for Development" that would extend the international peace and security dialogue generated by the secretary general's *Agenda for Peace* to the sphere of economic development to help overcome the marginalization of this issue in the UN system.[18]

Keating notes that Canada has an immense stake in preserving the United Nations as a credible forum. It should therefore seek to prevent the UN from taking on tasks for which it does not have an effective capacity or resources and ensure that a task is undertaken only if the requisite conditions for its successful management exist. Canada will lead the open-ended Working Group which will make recommendations to the UN General Assembly in 1994 on the reform of the Security Council. By providing permanent seats not only to Germany and Japan, the principal contenders, but also to major Third World states such as Brazil, India, and Nigeria, the Security Council would become a more representative body reflecting the power configuration of the post-Cold War rather than the victorious coalition of 1945.

The Change of Government in Ottawa

It is difficult to assess Prime Minister Mulroney's legacy to Canadian politics because his departure from office is still recent and because of the enormous controversy generated by his political style as much as by the substantive content of his policies. Even though he had had no personal background in international affairs, Mulroney demonstrated a more sustained interest and day-to-day direct involvement in foreign policy than any other Canadian peacetime prime minister.

Lester Pearson's illustrious career in international affairs had been made as a public servant and foreign minister. As prime minister he was essentially preoccupied with surviving the debilitating day-to-day domestic battles of his minority government and left most of the direction of foreign affairs in the hands of External Affairs Minister Paul Martin.

Trudeau's involvement in foreign policy was sporadic in nature. His foreign policy interventions, when they did occur — as for example on issues such as nuclear safeguards and the so-called peace initiative — attracted considerable attention and controversy both in Canada and abroad.

Mulroney's foreign policy role has largely been identified with cultivating a close personal working relationship with American presidents Reagan and Bush and with other world leaders such as Prime Minister Margaret Thatcher and Chancellor Helmut Kohl. Mulroney must also be credited, or blamed, for the initiation, negotiation, and ratification of the momentous Canada-U.S. Free Trade Agreement.

Mulroney's involvement in multilateral foreign policy issues has received less attention and deserves to be studied seriously. During his last year of office three major international issues, in particular, commanded his attention: the political and economic situation in Russia and Eastern Europe; the civil war in the former Yugoslavia; and the humanitarian catastrophe in Somalia. The foreign policy machinery, if left to its own devices, would not have produced the same initiatives and outcomes that resulted from strong political leadership from the Prime Minister's Office.

One of the international causes which Mulroney espoused most enthusiastically was Canada's commitment to the reform process in the former Soviet Union and Eastern Europe. In this context the prime minister was not only responding to wider international political and security considerations but also to pressures from the Canadian business community for the government to involve itself in the region where businesses saw significant long-term prospects for Canadian trade and investment. Aid to Russia had in common with other Mulroney undertakings that it involved

Canada in a close working partnership with the United States, emphasized that Canada could be a trusted and important team player on the international scene, and helped cement still further the already close relationship between the president and the prime minister. In 1992, as the result of pressure from the prime minister, the Canadian government established the Task Force on Central and Eastern Europe whose operations are discussed in Jeanne Laux's chapter. On the eve of the March 1993 Clinton-Yeltsin Vancouver summit, the Canadian government announced an aid package which amounted to a $200 million increase in bilateral assistance to Russia. The measure of Mulroney's achievement was that he pushed the aid package through the bureaucracy at a time of rising budget deficit and fiscal constraint.

During the past two years, the unresolved situation in the former Yugoslavia, and in particular the continuation of the brutal civil war in Bosnia, has remained the number one issue on the diplomatic agenda of Western leaders. Canada has been directly involved in the issue as the result of its peacekeeping contingents in Bosnia and Croatia, and its membership in the UN, NATO, and the CSCE, three of the four international organizations which have been primarily concerned with the conflict. The Canadian government has consistently opposed lifting the arms embargo for Bosnia for fear that this would escalate the overall level of military fighting. On the diplomatic front, Canada has supported the Vance-Owen peace process, as distinct from the actual Vance-Owen plan which it has viewed with some scepticism, as the best hope for a peaceful outcome to the war.

Apart from a natural empathy for the immense human tragedy, the Canadian government has been concerned with the safety of its peacekeepers in the civil war zone and has been politically frustrated by repeatedly being left out of the critical decision-loop, despite the size of its peacekeeping forces. The most important military and political consultations concerning the conflict are held by the UN Security Council, on which Canada does not currently have a seat; by the Council of Ministers of the EU, to which Canada does not belong; and by NATO, where our influence is overshadowed by the military Big Four (the United States, Britain, France, and Germany).

As with most other Western governments, an element of schizophrenia seems to characterize Canadian policy toward the civil war in Bosnia. On the one hand, in his Harvard University speech of December 1992, Prime Minister Mulroney suggested peace enforcement action on the model of Kuwait; in his London speech of May 1993 he set out detailed criteria for military action and he criticized President Clinton for not taking tougher action. However, in the discussions on the actual use of military strikes by NATO, Canada has been a voice of caution. The question of NATO air strikes in Bosnia became the dominant foreign policy issue of the short-lived Campbell government.

While the Mulroney-Campbell-Chrétien governments have not categorically ruled out NATO air strikes as a measure of last resort, they insisted that air strikes not be used simply as a military reflex action but form part of a more comprehensive peace plan; that maximum precaution be taken to ensure the safety of UN peacekeepers on the ground; and that the ultimate decision to use force be taken by the United Nations. In the prolonged UN-NATO negotiations during the summer of 1993, Canada was successful in getting agreement that the commander of the UN Protection Force (UNPROFOR) would have to "sign off" before any NATO air strikes could commence. As the Keating chapter argues, Canada not only had a general ideological preference for the principle of UN, rather than NATO, control, but also had greater confidence that a UN decision would take all necessary precaution to safeguard its own peacekeepers, while a decision by NATO would, in all likelihood, be dominated by the United States whose own soldiers are not serving as peacekeepers in the region.

Prime Minister Mulroney agreed to requests from President Bush to provide a contingent of over thirteen hundred military personnel to serve with the hastily assembled Unified Task Force (UNITAF) in Somalia under American rather than UN command. The action was defined as an international humanitarian enforcement measure under Chapter VII of the UN Charter that was justified by the enormity of the human catastrophe unfolding in Somalia. It was an unprecedented action, although there are certain parallels with the international Kurdish relief operation after the Gulf War. The Canadian bureaucracy had considerable doubts about this particular operation, but the prime minister had his way. Critics within the government were leery of the seeming open-endedness of the commitment, unenthusiastic about coming in the wake of the American man o'war — never popular with the

Canadian public as was witnessed by the Gulf War—and reluctant to depart from the well-tested ground rules for blue helmets that had a good chance of getting the cooperation of the local population. On the other hand, it could not be denied that a critical emergency existed and that Canada was better equipped than most countries to be of help. These latter considerations overrode formal criteria and traditional concepts of peacekeeping. Canada had made it clear at the outset that its participation was temporary, and it withdraw its contingents after UNITAF was succeeded by the UN Operation in Somalia (UNOSOM II) in May 1993.

Canada had no political, strategic, or economic national interest to serve in Somalia. Had there been less pressure for an immediate emergency action, the opportunity might well have been taken to tie the Canadian contribution to a developed and coherent doctrine on how peacekeeping should be conducted and financed, built on the principles enunciated in the secretary general's *Agenda for Peace.* This was hardly feasible under the emergency conditions, although under less pressing circumstances in future Canada might be able to pursue this reform-minded strategy. Canada's role in Somalia was a case of policy-making on the fly, and its best defence was that the situation was sufficiently pressing to leave room for no other response. An incident, in which several Canadian peacekeepers tortured and killed a captured Somali youth, received nation-wide publicity in Canada. Initially, it was little more than a political issue to embarrass Prime Minister Campbell during her election campaign. But this incident, and other less dramatic ones, which have tarnished the hitherto impeccable reputation of Canadian peacekeepers, have led to a wider soul-searching on peacekeeping, military training, and military accountability. As Nancy Gordon observes in her chapter, the Canadian incidents in Somalia demonstrated that conventional professional training for peacekeepers was not sufficient, and that it would have to be supplemented by cultural sensitivity training and better knowledge of the local situation. In a microcosm, the incidents underlined the enormity of the Somali catastrophe and the problem of trying to cope with a humanitarian crisis by relying on military enforcement measures.

Having held virtually every major federal portfolio, including briefly that of foreign affairs, Jean Chrétien assumed office in late 1993 as the most experienced prime minister in Canadian history.

Foreign and defence policy issues did not figure prominently in the 1993 election campaign. Mr. Chrétien promised to cancel the controversial EH-101 helicopter program and to negotiate some improved terms to NAFTA with respect to environment, energy, and a subsidies code. The first promise was realized as soon as he assumed office. It was to be a doubly symbolic decision, which signalled that the government would honour its election promises and that it was serious about fiscal restraint. On the second issue, Chrétien was less able to deliver. After the enormous difficulty of getting congressional ratification, the Clinton administration showed little disposition to renegotiate sections of NAFTA, as desired by the Chrétien government. What the new prime minister wanted was the renegotiation of the energy provisions of NAFTA so that Canada would maintain control over its oil and gas exports in time of crisis, a side agreement on the protection of Canadian water, subsidies and anti-dumping codes, and a more effective way to resolve cross-border disputes; what he got as a result of Trade Minister Roy MacLaren's late November 1993 visit to Washington, as Alan Alexandroff's paper notes, was an American refusal to change the energy chapter and a commitment to discussions on the other matters of concern.

Similarly, the Chrétien government has not been able to deliver on its, admittedly less important, NATO agenda. At the NATO summits in January and February, Canada was virtually isolated in its opposition to NATO air strikes in Bosnia and could not get NATO to endorse the principle that countries in Central and Eastern Europe would be allowed to join the alliance at a later date. Canada ultimately yielded in the face of concerted pressure from its American, British, and French allies who were determined to issue a strict NATO ultimatum allowing Serb forces ten days to withdraw their heavy artillery from the immediate area of Sarajevo. In a similar vein, the Canadian government accepted the NATO decision in mid-April to launch limited air strikes against ground targets in the vicinity of Gorazde. The risk of air strikes to UN peacekeepers on the ground was immediately confirmed when the Bosnian Serbs reacted by detaining two hundred UN peacekeepers, including sixteen Canadians.

The foreign policy section of the Liberal Red Book contains a very articulate Canadian commitment to multilateralism, in the best tradition of Louis St. Laurent, Lester Pearson, Paul Martin, and Pierre Trudeau;[19] new multilateral regimes are needed to address many emerging global issues, among them the management of global fish stocks, the protection of the world's atmosphere, the maintenance of biodiversity, the control of population growth, the resettlement of refugees, and the equitable sharing of global wealth and resources. A Liberal government will foster the development of such multilateral forums and agreements, including an improved Law of the Sea, a new agreement on global warming, an improved code of human rights, and a new agenda for development that matches the secretary general's *Agenda for Peace*.

The challenges confronting the current Canadian state managers are quite staggering as they seek to promote and harmonize diverse trade, security, human rights, and environmental objectives by means of multilateral regimes and institutional arrangements. Their most immediate task, as Alexandroff articulates, is to fashion policies to ensure the continuation of the economy recovery. Their task is greatly complicated by the crippling national debt with which the Liberal government is saddled and the diminished options that are consequently available. The troublesome question of whether Canada can make an effective contribution to the evolving multilateralism cannot be avoided when the intellectual debate in the departments of Foreign Affairs and National Defence is increasingly driven by resource constraints. The query can be posed whether Canadian foreign policy will come to approximate Oscar Wilde's definition of a cynic, as one who knows the price of everything and the value of nothing.

The dilemma facing the Canadian government reflects the one which plagues the UN system—that is, the need and desire to do more with a shrinking resource base. The foreign and defence policy reviews which are currently being conducted by the Chrétien government will probably focus less on proclaiming general international principles and defining broad national objectives, as did similar reviews by the Trudeau and Mulroney governments; instead, they will concentrate more on determining what international activities and commitments we will be able to afford. The review process will thus be guided by strict and sober accounting rules more than by idealistic philosophical principles of international relations.

In its February 1994 budget, the first one of the new Liberal government, both defence and development assistance bore a disproportionate share of overall spending cuts. The defence budget will be cut by $7 billion over the next five years and the size of regular forces will be reduced from 74,800 to 66,700.[20] The customary Canadian strategy of coping with a series of defence cuts during the past twenty-five years has been to reduce the size of the regular forces and to postpone defence re-equipment rather than eliminate principal defence missions. This has not exactly been an application of Mies van der Rohe's architectural law whereby "the less is more," but an attempt to do as much of the same with less. The forthcoming defence policy review may decide that such an improvisational approach is no longer possible, given the scope of defence cuts, and that the proper response will be to cut entire military missions. A report by a group of strategic and policy experts, released soon after the February budget, takes this radical approach when it recommends that Canada's future military role should concentrate on only two central missions — the defence of Canadian sovereignty and international peacekeeping — and disengage from all other missions, notably NATO.[21] A decision of this magnitude might be reconcilable with the recommendations contained in the chapter by Tom Keating, who prefers Canada's future security involvement in Europe to be channelled through the CSCE rather than NATO. But it would annul Alexander Moens's proposal that Canada give active political support to the Balladur stability pact while reinforcing it with a deterrence and military enforcement capability.

Defence Minister David Collenette has made it clear that, with the constraints of the February 1994 budget, Canada will not be able to increase its peacekeeping contingents, thus modifying a Liberal campaign promise to strengthen Canada's peacekeeping capacity.[22] Indeed, even without budgetary reductions, it is unlikely that Canada would ever match 1993 as the all-time record year for peacekeeping. For much of that year, more than four thousand Canadian peacekeepers served concurrently in the many peacekeeping missions around the globe; if we include rotation of contingents, approximately ten thousand Canadians performed peacekeeping duties during 1993.

The Liberal government's comprehensive foreign policy review process began with a March 1994 national foreign policy forum in Ottawa. Sponsored by Foreign Affairs Minister Ouellett and Defence Minister Collenette, representatives from academe, the non-governmental organization community, the business community, and the media debated the recent dramatic changes in the global environment and their impact on Canada. Evident throughout was the impossibility of separating foreign from domestic policy and the interconnections across components of Canada's international policies — for example, trade and aid, trade and the environment, and trade and human rights. Economic realities generated by globalization, the challenges to national sovereignty, alternatives to Canada's trade dependence on the United States, unemployment and the cynicism of youth not only in Canada but around the world, were among the subjects raised as necessary components of any review process.

In many respects the foreign and defence policy reviews are occurring at what may be seen as a critical juncture. The world is a very different place to what it was when the Mulroney government's foreign policy review appeared in 1985,[23] as is the position of Canada in it. Moreover, as many of the chapters in this volume suggest, the time is apposite for a serious assessment of many of the fundamentals of Canadian foreign policy. *A Part of the Peace* addresses many of the subjects and options that the review processes will consider. Whatever the choices Canada makes, there will remain both the responsibility and the hope that the peace will be of an ever larger part.

2 Global Economic Change: Fashioning Our Own Way

Alan S. Alexandroff

THE NEW LIBERAL GOVERNMENT, elected on October 25, 1993, faced an immediate and pressing trade agenda. Assuming U.S. congressional approval of the North American Free Trade Agreement (NAFTA), Prime Minister designate, Jean Chrétien, and his advisors had to decide whether, or how and when, a Liberal government would have NAFTA apply to Canada. Equally important, the new government was left with the task of concluding the eight-year-long Uruguay Round negotiations of the General Agreement on Tariffs and Trade (GATT). There were significant potential gains for Canada in a successful GATT accord, but there were also identifiable losers, most notably farmers reliant on Canada's decades' old supply management system. For the new government, as for most other advanced industrial countries, these trade negotiations required adroit handling at the international level combined with careful political management of powerful domestic interests.

If these immediate regional and global trade issues were not enough, the Liberal government and its new key ministers sworn in quickly following the Liberal election—Roy MacLaren, minister for international trade, John Manley, minister of industry, and Paul Martin, minister of finance—were faced with the need to fashion trade and economic policies where the line between domestic and international policy had all but disappeared. If that was not difficult enough, these politicians found themselves highly

---

I would like to acknowledge the assistance of both Dr. Sylvia Ostry and Dr. Leonard Waverman, respectively the chair and director of the Centre for International Studies. Both have been invaluable in deepening my understanding of the development of the global economy. I would also like to acknowledge the assistance of the Canada 21 Project and particularly its research director, Dr. Janice Stein. It was the opportunity with Sylvia Ostry to prepare the background research paper on the global economy that turned my attention to examining closely the response of the new Canadian government. It goes without saying that any errors or omissions in this chapter are mine alone.

constrained as a result of the past fiscal management of federal and provincial economies.

All of this was daunting. But even beyond these challenges, the pace of globalization, notwithstanding the marked global economic downturn, was accelerating. The internationalization of production by global corporations was expanding and deepening; direct foreign investment continued and increasingly focused on the emerging markets in Asia, especially China, but also in Latin America and Asia Minor. Finally, there was a widening circle of strategic alliances, between and among transnational corporations (TNCs), reflecting the driving force in the global economy of technology and its diffusion through these global firms. This apparently ceaseless global economic dynamic continued even as Canada struggled to find an adequate response to these competitive pressures. Notwithstanding the end, at least technically, of the recession, the twin evils of a wide and deep national recession and significant industrial restructuring raised fears over the adaptiveness of Canada's industrial structure and the effectiveness of Canada's political institutions. Fear was growing over the country's ability to fashion effective economic strategies to match the pace of global economic change.

The Context of Constraint

Into this tightening political and policy context, the new prime minister and his government arrived fresh from a significant election victory that saw two national parties, including the Progressive Conservatives, who had been the governing party for the previous nine years, reduced to parliamentary insignificance. The Liberal party won a majority government on the strong performance of its leader, Jean Chrétien. Although the Liberal election platform had made much of its Red Book, *Creating Opportunities*, Liberal success was taken far less from that document than from the leader's repeated commitment to integrity in government and the job-creating infrastructure program.

These commitments placed the Liberal party, now the government, in a difficult position with respect to tackling global economic change. Liberals had grown accustomed to reacting to trade policy, not to making it. The party had fought the 1988 election as a crusade against the Canada-U.S. Free Trade Agreement

(FTA). Deficiencies in NAFTA remained. Just beyond NAFTA there loomed the need for the new minister of international trade, Roy MacLaren, to fashion and implement a Canadian trade policy. And beyond that, Chrétien, MacLaren, indeed all the ministers, had to elaborate a Canadian policy that would be more consciously independent of the United States. All of this would need to be accomplished while the United States remained Canada's key market and with an administration in Washington that was becoming increasingly aggressive in its trade strategy.

The Liberal government had received a mandate, seemingly focused on domestic economic issues, particularly jobs. Yet the new government was beset by international economic pressures, with probably less manoeuvring room than any previous national government. And the government might well have to try and tackle an economic agenda while at the same time facing another wrenching round over the place of Quebec in confederation.

In short, the challenges the Liberal government faces appear daunting and go beyond just those posed by the global economy. But these global economic challenges could well determine the jobs and the standard of living for most Canadians. The global economy, then, is critical to a Liberal administration if it hopes to secure a second mandate. For the Liberals the dynamics of global economic change are crucial to their collective political future. They must find ways of grappling with at least two challenges:

> to fashion a medium-term trade and investment strategy in light of the conclusion of NAFTA and the Uruguay Round. This means, in particular, designing a strategy that can cope with the key economic actor and market, the United States; and second, to integrate domestic and international economic policy successfully so that government efforts reinforce private sector trade and investment initiatives to create good high value added jobs.

What follows is an effort to describe these challenges and to assess, in a preliminary way, the possibility and scope for response from the Chrétien government.

The Diminished American Giant

In the American electoral politics of 1992, Bill Clinton, the candidate, emphasized the need for the United States to address domestic priorities. He stressed that the end of the Cold War afforded the United States the opportunity to redirect its energies to rebuilding the country. The United States had to focus on solving its domestic problems—decaying cities, crime, deficits, R&D strategy—and in doing so make the United States economically strong again as a necessary condition for retaining leadership in the world.

Recasting the politics of the "new world order" largely in economic terms, Clinton approached American world leadership in terms of the economic sacrifices the United States had made during the Cold War to maintain solidarity against a now defeated foe. Clinton supported the demand to get more aggressive with nations in Europe and Asia, many former Cold War allies that had failed to play fairly in the global economy. *Putting People First*, the Clinton campaign's platform document, demanded that these nations abandon unfair trade subsidies and assure a more level playing field. To that end Clinton advocated, among other things, that his administration would propose passage of a stronger and sharper "Super 301" trade bill provision.[1] As the campaign document stated, "if other nations refuse to play by our trade rules, we'll play by theirs."[2]

In focusing on the unfair practices of other nations, Clinton adopted a well-developed explanation for the failure of U.S. competitiveness, pointing to others as the principal source for American decline as opposed to any internal failures. This debate over the failure of U.S. competitiveness had grown increasingly loud and accusatory in the latter part of the 1980s as the country's trade imbalance exploded. This imbalance had been particularly large with Japan, reaching a "whopping" US$52 billion in 1987. While the imbalance had declined thereafter, it began to rise again in the 1990s, exceeding US$43 billion dollars in 1992 with Japan alone. Analysts were quick to point to Japanese barriers, including culture and a complex industrial structure, all leading to a lack of import penetration in many key sectors and asymmetric flows of foreign direct investment (FDI). These and other arguments from analysts, who came to be known as the "Japan bashers," reinforced the view that the United States had been unfairly taken advantage of by its allies. Without a level playing field, so the argument went, the United States would be unable to reduce this yawning American trade imbalance. Therefore, the United States would have to be significantly more forceful in trade negotiations in order to create a more level playing field.

Trade expert and former economic policy advisor to the secretary general of GATT, Jagdish Bhagwati, named this critique of the trading system, and the criticism of Japan and other rapidly developing economies, as the "diminished giant" syndrome.[3] This approach, suggested Bhagwati, arose in response to declining American economic dominance in the global economy. The attack by the United States on the rising economic states, in his view, paralleled the British reaction to its decline in the face of a rapidly industrializing Germany and the United States in the late nineteenth century.

The adoption of a "declinist" position by candidate, and then president, Clinton had significant implications for his administration.[4] Like the two earlier Republican administrations, this stance allowed the government to call on significant corporate and union players. These private sector actors were only too willing to support a government view that focused on the unfair practices of other countries as opposed to closely examining competitive domestic practices. Further, it enabled the government to act in concert with these domestic interests to press trade initiatives, acting aggressively for commercial interests.

The adoption of an aggressive trade strategy, in line with these earlier Republican initiatives, was to further undermine the role of the United States as the key global economic actor championing the liberalization of the global economy. It was the United States after World War Two that had forced the pace in creating a liberal trading regime. It had also been at the forefront in pressing for each new round of trade negotiations under GATT, including the last and difficult Uruguay Round.[5] But a willingness to press for regional trade agreements, such as in North America, combined with a broadened array of aggressive trade practices, increasingly called into question the U.S. commitment to retaining, and more importantly, improving the open multilateral trading system under GATT. If the key economic player was no longer prepared to maintain the open system, there was an ever-present threat that the global economy would be tipped over into regional and potentially highly protectionist trading blocs. In such a system Canada would find itself with dramatically limited options.

An Aggressive Trade Agenda

The Clinton administration's adoption of an aggressive trade strategy was not a break in trade and investment policy, notwithstanding the free trade rhetoric of both the Reagan and Bush administrations. But the Clinton team added its own new Democratic perspective to American trade policy.

This aggressive policy consists of a number of instruments. First, there has been encouragement, or tacit support, for the use of U.S. trade remedy law, including anti-dumping (AD) and countervail against alleged subsidies (CVD) by the private sector. This reliance on national trade remedy laws has been most evident in the United States-Canada relationship and was central, as is described below, to the actions taken by the new Liberal government in the negotiations over the application of NAFTA to Canada. Next, the immediate past U.S. administrations had employed an array of managed trade instruments, including Voluntary Export Restraints (VERs) and Orderly Market Arrangements (OMAs). Finally, and most troubling, has been the willingness of U.S. administrations to extract unilateral concessions from other states and to threaten trade retaliation on the failure to achieve a satisfactory resolution. The abandonment of reciprocity and the turn to unilateral concessions has been labelled "aggressive unilateralism."[6] Such unilateralism has included use of Section 301[7] actions against the practices of various states, as well as actions to open the markets of offending states described as Voluntary Import Expansion agreements (VIEs). Such initiatives have both narrow and broad sector and market access targets.

The Clinton administration's trade policy appears to be built on the belief that there is no contradiction between aggressive trade policy and free trade. The president, and others in his administration, are also attracted to an active and strategic role for government, including a willingness to accelerate investment in advanced manufacturing technologies as well as to assist sectors (like the automobile sector) re-establish U.S. competitive leadership.[8] As a result, this administration has been an advocate for the electronic highway; in the 1994–95 budget, it signalled its intention to assist in harnessing science and technology in the service of economic recovery. In particular, the budget increased a number of commercial research programs; for example, it provides for a 78 percent increase, to $874 million, for the National Institute of Standards and Technology (NIST) which funds a variety of commercial research and development ventures in electronics, computers, and other programs under the Advanced Technology Project.[9] It does not take much imagination to identify the strong industrial policy flavour to Clinton administration policy and to identify NIST as the nerve centre of this policy.

The Clinton administration has been highly motivated to remove barriers to trade and gain enhanced market access for American companies (although its negotiators have frequently cast the negotiations as access for all foreign companies and not just U.S. ones). The key focus for the administration is Japan. On the first visit to Washington of then Japanese prime minister, Kiichi Miyazawa, in April 1993, the administration insisted on an agreement to draft a new framework for discussions of Japan's persistent trade surplus with the United States. While charges passed back and forth in the intervening months over the motives and intentions of the two governments, the United States and Japan reached a framework agreement shortly after the conclusion of the Group of Seven (G-7) summit in Tokyo in June of 1993.

Throughout these negotiations, the United States made clear that it had entered the talks to secure from Japan identifiable targets for imports and a targeted reduction of the Japanese surplus, thereby committing the Japanese government to a reduction of its surplus as a percentage of Gross Domestic Product (GDP). With the framework agreement the Japanese agreed to negotiate objective criteria to measure progress in improving market access. Further, Japan offered a highly significant reduction of its trade surplus.

This agreement is the centrepiece of the Clinton administration's efforts to reduce the Japanese trade surplus and increase Japanese imports of foreign goods. In fact, it is an agreement to continue negotiations with the intent of securing, first, a statement of directions and principles for negotiations over more specific negotiations to open sectoral markets; and second, a mechanism for continuing consultations over two years including twice yearly meetings between the prime minister of Japan and the U.S. president. But the negotiations have stumbled over interpreting the language of the agreement with respect to targets and the commitment of the Japanese to reduce their surplus. The breakdown of the negotiations came in a very public way with the meeting of President Clinton and Prime Minister Morihiro Hosokawa in

Washington on February 11, 1994. The two held a news conference where they admitted failure and President Clinton indicated that the United States was prepared to look at other options. Among these is the reinstatement through Executive Order of Super 301. Additionally, the administration is prepared to retaliate against Japanese cellular telephone manufacturers for the perceived failure to carry out a 1989 agreement to open the cellular phone market around Tokyo to Motorola Inc.

The failure to date to elaborate the framework agreement with Japan has underlined the insistence of the United States on a trade relationship governed by the "management of results"—specific numerical targets and objective indicators of progress. Japan has objected to this approach, arguing that it will destroy the liberal trade system. The Japanese have underscored the detriment to trade relations of such numerical targets by referencing the Semiconductor Trade Agreement (STA) entered into in 1986 and then revised in 1991.[10] To Japan, the United States focused increasingly on the 20 percent benchmark, that, on U.S. insistence, became part of the 1991 STA. The Japanese suggested that the benchmark became a minimum and an immediate tripwire for American complaints about the bilateral relationship. The United States has become increasingly reliant on short-term indicators and targets to measure the success of the relationship. The United States has seemingly moved a long way in the direction of a trade war with Japan to secure a change in Japanese practices.

The aggressive trade policies of the last three American administrations have had serious consequences in the evolution of global trade. Recourse by U.S. private parties to national trade remedy laws against Canadian competitors has raised serious questions in Canada over the value of the FTA. It has also fed Canadian opposition to the maintenance of the FTA or its extension to NAFTA. Managed trade actions and equally aggressive unilateral actions have done much to raise doubts over the intentions and commitment of the United States to the maintenance of an open global economy.

Managed trade initiatives and aggressive unilateralism also have had investment-related trade measure (IRTM) consequences, many unintended. In a number of instances, for example in the automobile industry, the VERs against Japanese car companies in the 1980s led these global competitors to invest heavily in the United

States and to establish large-scale Japanese transplants to avoid the quotas. A further unintended consequence of this managed trade initiative was to add to the overcapacity in the auto industry that exacerbated the difficulties of that industry in the downturn of the 1990s. In another instance, the 1986 STA rationalized the cartelization of the Japanese semiconductor industry, assisting it in substantially increasing profits.

Other unintended consequences have arisen. As competitive pressures built, the United States began to experiment with a number of programs aimed at supporting American industry, particularly in the advanced technology areas. Possibly the most innovative, and certainly the most controversial, was the establishment of SEMATECH (Semiconductor Manufacturing Consortium) in 1988. It was designed as a means to maintain the technological competence of American firms in the dynamic random access memory (DRAM) and semiconductor equipment industry. As a result, the United States prohibited the inclusion of foreign companies in the consortium. But global corporations were unwilling to forego access to potential technological advances, and many have established strategic alliances that have leap-frogged the prohibition. Thus, IBM formed a strategic alliance with Siemens to overcome a prohibition aimed at American and other foreign entry into the European JESSI consortium. This alliance, in turn, gained "unofficial" Siemens' access to SEMATECH.

These international corporate alliances represent the continued force of technological change and a deepening of globalization by transnational corporations. This deepening of globalization, however, is an unintended consequence of national industrial policy. The impact of strategic alliances poses a critical problem for national economic development in Canada. There are a limited number of Canadian players to maintain access in such strategic alliances and thereby gain technological development arising from participation.

As a last consequence, aggressive unilateralism has focused the attention of American policy makers and powerful domestic interests increasingly on the management of results. This growing obsession with short-term targets and benchmarks has heightened tensions and raised the possibilities for the extension of market-sharing agreements through the global economy, presumably at the insistence of the United States, but now possibly arranged by other players such as the Europeans. Finally, and most seriously, the determination of the United States to open the Japanese market has led the Clinton administration to the brink of a trade war with its second largest trading partner. In this effort, the United States has completely ignored the multilateral trading context and is determined to force changes unilaterally.

Concluding the Uruguay Round

While the most prominent feature of the Clinton administration in the global economy is an aggressive trade tilt, there has not been a complete abandonment of free trade initiatives. Indeed, it would appear that the administration has lurched at aggressive trade only to trumpet the success of its efforts to expand a liberalizing global economic environment. The Clinton administration hailed the passage of NAFTA. In the fierce political debate over the passage of NAFTA, the Clinton administration relied frequently on classic free trade arguments to secure NAFTA support. And significantly, the administration was able to report to Congress on the mandated final date, December 15, 1993, that it was going to be able to reach a successful conclusion to the Uruguay Round. While critics were quick to identify both agreements as far less than free trade, there is little doubt that they were not likely to aid protectionist forces either regionally or globally.

The Uruguay Round is a significant achievement bringing services, investment measures, agricultural, and intellectual property, among other areas, under multilateral agreement. The Final Accord[11] will reform anti-dumping, subsidies, and the dispute resolution system, as well as creating a common institutional framework for the conduct of trade relations among its members, the World Trade Organization (WTO). The WTO in particular, has been identified as a major boost for multilateralism and places trade, really for the first time since the end of World War Two, at the same level, institutionally, as monetary issues or economic development. Yet while experts generally have applauded the significant economic gains of the Final Accord, American support for multilateralism remains clouded. Indeed, there had been a continuing effort on the part of both the Bush and Clinton administrations to protect national trade remedy law in the face of reform of the dispute resolution provisions of GATT. At the time of writing, it is unclear exactly how the United States views the impact of the Final Accord. The nature of the constraints placed on the United States will remain unclear until the implementing bill is formally submitted to Congress by the president. Even with the legislation, it may well take an American effort to use a Section 301 action within a trade-related GATT area to understand how the United States views the constraints on it as a result of this multilateral accord.

The Canadian Export Challenge

The global economy of the 1990s is a far cry from the world presented to Canadians following World War Two. The intervening decades have been good years for Canadians. We retain a very high standard of living in comparison to most countries (in fact we are fourth after the United States, Switzerland, and Luxembourg, although under revised calculations we have only the eleventh largest economy in the world in contrast to the older calculation which pegged Canada as seventh).[12] Between 1960 and 1990 Canada created jobs faster than any other industrialized country. In fact, in the period between 1984 and 1989 the Canadian economy grew faster than any other G-7 economy. At the same time Canada's economy became more integrated internationally with our foreign trade, representing over 30 percent of GDP.

Politically, Canada's leadership has recognized and benefited from a strong commitment to multilateralism. Our post-war leadership has supported an open, liberal trade and payments system and the multilateral institutions of the global economy, including GATT, the International Monetary Fund (IMF), and the World Bank. Canada has been significantly involved with the succession of liberalizing trade rounds under GATT. And it has had the good fortune of participating in the economic summits with the other G-7 members since the Puerto Rico summit in 1976. As the Macdonald Commission commented in its evaluation of Canada in the global economy, "The multilateralism practised over the past 40 years has served our country well: it has nurtured a trading nation with a much stronger industrial base, more capable of confronting the pressures emanating from the international economic environment."[13]

Yet the accelerating pace of globalization of the world economy has imposed increasing pressure on the Canadian economy. And while the Canadian economy grew over the 1980s, disturbing signs appeared that raised questions over Canada's ability to compete globally. Of highest concern was the significant alteration in Canadian productivity beginning in the 1970s. From the 1960s to about 1973 or 1974, total factor productivity grew at an annual rate of 2 percent. From 1973 to 1979 this rate of productivity slowed to an annual rate of .8 percent, and thereafter to 1990, Canada's total factor productivity failed to increase at all. While other industrialized countries suffered declines, only the United States rivalled Canada's precipitous fall.

While there has been a substantial expansion of Canada's manufacturing base, we remain highly dependent on natural resources. Unprocessed and semi-processed resources represent approximately one-third of Canadian exports. Processed resources add another 10 percent. As the 1993 Report of the National Advisory Board on Science and Technology noted, the resource sector is almost the only one whose exports contribute to a positive trade balance.[14] Meanwhile, there has been an inexorable downward trend over the past twenty years in commodity prices in real terms. In other words, Canada is having to run faster to just stay in place.

The main force driving the globalization process is the broadening application of technology and knowledge to production, marketing, and distribution. While high technology sectors represent the cutting edge of this economic revolution, the application of science and innovation across all economic sectors is vital to achieving a competitive economy. It is essential in creating high value-added jobs that have increasingly become the touchstone of all advanced economies. Notwithstanding the efforts of the federal and provincial governments to improve innovation through an attractive R&D environment, especially through tax expenditures, Canada's total expenditures on R&D are a fraction of comparable spending in Japan, Germany, or the United States. Private sector R&D spending performs even more poorly. In 1991, only .4 percent (3,566 firms) of businesses were engaged in R&D activities; further, this activity is highly concentrated, with twenty-five firms accounting for 48 percent of the spending.[15]

If the structure of Canada's industry challenges us in adapting to globalization, Canada's integration in the global economy poses significant problems as well. Canadians see themselves as a nation of traders, and point to the high volume of export trade. But Canadian trade is highly concentrated. Canadian exports to, and imports from, the United States represent over 70 percent of Canada's two-way trade. In dollar terms, Canada's exports to the United States have increased over 112 percent between 1983 and 1993 on a very large base of exports. In the same period, exports, on a much smaller basis, to Japan have increased only 67 percent, while to China, currently one of the fastest growing economies in the world, Canada's exports have not increased at all in the ten-year period to 1993.[16]

Not only is Canada's trade concentrated with the United States, it is highly restricted in the range of companies actively exporting. Recent trade analysis has demonstrated that the one hundred largest firms in Canada, mainly resource companies, account for 60.4 percent of all of Canada's exports. Moreover, only 7.6 percent of all Canadian firms export, and of this only 15.4 percent of those firms are identified as manufacturing ones. Finally, statistics point to the fact that only 9 percent of small and medium-sized (SMEs) Canadian manufacturing firms export.[17] This has raised particular concern, as most analysts suggest, though not without some controversy, that SMEs have been the only segment of the Canadian industrial structure where employment has been created in recent years.

The unfolding of globalization has also, seemingly, placed us at a disadvantage. Sylvia Ostry has noted that globalization has moved through stages. As she describes it, "the present phase of accelerating world integration is dominated less by increasing trade linkages than by growing investment and technology flows facilitated by the exploding financial linkage of the 1980s."[18] There has been a growing array of strategic alliances between global companies particularly in regard to technology flows. Strategic alliances differ from traditional corporate arrangements by the fact that they are two-way relationships and focus on joint knowledge production and sharing. These relationships involve little or no equity and they represent generally longer-term activity for these firms. Lynn Mytelka, who reported on three high technology areas (biotechnology, information technology, and the new materials sector), identified a steep rise in such alliances. However, Mytelka's investigations also identified that Canadian firms, "spontaneously engaged in far fewer strategic partnerships than European firms, even those from considerably smaller European countries such as the Netherlands and Sweden."[19] Though it is unclear what has caused this pattern, it is reasonable to assume that the factors noted above on R&D, the number of companies exporting, and the type of companies exporting, all contribute to the limited Canadian involvement in strategic alliances. Added to that are the barriers that individual nations have erected to the involvement of foreign firms. Here, too, it appears that we have few Canadian firms able to circumvent these national restrictions.

The challenges to Canada are evident. We have an industrial structure that appears to be imperfectly adapting to the broad, and increasingly deep, process of globalization. Further, Canada—and indeed all the major industrialized and industrializing countries—are facing a challenge to multilateralism and the liberalizing trend in the global economy. The United States is increasingly subject to bouts of aggressive unilateralism and unwilling, as the still dominant economic player in the global economy, to bear some of the costs associated with the maintenance of such an open multilateral rules-based global economic system. Even bilaterally, American trade policy has undermined, or at least raised the cost, of the free trade arrangements.

Securing Access

The relationship with the United States remains the key to Canada's global trading and investment health. It was the rising call for protection in the United States in the 1980s that initiated Canada's search for a new trade policy and led the Tories under Brian Mulroney to open free trade discussions with the United States. The product of these discussions was the Free Trade Agreement with the United States which took effect on January 1, 1989, after what was little short of a referendum on free trade with the United States in the fall 1988 Canadian federal election.

The Liberals, who had fought what the then leader of the party, John Turner, called a crusade, failed to signal any trade policy change until after not only a leadership change but a full year beyond that. Then Jean Chrétien brought together experts and Liberals for a conference at Aylmer, Quebec, in November of 1991. There, in his closing remarks, Chrétien indicated, if only indirectly, that the Liberal position on trade was moving on. He signalled his intention to put the 1988 election behind him by stating: "Protectionism is not left-wing or right-wing. It is simply passé. Globalization is not right-wing or left-wing. It is simply a fact of life."[20]

What emerged as Liberal trade policy was a call to renegotiate what the Liberals described as the flaws of the FTA and then the NAFTA. In their Red Book the Liberals argued the need to renegotiate, to correct the lack of a common subsidies code, an anti-dumping code, an inadequate dispute resolution mechanism, and to secure the same arrangements for Canada in energy that had been provided to the Mexicans in NAFTA. The heart of the Liberal reaction to the Progressive Conservative's trade policy was a view that the key benefit that the Mulroney government had offered Canadians in the FTA—secure access to the American market—had not been achieved. The Liberal party and its leader identified the repeated recourse by U.S. industry to trade remedies to deal with Canadian competition. Both the Tory government and the Liberals suggested that U.S. trade law procedure was a political process favouring its own petitioners. Liberals also pointed to visible requests for binational panels under the dispute resolution mechanism of the FTA and the seemingly endless disputes in highly public cases such as softwood lumber. The Liberals concluded that these, and other actions by the United States, proved that the FTA had to be renegotiated and access secured.

The Clinton administration's late adoption of the NAFTA agreement and its success in obtaining congressional passage in November 1993 placed before the new Liberal government a trade policy dilemma. While the 1993 Canadian election campaign had not focused in a fundamental way on trade, the Liberals hesitated over whether as a government they would enter into NAFTA on January 1, 1994. Liberal M.P. David Dingwall, speaking for the party at a news conference called on September 22, 1993, to rebut criticisms by Prime Minister Campbell, suggested that Canada would not enter into NAFTA until the key flaws of the agreement were renegotiated and that such negotiations could well go beyond January 1, 1994. A week later, on September 30, 1993, Roy MacLaren, a strong advocate of free trade (and now minister for international trade), implied that a Liberal government might not block implementation suggesting, that a "Liberal government would implement the agreement when it is in Canada's interest."[21] Jean Chrétien continued to insist that a Liberal government would demand renegotiation of NAFTA, notwithstanding the pointed statement by the United States' trade representative, Mickey Kantor, on the first day of the Canadian election campaign, repeated periodically and supported openly by President Clinton, that the United States would not consider reopening the talks. Further, in Prime Minister Chrétien's first news conference, held just days after the Liberal victory, he warned that his government might not implement NAFTA if the United States refused to renegotiate. He insisted that NAFTA needed to be changed to include, among other things, an agreement on what constituted an acceptable subsidy and clearer rules on the use of countervail trade sanctions.

Was the Liberal government's concern about American recourse to national trade remedy law valid? A review of all the recent trade cases and binational panels under the FTA reveals that the number of initiated anti-dumping cases in Canada or the United States dropped when comparing the period 1986–88 (before the FTA) with 1989–91 (the period just after the FTA). However, there has been a significant increase in the number of initiated anti-dumping cases in both Canada and the United States when 1990–91 is compared with 1992–93. Moreover, the number of binational panels, requested by either the United States or Canada, has increased in a comparison of the same periods. This is particularly striking in the number of American requests. In both countries, the number of investigations of anti-dumping cases initiated by the appropriate national administrative agency has shot up, but particularly so in the United States. Finally, there are far fewer countervail cases concerning alleged subsidies. In fact there are only five such cases, all of them American, that have been initiated since the implementation of the FTA. While the number of countervail cases is small in comparison to anti-dumping cases, they are high-profile and concern high dollar value exports such as softwood lumber or magnesium. This evidence would appear to underline the Liberal view that there is a rising volume of U.S. cases, although it also reveals that Canadians have not been unwilling to initiate anti-dumping actions against their American competitors. What the evidence underlines is that the pattern of cases and panels does appear to substantiate the perception of harassment by Canadian interests and the Canadian government, and could well undermine confidence in the dispute resolution system on both sides of the border if the trend is not blunted.

Following the statements during the election campaign (including the addition of the subject of the export of water shortly before the November Asia-Pacific Economic Cooperation forum summit), Prime Minister Chrétien dispatched his new minister of international trade, Roy MacLaren, to Washington to negotiate changes to NAFTA. MacLaren was briefed to deal with a side agreement on subsidies, a side agreement on anti-dumping, a side letter on restrictions on the wholesale transfer of water, and security of energy supplies.

MacLaren returned to Ottawa to present to cabinet the framework of an agreement, allowing the prime minister to announce on December 2, 1993, that Canada would be able to enter NAFTA on the appointed January 1, 1994 date. The United States and Canada agreed to reinstate, for all practical purposes, the working group established in Article 1907 of the FTA (this section had effectively been eliminated by the NAFTA). This working group will now conclude a report on unfair trade codes by 1995. The Liberals have found a way, it would seem, to keep alive the Canadian goal of confining American trade remedy law on the matter of subsidy. With the conclusion of a subsidies code in the Final Accord in GATT, there would appear to be the basis for moving at least to a common definition of what constitutes a subsidy. While critics suggested that the government had achieved nothing, there remains a locus for the two countries to continue efforts to reform trade remedy law and, potentially, to resolve the question of trade harassment. Unfortunately the progress achieved in this area was muddied as a result of Prime Minister Chrétien's insistence on seeking changes in Canadian obligations on energy. Questionable in its goal, the government effectively received nothing from the United States. The prime minister had to be content with a largely meaningless unilateral declaration that Canada had not given up its energy security. The evident American rebuff on energy undermined the success, limited but real, that had been achieved on the questions of anti-dumping and countervail duties.

Reinforcing Multilateralism as a National Strategy

The appointment of Roy MacLaren as minister for international trade placed a highly knowledgeable player in a critical economic portfolio. A former foreign service officer himself, MacLaren has been a consistently strong voice in the Liberal caucus for free trade and multilateralism. As critic for international trade when in opposition, MacLaren had spoken and written extensively on the impact of the FTA on the future of Canada. In a 1991 discussion paper, entitled "Beyond Continentalism: In Search of an Independent, Global Trade Policy for Canada," MacLaren attacked the Mulroney government in the following terms: "Both actively and passively, the government's whole approach to trade points to a fundamental drift (if not shift) towards continentalism." He directed his attention to the traditional bases of Liberal trade: support for liberalization as a small, open, trading nation; and multilateralism as a response to concerns about Canadian sovereignty, especially with respect to the United States. Based on these principles, the paper put forward an alternative option to the Progressive Conservative government's trade policy: to expand Canada's trade and links beyond the United States and, indeed, beyond the western hemisphere. As MacLaren suggested, "given Canada's decision to pursue free trade with the United States, it should take the next logical step and pursue free trade with the world—as the title of the paper suggests, move 'beyond continentalism' and become aggressively global."[22]

Much of the logic presented in the 1991 discussion paper remains valid today. What is clear is that the twin pillars of liberalization and multilateralism are under attack principally, but not solely, as a result of the aggressive trade strategy of the United States. The Liberal party's inclination to support multilateralism is important. The question remains how to act in an effective way with the key economic player exhibiting unilateral behaviour.

The new multilateral trade institution, the WTO, which was originally a Canadian proposal, would appear to afford the Liberal government an ideal setting to press for an agenda to reinforce multilateralism and an open trading system. It is critical for Canada, as an important but non-strategic player in the global economy, to ensure that a transparent rules-based regime is reinforced in fact and not just in principle. As the various national industrial strategy restrictions reveal, Canada could be seriously hurt by national non-MFN (Most Favoured Nation) and non-national treatment rules. Even conditional reciprocity may well threaten Canadian prosperity in the global economy. It is therefore vital that Canada use the WTO to reinforce a rules-based multilateral system. Given the very recent creation of WTO, the government has not necessarily had time to understand how this institution can assist Canadian global economic policy.

To make the WTO an effective multilateral instrument, capable of drawing the United States into the multilateral circle and blunting potentially unilateral initiatives, Canada will have to work in concert with other actors, particularly strategic actors such as Japan. This a significant task. Japan, like other players, has been a supporter of the multilateral trading system but has generally preferred bilateral negotiations to resolve problems. It has also been slow to recognize the barriers that hinder greater imports. Thus, in the case of the United States, Japan has preferred to undertake bilateral negotiations and has eschewed multilateral solutions. The new Canadian government, for national interest reasons, as well as the promotion of internationalism, may now have the opportunity to encourage the Japanese to support, and take a lead in promoting the effectiveness of the WTO. In this contentious trading environment, strategic players such as Japan may well be more inclined to see the value of collective action.

What then could the agenda be? How effective is the WTO likely to be? The evidence from the negotiations over NAFTA and the work in GATT and the Organization of Economic Cooperation and Development (OECD) demonstrates that trade is now intimately linked with a broad range of issues, including the environment, competition policy, investment, and technology transfer rules. These are issues which should not, and cannot realistically, be resolved in bilateral settings. Further, resolving them in a multilateral context will be vital in reinforcing a rules-based global system. As for the question of effectiveness, it remains unclear how the United States views the WTO. This will be of crucial importance to the institution. However, the U.S. attitude may well depend upon clear international community support for this multilateral institution. Here Canada can be a significant player, helping to ensure the effective participation of key players such as Japan and the European Union.

Trade Strategy versus Trade Promotion

As Trade Minister MacLaren noted, for Canada the question of multilateralism is also a question of sovereignty. Our adoption of a global trade approach, even examining the possibility of a comprehensive agreement with Japan, should be understood in the rejection of continentalism, Canada's trade dependence, and the concentration of our trade with the United States. As the minister argued, "the further integration of Canada into the world economy would serve to diminish Canada's relative dependency on the United States." Global trade policy, then, is intended to show that Canada is "prepared and eager to enter into reciprocal free trade relations."[23] This view is underscored in the "Red Book" in a call to limit American domination:

> If a Western Hemisphere free trade bloc evolves, Canada must play an active independent role in defining that bloc instead of merely reacting to Washington's hub-and-spoke approach to trade in this hemisphere. Canada should be working with other countries to minimize dominance by the strongest partner. . . . While we must seize opportunities for trade in the Americas, a Liberal government will not turn its back on the rest of the world. Expanding trade and investment with the Pacific Rim is crucial to our economic future.[24]

The extension of Canada's trading relationships is a theme to which MacLaren has returned since becoming minister. Shortly after the Asia-Pacific Economic Cooperation forum meeting in Seattle in November 1993, he suggested that he would consider a bilateral free trade deal with an Asian country: "I think there are Asian countries with which we could take steps to liberalize our trade faster than we could with other countries."[25] MacLaren has undertaken a strenuous travel schedule, including stops in Mexico, Chile, South Africa, and Asia.

Advancing a strategic trade policy does engender criticism. There are those within and outside the government who believe that Canada has absorbed as much trade policy as necessary with the successful conclusion of the Uruguay Round and NAFTA. What should now absorb Canadian policy makers is a concerted trade promotion effort intended to take advantage of the opportunities established by these trade arrangements. Thus, for example, governmental effort should be focused on supporting increased trade between Canada and Mexico rather than designing new trade initiatives. Moreover, government trade initiatives are not particularly meaningful. They represent diplomatic steps, as opposed to hard economic initiatives. Previous efforts, for example the Third Option, were largely divorced from trade and economic reality.

At the end of the day, however, it is likely not an either-or proposition. The government does need to ensure that it is effectively assisting the expansion of Canadian trade. However, the increasingly competitive global environment requires more than just a generalized effort to promote trade. Under the Clinton administration there is planning under way to advance the interests of the United States. The administration is already looking at a meeting in December, 1994 to include all democratic leaders from the western hemisphere. On that occasion the Clinton administration is hoping to release a plan to create a wider hemispheric free trade zone in the next 10 to 15 years, and, possibly indicate how, or whether, Chile will be invited into NAFTA in the very near future. The American undersecretary of commerce for international trade, Jeffrey Garten, has suggested that U.S. foreign economic policy is being revised based on American calculations of where global growth is likely to occur to the end of the decade. The undersecretary and his staff have already identified ten large emerging markets. In Garten's estimation, expanding American exports is the goal, and "this is where the efforts of government will pay off the most."[26]

Unless the Canadian government wishes to find itself responding to another U.S. trade initiative, as occurred with Mexico, Canadian policy is going to have to be more proactive and strategic. Put more positively, the Liberal government needs to undertake the exercise, in partnership with the major interests in Canada, especially the business community, to determine where Canada's trade and investment future should lie. Having established priorities, the Canadian government can then undertake the difficult task of promoting comprehensive trade relations with priority countries and integrate policy and commercial activity to achieve national ends. Such planning will mark an end to policy drift by identifying for Canadians a positive trade strategy. From all indications, Trade Minister MacLaren recognizes the importance of such a global trade strategy.

There Is No Foreign Policy: There Is No Domestic Policy

While Roy MacLaren recognizes the importance of an effective trade policy, he is fully aware, as is his party, that success can only be built on the growing strength of the Canadian economy. As the Red Book describes contemporary Canadian trade: "The Liberal Party does not see trade policy as a substitute for domestic policies. Monetary, fiscal, investment, training, education, and research and development policies go hand-in-hand with a nation's trade policy."[27] There is a general recognition that to create a successful trade policy, the Canadian economy must become increasingly competitive. In that regard, the Red Book examines steps to address fiscal and monetary policy and to improve human capital. And it devotes an entire chapter to the creation of an innovation economy, where it argues for a working relationship with the private sector to:

> identify strategic opportunities for the future, then redirect . . . existing resources towards the fulfilment of those opportunities. Research and development, small business policy, education and training, taxation policy, environmental regulation, community economic development, and the availability of venture capital are all areas where the federal government can focus its efforts to achieve strategic economic opportunities and promote economic growth. Our future success will come when we coordinate all these policies with the single-minded goal of producing greater wealth and more good jobs for all Canadians.[28]

While a number of goals are identified, a key objective in development of an innovation economy is a policy to foster a more active small and medium-sized business community. Besides undertaking initiatives to draw these companies into an R&D environment, the Liberal party argues for a directed trade policy:

> Canadian firms, especially small and medium-sized businesses, must adopt an aggressive trading mentality and a strong outward orientation to take advantage of export markets. More Canadian businesses must become exporters, and government must develop the knowledge and skills to make that possible.[29]

The approach described in the Red Book is broad and encompasses a wide range of policies, from macro- to micro-economic.

From the prime minister to the cabinet there is the intent to promote fiscal responsibility, to cooperate with other levels of government to fashion a more coherent and determined attack on economic policy, and to reduce internal barriers to the movement of goods and services. There also appears to be a genuine interest in building a "Canada Inc." or "Team Canada" approach. However, the changes to the structure of the federal government and of the ministers' offices do not appear to have taken into account the demands of a Team Canada strategy. In particular, no steps were taken to link more closely the departments of Industry and Trade, though that was a possible option. Even more serious was the decision to encourage Paul Martin to take up the Finance portfolio. Martin was, along with Chaviva Hosek, the principal source behind the Red Book. Many of the initiatives, particularly the industrial policy recommendations, came from Martin. It was anticipated that Martin would be a prime figure in implementing the Team Canada growth agenda from the Department of Industry. The decision to place Martin at Finance has limited, at least on initial examination, a key figure in the development of a growth agenda. Indeed, by early 1994 the government appears not to have spoken or acted on the growth agenda as described in the Red Book.

Conclusion

The global economic challenges that face the new government are enormous. For better or worse, this government has had to deal with these matters almost from its first day in office. This placed an immediate burden on ministers and officials responsible for fashioning trade and economic policy. While it is early in the Liberal government's mandate, there are some tentative conclusions that can be drawn. Notwithstanding criticism levelled against the government in its determination to renegotiate aspects of the free trade arrangements, the Chrétien government has been able to keep on the negotiating table with the United States the damage that recourse to national trade remedy law has for both countries. In a bilateral relationship of such marked asymmetry, the agreement to maintain a working group on subsidy and anti-dumping must be seen as a positive achievement.

With respect to the question of the reinforcement of a rules-based multilateral trade and investment regime, the conditions are present to design and implement a Canadian strategy. The minister for international trade, Roy MacLaren, favours a global trade policy and is committed to multilateralism. There is, as a result of the successful completion of the Uruguay Round, a potentially effective multilateral institution, the WTO. What remains to be determined is whether the government can recognize the potential of, and then implement a strategy for reinforcing multilateralism as well as achieving Canada's national interests through this new institution.

In examining the early efforts to fashion a trade strategy, there is a debate between those who favour trade promotion as opposed to those who desire a strategic trade plan. In reality both objectives are required. To assist the expansion of exports, the Canadian government needs to review, and revise where necessary, trade promotion initiatives. However, it is equally the case that Canada must develop a trade strategy. If Canada is to diminish its dependence both economically and politically on the United States, it will have to identify priorities and possibly seek comprehensive trade relations. It would appear that the current minister for international trade has long understood the need for Canada to establish a global trade policy. We must now await ministerial direction.

Lastly, there is little evidence that the government has begun a concerted effort to act on the severest challenge: to fashion an integrated economic policy that builds on what has been referred to as a Team Canada approach. Such an approach avoids the traditional barriers separating foreign and domestic policy. It recognizes the critical relationship of prudent fiscal management with economic competitiveness. It acknowledges the critical need to stop talking about internal barriers and actually begin to dismantle them. Further, it requires the provincial and federal levels of government to do more than talk about partnership and harmonization. Finally, and dramatically, it needs to orchestrate a microeconomic strategy that builds an innovative economy: by acting in partnership with firms, especially small and medium-sized companies; providing training for workers; applying commercialized innovation; and establishing the appropriate institutional forms, knowledge, information, and financing to trade and invest.

All of this requires a significant change in the way the federal government functions. It will take time. The interest of the government and individual ministries appears to be there, but there is little indication that the appropriate planning and decision making structures have been put in place to allow for such a change. It is also not clear that responsibilities have been optimally assigned. Good intentions will surely fail without the ability to advance such a significant agenda. The reward for such a successful transformation is the greater competitiveness of the Canadian economy and then, hopefully, jobs and a rising standard of living. Greater Canadian integration into the global economy can provide Canada with the contemporary currency of power and influence on which the new world order depends—economic power. Canada can, really for the first time since the onset of the Cold War, affect its own place in this order. We can fashion our own way.

THE FUTURE OF MULTILATERALISM

3 The Future of Canadian Multilateralism

Tom Keating

MULTILATERALISM IS APPROACHING a critical juncture, and its future direction is intricately linked with Canadian foreign policy. Since the 1940s Canadian foreign policy has developed in and around multilateralist associations. Recent demands and expectations, however, have far outpaced the capacity of these institutions, many of which have also been shaken by the turbulence that has defined international politics in recent years. This chapter reviews some of these developments and argues that the future viability of multilateralism depends on the ability of institutions, and more precisely their member governments, to respond effectively to the pressing demands for adaptation and change. Given the continuing significance of multilateralism for the pursuit of Canadian foreign policy objectives, this becomes a particularly important issue for the newly elected Liberal government. While there will be many opportunities for Canadian policy makers to contribute to this process of adaptation and change, an effective response will require a degree of creativity and commitment comparable to that displayed in the 1940s.

In recent years multilateral institutions, and especially the United Nations (UN), have moved to the centre of the international political arena. One of the distinguishing features of this renewed multilateralism has been an increase in the opportunities and demands for more assertive and interventionist activity. The passing of the Cold War has brought a fundamental change in the political and security environment in which the institution has operated. Removed from the constraints of the Cold War, the UN has become more actively involved in dealing with regional and intra-state conflicts. On the practical side, there is now a greater likelihood that the permanent members of the Security Council will be able to agree on collective action. There have also been indications in recent years of an emerging consensus, at least among a core group of members, on the desirability of adopting a more assertive and interventionist approach to deal with a whole range of problems, from sources of conflict to human rights and the environment. Finally, for a number of years there have been many social, economic, and political problems that defy national solutions; accordingly, demands for multilateral action have intensified. As a result of these developments, multilateral institutions have been viewed as the primary instrument for the establishment of a new world order that would usher in a more peaceful, prosperous, and progressive age.

Indications of these changes could be found in various associations in addition to the UN, including the Organization of American States (OAS), the Conference on Security and Co-operation in Europe (CSCE), the annual economic summits of the G-7, and the World Bank. Nowhere, however, has the promise of real change been more apparent than in the corridors, lounges, and assembly halls of the United Nations. For some observers the Gulf War was an indication that the UN would soon be able to implement the collective security provisions that had been stillborn in 1945. The Security Council summit of January 1992, and subsequent release of the secretary general's report, *An Agenda for Peace,* later that year were also signs of an institutional renewal. Finally, the unprecedented Security Council decision of December 1992 to intervene militarily in Somalia seemed to confirm that the international community was moving in the direction of a more intrusive form of multilateralism, one that would place less emphasis on state sovereignty and more on alternative values such as democracy, human rights, and environmentalism.

The former Conservative government in Ottawa strongly supported these changes. Early in the 1990s it identified good governance as one of the guiding principles of Canada's foreign policy. Multilateral associations were to be employed to achieve these noble, if (in the context of traditional international politics) revolutionary, objectives. Many of that government's specific proposals concerning human rights and responsible government were articulated in multilateral associations such as the Commonwealth and la Francophonie, meetings of the CSCE and the OAS, and before the UN General Assembly. The interest in using multilateralism to pursue substantial foreign policy objectives was also evident in the government's strong support for the proposals in *An Agenda for Peace*. Nor was this support merely rhetorical. Canada's former UN representative, Yves Fortier, was the first to advocate UN intervention with Canadian troops in the disintegrating republic of Yugoslavia in the fall of 1991. Former prime minister Mulroney also initiated a multilateral response to the overthrow of President Bertrand Aristide in Haiti in February 1992. In addition, the government supported the Security Council's first explicit venture in humanitarian intervention in Somalia in December 1992 and committed Canadian armed forces to the cause.

As 1993 drew to a close the optimistic soundings of the potential for multilateralism had yielded to a more discordant tone. Once again the UN received most of the attention. The promise of a new world order fading with the persistence of bitter nationalist conflict in Bosnia, continuing anarchy in Somalia, an aborted mission to Haiti, and the resumption of civil war in Angola. Bold initiatives have left the United Nations and many member governments over-extended and over-exposed. It became evident that there were substantial costs and risks inherent in this more assertive multilateralism—for institutions, member governments, and perhaps the entire process of multilateralism.

There was also cause for concern in other areas and institutions. It could be seen, for example, in the tortoise-like pace of trade policy reform under the General Agreement on Tariffs and Trade (GATT) and the creeping bilateralism and unilateralism in international economic relations. The limited results of multilateral conferences on the environment in Rio de Janeiro in 1992 and human rights in Vienna in 1993 also made it clear that independent states were not yet ready to yield sovereignty to multilateral regulations and that consensus on basic principles would not be easily achieved. The hesitant and uncertain response of the North Atlantic Treaty Organization (NATO) to the collapse of the Warsaw Pact and the Soviet Union, and the problems the CSCE has experienced in defining an effective alternative to alliance structures are further indications of the uncertainty surrounding the future of multilateralism. The new world order has, for many, become a term of derision. The multilateral organizations that were going to oversee the transformation, and especially the United Nations, have fallen far from the optimistic hopes of the early 1990s. Increased, and arguably unrealistic, expectations have not been met and as a result the institutions have been castigated. For Canada, which has traditionally supported and relied on multilateralism, these developments are particularly worrisome for they call into question not only specific policies but the processes and institutions on which multilateralism rests.

John Ruggie has written that one of the distinguishing features of multilateralism "is that it coordinates behavior among three or more states on the basis of generalized principles of conduct."[1] There is, in Ruggie's view — and it is one that I share — more involved in multilateralism than the purely nominal activity of three or more states collaborating together. There is also a qualitative dimension to multilateralism reflected in generalized principles of conduct. These principles "specify appropriate conduct for a class of actions, without regard to the particularistic interests of the parties or the strategic exigencies that may exist in any specific occurrence."[2] Multilateralism is also not limited to general purpose universal institutions. Instead, as Ruggie writes, "the attributes of multilateralism characterize relations within specific collectivities that may and often do fall short of the whole universe of nations."[3] This is evident in Canada's case, since the more important elements of post-war multilateralism in Canadian foreign policy have been associations such as NATO and the GATT which started with a limited number of committed members.

Multilateral cooperation has been a prominent feature of post-World War Two international politics and has played a significant part in Canadian foreign policy. For much of this time multilateralism has been rooted in transatlantic cooperation in which Canada's interest in sustaining the North Atlantic triangle converged with a wider interest in preserving western security. Today the triangle no longer defines Canada's foreign policy interests. Shifting interests in trade and security and changing immigration patterns have brought about an interest in hemispheric and Pacific connections. As a result, the transatlantic connections no longer provide a sufficient foundation for multilateralism. In addition to its geographical characteristic, post-war multilateralism was also supported by an overriding concern with security interests. Today security concerns are less immediate and the threat of general war more remote. Other issues, principally commercial ones, have assumed greater prominence. It is no longer self-evident that under these changed conditions existing multilateral structures will be sufficient to serve Canadian interests effectively.

Beyond encompassing a broader array of states and issues, the character of multilateralism has also changed. It has become increasingly intrusive, encroaching on more and more areas that were formerly the responsibility of national governments. Since the end of the Cold War it has also taken on coercive overtones, as leading supporters of the post-war liberal order, including Canada under the Mulroney government, have sought to extend the geographical scope of these liberal principles to other parts of the globe. The overriding objective in the past was to further an international order that was peaceful and stable. In recent years a concern with peace and stability has been superseded by advocates of economic reforms, human rights, political liberties, and environmental practices. Despite, or perhaps because of, these changes, there has remained in Ottawa a strong commitment to multilateral cooperation. The principal institutions that have been used may be changing and the geographical scope and substantive content may be altered, but the principles and practices of multilateralism seem well entrenched in Canadian foreign policy. Recent developments have, justifiably, created a considerable amount of uncertainty and anxiety around the future of multilateral cooperation. As is argued below, in this period of risk and uncertainty, concerns over the capacity, credibility, and legitimacy of existing institutions, and the policies of key states such as the United States, Germany, Russia, and others, will play a critical role in determining the future viability of multilateral cooperation.

Assertive Multilateralism

The 1990s have witnessed a revival of UN-sponsored peacekeeping operations. As a result of the unprecedented cooperation of the permanent members of the Security Council, thirteen operations have been initiated since 1989. During 1992 and 1993 the organization deployed its largest operations ever in Cambodia, the former Yugoslavia, and Somalia. These missions — each of which has had significant Canadian involvement and which are discussed in detail in subsequent chapters — were unprecedented not only in the number of troops involved, but also in their mandates. The range of activities included everything from the more typical monitoring of cease-fires to such non-traditional duties as election-monitoring, protection of minorities, humanitarian relief, and social and political reconstruction. There has also been a shift at the UN to more permissive attitudes about the necessity for mutual consent before initiating these operations and bypassing sovereign authorities. By 1993 peacekeeping as traditionally understood no longer accurately defined the activities of many of the blue berets deployed around the world. New designations such as peacemaking, enforcement, and humanitarian intervention more accurately described these operations. In Cambodia, Bosnia, and Somalia the UN undertook missions that intervened more directly and assertively in the domestic affairs of member governments and did so, at times, without the support of local authorities.

The shift in UN operations toward a greater emphasis on enforcement measures has not been the result of a consistent set of factors. At times the initiative has come from member states, as it did for example in the aborted mission to Haiti. On other occasions, such as with Somalia, the organization has responded to pressure from the secretary general, Boutros Boutros-Ghali. It would seem, however, that support for these missions is indicative of a developing consensus among member governments, and especially the permanent members of the Security Council, on the desirability and potential for humanitarian intervention. Some governments, including Canada's, have been in the forefront in advocating this more assertive and interventionist role. David Cox said that "no government, to my knowledge, has been more emphatic about the limitations on the principle of sovereignty than the current government of Canada."[4] The Canadian government's support is reflected in the fact that the relative size of its contribution to these operations is far greater than any other UN member.

The growing political support for enforcement operations, at least in principle, can also be seen in other institutions. The OAS, for example, has adopted provisions that support unspecified interventionary measures to restore democratically elected governments that have been overturned through non-democratic means. At the OAS General Assembly in Santiago, Chile, in 1991, in a decision supported by Canada, member governments adopted the "Santiago Commitment to Democracy and the Renewal of the International System." This document is a statement of principles and selected measures designed to restore democratically elected governments to power in the face of rebellions or coups. These measures were employed in response to threats to democracy in Peru and Haiti with negligible results. Institutions such as the CSCE have also favoured more interventionist practices. For instance, officials at the CSCE's 1992 summit not only adopted changes that would provide it with the potential to intervene in a greater variety of issues, but also enlisted the forces of NATO to provide the necessary military force to make this potential more credible. The principle of humanitarian intervention has also received support at the annual economic summits of the G-7. Calls for enforcement measures have not been limited to armed conflicts or security issues. There have, for example, been demands that the World Bank should use interventionist measures to further human rights or protect the environment. Both the Bank and the International Monetary Fund (IMF) have been intervening in domestic economic policy for years. Recent trade agreements such as the North American Free Trade Agreement (NAFTA) provide for greater involvement in domestic affairs, including environmental and labour standards, and incorporate enforcement provisions as part of the agreement.

The Risks of Intervention

A greater emphasis on enforcement, and especially enforcement measures that take multilateral institutions into the domestic affairs of member states, raises a number of practical, political, and institutional risks. The risks for Canada are considerable. The increase in the number and scope of UN operations in recent years has required more troops and money. In comparison with 1990, the costs of UN peacekeeping in 1993 had escalated from about $700 million a year to more than $2.4 billion. As these increased expenses have not been met by member governments, the UN has had to squeeze other expenses to the point where it was forced to end daily sittings of the forty-sixth General Assembly early to save money on its power bill. Andy Knight provides greater details on these problems in the following chapter. The Canadian delegation, and others, continue to press for more effective financing of UN peacekeeping operations. Yet when major donors such as the United States balk at paying their assessments and owe more than a quarter of a million dollars on peacekeeping costs alone, the prospects for reform look as bleak as ever.

These new operations require more than a financial commitment. In 1993 more than eighty thousand individuals were serving under UN command around the world, nearly ten thousand of whom were Canadian. In addition to the numbers, the complement of nations involved in UN peacekeeping operations has changed. Once limited to impartial middle powers, the major powers are now assuming a greater role in these operations. While Britain and France are not strangers to UN operations, they have become quite prominent in the United Nations Protection Force (UNPROFOR) in the former Yugoslavia. For the first time in Somalia, American troops have been operating under UN command structures following the transfer of authority from the Unified Task Force (UNITAF) to the UN Operation in Somalia (UNOSOM II) in May 1993. Russian troops and those from other Commonwealth of Independent States (CIS), such as Ukraine, have also participated in recent UN operations. In addition, both Japan and Germany have broken with post-war tradition and strong constitutional and political inhibitions in contributing to UN forces in Cambodia and Somalia respectively. Japan has also contributed forces to the UN's operation in Mozambique. Despite this increased involvement on the part of the permanent members and other major powers, the contributions of middle powers such as Canada remain a significant part of these multinational forces.

Enforcement missions are obviously more dangerous than traditional peacekeeping operations. It is not at all clear that contributing states are willing to accept these risks or that their support will remain in the face of casualties. The experience of American forces in Somalia, discussed by Nancy Gordon in chapter 13, provides a clear indication of these problems. In response to American casualties in Somalia the U.S. Congress began to put pressure on the Clinton administration to withdraw American forces from this UN operation. The fallout was not limited to Somalia and the effects may constrain the administration's ability to contribute to multilateralism through the UN and in other areas. Congress adopted legislation that reflected its "hostility toward the mounting cost and complexity of United Nations peacekeeping operations, a belief that the American share of these bills is too large and a concern about waste and corruption in the organization." The legislation "killed a proposed $175 million fund for unforeseen peacekeeping costs; withheld 10 percent of its regular budget contributions until Secretary General Boutros Boutros-Ghali appoints an Inspector General to fight waste and corruption; cancelled the fourth of five special payments to eliminate existing arrears, and told the Clinton administration to cut the American share of new peacekeeping bills from 31.7 percent to 25 percent."[5]

These measures effectively undermined the administration's earlier demands for a more assertive multilateralism and reaffirmed the position of the United States as the UN's biggest debtor. It was, perhaps, in anticipation of this that Clinton informed the General Assembly that the United States would view its commitments to the UN selectively: "If the American people are to say yes to the U.N. peacekeeping, the United Nations must know when to say no."[6] The message according to Thomas Friedman, reporting in the *New York Times* and paraphrasing President Kennedy's inaugural address, was that the United States would "pay only some prices, fight only some foes, and . . . bear only some burdens in the defense of freedom."[7] By the end of the year the Clinton administration was revising its plans for participation in UN peacekeeping operations.

The Americans are not the only ones to be affected by these developments, the commitments of other member governments may also be at risk. The German government, for example, took considerable political risks in supplying troops to the UN operation in Somalia. If UN forces there are destined to a humbling withdrawal, it may make it more difficult for Germany to make a similar contribution in the future and encourage a more isolationist policy. In Ottawa similar concerns, and others unique to Canada, have given rise to political and financial problems. The greater risks involved in these more assertive operations raise concerns among the military about the proper level of training (for reserves) and the quality of equipment. Political leaders share these concerns and the possibility of declining public support in the face of the increased risks that Canadian forces may face in the field. Operating under severe budgetary constraints, the Canadian armed forces have been stretched to the limit in meeting existing UN commitments. Despite its campaign promise, it is not at all clear what additional financial support a Liberal government will supply to maintain, let alone expand, these commitments. Any policy to save defence dollars may substantially impair the government's ability to respond to requests for additional peacekeeping contributions. On the political side, contributions to the UN have generally been viewed as a positive commitment Canada makes to international order that also distinguishes the country's foreign policy from that of the United States. As Jockel and Sokolsky have argued, recent UN operations, such as the one in Somalia, require a revision of these assumptions, but the effects that this might have on policy choices are as yet unclear.[8] Not only might these contributions now be seen as an extension of United States' policy, they might also alienate UN members such as India who are opposed to these interventionist measures.

The most important effects of developments in Bosnia and Somalia and of the shift to a more critical view of the UN in American policy are likely to be on the credibility of the UN. Already condemned by some as accomplices to aggression in Bosnia, American criticisms of the UN's role in Somalia brought a quick response from the secretary general. "The United States has no credibility until it pays and stops hiding its incapacity to pay behind complaints about the need for more United Nations reforms."[9] On the more substantive issue of the problems in Somalia that had precipitated the American policy shift, he cautioned that this new form of intervention would not be simple, straightforward, or always successful. "It must be understood that there will be failures as well as successes. The UN is not a magic wand. The problems before us cannot be solved quickly. Staying power is crucial. If the forces of chaos and confusion conclude that the UN is short of breath, they will prevail simply by waiting for the world to turn its attention elsewhere."[10] It thus becomes imperative that governments in countries such as Canada, which have a stake in preserving the UN as a credible forum for conducting multilateral negotiations, must attempt to prevent the organization from taking on tasks where it lacks the capacity to be effective.

The debate between the UN and the United States over Somalia is indicative of the problems the organization will face as it conducts these new operations. The credibility of the organization is being tested and it is not doing well. At risk are not only these more interventionist practices but the full range of UN activities, including more traditional forms of peacekeeping. For example, one analyst has recently described peacekeeping as "a hopeful enterprise that stands on the brink of being ruined by the unrealistic expectations of UN member states who send the Organization into some of the world's most intractable trouble spots without strong and consistent political and financial support."[11] There is the very real risk that the UN will become the dumping ground for problems that member governments find too difficult to resolve and subsequently will be blamed when the problems continue.

This is not to suggest that the UN is without fault. Its problems include inadequate infrastructure, the lack of effective command and control in New York, inappropriate equipment, and ambivalent rules of engagement. There have also been numerous allegations of corruption and abuse of privilege in the field, ranging from black marketing activities and prostitution to acts of violence in both Bosnia and Somalia. Jocelyn Coulon's chapter touches on the apparent lack of impartiality of several UN peacekeeping contingents in Cambodia. On the other hand there have been proposals to improve this performance—everything from a special peacekeeping fund of US$50 million to get forces in the field as quickly as possible, to the prior positioning of equipment, to a proposed UN stand-by force comprised of troops from various member states. As discussed in the next chapter, there are many proposals for radical reforms. However, given the limited amount of experience and the uncertain consensus, a more reflective or reformist approach seems preferable. In the final analysis a good deal of the responsibility for the UN's recent problems must be borne by member governments. "It is not some disembodied 'UN' that has brought the organization to this tortured pass. Nor is it its secretary general, who has ambitions for the institution but not independent authority. It is the collective decisions of the U.N. membership, especially the top dogs."[12] If the credibility problem is to be effectively addressed, member governments will have to demonstrate a good deal more political will and practical support than they have to date. Until this materializes Canadian policy makers might be wise to argue for greater caution and a clearer mandate before advocating more intervention.

The Demise of Atlanticism

The assertive multilateralism displayed by the United Nations stands in sharp contrast to the more timid response of NATO. In recent years the United Nations has replaced NATO as Canada's primary multilateral security connection. While the UN has had difficulty in adjusting to its new role, the problem for NATO has been in defining any role amidst the rapidly changing security situation in Europe. Alexander Moens provides a more thorough discussion of this issue in chapter 7, but a few considerations are worth raising here.

For years NATO served as the principal stabilizing feature of European security and a fundamental part of Canada's multilateral security structure. In the late 1940s Escott Reid viewed NATO as an initial step on the road to an expanded collection of liberal democracies. Article 2 of the North Atlantic Treaty was designed, in part, to facilitate the non-security dimensions of multilateralism. This vision for NATO never materialized. Instead it became primarily a military alliance and its main task evolved into one of deterring Soviet advances in Europe. NATO has as yet been unable to overcome its Cold War legacy. Four years after the collapse of the Berlin Wall, the alliance still lacks a coherent plan for its future role in regional security. Continued instability in Russia and persisting concerns about the disposition of nuclear weapons in that country and other republics of the former Soviet Union have provided one source of sustenance. Beyond this, however, there are no clear directions for the future. On paper it would seem to be the only multilateral institution with the necessary capacity to provide security guarantees. Indeed its capabilities are sufficiently impressive that both the UN and the CSCE have enlisted NATO forces as stand-by units.

It is unlikely that this will be a sustaining role. For one thing, it is not clear that member governments will support it. On balance, what NATO possesses in capability it would seem to lack in legitimacy. After all, it was designed for inter-state conflict of a particular type. Present indications are that conflict is more likely to be civil than international and may be as likely to occur within member governments as between them and some outside power. In the immediate term as discussed by Teresa Rakowska-Harmstone in chapter 11 and Alexander Moens in chapter 7, NATO's major dilemma will be how to respond to the governments of Eastern Europe.

One of the problems in defining a new role for NATO reflects the competition between institutions in Europe. This poses a particular difficulty for Canada. Efforts to reinforce transatlantic connections depend very much on the response of Europeans. Yet for the time being Europeans have not clearly defined which is to be the lead institution in security matters. Each of NATO, the

European Union (EU), the WEU (Western European Union), and the CSCE have failed to demonstrate the capacity to respond effectively to security threats in the Balkans. As a result, the multilateral European security structure is in disarray.

The CSCE has failed to fill the security vacuum in Europe. It has been as inconsequential in responding to the war in the former Yugoslavia as have other European institutions. The fact that it lacks the capacity to respond with force may be alleviated somewhat by NATO's willingness to support CSCE-sanctioned activities, but at the present time the institution is not able to settle these issues alone. Nonetheless the Canadian government continues to support the CSCE, suggesting that it sees the organization as still offering a promising option for the future of European security. The CSCE may very well remain Ottawa's best chance for securing a transatlantic multilateral connection. It may also remain an important institution for strengthening East-West relations. Unlike NATO, which seems unable to shake its Cold War heritage, the history of the CSCE has been marked by bridging and confidence-building measures that have effectively overcome the barriers resulting from Cold War alliance structures. What the CSCE lacks in military capacity it may compensate for with political credibility and legitimacy. It may also be worthwhile to explore expanding the CSCE's economic role.[13] More than other institutions, the CSCE would seem to retain the potential to bridge both the transatlantic and the West-East divides.

The problems in Europe have been complicated by the erosion of the transatlantic basis for multilateralism. The post-war consensus on security and trade issues has become more difficult to maintain as states on both sides of the Atlantic display a penchant for unilateral and regional initiatives. The lack of cooperation and consultation is especially noteworthy on the GATT negotiations and over the war in the former Yugoslavia. The breakdown of order in Yugoslavia and the developing war in Bosnia were claimed by the European Union as European issues that required and would receive a European response. The failure of the EU to resolve the conflict in its early stages led many in Washington to blame the Europeans. The American reaction, however, was also problematic. Rather than pursue solutions through transatlantic institutions such as NATO or even through the UN, the United States instead turned to public diplomacy in threatening air strikes and conducted bilateral meetings with European governments to win support.

Trade negotiations have been equally problematic and retaliatory threats have been as common as constructive diplomacy. The successful completion of the Uruguay Round may ease transatlantic tensions in this area. The difficulty in reaching an agreement, however, was partly a result of a more inward-looking policy on the part of all the major partners. The attention devoted to regional agreements in the European Union, the Free Trade Agreement, and NAFTA required enormous political energy that seemed to detract from broader multilateral negotiations. Canada's ongoing preoccupation with protecting marketing boards, for example, constrained the government's ability to put forward compromise proposals.

The differences between the European and American interests reached a climax in October 1993 when the Clinton administration publicly criticized the Europeans. Much of the criticism was in response to European complaints over Clinton's Bosnia policy, but the reaction was unexpected and highly visible. Clinton complained that the British prime minister, John Major, was more worried about the fall of his own government than the human suffering in Bosnia, and the American secretary of state, Warren Christopher, suggested that Washington might need to re-think its foreign policy because "Europe is no longer the dominant area of the world."[14] The differences may have been a reflection of frustrations brought on by domestic pressure on the Clinton administration to do something in Bosnia, and they were subsequently smoothed over. They are, however, suggestive of the shifting interests in North America to both the hemisphere and to the Pacific Rim.

It is perhaps inevitable that the transatlantic character of post-1945 multilateralism should give way to other options. In some cases it is a measure of the success of this process that it should now encompass states from various regions of the globe. From a Canadian perspective, shifting priorities in security and trade have brought about a relocation of resources. This has been encouraged by changing demographic patterns as immigration flows now tend to cross the Pacific to a much greater extent than the Atlantic. The result has been greater attention to the western hemisphere and the Pacific Rim. In these regions the multilateral foundation is less secure, but Canadians have taken an interest in supporting it. Transatlantic cooperation has also been complicated by the emergence and strength of bilateral and unilateral initiatives in areas such as trade policy. It is further compounded by governments confronting high debt loads, persistent deficits, and considerable domestic pressure to deal with problems at home. The future health of multilateral cooperation with Europe will not simply be maintained by default because of the existence of institutions. It will require states to turn away from the isolationism that is gaining support on both sides of the Atlantic, to identify key institutions such as the CSCE as the basis for future cooperation, and to identify areas in which multilateral procedures are likely to yield mutually beneficial outcomes.

Legitimizing Multilateral Institutions

One of the biggest challenges facing organizations such as the UN, the OAS, the World Bank, and others will be in maintaining the support of their membership. Multilateral institutions have become more assertive and more intrusive. Sovereignty is becoming less and less effective as a barrier to the regulation of multilateral regimes. In areas as disparate as trade, human rights, and the environment, multilateral institutions now take a direct interest in the domestic policies of member states and increasingly attempt to intervene to redress problems that have been identified. As the activities of these organizations have expanded and encroached more and more into the domestic affairs of member states, questions have been raised over the legitimacy of these decisions, the procedures by which they were made, and the organizations that make them. In recent years representatives from African and South Asian governments have, for example, questioned the UN's authority to intervene in the sovereign affairs of member governments. Their concerns reflect an anxiety that a handful of western states are determining when and how the UN should intervene and fear that their interests and priorities for organizing domestic economies and polities were being excluded.

Similar concerns have been expressed about the World Bank's attempts to impose environmental or human rights standards on recipient countries and trade policy priorities in the GATT. It will be important for multilateral institutions to address these apprehensions if they are to succeed in expanding the scope and authority of international regulations and in enhancing the ability of institutions to enforce these regulations. There may, for example, be a need to develop a supportive consensus among key states in a region before assertive action is taken there. In addition, it will be necessary for institutions to be as consistent as possible in the application of these regulations. "The concept of the neutrality of the United Nations," noted one observer, "must be maintained if the UN is to avoid being perceived as a tool of narrow national interest. The United Nations must not only be neutral but must be perceived to be neutral."[15] In order to maintain this neutrality, it may be beneficial on occasion to turn to other institutions or a selected group of states to enforce decisions taken by the UN. In that way the UN can remain apart from the actual conflict and be used as a forum for negotiating a resolution of the conflict.

The domination of multilateral institutions by western states also raises concerns about the representation of alternative views within the UN and other institutions. In organizations like the United Nations it will not be sufficient for western governments, however noble their intentions, to dictate what is and what is not acceptable behaviour. If they cannot resist the temptation to proselytize their own moral values, then this would better be done on a bilateral basis. To use multilateral organizations for such purposes runs the risk of undermining the legitimacy of these organizations and further reducing their room for effective action. If the UN is to take a more active role in the area of human rights, for example, in the longer term it will be more effective if it has built a consensus for such action in the General Assembly rather than have it imposed by the Security Council. If universal organizations such as the UN, the GATT, and the World Bank are to maintain (or regain) their legitimacy, they must retain the support of all their members, rich and poor alike. As the East-West conflict becomes an historical footnote, the North-South divide assumes greater significance. The fact that western values prevailed in the Cold War does not mean that they now become the preserve and the raison d'être of multilateral institutions.

There is still a great diversity of ideas and programs in the international community that institutions such as the UN should reflect. Adam Roberts criticized *An Agenda for Peace* on this very issue when he wrote: "It makes too little allowance for the real differences of perspectives among states and for their narrow often competing interests."[16] At a minimum it will be necessary to recognize, respect, and respond to these different perspectives. If multilateralism is to be effective in addressing contemporary global concerns, the Canadian government and others must bridge this divide and develop mechanisms that will incorporate the interests of these states and peoples. This will ultimately strengthen the work of these international institutions.

One way of enhancing the legitimacy of multilateral institutions is to make the decision-making structures of the organizations more representative. In the United Nations this has generally been addressed in terms of institutional reform and much of the attention has focused on the Security Council. There is a widespread view that the Council is in need of reform and that its permanent membership needs to be expanded to account for the changes that have occurred since 1945.

A number of special interests have emerged in this debate. For some, it is necessary to recognize the economic power of Japan and Germany. This would, however, do little to silence opposition to the North's over-representation and, if anything, might have a detrimental effect on the institution's legitimacy in much of the world. Alternatively, or additionally, an expanded Security Council might include as permanent members representatives from the South such as India, Nigeria, Brazil, or others. This would seemingly alleviate some of the concerns over the dominance of the West within the institution, but it is important to keep in mind that dominance is not simply a result of having a seat at the Security Council. An expanded and more representative Security Council may thus not completely satisfy the concerns of some Third World governments about western bias in UN operations. It would, however, increase their opportunities to offer alternative views. Its effects on Canada would likely be negative in that the opportunities for Canadian participation and influence might be reduced.

During the 1993 election campaign the Liberals indicated their support for a Charter Review Conference in 1995. Security Council reform has been identified as a priority in this area, and the Canadian government will be in a position to play a significant role in this process. Canada's interest in reform and its long-standing commitment to the UN are likely the reasons why it will lead the open-ended Working Group that will examine the issue of Security Council reform and make recommendations to the General Assembly in September 1994.[17] As part of this important process, Canadian officials should keep in mind the principles that guided the government's approach in 1945, and they should emphasize among the criteria to be considered a state's potential contribution to the objectives of the organization.

Another method for enhancing the legitimacy of multilateral decision making might be to expand the membership of multilateral associations. In some, such as the OAS, this may be limited by geographic or other special considerations. In others, such as the G-7, it may be constrained by political pressures. Where possible, however, expanding the membership may add new ideas and interests to the association. It might also generate a greater commitment to multilateralist principles on the part of these new members. It would seem, for example, that despite the problems, the GATT has become a much more influential association as a result of its expanded membership and that its governing principles have gained wider support. There are indications that other institutions are also making changes to accommodate new states with new interests. Canada has registered its support for such moves, as reflected in former trade minister Michael Wilson's comments to the Organization for Economic Co-operation and Development (OECD). "Expanding the OECD's relations with non-member countries is in the best interests of all members...Canada strongly supports continuing this open yet differentiated approach. We have seen that a number of countries have moved toward much closer economic cooperation with the OECD as their economies have developed. Mexico and Korea . . . have become active participants in many OECD committees, making valuable contributions and drawing benefit from the experience."[18]

Larger membership can sometimes delay and complicate the decision-making process, but in the long term it would seem both to strengthen and legitimize the institution. As Miles Kahler has shown, there are also effective strategies for addressing concerns over the decision-making process.[19] This could be done in various ways, such as different voting procedures, concurrent majorities by different groups, consensus decision-making procedures such as were used during the UN Conference on the Law of the Sea

(UNCLOS III), or limited consensus-building in small groups prior to advancing issues to the full membership. The past success of Canadian delegations in coalition diplomacy in UNCLOS III and the GATT would suggest that these methods may well be an effective strategy for building support for the necessary reforms.

A final critical requirement for retaining support for multilateralism among governments from the South involves responding to their interests and demands. The degree of involvement and commitment that states are willing to invest in multilateral practices are determined in large measure by their interests. Multilateralism designed for the exclusive benefit of the rich and powerful will not be a source of stability and peace, let alone justice, in the future. Institutions that have sought and acquired the support of Third World states, such as the UN, the World Bank, and the GATT, cannot expect to retain this support if they ignore the interests of these states or violate multilateralist principles in a way that disadvantages these states. An example of this problem has been the persistent use and abuse of the Multi-Fibre Agreement by GATT members. It is also evident in the overwhelming concentration of UN activities in recent years on issues such as peacekeeping, human rights, and the environment and the concomitant lack of attention to an agenda for development.

Multilateral associations will not only have to address the concerns of governments. Increasingly it will also be necessary to make more room for non-governmental organizations. Representatives of non-governmental interests have been prominent among those advocating a more intrusive form of multilateralism. In the past they have worked through national governments. More recently they have sought a place at the multilateral table. At UN sponsored conferences in Rio in 1992 and Vienna in 1993 on the environment and human rights respectively, non-governmental organizations were active and influential. They received a great deal of support from the Canadian delegation on both occasions. Incorporating these interests into the multilateral process will present a formidable challenge given the statist bias of most multilateral institutions. It is becoming increasingly evident, however, that non-governmental organizations represent a potentially significant constituency for those institutional interests that favour continued intervention in the internal affairs of member governments in such areas as human rights and environmental protection.

They are also a source of pressure that can be used to encourage critical member governments such as the United States to maintain their multilateral commitments. As a result, the successful integration of these interests into the multilateral process may assist in legitimating these institutions and their decisions in the future.

Multilateralism and Canadian Interests

Canadian policy makers have consistently been at or near the forefront of multilateralist activity for the past fifty years. Based on recent policies Canadian support for multilateralism remains as strong as ever. The Liberal government gives every indication of continuing, if not strengthening, this support. It is, for example, suggestive that one of the government's first foreign policy initiatives was a visit by the foreign affairs minister, André Ouellet, to the United Nations. On this occasion he emphasized "the high importance the new Canadian government gives to the United Nations, and to the peace and security issues that must be dealt with by the United Nations."[20]

The future role that multilateralism will play in Canadian foreign policy is, however, dependent on the way other governments react to multilateral activities and the way in which institutions weather the storms that currently beset them. It will likely be necessary to redesign Canada's multilateral commitments to account for new policy concerns, shifting power balances, and the changing character of international institutions. This has been occurring already with the greater emphasis on hemispheric connections and a persisting interest in initiating multilateralism in the Pacific Rim. As a result, Canadian officials may find it necessary to work with a different array of states or in new institutional settings. At the same time, it will be essential to secure the support of key states such as the United States, Japan, the European Union, and, in some instances, Russia, to multilateral procedures and institutions. We probably do not have a great deal of influence in this area, but it would be beneficial to exercise whatever leverage is possible. Finally, it is critical to look after the longer-term health of these institutions. The potential that we see today for multilateralism rests in part on the past maintenance of institutionalized fora for cooperation even when cooperation was not possible.

It would be wise for Canadian policy makers to continue to favour a multilateral structure in which rules matter more than the arbitrary use of power, where weaker states have the ability to form coalitions that can influence both agendas and outcomes, and where decisions are made on the basis of expertise and bargaining instead of brute force. Multilateralism provides such a system, but it must be cultivated. In the face of the turbulence that has recently affected multilateral institutions, it may be time for a good dose of moderation. The circumstances would also appear conducive to some middle-power initiatives in areas such as UN reform, NATO's relations with Eastern Europe, and expanded mandates for international financial institutions. Cooper, Higgott, and Nossal have recently argued "that states with a tradition of middle power internationalism had substantial and largely untapped institutional capabilities for international coalition-building for the management of global problems."[21] There will be many opportunities for Canadians to apply these capabilities in support of multilateralism in the future.

4 United Nations Structural and Financial Reform

W. Andy Knight

THE SUDDEN OUTBURST OF EUPHORIA about the prospects for a rejuvenated United Nations after the "success" of the 1991 Gulf War did not last long. During 1993 not only was the world body unable to address effectively conflicts in Somalia and the former Yugoslavia, but assessments revealed a complex transorganization lingering on the brink of financial insolvency, with its programs in the economic and social fields in a paralytic state and with a record of mostly failed attempts at restructuring its institutional arrangements.[1] This chapter examines efforts to change the UN's administrative and financial structure and offers suggestions about the type of change process and the kinds of reform the new Canadian government could advocate over the next five years and beyond. I argue that there are two distinct change processes operating within the UN. Each one has particular weaknesses that might be overcome through synthesis.

Multilateralism and International Institutional Adaptation

The most promising conceptual approach for understanding the place of international organization within the broader context of world politics is multilateralism. It also provides a good theoretical framework for the analysis of adaptation and transformation processes in international organizations. Unfortunately, multilateralism, "has been relatively neglected in international relations theory."[2]

There are at least two competing approaches to the study of multilateralism. One emphasizes the importance of analyzing that nexus between the evolution of global order and changes to

---

The research for this chapter was funded in part through a grant from the now-defunct Canadian Institute for International Peace and Security (CIIPS). The author would like to thank Professor Andy Stritch and Professor Marc Desjardine for helpful comments on an earlier draft.

the concrete manifestations of the multilateral process. This view sees the multilateral process as a *longue durée* historical one in which the UN system is the most recent universalist attempt at institutionalizing a particular form of world order, namely the immediate post-1945 world order.[3] In accordance with this view, the UN system is not treated as a given. Its institutional arrangements are relevant only for a specified period and must, inevitably, be transformed over time as material circumstances change or as prevailing meanings, practices, and purposes are challenged by a new intersubjective consensus.

The other approach to multilateralism, because it accepts uncritically the existing configuration of state and economic power, opts for piecemeal reforms to existing structures of international organizations so long as they are in accordance with the overall visions of existing elements within these organizations. This view is less sensitive to the impact of the exogenous forces on the UN and focuses more on the organization's endogenous incremental and reformist agenda. In other words, it attempts to adapt the existing institutional framework without questioning the constituted principles or underlying ideas of world politics embodied in the UN.

Two Change Processes at the United Nations

What is clear from the historical and empirical record is that preoccupation with adapting the UN system is not new. Careful study of the literature reveals at least two change processes operating within the organization: a *reflexive* and a *purposive* one. They correspond roughly to the two distinct conceptualizations of multilateralism proffered above.[4]

The Reflexive Adaptation Process

The reflexive adaptation process is characterized by its relatively uncoordinated responses to systemic forces. It operates in an ad hoc, non-purposive fashion, adapting the organization's structures and processes to meet changing demands of the international system. It can be described as unconscious cognitive learning that is, through innovation and organizational creativity, a response to various challenges.

Since its founding the UN has experienced a number of specific exogenous challenges to its original vision and mission. The primary ones came from five sources: the Cold War environment;

decolonization; a changing conception of socio-economic rights; demands for wider application of human rights norms; and, agitation for multilateral action on the ecological and sustainable development front. In each case, the UN system was pressured to adjust its structures, processes, and goals to meet the challenge of relevance.

Immediately after World War Two the presumption that the victorious wartime allies would remain united in their fight to preserve a stable international security environment proved false when the leading powers, the Soviet Union and the United States, drifted apart in a Cold War environment. East-West tensions and rivalry quickly dominated both the international system and the UN Security Council. Global politico-military relations were instantaneous and decisively affected by the bi-polar structure that emerged. Balance-of-power concepts and preoccupation with spheres of influence and containment combined with the advent of nuclear weapons, and their vertical and horizontal proliferation, to limit the available options for the UN's role in maintaining international peace and security. Excessive use of the veto in the Security Council paralysed the UN and further marginalized the organization.[5] How did the UN respond?

First, in 1947, there was an attempted shift in decision-making power with respect to security matters away from the Security Council to the General Assembly. This involved the creation of an Interim Committee, the adoption in 1950 of the Uniting for Peace resolution,[6] and the establishment of a Collective Measures Committee to advise the Assembly on ways to further strengthen the UN's peace and security role. Secondly, a number of permanent and ad hoc bodies, means, and techniques were created to grapple with the escalating superpower arms race and the global arms trade.[7] This was preceded and followed by a number of disarmament and arms limitation treaties.[8] Thirdly, the Canadian Lester Pearson's innovation of peacekeeping was conceived and made operational.[9] Parallel to this development was the imaginative introduction by Dag Hammarskjöld of preventive diplomacy. This proactive approach depended heavily on the secretary general's expansive interpretation of the discretionary good offices powers granted under Article 99 of the Charter. Preventive diplomacy was conceived as a means of reducing or restricting the Cold War arena.[10]

The UN's reflexive change process was also evident during the period of decolonization. In 1945 the UN was created by 51 states; today there are 184 member states. With the influx of decolonized entities, a challenge was launched to the vision prevailing in the organization at the time. The Non-Aligned Movement (NAM) and the Group of 77 (G-77) were expressions of this counter-hegemonic force. How did the UN respond?

The initial response was to adapt existing institutional structures and processes; for example, the Trusteeship Council modified its function in order to expedite the independence process.[11] The Assembly also approved a number of resolutions, declarations and "action plans" and created new mechanisms, such as the Committee of 24, to speed up the end of colonialism. In many respects, these actions allowed the UN to become "an instigator, a catalyst, a face-saver for the colonial powers" and "a bridge between the old and the new countries."[12]

In response to the demands of the Third World states for greater representation at all levels in the UN, structural adjustments were made to the Security Council and the Economic and Social Council (ECOSOC) via formal amendments to the UN Charter. In 1963 and 1973 ECOSOC's membership was increased from eighteen to twenty-seven and from twenty-seven to fifty-four, respectively. In 1965 the Security Council's membership rose from eleven to fifteen. Thus the influx of new states into the UN system brought about both process and structural changes to some sub-systems of the organization.

The numerically strong bloc of developing countries brought into the UN system a plethora of demands and pressures which the organization's post-1945 structure was ill-prepared or not designed to handle. The Third World demand for speedy economic development challenged the established liberal economic order. In 1964 the call for a New International Economic Order (NIEO)[13] at the first UN Conference on Trade and Development (UNCTAD) meeting in 1964, signalled not only the desire by the "new" states to change the rules of the game, but also caused a marked divide in the UN between the North and South. Reaction to the South's economic and social demands led to an expansion in the UN's socio-economic machinery.[14] This was accompanied by an augmentation of international legal mechanisms to accommodate the "changed" situation.[15] One should note, however, that there was little change to the Bretton Woods institutions[16] which had exerted much control over developing countries' economies, except, perhaps, a slight shift in their mission in response to a UN agenda that was now dominated by Third World concerns.

Throughout this period, the UN Charter provided a base for the development of international human rights law,[17] which progressively moved from standard-setting and treaty-making to the creation of a proliferation of unprecedented mechanisms for encouraging and producing compliance towards human rights norms among sovereign state actors.[18] In response to blatant human rights violations, a human rights committee structure was set up in accordance with the twin covenants—on Civil and Political Rights, and Economic and Social Rights.

This structure consists of the Committee on the Elimination of Racial Discrimination; Human Rights Committee; the Committee on Economic, Social and Cultural Rights; the Committee on the Elimination of Discrimination against Women; the Committee against Torture; the Convention against Torture and other Cruel, Inhuman and Degrading Treatment or Punishment; the Group of Three and the Commission against Apartheid in Sport; and several ad hoc committees, sub-commissions, special rapporteurs, independent expert panels, advisory services, working groups, and instructed and uninstructed bodies.

During the late 1960s growing international concern about the state of the earth's increasingly fragile environment sparked discussion within and outside the UN about the need for multilateral action on this issue. As one commentator put it, the problems of spaceship earth begged for global solutions.[19] In 1968 ECOSOC passed a resolution calling for a UN Conference on the Human Environment. Important outcomes of that 1972 Stockholm conference were the creation and adoption of the UN Environmental Programme (UNEP),[20] the "Declaration on the Human Environment" and an "Action plan." Since 1972 UNEP has initiated programs such as Earthwatch;[21] the Sudano-Sahelian Plan of action to combat desertification in the Horn of Africa;[22] long-term strategies for a world Environmental Perspective to the Year 2000 and beyond; anti-marine pollution efforts;[23] and codification of international environmental laws. The globalization of environmental and sustainable development politics drives the demand being placed on the UN to improve its environmental bodies, policies, and capacity to deal with environmental problems. The Earth Summit, the 1992 UN Conference on Environment and Development (UNCED), was a further response to this demand.[24]

What can we learn from the UN's reflexive process? Clearly, the organization is capable of responding to systemic pressures for change. In each of the above cases, the UN adapted in response to systemic forces in a way that can only be described as unplanned, reactive, innovative, and expansive. This ad hocary, creativity, and ingenuity was often sparked by individual diplomats and UN officials determined to harness the strength of the organization and to salvage the original dream of its founders.[25] Organizational theorists Connor and Lake describe reflexive change processes this way: "With no guidance or direction from management, the form of those adjustments will develop according to custom, convenience, (path of least resistance, for example), power differences among groups affected, or whim."[26] Certainly one of the change processes within the UN fits that description.

But as a direct consequence of this reflexive approach to change, the UN system has evolved more by default than by rational design. It is the unbridled, organic-like growth in the organization's tasks, programs, personnel, and budget—much to the chagrin of the major donor member states—that the purposive approach to change was expected to counter.

The Purposive Change Process

A purposive or "managed change" process,[27] usually labelled "reform,"[28] has existed alongside the UN's reflexive process. It involves conscious, deliberate, and collaborative efforts to improve the operations of the system through a selection of strategies at key intervention points in the change-management process.[29] The following section is a cursory examination of the reforms attempted through this "planned change" process. For analytical purposes, a distinction can be made between micro and macro purposive change efforts. Macro level reform efforts are so labelled because their implications are broader than that of the micro reform attempts.

Table 1
Growth of the UN Secretariat*

Date	From Regular Budget	From Extra Budget	Total
June 30, 1977	9,531	2,590	12,121
June 30, 1978	9,655	3,935	13,590
June 30, 1979	9,960	4,651	14,611
June 30, 1980	10,368	4,538	14,906
June 30, 1981	10,517	4,801	15,318
June 30, 1982	10,902	5,253	16,155
June 30, 1983	11,118	5,101	16,219
June 30, 1984	11,263	4,598	15,861
June 30, 1985	11,850	3,428	15,278
June 30, 1986	10,682	3,539	14,221
June 30, 1987	10,235	3,846	14,081

*Staff in the UN Secretariat with appointments for a year or more, by source of funding (posts financed in whole or in part from the UN regular budget and posts financed from extra-budgetary sources).

Source: Marjorie Ann Browne, United Nations Reform: Issues for Congress, *Congressional Research Service Report for Congress* (September 6, 1988).

Micro-level reform efforts in the UN were aimed at improving or making changes to the organization's recruitment, salary, allowance, and leave system; financial operations; peacekeeping operation; Secretariat activities; Charter and global role, and administrative, financial and personnel structure. The first such recorded attempt began in 1949.

The need to make changes to the UN's salary, allowance, and leave system was in large part a reaction to the reflexive expansion of the Secretariat (Table 1).[30] Typical of the purposive change process, committees of "experts" were set up in 1949, 1955, and 1970 to review this question and make suggestions for institutional modifications.

The Committee of Experts on Salary, Allowances and Leave System in 1949 recommended reductions in salary grade levels and a modification of UN posts into four main categories (replacing the old structure of nineteen grades under one category).[31] In 1955 a Salary Review Committee decided that UN staff salaries and allowances needed downward adjustment; that recruitment practices ought to be revamped; and that the conditions of service throughout the UN common system should be better coordinated. An eleven-member committee of "experts," the Special Committee for the Review of the United Nations Salary System, in 1970 reviewed the criteria and principles governing UN salary levels and concluded that pension provisions were too generous, that the number of higher graded personnel was too high, and that the post adjustment system was unacceptable.[32] A recommitment was made to the Noblemaire principle as a formula for establishing professional salary levels[33] and an International Civil Service Commission (ICSC) was created in 1975, based on two Assembly resolutions.[34]

The rapid expansion of the UN system led to frictions between the organization's main "donors" and its "recipient" member states (most of whom contribute between 0.01 and 0.02 percent to the total UN regular budget). By the late 1950s we begin to see the first signs of a financial crisis in the UN, brought on by a major disenchantment with UN peacekeeping operations and some states' refusal to contribute to these missions, a top-heavy Secretariat,[35] and mismanagement in the implementation of technical cooperation activities.

By the mid-1960s the financial crisis in UN peacekeeping operations had spread to the entire UN operation, as more and more member states withheld their assessed contributions for other activities they did not wish to support. The Assembly, acting on the leadership of the French delegation, set up a Committee of 15 to analyze and tackle this problem. The resulting reports from this committee noted that, between 1956 and 1965, UN expenditures had more than doubled, primarily as a result of the influx of new states into the organization. Some committee members felt that spending ought to be brought under control and that, beginning in 1973, all member states should pay their assessments in full.

Further to this, there were recommendations to create a UN planning, programming, budgeting and evaluative system (PPBES), to reduce conference servicing and documentation, and to standardize the financial operations of the organization. The committee was successful in getting its proposed six-year programming plan, consisting of a biennial program budget, adopted. But it was less successful in improving the conference servicing situation and in limiting excessive duplication of documentation. The persistence of the financial crisis led to a renewed effort in 1975 to bring the situation under control.[36] The fact that there remains a financial crisis in the UN system is testament to the failure of these reform efforts.[37]

Meanwhile something had to be done about the near-insolvent financial position of the peacekeeping operations. In 1962 the UN had issued long-term bonds to member states to cover shortfalls in the cost of the UN Emergency Force (UNEF) and the UN Operation in the Congo (ONUC) operations. However, the controversial practice of taking from the regular budget the annual payments required to service UN peacekeeping loans resulted in withholdings from the regular budget by those states who, on principle, opposed the peacekeeping concept.[38]

A number of specific efforts were made to improve the financial arrangements for peacekeeping. In 1963 a special session of the Assembly made peacekeeping financial assessments separate from those of the UN regular budget. Troop contributing countries agreed to cover the cost of their own participation in UN peacekeeping efforts. Additionally, a Special Account for peacekeeping was initiated to serve as working capital for pressing shortfalls in the peacekeeping operating expenses. As a result of this change peacekeeping operations were placed firmly in the control of those member states that were able to pay (primarily Western capitalist states), and those member states who disagreed with a particular peacekeeping mission were simply allowed not to contribute to it.[39]

Despite the agreement to set up the Special Account for peacekeeping, financial problems persisted. By 1964 the UN peacekeeping account was $100 million in arrears. A Special Committee of 34 member states undertook a comprehensive review of these operations and, although unable to reach consensus, agreed upon the following informal rules regarding future operations: any new peacekeeping force would be established by the Security Council; each member country would be assessed a given amount for these operations, whenever voluntary contributions could not be agreed upon; a formula reflecting a scale of assessment similar to that used for the UN regular budget would be instituted for peacekeeping—this formula would reduce contributions from developing states and increase those from the permanent five countries on the Security Council.[40] The committee's work continued into the late

1980s, widening its scope to include such matters as requirements of facilities, services, and personnel for peacekeeping operations.

Linked to the concern with financial arrangements in the UN was the question of effectiveness and efficiency of UN personnel. To this end, another expert Committee of 8 was appointed in 1961 to review the activities and organization of the UN Secretariat.[41] Like many of the other UN expert committees, members disagreed over the final recommendations. The Soviet committee member pointed out serious defects in the organizational structure, such as its cumbersome and ill-defined structure, the unduly large number of senior posts, the unjustifiably large staff, and the excessive division of functions. His proposal of a troika to head the Secretariat in place of the singular head (the secretary general) was soundly criticized by Western members of the committee.[42]

Some minor changes were made, however, to the allocation of top-level responsibilities so as to achieve a more equitable and geographically balanced distribution of staff. Among some of the recommendations of this committee were proposals to limit budget increases, reduce the number of staff in the Department of Trusteeship and Information for Non-Self-Governing Territories, develop a UN library service, and better schedule and service UN meetings.

By 1968 a Committee of 7 was struck to do a similar review, including not only the Secretariat in New York but also offices in Geneva, the staff of UNCTAD, United Nations Industrial Development Organization (UNIDO), and the regional economic commissions. The committee's final report covered a number of issues, including grading senior officials, reducing documentation and the number of conferences, avoiding unnecessary increases in staff work load, completely reorganizing the secretary general's executive offices, decentralizing the economic and social activities and institutions, improving the financial management of UNDP, pooling and reducing the expenditures of the Department of Public Information (DPI) and the information centres, establishing a budget review committee, calling for a systematic study of the utilization of Secretariat manpower, creating a management service to review administrative procedures, improving recruitment procedures, rotating senior officials, increasing staff mobility, institutionalizing staff training, and improving promotion and retirement policies. Most of these recommendations were implemented but failed to reduce the overall UN budget.[43]

In light of article 109 of the Charter, in 1975 the General Assembly created the Special Committee on the United Nations Charter and Strengthening of the Role of the Organization. This body meets yearly to consider proposals for strengthening the role of the organization, primarily in the area of the maintenance of international peace and security. So far, however, only a few modest changes have been recommended by this committee for implementation by the Assembly.[44] Issues such as dropping the "enemy states" references in the Charter and changing the composition of the Security Council to address the "democratic deficit" in the organization will most probably be subjects for this committee to ponder leading up the Charter review conference in 1995.

In continuation of efforts begun by U Thant in 1968, Kurt Waldheim asked the Assembly in 1980 to establish an expert body to evaluate the Secretariat's administrative structure and recommend ways of reorganizing that body. The Committee of 17 appointed to address this issue continued its work into the next secretary general's term before recommendations were brought forward. But when Javier Pérez de Cuéllar took office in 1981 he initiated a number of administrative changes outside of the Committee of 17's recommendations. These included the creation of a Programme, Planning, and Budgeting Board (BBPP); the establishment of an internal senior level board to review and approve program budget issues; and the institutionalization of a Central Monitoring Unit whose task it was to supervise program performance.

By 1983 de Cuéllar had established an internal mechanism, the High-level Advisory Group on Administrative Reform, to identify issues and areas for administrative reform. The final report of this committee had among its proposals measures to modernize the Secretariat's communication system, further changes to UN peacekeeping operations, the establishment of a staff incentive program, and new procedures to control travel costs of Secretariat members and to dispose of excess UN property. Many of these measures were implemented, although they did little to improve the administrative functioning of the Secretariat.

Macro reforms attempted to date have dealt with improving the capacity of the UN system (the Jackson reforms), the economic and social sectors (the Dadzie reforms), and the UN system's administrative and financial functioning (the Group of 18 reforms).

The proliferation of organizations, committees, units, programs, and funds dealt with in the previous section had a negative effect on the UN's delivery system.[45] Despite the creation of the UNDP in 1965, problems of poor inter-agency coordination continued because the fragmented development assistance structure of independent and semi-independent agencies, units and funds had essentially remained intact. To redress this problem, the UNDP Governing Council commissioned Sir Robert Jackson and a group of experts to undertake a study of the capacity of the UN system to handle the resources that were made available to the organization.

The recommendations of this group included enhancing the role of UNDP and ECOSOC and improving inter-agency co-ordination of funds and other resources as well as aid delivery and technical assistance to the developing world. The failure of the Jackson reforms is fairly evident. The relative importance of UNDP resources vis-à-vis those of the specialized agencies has declined rather than increased, and inter-agency rivalry and lack of coordination has continued unabated.[46] As a result of the Jackson reform effort, the UNDP did, however, develop a system of country programming based on indicative planning figures and managed to limit the autonomy of specialized agencies by placing UNDP resident representatives in charge of coordinating all UN agency field activities. But any proposal that potentially threatened the position and power base of the specialized agency heads seemed doomed to failure.

Responding to the perceived failures of UNDP and UNCTAD,[47] the G-77 used its voting majority in the Assembly to force the establishment of a high-level group of experts, the Group of 25 to recommend structural changes to the UN economic and social sector. Recommendations from this group included creating the post of director general to coordinate socio-economic activities in the UN, establishing a new consultative procedure to achieve consensus on controversial socio-economic issues being confronted by the world body, replacing UNCTAD with an international trade organization, revitalizing ECOSOC, redefining the role of specialized agencies, and consolidating pre-investment funds.[48]

Most of the G-77 countries were unhappy with the recommendations.[49] They wanted to strengthen the role of UNCTAD, not eliminate it. They also hoped to see the General Assembly empowered to issue directions to the IBRD and the IMF. The G-77 opposed attempts to consolidate development funds, believing that this would lead to a decrease in such funds. On the other side of the coin, the United States and some of the major donor countries opposed any attempt to limit the autonomy of the IBRD, the GATT, or the IMF. The United States in particular did not like the proposal to create the post of director general.[50]

In December 1977 the Assembly finally approved the implementation of a watered-down version of the Dadzie recommendations in order for it to gain the acceptance of the various dissenting groups.[51] Although the Office of Director General was created, for instance, it was given insufficient resources and authority to fulfil its mandate effectively. One of the successes of this reform effort was to streamline the Administrative Committee on Co-ordination (ACC) machinery, which placed it in a better position to oversee inter-agency coordination in the developmental field. Both the ACC and ECOSOC were given a Secretariat, the Office of Secretariat Services for Economic and Social Matters (OSSESM). A new Department for Technical Co-operation and Development (DTCD) was formulated to coordinate all staff dealing with developmental issues. In addition, country coordinators replaced UNDP resident representatives as overseers of UN assistance activities in development countries.

The commitment of the developed countries to the Dadzie and Jackson reforms was lukewarm at best. The OECD leaders in particular agreed with the developing world on the need for restructuring the world economy. However, they demonstrated a need to control the plan to accomplish this. For them the best strategy was one of coordinating their economic policies through the the Group of Seven, which has since become a bi-annual feature of international relations.[52] For all intents and purposes, as Saksena notes, "the so-called North-South dialogue has reached, it seems, a dead end." And, as far as international economic decision-making goes, the UN was "actually reduced to a non-factor."[53]

By the late 1970s it was quite evident that the strain on the UN's administrative and financial structures was, in part, a by-product of North-South conflict. The South, by virtue of its voting majority in the Assembly, forced the organization to institute new programs and entities to serve its interests. The North, on the other hand, used its financial clout to deny the resources that would be necessary for these new programs and organs to operate adequately.

Evan Luard predicted in 1979 that "conflicts about the level and type of expenditure" within the UN would become "frequent and fierce in the future," and that this issue "could become perhaps the central issue of international government."[54] It took less than five years for this prediction to become a reality. In fact, each year since 1976 a "financial emergency" item has been placed on the Assembly's agenda. By the mid-1980s representatives of the United States and some other major donors blamed this crisis on internal UN mismanagement. Some of them described the organization as an expensive, ungovernable, ever-expanding bureaucracy with severe management and personnel problems brought on by the Third World tyrannous majority. It was at this point that we notice a number of questionable tactics being used, particularly by the United States, to force predetermined reforms on the organization.

In 1985 several pieces of U.S. legislation (for example, the Kassebaum Amendment and the Gramm-Rudman-Hollings Act) were passed, effectively reducing the level of U.S. financial contribution to the UN's regular budget or linking full payment of UN dues to such changes as progress on financial and budgetary reform in the UN, a 15 percent reduction in UN staff, reorganization of budgetary methods so that larger contributors could have a bigger say in the allocation of the organization's funds, and reduction of the number of Soviets working within the UN system on a short-term contractual basis.

It was at this point that UN officials began to realize that organizational growth would no longer be a self-evident fact in the life cycle of the UN. Managers would have to learn to cope with dwindling resources, as many states were trying to do in the mid-1980s. A deliberate zero-budgeting policy was advocated by the United States and other western developed states to demonstrate this new thinking. The organization's major donors obviously intended to produce a leaner UN that might also prove to be more efficient and effective than it had been during the growth years. But what followed was a severe financial crisis that threatened the viability and survival of the UN system during the mid-1980s.

The official administrative response to this crisis was the initiation, on December 18, 1985, of the most extensive administrative and managerial reform effort in the UN's history.[55] It lasted five years and had a profound effect on the entire UN system. The primary goals of this effort were to reorganize the Secretariat, cut staff levels, reduce the number of meetings and reports, cut back on official travel, and streamline the central budgetary and administrative operations.[56] Tapio Kanninen calls this a classic case of "retrenchment" and "downsizing."[57] Between February and August 1986, this Group of 18 met sixty-seven times in closed session. Its final report was, according to one commentator, more of a disparate list of recommendations than an agreement on what was to be reformed.

Most of the seventy-one final recommendations of the Group essentially reflected what the United States wanted. That included a consensus procedure for all UN budgetary decisions; the expansion in the mandate of the Committee on Program and Coordination (CPC) over the budget process, a 15 percent reduction in the overall UN staff, and a 25 percent staff reduction at the under-secretary general and assistant secretary general levels. Between 1985 and 1987, the number of posts at those levels were in fact reduced from eighty-seven to fifty-six and, in April 1990, the secretary general reported a 12 percent overall reduction in staff levels.

In a further cost-cutting move, Boutros Boutros-Ghali, following on from his predecessor in implementing the Group of 18 recommendations, announced on February 6, 1992, that external recruitment for posts in the professional category would be suspended until further notice and that maximum restraint should be exercised in making appointments to posts in the general service and related categories.[58] The secretary general also made a number of sweeping and downsizing changes to the Secretariat, particularly in the top echelons. Effective February 29, 1992, a number of offices and departments were discontinued as separate entities, and their functions and programs were to continue under new administrative arrangements.[59] A number of top-level secretariat positions were also axed by the secretary general at the same time.[60] In total, Boutros-Ghali's reorganization effort resulted in a net reduction of fourteen high-level posts in the Secretariat. The UN's 1992-93 regular budget of just over $1 billion a year made

Table 2
Breakdown of Senior Posts by Budget Category
1992–93

Budget Category	ASGs	USGs	Total
1. Policy-making/direction	2	3	5
2. Political Affairs	3	5	8
3. International Law	1	2	3
4. International Development	9	6 + DC	15 + DC
5. Economic Commissions	0	5	5
6. Human Rights/Humanitarianism	2	3	5
7. Public Information	0	1	1
8. Common Services	3	2	5
Total Established Posts	20	27 + DG	48 + DG
Temporary Posts			
9. Good Offices (Afghanistan)	1	0	1
10. Disarmament	1	0	1
11. Earth Summit	1	1	2
Total Temporary Posts	3	1	4

Source: Office of Human Resources Management (OHRM), United Nations, New York.

provision for a total of forty-eight posts at the top level within the Secretariat, down from sixty-two in the previous budget. The established posts were for one director general (DG), twenty-seven under-secretaries general (USGs), twenty assistant secretaries general (ASGs). In addition, provision was also made for temporary posts for one USG and three ASGs (see Table 2).

Despite these seemingly sweeping changes, the Group of 18 had failed to agree on several issues which lay at the heart of the administrative and financial problems of the organization—in particular the planning, programming and budgeting process, and the restructuring of the intergovernmental machinery. In the final analysis, these reform efforts can be considered at best of only limited success. Indeed, the implementation of this planned change effort could not have come at a worse time for the organization. The fact that the serious financial crisis facing the UN would have to be addressed at the same time as the proposed retrenchment reforms were being implemented obviously placed a severe strain on the ability of the UN to accomplish even the most basic of its mandated tasks. The organization found itself on the brink of insolvency, trying to do more with less.

The Persistence of Problems

In spite of the purposive attempts at changing the organization, there continue to be major administrative and financial problems throughout the UN system. At the moment, the organization is obviously overstretched, saddled with too heavy a burden of intervention and peacekeeping. These new demands require greater financial contributions from member states, most of whom are facing severe budgetary problems of their own. But there are other serious problems in the organization that need to be addressed urgently.

Dick Thornburgh, the former U.S. attorney general who recently completed a year's service as UN under-secretary general for administration and management, complained that the UN was suffering from the kind of bureaucratic inertia that plagues most governmental agencies.[61] Poor management, recruitment, and hiring practices, wanton nepotism and the large number of "deadwood," lack of accountability, efficiency, and effectiveness, duplicative and obsolete functions, rampant waste, fraud, and abuse of the system—all these factors combine to make the world body less able to cope with the increased demands of the international community.

Other recent observations come to similar conclusions. It seems that institutional inertia, lack of accountability, and poor coordination that verges on administrative chaos still plague the system. Charges of corruption in specialized agencies and various peacekeeping and humanitarian missions are persistent. There is seemingly no mechanism for effectively addressing such problems.[62] In addition, it is becoming increasingly obvious that many UN organs are sustained solely because of bureaucratic and member-state vested interest. Several of them are, to put it euphemistically, "marginally useful." Often these bodies measure success by the number of conferences they hold or the number of reports generated. Some bodies persist even when their mandate has evaporated. Others promote declaration of "decades" in order to stay in business.[63]

Some once vital cogs in the UN machinery have become anachronisms. For instance, the department responsible for trusteeship and decolonization has been rendered largely irrelevant primarily because of its own success. More than eighty former colonies have been admitted into the UN since the founding of the organization in 1945. Of the eleven trusts territories that were originally administered by states under UN supervision, only a fraction of the last one is left. This is the tiny Pacific island of Palau, which is still under U.S. jurisdiction. Yet the department still employs about fifty-six staffers and spends roughly $9.5 million over two years, including more than $114,000 to send nine people on "visiting missions" to Palau for two weeks a year.

A special committee still oversees eighteen "non-self-governing territories," including Bermuda, the U.S. and British Virgin Islands, Guam, American Samoa, and Pitcairn Island. Roughly 88 percent of its $618,000 biennial budget is used for visits to these territories. The committee then issues annual reports drawn largely from press clippings.

Another marginally useful body is the Centre on Transnational Corporations (CTC). While it is now downgraded to a division and has lost its director, the CTC still has a biennial budget of $12.8 million. It has spent fifteen years trying, unsuccessfully, to draft a code of conduct for transnational corporations. Critics say that this centre has done more to discourage foreign investment than anything else.[64]

According to one UN official, the greatest waste in the UN stems from the mountains of published material that are of negligible value and the large number of conferences which perpetuate the production of those materials. Within the current two-year regular budget, nearly $101 million is allocated for public information and more than $422 million for conference services. Many of the reports issued by the UN may be useful, but many others are not read by anyone and can take up to a year to produce (in some cases translated into the six official languages of the organization). In spite of the Group of 18 recommendations, the flow of paper continues unabated. In 1991 the UN headquarters and its offices in Geneva and Vienna produced 164.1 million documents totalling approx 2.12 billion pages, according to UN statistics. This cost the organization about $275 million—a figure that does not include the cost of writing the documents nor the millions of documents published by other agencies of the UN. Among the costliest publications are the yearbooks that are usually out of date by the time they are produced. Similarly the Yearbook of the Human Rights Committee—a 657-page document—was produced in 1992 to cover the years 1983–84. Ironically, a number of the governments that issued reports for that yearbook are no longer in existence.[65]

The above predicament is compounded by the organization's constrained capacity—a direct result of the UN's continuing financial crisis. A recent study of its financial state concluded that the UN's financial system does not provide "the capacity or the flexibility to respond effectively and expeditiously to the many challenges that now confront it."[66] First of all, the UN has no system for tracking daily cash flow. It has no inspector general to perform surprise audits or evaluate the financial and management performance of the many sub-parts of the organization. But worse, the financial withholdings to the UN regular, voluntary, and peacekeeping budgets by several member states, compounded by the depletion of the reserves in its Working Capital Fund and Special Account since the middle of 1991, have left the organization on the brink of insolvency.

The Continuing Financial Crisis

Underlying the financial crisis is the unconstitutional practice by member states of withholding assessed contributions to the UN regular budget. As this became increasingly widespread, a major cash flow problem further crippled the organization.[67] Unpaid dues rose from US$120.9 million in 1976 to US$504 million by January 1986. Of this, $162 million represented unpaid contributions to the peacekeeping account, which is separate from the regular budget, and $242 million represented unpaid contributions to the regular budget.

In 1989, 1990, and 1991 the total amount outstanding in the UN regular budget was $461,238,000, $402,952,000, and $439,384,000 respectively. Some of the major financial delinquents as of June 1992 were Brazil ($33,482,499), Iran ($11,371,832), the Russian Federation ($138,110,295), South Africa ($49,044,904), Ukraine ($17,308,974), and the United States ($555,026,876). The total amount outstanding in the UN regular budget as of that date was $910,597,591.[68] Over the course of 1992, member states paid $976 million of the $1.04 billion owed to the UN regular budget, yet by December 31 of that year, eighty-seven member states still owed altogether $500 million in past arrears, with fifty-two of these owing more than their full assessment for the year. In January 1993 only eighteen states (providing 16 percent of the overall regular budget) have paid up in full. The status of financial contributions by member states in other budgetary areas is equally bleak.

As of June 30, 1992, the total amounts outstanding in the UN peacekeeping operating budgets were as follows: the UN Emergency Force (UNEF) and the UN Disengagement Observer Force (UNDOF), $26,182,107; the UN Interim Force in Lebanon (UNIFIL), $269,337,619; the UN Iran-Iraq Military Observer Group (UNIIMOG), $1,065,293; the UN Angola Verification Mission (UNAVEM I and II), $17,936,899; the UN Observer Group in Central America (ONUCA), $12,913,658; the UN Iraq-Kuwait Observation Mission (UNIKOM), $14,149,862; the UN Mission for the Referendum in Western Sahara (MINURSO), $21,064,797; the UN Observer Mission in El Salvador (ONUSAL), $22,284,792; the UN Advance Mission in Cambodia (UNAMIC), $5,337,167; the UN Transition Authority in Cambodia (UNTAC), $465,286,763; the UN Protection Force (UNPROFOR) operations in the former Yugoslavia, $83,579,467. The total amount outstanding for UN peacekeeping operations and observer missions came to $939,138,424 that year. Only the Namibian operation, the UN Transition Assistance Group (UNTAG), has a surplus of $14,636,525.[69]

In short, the serious financial crisis has had an impact right across the system. Today, the UN Fund for Population Activities (UNFPA) has lost $10 million a year because the U.S. administration claimed that the Fund supported a "coercive" birth control program in China; the International Atomic Energy Agency (IAEA) is short $3 million in dues and another $39 million will arrive a year late; the World Health Organization (WHO) is waiting for $17 million in back dues and at least $10 million will be carved out of this year's $75 million U.S. contribution because of a budgetary agreement with Congress; a plea by the IBRD for an additional $71 million to help the poorest countries' economies has fallen on deaf ears in the Congress.

The large amount of withholdings from the regular budget, in addition to the cash flow problem created by the tardiness of several member states in paying their assessed contributions and the low limit on the organization's working capital fund of only $100 million, seriously threatens the financial viability of the organization and its ability to carry out the new tasks being assigned to it by the international community.[70]

Conclusion: What Can Canada Do?

The basic thrust of the argument running through this chapter is that there are problems with both change processes operating within the UN system. The reflexive one pays insufficient attention to the internal limitations of the organization and as such jeopardizes the UN's future survival. Those who advocate this approach to reform tend to ignore the issues of efficiency and effectiveness. On the other hand, the purposive approach tends to constrain needed change by limiting the parameters of what can be changed or what is considered for adaptation and to favour status-quo forces over the more progressive and dynamic elements. In many respects, those who advocate this approach to change have an obsession with organizational efficiency and effectiveness, almost to the exclusion of the relevance issue.

Leading up to 1995, it is important that a new agenda for UN reform be put into place. This agenda must have two tracks. While it will be important to deal with immediate reform issues such as making the system more efficient and effective, it is perhaps more important at this critical juncture to adopt a long-term reform agenda and strategy that focus on the needs of international society and the means by which the UN can be adjusted to help. As Maurice Bertrand points out, despite various efforts at reform, "no real restructuring or rethinking of the role of the Organization has ever been achieved. . . . A reappraisal of the role of the world organization has now become crucial."[71] Thus relevance should become the watchword in any future Canadian efforts to reform the UN system. This would mean that Canadian representatives at the UN may have to move beyond their penchant for strictly "reformist" types of organizational change to consider more radical ones.

The potential items for the new reform agenda will look much different from the previous one dealt with in this chapter. Given the tasks that the UN is currently being asked to perform, the list of reform agenda items would have to include collective security and enforcement; arms control and disarmament; peacekeeping and field observation; preventive diplomacy; early warning devices and mechanisms; refugees and humanitarian assistance; economic and social policy; environmental and sustainable development; and burden-sharing regionalism.

Developing an operational UN military capability to meet current political demands will be the key to cooperative security in the future.[72] But this raises a number of questions about what changes will be needed in order to bring this about. Should the UN Military Staff Committee be revitalized? Is the creation of a permanent UN police force the answer? How will the UN overcome the tension between the protection of sovereignty and the need to deal with conflicts that are essentially within the jurisdiction of states? What should the composition of the Security Council look like in this post-Cold War era? We note that attempts at demilitarizing Iraq in the wake of the Gulf War constituted a major change in the way the UN has dealt with questions of disarmament in the past.[73] Will this be one of the organization's roles in the future? Is there a need for refinement in the approach that was used in the Iraqi case? What impact will this have on the non-intervention principle in Article 2 (7) of the UN Charter? Should this article be challenged in 1995 when the Charter is being reviewed? How will the UN handle the conflict between enforcement action and non-intervention?

With respect to peacekeeping, several reform questions need to be addressed. Are the UN's military and civilian peacekeepers adequately trained to deal sensitively with socio-cultural differences? Is there any UN training procedure for such? Should there be a greater institutionalization of peacekeeping training, with a permanent training centre for international peacekeepers? Given Canada's credibility in this area, the Liberal government should consider the possibility of Canada being a centre for peacekeeping training. On the issue of preventive diplomacy, it would be worthwhile to consider reforms which would elevate the status of the UN's proactive and early warning devices over the conflict management and reactive mechanisms.

On the subject of human rights and socio-economic issues, it is becoming clear that the relationship between the state and its civil society is in a process of renegotiation. The Canadian government might want to consider how the UN's human rights machinery can be reformed to address this problem. For example, should there be a permanent international criminal court with the capability of bringing even state leaders who grossly violate the human rights of their civilians to justice? How can this be effectively done?

The globalization of the world economy obviously calls for a more cooperative, integrative and holistic approach to questions of economic and social policy. Can the UN take the lead in this coordination, or are the obstacles too great to be overcome? Is the UN the correct institution to deal with this? It is clear that what is required is a global negotiating forum to deal with such issues as trade, production, and economic development. Is this a function for the existing Bretton Woods institutions, UNCTAD or ECOSOC, or should reforms such as the recent creation of an international trade organization be considered? Should there not be greater collaboration among existing regional, non-governmental and transnational groups to create a socio-economic regime to coordinate this policy globally, rather than trying to do this through the UN system? Similar questions can be raised about the environmental and sustainable development issue. But perhaps, given the nature of this item, even more radical reforms might be contemplated which would institutionalize the nascent link between non-governmental organizations working in this issue area and the UN system.

Finally, with the developments toward European integration, questions about burden-sharing between the universal and regional bodies are being asked. One of the UN reform concerns raised repeatedly these days is whether the UN should be so heavily engaged in regional disputes or whether regional organizations ought to be taking more responsibility in this area. Should such division of labour be done through formal constitutional arrangements, or can some other informal plan be devised to share the cost of international governance? The UN was never intended as the only body capable of addressing global issues. How can Chapter VIII of the Charter (on regional arrangements) be made operational? Would the concept of subsidiarity now being adopted by the Europeans be useful in this context?

To address the above reform items properly, it might be worthwhile for the new Canadian government to consider an approach to change in the UN that synthesizes the reflexive and purposive approaches to change dealt with in this chapter. This combined approach would begin with a strong normative vision of the future of global order and would adopt a "modified" purposive approach to redesigning the UN system. It is modified in that it jettisons the notion of comprehensive rationality in favour of a "bounded rational" approach to change. It also views any management of change as an attempt to "facilitate" rather than "control" it. In other words, this third option for changing the UN system would adopt a purposive approach only in so far as it helps to expedite the creation of administrative and financial structures that are relevant to the emerging global governance order. The UN system would therefore not be treated as a given, but as an organic entity that can be transformed by the structure/agency interplay of both exogenous and endogenous forces.

Organizations like the UN cannot hope to function independently of the ebb and flow of political activity in the world in which they operate. In fact, "universal intergovernmental organizations are particularly sensitive to the movement of world forces."[74] The problem for the UN is that while it is increasingly being called upon to address new issues, its administrative and financial structures are proving to be inadequate for the task at hand.

The global upheavals and dislocations we have witnessed since 1989 seem to indicate that the emergence of a new world order will be far more complex and protracted than at first anticipated. The role of the UN in any new global arrangement is thus very much unclear. It will be important for the new Canadian government to make a serious assessment of the changing international political, security, and socio-economic environment[75] in order to determine what impact the turbulent exogenous forces are having on the UN system.[76] It would be equally important for the government to do a realistic assessment of the extent to which the UN system's internal apparatus is adjusting to meet the challenges of the emerging world order.

So while reforming and changing the UN's structural and financial arrangements is still critical at this stage, it is only one small step in what could be a much longer journey in a major transformation of the world body. If the organization proves unwilling or unable to adjust its administrative and financial structures to ensure that it will be able to cope with the new demands being placed on it by the international community, then how will it ever succeed in responding to the more transformative and radical demands for change that can be expected in the future? Failure to adjust now could mean that the United Nations may find itself, as the League of Nations did back in the 1930s, relegated to the dustbin of history or perhaps replaced by a third-generation international organization.

Canada has a major stake in UN reform primarily because it has sunk a substantial amount of human and financial resources into this organization. Its declared and substantive commitment to multilateralism explains in large part this country's continuing interest in adapting the UN system. However, saddled with a $46 billion debt left by the Conservative government, the newly elected Liberal government will find it necessary to make some hard choices about where and how future Canadian resources will be allocated. Unless the UN proves capable of adjusting, it may also find itself being abandoned by even those states, like Canada, that have given it unconditional support in the past.

5 Nothing is Agreed until Everything is Agreed: First Thoughts on the Implications of the Uruguay Round

John M. Curtis
Robert Wolfe

THE LARGEST AND MOST COMPLEX international economic negotiation ever attempted finally came to a dramatic conclusion on December 15, 1993, in Geneva when all 117 participants in the Uruguay Round agreed that everything had been agreed. The world's trade ministers will now meet in Marrakesh in April 1994 to sign the agreements. As part of the outcome of the Round, the ministers will also create the World Trade Organization (WTO), thereby fulfilling the dreams of the architects of the post-World War Two international system.[1] In this chapter we try to place this historic achievement in perspective by asking three questions about the Round: Why was it different from previous trade rounds? What happened substantively? What does the outcome mean for Canada and for the world trading system? The analysis will focus more on the outcome than on the history of the process, but we begin by setting the stage for the long-awaited conclusion of the Uruguay Round.[2]

The Setting

In Becket's famous play, Estragon suggests that it is time to go, but Vladimir says they cannot. When asked why not, he says, because we're waiting for Godot. Since the early 1980s the world trading system has been waiting for one or another country to agree to consider follow-up to the Tokyo Round, or to launch a new round, or accept the inclusion on the agenda of agriculture, or services. There have been delays caused by elections, recessions, differences of view on substantive matters, and the need to obtain fast-track authority. The General Agreement to Talk and Talk has seemed a fair characterization of the General Agreement on Tariffs and Trade (GATT). Actors touted for the role of Godot have included various American presidents (who were thought capable of single-handedly turning back a perceived drift to protectionism), Japanese prime ministers (who had only to say the word to reduce their trade surplus by opening the door to American rice), and the German chancellor (who could have put the French *paysan* in his place by turning Germany's back on decades of carefully nurtured Franco-German collaboration). Others thought Godot would never arrive, having been missing in action since the end of the Cold War.

The Round was first supposed to end in December 1990 in Brussels. After that failed ministerial meeting, the Round almost concluded with an agreement on Arthur Dunkel's Draft Final Act of December 1991. In late 1992 many people thought that the prospect of a new American president would force Godot to appear by December 1992. One wag described the renewed activity during the fall of 1993 as the Fourth Annual Final Push to Complete the Uruguay Round. In this chapter we offer no explanation for the arrival of Godot—perhaps she was frightened by the heads of the International Monetary Fund (IMF) and the World Bank who joined the director general of GATT in September 1993 in issuing an unprecedented appeal to governments to take decisive action because "failure to conclude the Round would lead to greater protectionism and loss of confidence, with major economic and social implications for high and low-income countries alike."[3] They were right to make that judgment about the importance of the Uruguay Round in September 1993, but the statement would have been just as accurate in previous years. Explanations of how this historic agreement was achieved will be found in the domestic political economy of the participants and in the changing structure of the international system. Our approach in this chapter, however, is not rooted in rational choice, pluralist, or systemic theories; we do not seek an explanation of the outcome in the interests of individuals, groups, or states.[4] Instead we concentrate on the institutional norms that shaped this outcome and on how the new WTO might shape the future evolution of the trading system.

Why the Uruguay Round was Different

The Uruguay Round of multilateral trade negotiations was the eighth held under the auspices of GATT. Each round in effect modifies and extends the existing agreements embedded in the trade regime. Even the 1947 General Agreement itself was a codification of practices that had been evolving since the nineteenth century.[5] The trade policies of governments, the only matters regulated by GATT, have both facilitated and impeded the considerable expansion of world commerce since World War Two. The GATT has made two regulatory contributions as it has evolved since 1947. First, it has tended to restrict the number of national policies that impede the further expansion of trade. Secondly, and more important, it has increased the transparency and predictability of government policy, which reduces the chances of conflict among governments while creating more stable expectations for economic actors engaged in international commerce. The Uruguay Round is part of the tradition of continuity in the evolution of the trading system, but it is also different from all previous rounds, most notably in the scope of issues covered, the large increase in the number of participants, and the unusual role of coalitions.

The need for a new round was apparent almost before the ink was dry on the Tokyo Round agreements in 1979. Trade negotiators knew that many issues had not been dealt with properly—especially agriculture and textiles—while others had been pushed into "minilateral" codes, fragmenting the trading system. (Agreements with limited membership, like the Tokyo Round codes, are often called minilateral. In the Uruguay Round such texts are called "plurilateral.") Politicians feared that GATT would be unable to contain the rise of the so-called new protectionism. It soon became apparent that GATT was ill-equipped to respond as new technologies, new activities, especially services, and newly dynamic countries transformed the world economy during the 1980s. The GATT ministerial meeting of 1982 launched the arduous process of shaping an agenda for a new round of negotiations whose goal would be nothing less than the complete modernization of the trading system. The process culminated in a ministerial meeting launching the new round in Punta del Este, Uruguay, in September 1986.

The negotiating agenda established by the Punta Declaration was larger than that of any previous multilateral trade negotiation.

It included issues left over from previous rounds (like agriculture), issues of specific interest to developing countries that had not been properly covered in the past, and the "new issues" created by global economic change. The agenda also included institutional matters designed to strengthen the policy capacity of GATT, which has never been properly constituted as an international organization. It would not have been possible to get agreement to launch the round if all of these issues were not included; some also thought that it would not be possible to conclude the negotiations if there were not a big package with something for everybody.

The Uruguay Round can be portrayed as a response both to economic change and to the unfinished agenda of the Tokyo Round. But for developing countries it was also a sharp break with GATT's past. In the negotiations leading to the Havana Charter of the ITO, the question of development was almost overlooked. The problems of developing countries in the trading system were first addressed in the Haberler report of the 1950s, but GATT did not seem to provide many opportunities for developing countries through the first seven rounds. The long history of Part IV of the General Agreement, which institutionalized "special and differential treatment," the efforts of UNCTAD to play a role in trade negotiations, and the attempts to "launch global negotiations," all failed to change the marginalization of developing countries in the trading system.[6]

The emergence of the developing countries had created a situation where there was a two-tier GATT. Although these countries were rapidly increasing their formal participation during the 1980s, in effect joining the world economy as their attitudes to trade liberalization were being transformed, they were not receiving the full benefits nor, in some cases, making a full contribution. A central theme of the Uruguay Round, therefore, was a desire to integrate all countries as full participants. The Round featured a larger number of participating countries than ever before, a number that kept growing as the negotiations progressed.[7] There have also been a number of "observers"—countries not ready to be or not yet accepted as Contracting Parties, some of which, like China, have been active participants in the negotiations.

The Uruguay Round was an indicator of a profound shift in how developing countries regulate their own economies and manage their relations with the world.[8] The successful outcome of the

Round in effect locks in this shift, with potentially major implications for the future management of the trading system.

It is now commonplace to assert that the governance of the world economy is fragmented. No country has the dominance exercised by the United States before 1971. Issues are also fragmented; money matters, for example, are pursued in the IMF, the World Bank, the Organization for Economic Cooperation and Development (OECD), and the Bank for International Settlements (BIS). Developing countries learned in the 1950s that they could have more influence if they banded together—for example, in what became known as the Group of Seventy-Seven (G-77). Large countries learned a similar lesson in the 1970s, banding together in annual economic summits. This coalition of the powerful developed an operational role in the 1980s, first by formalizing long-standing cooperation in GATT with the creation of the Quadrilateral Group of Trade Ministers (European Union [EU], United States, Japan, and Canada) and later by creating the Group of Seven (G-7) Finance Ministers to manage more active economic policy cooperation.[9]

Efforts to launch the new round of trade negotiations in the mid-1980s stimulated a new form of coalition activity, groupings that crossed the normal boundaries of international economic relations erected on "North/South" or "rich/poor" lines.[10] (Before and during the Uruguay Round, for example, a large and informal group of developing and developed countries met irregularly at ministerial level to review progress.[11]) Canada was a member of many of these groups because we have learned that we have interests in common, not only with the G-7 or the other industrial economies, but also with other small states, other resource exporters, and so on. As countries contemplate the post-Uruguay Round agenda and the role in the world economy of countries in transition and newly dynamic economies, new regional groupings are emerging, with the Asia Pacific Economic Cooperation (APEC) forum the most prominent example.

The best-known illustration of the substantial coalition activity in the Uruguay Round, other than the Quad, has been the development of the Cairns Group of Fair Trading Nations as a "third force" in the conduct of the agriculture negotiations.[12] The now thirteen countries first met as a group of five in Uruguay in early

1986; the group was formally constituted at a ministerial meeting in Cairns, Australia in August 1986. The United States, the European Community (EC), and Japan were invited observers, at least at the early meetings. The group's supporters claim that the Cairns Group represents a unique evolution in the process of coalition-building in multilateral trade negotiations. Its critics counter that the endeavours of the Cairns Group to stimulate international agricultural reform must be seen as quixotic in practice and overstated in theoretical significance. The Cairns Group has tried to be each sort of potential coalition (agenda-moving, proposal-making, blocking, and negotiating), depending on the stages of the negotiations, with varying degrees of effectiveness. It is clear that the Cairns influence was greatest up to, but not at or since, the Brussels ministerial meeting in 1990, for reasons that have more to do with the nature of the Round than with the Group itself.

The Uruguay Round was a departure from past GATT rounds because of the importance of institutional issues. Although market access negotiations define the negotiation by the market power of the participants, negotiations on rules and principles allow a greater role for skill and perseverance, creating an opening for new kinds of coalitions.[13] The members of the Cairns Group showed both elements. They accounted for roughly 10 percent of world trade in 1992, but represented over one quarter of world agricultural exports at the time of Punta del Este.

In the GATT context, this sort of market weight buys a certain amount of influence. That influence was used first to influence the *shape of the agenda* for the Uruguay Round, then to advance *negotiating proposals*, and finally to ensure that a big agricultural package acceptable to the Group could not be pushed off the negotiating table, a *blocking* role. The Cairns Group relied on the aggregate strength of the group in international agricultural trade: tightly defined group goals; a degree of discipline, notwithstanding the heterogeneity of group membership; and strong technical and entrepreneurial leadership, especially, but not exclusively, from Australia. Canada's relations with the Group were occasionally strained by our need to accommodate the interests of our more diverse farm sector; other members of the Cairns Group did not share our views on Article XI, for example. The Group remained active throughout the Round, but its influence on the final negotiating or bargaining was minimal, although the Australians certainly reaped domestic political benefits from the appearance of influence on the big players in Washington and Brussels.

The Quad, in contrast, played a significant role at all stages of the negotiations, as it did in a more informal way during previous rounds.[14] Quad ministers have met two to three times a year since the early 1980s, officials have met informally half a dozen times a year during the Round, and there was constant communication by phone. Once the rules negotiations neared completion, the Quad played an especially important role during the final six to eight months of intensive bargaining on market-access issues in order to reinvigorate the Round and to ensure that a big package could be assembled. Ministers prepared the trade issues for the Tokyo Summit in July and came together in December as the final package of bilateral market-access agreements was multilateralized to all participants. The size of that package was vital. Since one or another of the Quad members tends to be the largest trading partner for all other participants, momentum in the Quad was the key to the rest of the package. As other countries came to realize this dynamic, pressure on the Quad to reach an agreement was intense, even from developing countries. Canada played a leadership role within the Quad, but was also seen as an *interlocutor valable* by other countries because of our unique and privileged access to the three largest players in the Round. This credibility had been established early in the Round in the de la Paix Group (named after a Geneva hotel) which played an important North-South bridging role at a time when developing countries were still hesitant about the competence of GATT to move into new areas while being unsure whether the Round would address issues of interest to them such as market access for resource-based products.

The Quad allowed the largest trading countries to play a more organized role in the management of the Uruguay Round than they had in the Tokyo Round. This emphasizes the theme of continuity, but the role of developing countries at the end of the Round demonstrates the break from the past. At the end of the Tokyo Round, developing countries were simply excluded from membership in the codes. In contrast, it is striking that in the final stages of the Uruguay Round, as developed countries agonized over details, developing countries were largely prepared to accept the package. In the spring of 1993 Argentinian President Carlos Menem wrote to the leaders of the major countries on behalf of a group of thirty-seven developed and developing countries making the case for a sense of urgency in the negotiations. In November 1993 a group of Commonwealth representatives toured European capitals and Washington, calling on the industrial countries to settle their differences and conclude what had become the most multilateral round ever.

Also indicative was the demand for action to complete the Round in the "Declaration of APEC Ministers on the Uruguay Round" released in November 1993 after their annual meeting in Seattle. One consequence of the diverse participation, and the cross-cutting alliances, was a huge package containing something for everybody. When the French made a last-ditch suggestion to remove agriculture from the package, there may have been some temptation to do so in Washington, but, as one American is reported to have said, "We've gone over the waterfall in a barrel. There is no backing down. Even if the U.S. would agree to it, the Cairns Group would not."[15] Similar statements could have been made about other groups and both other market-access issues (e.g., textiles) and other rules issues (e.g., safeguards). The interests of developing countries after the Uruguay Round must be accommodated at the main table rather than being pushed off to a side table labelled "special and differential," as in the Tokyo Round. The trading system will not be the same.

Snapshot of the Results

The Final Act of the Uruguay Round contains over thirty agreements, understandings, and declarations, capped by the agreement to create the WTO. The agreements include an enormous package of national commitments to lower tariff and non-tariff barriers to merchandise trade, a thorough reform of trade rules, and the extension of the system to cover such new issues as trade in services and intellectual property.[16] Each of the areas will have a general impact on the world economy as well as a particular impact on national economies, such as Canada's. Some, such as the effect of tariff reductions, will be readily quantifiable. Others will be harder to assess, such as the way new disciplines, from agriculture to financial services, will lead to more predictability and confidence in the world economy. The following assessments of the implications of the Uruguay Round package, therefore, are necessarily preliminary.

Opening Markets For Goods

After seven multilateral trade rounds since 1947, tariffs (customs duties) were on average already low — around 5 percent for the main industrial countries before the Uruguay Round. Some very high tariffs remained, however, particularly in sectors such as textiles and clothing, footwear and agriculture, and more generally in certain developing countries that are important emerging markets. The Uruguay Round target, set by the Montreal ministerial meeting in 1988 after pressure from Canada to have as ambitious a market-opening agreement as feasible, was to bring the average level of tariffs down by more than 30 percent and to increase the number of tariffs "bound" against subsequent increases. This target was substantially exceeded. Estimates vary, but the average reduction will be over 40 percent.

At the Tokyo summit in July 1993 the Quad countries agreed to reduce tariffs to zero in nine sectors and to make deep cuts in a range of natural resource, agricultural, and other industrial sectors. These reductions were then "multilateralized" to other participants under the Most Favoured Nation (MFN) principle, which requires that a tariff applied to one party be available to all.[17] Other sectors will see tariffs harmonized at low levels and, in the area of high tariffs, substantial reductions of up to 50 percent will be realized, for example, in chemicals.

Further, not only will tariffs fall, but many other kinds of border restrictions, such as import quotas, will be wholly or partly liberalized. For Canada, this aspect of the package will mean improved and more secure access to major export markets, including the United States. European industrial tariffs facing Canadian exporters will on average decline by 60 percent by the time the Round is fully implemented; Japanese tariffs will fall somewhat more; and there are significant reductions in dynamic new markets such as Republic of Korea. Sectors affected include wood, paper, non-ferrous metals, chemicals, as well as export-oriented Canadian agricultural products sectors such as wheat, barley, canola, flaxseed, pork, and beef. This outcome goes a long way towards Canada's long-standing commercial policy objective of reducing or eliminating high levels of effective protection against our resource-based industries.

Rewriting And Extending The Rules

The Uruguay Round devoted far more attention than previous rounds to the GATT rules concerned with ensuring fair competition within and between markets. For Canada, reducing administered or "legalistic" protection has been a fundamental objective in multilateral, bilateral, and regional trade negotiations in recent years. The central agreement, the result of a Canadian proposal, is the first internationally agreed definition of subsidies. The agreement also includes new disciplines on the use of countervailing duties (which can be imposed by the importing country to offset the effects of subsidies in the exporting country).

The Uruguay Round agreements also include improvements to rules on measures that attempt to counteract selling below cost in foreign markets (anti-dumping), a comprehensive agreement on emergency import control measures where industries are under real threat from foreign competition (safeguards), and a new code on the way in which the origin of imports is determined by customs authorities (rules of origin). Many other rules of the original GATT will also be clarified and improved, including tightened disciplines on national investment regulations which distort trade (Trade-Related Investment Measures — TRIMs).

The comprehensive subsidies/countervail agreement will reduce the vulnerability of Canada's federal and provincial subsidy programs, particularly regional development, to countervail and will provide a basis to challenge subsidies elsewhere. Although subsidy discipline will continue to expose some Canadian subsidies (especially large one-time packages) to countervail and to increased multilateral remedies, countervail reforms will be entrenched in the GATT rules and will require the United States, a major user of countervailing duties, to follow fairer procedures. The agreement provides a good basis for follow-on negotiations in the trade remedy working groups recently established under the North American Free Trade Agreement (NAFTA).

Returning Textiles and Clothing to Normal GATT *Rules*

The textiles and clothing sector has been governed by a system of world-wide quota controls affecting the exports of developing countries to industrial countries for more than thirty years. The Multi-Fibre Arrangement (MFA), which provides the current framework for the system, has been in place since 1974, effectively removing this sector from GATT. The Uruguay Round outcome will lead to the progressive phasing out of the MFA, and other similar restrictions, over a period of ten years.[18] This agreement does not mean that trade in textiles and clothing will be completely free. It does mean, however, that the same GATT-based rules will ultimately apply in this sector as apply to other sectors. It also means that there will be increased pressure on Canada's domestic producers to adjust, with consequent probable losses of employment. The transition period will be sufficiently long and gradual, however, to permit the industry to adjust to the new competitive conditions, with benefit to Canadian apparel manufacturers and to individual consumers.

A Ceasefire in the Farm War?

Agriculture was the most contentious part of the Uruguay Round from start to finish.[19] The Uruguay Round agreement on new trade rules and more open access for agriculture will have four components. The first three represent a program of commitments for reform which will lead to substantial changes in policies but very gradual changes in effective support for farmers. The fourth part will be an agreement on the use of regulations related to animal and plant health and safety standards which should result in an overall improvement and some harmonization in the use of such standards while ensuring that they are not used as arbitrary and unjustified barriers to trade.

The core of the complex agriculture agreement is simple: measures that distort trade in farm products should be brought under GATT disciplines. Many evolving GATT principles and practices—the ones that make the trade regime multilateral in form—are reflected in the text, including provisions for safeguards, MFN, mutual surveillance, and dispute settlement. The text also creates new market-based obligations in three areas of trade distortion corresponding to the three ways in which all industrial states help their farmers. The first is market access. Here participants agreed to "tariffy" all measures that restrict access to their own markets, including the U.S. Section 22 waiver, the EU variable levy, the Japanese and Korean bans on the import of rice, and the import quotas imposed under GATT Article XI (2) (c) in support of domestic supply management systems. (Canada had been pressing instead for the strengthening and clarification of Article XI.) The resulting tariffs, together with all existing tariffs, would be bound against further increase, and then subject to 36 percent reduction during the six-year transition period. Tariffication is significant because it is an aggregate measure, leaving states scope to craft the implementation details to suit domestic purposes, and because it is multilateral in form, unlike the codes adopted in the Tokyo Round. The second area is export subsidies, where the text now requires reductions over the transition period of 36 percent in budgetary terms and 21 percent by volume, which should considerably lessen the fiscal cost and market disruptions of the export subsidy war of recent years.

The third and most contentious area is domestic support measures. In agriculture, border measures and export subsidies are the residual of domestic policies. There is no point reducing these other distortions if the principal source of the problem is not brought under control. The basic agreement is that only those domestic measures that distort trade would be reduced. For convenience the negotiators refer to the categories of domestic measures as "boxes" into which all domestic programs could be put, although these terms do not appear in the text. The boxes are given colours by analogy to traffic lights.[20] The most important Box is Amber, for trade-distorting policies that will be subject to agreed reductions over the six-year transition period.

The major conceptual innovation of the Round has been the agreement on the Aggregate Measure of Support (AMS), which allows a single value to be placed on all trade-distorting support received by a specific product. The AMS will be reduced by 20 percent during the transition. The Blue Box is defined as measures that are in the Amber Box because they may have production or trade effects, but which need not be included in the calculation of the total AMS. The Blue Box is designed to let the European Union get credit for implementation of reform of its Common Agricultural Policy (CAP), although the provisions would also be available to other countries.

Finally, the soul of the agriculture agreement is the Green Box, which sets out the principles under which states may claim exemption from the general commitment to reduce domestic support policies for farmers. The fundamental requirement is that such policies "have no, or at most minimal, trade distortion effects or effects on production." The kinds of policies that may go into this Green Box include services which are generally available to the rural community, such as research, pest control, and infrastructure, and direct "de-coupled" payments to producers for such things as structural adjustment or regional assistance. Such direct support must not involve either price support or implicit support from consumers. Governments can do whatever they think necessary to support the income and general standard of living of farmers, but such support must not be related in any way to price levels or production volumes. There is implicitly a Red Box, to complete the analogy; it contains the export subsidies.

These provisions are a major improvement over previous GATT treatment of agriculture, but obvious inconsistencies remain. Under American trade remedy law, for example, some Amber and Blue subsidies would normally be countervailable. The Europeans would not agree, however, to take the pain of changing the CAP if they were to be at risk of American harassment. The text contains, therefore, both a "continuation" clause, recording agreement to begin further negotiations one year before the end of the implementation period, and a "peace clause," specifying that measures covered by the agreement will not be subject to trade remedy action for the first nine years of the transition. The Amber Box has an indefinite life; the Blue Box might come to an end after six years; and the Green Box will likely be continued after the transition. All participants, therefore, have an incentive to return to the table after six years to negotiate further reductions in Amber programs as the price for a continuation (in some form) of the Green and Blue exemptions. This part of the Uruguay Round was the hardest to conclude but may well be the most important, for world politics as well as the world economy.

Trading Creativity and Invention

The Uruguay Round agreement on Trade-Related Intellectual Property Rights (TRIPs), covering matters such as patents, copyright, trademarks, integrated circuit layouts, trade secrets, and appellations of origin (geographical indications), will create or reinforce jointly agreed standards of protection and enforcement in all areas of intellectual property. It will apply GATT principles, such as non-discrimination, equality of treatment, and transparency, to economic activities created by rapid technological innovation, a characteristic of today's world economy. Also important are provisions to enhance the enforcement of intellectual property rights at the national level.[21] Canada will benefit from removal of discriminatory features of U.S. patent provisions, although the agreement will limit future use by Canadian producers of certain appellations of origin.

Trade in Services

The fast-growing area of trade in services covers a multitude of sectors, from banking and insurance, through tourism, to the provision of labour. Though the data are weak, trade in these and other services is broadly estimated to account for US$2 trillion in world trade every year ($800 billion in cross-border commercial trade, $1.2 trillion mostly in investment). The service industry, currently the fastest growing sector in the Canadian and most other economies, accounts for 70 percent of Canadian jobs and 65 percent of Gross Domestic Product (GDP). Much of this trade is already open to international competition, but rules and disciplines were needed to guard against protectionism or discriminatory measures. By bringing it into the multilateral system of trade rules, services markets world-wide can be secured, and trade be subjected to multilateral dispute settlement arrangements.

Since the service sectors have not been covered up until now by GATT, a completely new set of rules has been established called the General Agreement on Trade in Services (GATS). While some of the rules on services find their roots in GATT itself, many reflect the fact that trade in services is normally less a matter of exchange across the border — there are no tariffs to be negotiated, for instance — than a question of the establishment of infrastructure (in the term of investment) in the "importing" country. The services agreement contains three elements: a body of general rules; a number of special conditions or exceptions related to the particular circumstances of individual service sectors; and a package of initial liberalization commitments by members of the agreement.

Areas where attention has focused have been financial services, transport services, telecommunications, audio-visual and other "cultural" services, as well as commitments on the establishment of commercial presence and the movement of skilled personnel.

Considerable progress was made in opening service areas of interest to Canada, including banking, construction, engineering, and environmental services.

The Trading System

The trade regime is both the regulation of governmental regulation of trade and the constitutional framework governing that regulation. GATT in effect tells states how to act so that their actions can be understood by other states.[22] GATT makes certain forms of behaviour comprehensible as a means of declaring them legitimate or not. The two halves of the definition of an international regime split, therefore, on the constitutive rules (conventions, norms, principles) by which states understand behaviour in an issue area and on the regulatory procedures by which states know whether their actions and the actions of others are in conformity with the rules. As Contracting Parties, states discuss specific trade problems, theirs and others, in the context of existing rules; they also hold periodic negotiations about the rules. By the end of the Tokyo Round, GATT had been fragmented, with some fundamental matters (e.g., subsidies) being dealt with under codes, of which only some contracting parties were members and which had autonomous dispute settlement mechanisms. There was no proper surveillance mechanism, and GATT itself was still an interim agreement, not a proper international organization. One of the priorities for the Uruguay Round, therefore, was strengthening GATT itself in order to withstand further fragmentation.

There are three major institutional agreements in the final Uruguay Round package. The first seeks to streamline and give more teeth to the dispute settlement procedure, one of the ways in which contracting parties agree on breaches of the rules and ensure compliance. Some reforms were introduced during the Round, but the final package provides even clearer timetables and deadlines, ensures more automaticity in the process (preventing blockages), and improves the implementation of adopted dispute panel reports. The creation of a comprehensive and integrated system for multilateral disputes improves the possibility for small countries like Canada to exercise influence within the regime, if more countries use it than has been the case in the past. There are also uncertainties for Canada, however, in the management of our most important trading relationship with the United States, where we now have two sets of dispute settlement procedures. The hope for all countries is that if the WTO meets expectations, it will be sufficiently effective that Americans will find the benefits of unilateral action (e.g., Section 301) not worth the costs, thereby strengthening multilateralism.

The second major institutional outcome of the Uruguay Round will be the formalization of the Trade Policy Review Mechanism which was introduced into GATT on a provisional basis in 1989. It has permitted GATT for the first time to undertake comprehensive, detailed reviews of the trade policies of individual members, thereby improving transparency and the exchange of information and analysis.[23] Economists believe that if the public knew the real costs of protection and subsidies, politicians would be less likely to make bad decisions. Such thinking underlay Fritz Leutwiler's group of "Wise Men," which recommended a public "protection balance sheet" and regular public surveillance in GATT of the ensemble of a country's trade-related policies.[24] Similar thinking underlies the decision to publish policy recommendations in the IMF *World Economic Outlook*, and the OECD *Economic Outlook*. The OECD Economic Policy Committee has argued that "Publicising the results of surveillance can broaden and strengthen support for reform, which is essential for sustained progress. . . . Closer public scrutiny will strengthen the political weight of broad economic considerations relative to that of special interests."[25]

Finally, a new World Trade Organization, the result of a Canadian proposal,[26] will be created to provide the institutional framework for the implementation of *all* the Uruguay Round results. The need for such a body has been apparent for many years.[27] The purposes of the WTO, as described in the agreement's preamble, are "to develop an integrated, more viable and durable multilateral trading system encompassing the General Agreement on Tariffs and Trade, the results of past trade liberalization efforts, and all of the results of the Uruguay Round of multilateral trade negotiations." The WTO will provide the forum for negotiations among its members on their multilateral trade relations, and a framework for the implementation of the results of such negotiations. There will be a Ministerial Conference composed of representatives of all the members, which is to meet at least once every two years, giving the WTO the kind of regular political guidance that the GATT has lacked. In the intervals between meetings of the Ministerial Conference, its functions will be carried out by the General Council, which will also discharge the responsibilities of the Dispute Settlement Body and the Trade Policy Review Body. Under this umbrella there will also be a Council for Trade in Goods, a Council for Trade in Services, and a Council for Trade-Related Aspects of Intellectual Property Rights. The various Uruguay Round agreements also provide for a variety of subsidiary committees under these bodies. There is provision for the head of the WTO to enter into regular consultations with the heads of the IMF and the World Bank. Most important, the WTO, like the Final Act of the Uruguay Round, will not be a Chinese menu. All participants, from the minnows of world trade to the whales, must accept the whole set of commitments, or opt out completely. The implications of this central feature of the Uruguay Round will shape the future of the trading system.

First Thoughts on the Implications of the Uruguay Round

The full implications of newly agreed trade agreements are not immediately apparent. Even in the oldest and most straightforward areas of market access, the negotiations proceed backward, by an exchange of "concessions," rather than forward, with an eye on structural adjustment. In consequence it takes time to see how economic actors will adapt. In the newer areas of changes to the rules, we will need time to see how states will use the new procedures and how the increased certainty and predictability will influence private sector decisions to invest and trade. In the newest and most important areas, like the GATS or the aggregate measures in the agriculture agreement, the full meaning and implications of the new system will not be apparent for some time. Countries will try to operationalize their commitments. There will be a process of mutual understanding of the results through the surveillance processes. Ultimately there will be disputes. It is only through the process of practice, discussion, and adjudication that the full meaning of the agreements will become clear. It is only as agreements are put into action that we begin to learn where mistakes were made, where clarifications are needed, and where gaps need to be filled. With the agreements only just signed as this book goes to press, the best that we can offer is some first thoughts. We consider four sorts of implications: the likely economic impact of what was achieved; the significance of the unfinished agenda; the prospects for containing regionalism; and the implications of how the deal was achieved for the WTO, for future negotiations, and for world politics.

The World Economy

By liberalizing world trade and strengthening international trade rules and institutions, most economic and trade policy analysts concluded that a successfully completed Uruguay Round based on the 1991 Draft Final Act and subsequent agreements would increase overall world and Canadian economic welfare — in other words, income would be higher than it might have been had the Round failed. With the details of the full market-access package still incomplete, no assessment of the actual Final Act can be completed, but estimates of the benefits will, if anything, be higher than those made over the past couple of years because of the way the extension of the Quad market-access package to other countries kept ratcheting up the overall package.[28] The successful outcome is also positive for global and national allocative efficiency; at the most fundamental level, trade liberalization allows a country to shift resources to areas where they can be better used, releasing resources from the production of goods and services that can be bought more cheaply from abroad. Liberalization may also raise the rate of economic growth as the environment for investment and innovation improves. Taxpayers benefit when the deadweight costs of subsidies are lessened, and consumers benefit when the price of the goods they buy reflects a reduction in indirect subsidies.[29] While these benefits will only emerge over time, the successful conclusion of the Round should provide some immediate stimulus to the world economy through its psychological effects on business confidence — what Keynes called "animal spirits."

While the overall effects of a liberalizing trade agreement such as the Uruguay Round, the Canada-U.S. FTA, or NAFTA will be positive, some firms, workers, and communities will be adversely affected. Trade liberalization in general and the Uruguay Round in particular will be politically and socially acceptable only if gains to the economy from a successful outcome are demonstrably greater than the losses and if the adjustment costs to those adversely affected are dealt with equitably in our national economies. The overall net economic benefits of a successfully completed Round seem to be demonstrably positive. A joint World Bank-OECD study concluded that the annual contribution to the world economy resulting from a success in the Uruguay Round negotiations could be about US$213 billion (US$2.5 billion for Canada) by the year 2002. The estimate for the world is the difference between world real income in the year 2002 based on known or expected economic trends, and world real income assuming a successful conclusion of the GATT Round, all expressed in 1992 dollars. The study assumes that a successful round is roughly equivalent to a 30 percent cut in effective protection both for agriculture and for industry. Because agricultural barriers are now much higher than industrial tariffs, the bulk of the gain comes from agriculture.[30]

The Unfinished Agenda

The Uruguay Round negotiations were enormously complex, yet some long-standing issues were never put on the table, for example, the environment, workers' rights, commodity arrangements, and restrictive business practices. Some issues that were in the Punta Declaration either did not receive a lot of attention (notably institutional links between GATT, the World Bank, and the IMF, and work on the interrelationship of policies that affect trade, debt, and growth) or did not make much progress. In addition to this unfinished agenda, there are also a host of new issues not envisaged at the time of Punta del Este. Some of these issues will be inscribed on the WTO work program by the Marrakesh ministerial meeting, notably government procurement, civil aircraft, and a series of services negotiations in such sectors as financial services, maritime transport, telecommunications, and movement of people.

Sustainable development will be the first challenge facing the new WTO.[31] The Round came to a conclusion at a time when environmental considerations were much more prominent than they had been when the negotiations began. Some of the environmental effects of the changes in trade policy contained in the Final Act could only be assessed as negotiations proceeded, not at the end, but such a review was not contemplated when the Round began in 1986. In Canada, for example, while there may be an expectation that there would be an environmental review of the Uruguay Round, a full NAFTA-type review, let alone an improvement on the NAFTA review, would be difficult if not impossible at this stage.[32] It is too late to consider the environmental effects of global trade flows, and of global trade liberalization in the context of this Round. Rather than endanger the overall benefits of this lengthy negotiation, the WTO will need to be working to make progress on developing an international consensus on the integration of environmental reviews into the process of international economic cooperation in future. In the interim, individual countries will need to review the proposed changes in trade policy in the context of existing legislative and regulatory environmental objectives.

There is also a growing understanding that as a result of globalization, continually evolving international rules of the game are needed for a cluster of micro-economic issues that were once considered domestic policy. There are three proximate causes of globalization: the post-World War Two growth and industrialization of what has been known as the Third World; a long process of investment and trade liberalization in the industrialized countries which continues today through regional integration agreements; and the impact of technological change in transport and communications technologies that have resulted in the dramatic compression of "economic space." The symptoms of globalization are growth in trade, foreign investment, and the emergence of the global corporation; changes in the structure of wages and income distribution; and the growth and internationalization of services.[33]

Another symptom of globalization is persistent calls for "harmonization" and "convergence" of domestic regulatory policies. Sylvia Ostry launched a major work program at OECD on this subject with an important insight: "The battle for market share in leading edge sectors involves not only competition among multinational enterprises but also rivalry among the different market systems which influence the enterprise's ability to compete."[34] She argued that competition among systems will lead to discord — "system friction" — which requires efforts to promote convergence or harmonization so that multinational firms can compete on the basis of the same domestic rules world wide. Attempts to end friction between divergent domestic regulatory systems will be high on the next agenda for trade negotiations.[35]

Regionalism and Multilateralism

One of the most commented upon features of the world trading system in recent years has been the apparent trend to regionalism. Asian regionalism, for example, is the focus of Wendy Dobson's chapter in this volume, while Charles Doran considers the North American variant. Whether economic forces show distinctive regional patterns is a different matter from whether governments try to use policy measures to the same end. GATT rests on certain fundamental norms and principles. The MFN principle requires Contracting Parties to extend to all participants any concession that it gives to one. The national treatment principle requires that once admitted to the market, all goods will be treated equally. GATT has always accepted the possibility of regional trade agreements, but such customs unions and free trade areas were seen as exceptions to the rules because they are inherently discriminatory, denying both national treatment and MFN to some classes of foreign goods. Regional agreements were to be allowed only if they were demonstrably trade-creating rather than trade-diverting, but this provision of the General Agreement has been thought to be weak. The Uruguay Round outcome is thus important for two reasons.

First, the Final Act contains agreements on strengthening the procedures for reviewing regional arrangements and on working toward harmonized rules of origin. Secondly, and likely more important, the general strengthening of the multilateral system represented by the success of the Round allows a rebuttal to claims that regional liberalization is necessary when multilateral liberalization is blocked, that the two forms of rule-making and market-opening cannot be pursued in parallel. This point is especially important when GATT is seen not as a body of law but as an international regime whose influence on the behaviour of governments depends on convergent expectations. An expectation that only regional negotiations are successful could have become a self-fulfilling prophecy.[36] The success of the Round influences those expectations, and shows how multilateral and regional negotiations can build on each other for both increasing market access and devising new rules.

Single Undertaking

In the section of the Punta Declaration on General Principles, the participants agreed that "the launching, the conduct and the implementation of the outcome of the negotiations shall be treated as parts of a Single Undertaking." The full import of that section was not appreciated at the time. The broader substantive scope and larger number of players participating in the Uruguay Round negotiations would have made success problematic, but the idea of a "Single Undertaking" made success doubly difficult. It is not surprising that the Uruguay Round was in consequence slower than the Tokyo Round.

As the Round dragged on, scholars wondered if minilateral deals might be possible. France suggested putting agriculture to one side when it was making its last stand in the fall of 1993. The structure of the Punta Declaration made all this moot, as had already been demonstrated in 1988 at Montreal when the refusal of six Latin American countries to accept partial results (among other things, on agriculture) caused the conclusion of the meeting to be postponed for four months. In the end all understood, in the words of the Dunkel text, that "no single element of the Draft Final Act can be considered as agreed until the total package is agreed." Participants accepted that the Uruguay Round agreements "shall be open for acceptance as a whole."

This stipulation clearly made the task of assembling a big package that much harder. There are no "minilateral" deals as there were in the Tokyo Round. This fact may initially have been a disappointment to those developing countries, led by Brazil and India, that forced the creation of a separate negotiating structure to keep services outside the GATT framework. The Single Undertaking has constrained the group negotiating services to move to the same timetable as the goods group, thereby making the linkages implicit rather than explicit.[37] Another consequence has been that many texts, notably those covering investment and intellectual property, reflect a broad consensus and not simply the wishes of OECD countries. The Single Undertaking is also a tool by which developing countries could ensure that progress was made on issues of interest to them which had been poorly handled in previous rounds, especially textiles, tropical products, and agriculture. This tool has been used to great effect, especially at the Montreal and Brussels ministerial meetings, and its potential use was on the minds of negotiators during the end game. The problems in farm trade may or may not have been more severe than at various points in the past, but this time they could not be pushed off the table.

The Single Undertaking changes how we understand the logic of multilateral negotiation in the GATT. Under the General Agreement, decisions are to be taken by a majority vote, but in practice decisions have been taken by consensus. Nevertheless, as Jackson shows, knowledge of the legal structure of voting has a real effect on the behaviour of the contracting parties.[38] On some issues, the interests of the largest countries take effective precedence. The early GATT rounds were largely centred on cutting tariffs. This important function of GATT, now part of a larger process called "market access," was certainly important in the Uruguay Round, especially in the final six months. In this domain GATT still proceeds by an exchange of concessions among principal suppliers which are then multilateralized by MFN to other participants. Lesser participants in a given sector must in consequence accept the deal struck by the larger ones—in effect, a form of weighted voting that was not affected by the Single Undertaking. On other issues, such as amending the agreement, the two-thirds rule inhibited attempts to alter existing language, which led to the code approach in the Tokyo Round. The Uruguay Round broke this logjam.

It might be argued that the Single Undertaking simply makes the inherent nature of multilateralism visible. Caporaso, basing himself on Ruggie's definition, says that "the institution of multilateralism is distinguished from other forms by three properties: indivisibility, generalized principles of conduct, and diffuse reciprocity. These three properties should be treated as a coherent ensemble. . . . "[39] If this interpretation is accepted, then previous rounds have been less than fully multilateral. The Uruguay Round attempted to make all the benefits and obligations of GATT indivisible and it did so on the basis of non-discrimination. The Single Undertaking required participants to negotiate on the basis of diffuse reciprocity, in that acceptance of new disciplines in one area was tied to the desire to obtain the general benefits of the agreement. Developing countries may not have wanted to accept disciplines on investment measures or intellectual property, but they had to accept something in these areas in return for new disciplines imposed on industrial countries in such areas as textiles and tropical products.

Specific reciprocity is the common meaning of the term, "my actions are dependent on yours." Diffuse reciprocity, in contrast, accepts that action is sometimes motivated by some sense of obligation for the general good; it "adjusts the utilitarian lenses for the long view, emphasizing that actors expect to benefit in the long run, and over many issues, rather than every time and on every issue."[40] Specific reciprocity may be facilitated by international regimes and in turn may promote greater cooperation, but diffuse reciprocity depends on the existence of the norms of obligation associated with regimes. Both forms of reciprocity may co-exist in the trade regime.[41] Keohane thinks that diffuse reciprocity requires concessions to be sequential, not simultaneous, while noting that conditional MFN makes reciprocity difficult. Winham worried that the experience of the Tokyo Round showed that specific reciprocity was difficult between unequal partners, impeding the integration of developing countries.[42] The Uruguay Round Single Undertaking forced simultaneous unconditional MFN, making diffuse reciprocity easier by ensuring that there would be no free riders, one of the common problems in diffuse reciprocity.

The Single Undertaking has affected all of the parties, large and small. Without a large and broad package, it would have been impossible to attract so many countries into the negotiation. Without an outcome that appears balanced, there would be no outcome at all. All the benefits are tied to acceptance of all the rules, which among other things explicitly extends MFN to all the agreements, including the minilateral codes of the Tokyo Round. The ITO had a similar provision, one which would have made it not the public good of hegemonic theorists but a private, because excludable, good. Viner observed at the time that "under the Suggested Charter [of the ITO] not only will there be no obligation to extend most-favored-nation treatment to non-members of the ITO, but member countries will not be permitted to extend to non-member countries, unless the Organization grants special permission, the concessions which they grant to the other member countries as a result of the tariff-reduction negotiations." He thought this provision important, otherwise high-tariff countries that failed to liberalize would by free riding discourage the whole process.[43] A country's status as a Contracting Party of what is now called the GATT 1947 will not be affected by a failure to accept the WTO, which includes all the Uruguay Round agreements, but the residual benefits of the old GATT without WTO membership will hardly be worth having.

Conclusions on First Thoughts

Canada was an enthusiastic participant in the Uruguay Round from the beginning until the end, when within weeks of taking office as the trade minister in a new government, Roy MacLaren was in Geneva working with his Quad counterparts and other trade ministers to complete the package. Canadians helped to set the agenda and later made important contributions to developing negotiating objectives in such areas as subsidies, market access, and the WTO itself. Official enthusiasm seems to be shared by Canadians generally, three-quarters of whom are said to support the reduction of trade barriers through GATT.[44]

GATT is the basis for the stability of the international trading system on which increases in world welfare depend, but it is also Canada's principal trade agreement with all but two of our trading partners. It is also the legal underpinning of the FTA and now NAFTA. The then Secretary of State for External Affairs, Allen MacEachen, chaired the GATT ministerial session held in November 1982, which was the first step toward the new round. At the celebration of GATT's fortieth anniversary in 1987, then Trade Minister, Pat Carney, invited the participating countries to hold the planned mid-term review meeting in Canada. The Montreal ministerial meeting was hosted by her successor as Trade Minister, John Crosbie, just after the 1988 election debates over free trade with the United States. Canada had five priorities for the round as articulated by Carney on the occasion of GATT's fortieth anniversary. Canada's first priority, forty years after the signature of the General Agreement, was strengthening the GATT system by creating a more policy-oriented organization with links to the other Bretton Woods institutions. Second was developing new rules for agricultural trade. Third was improved and secure market access for trade in goods and agriculture. Canada's fourth priority was the new issues of services, intellectual property, and investment. The final priority was greater participation and integration of developing countries into GATT.[45] These broad objectives have all been achieved.

The Uruguay Round represents a major step forward in the further opening of world markets and in strengthening and extending trade rules. While putting pressure on import-sensitive and domestically oriented sectors of the Canadian economy (such as poultry, dairy, textiles and apparel, furniture, as well as some machinery and equipment), the Uruguay Round on balance will contribute to making the Canadian economy more competitive internationally and more capable of taking advantage of global growth opportunities in the years ahead. This positive outcome is of even more importance for developing countries, including the transition economies, than it is for members of the OECD.[46]

The Final Act has turned out to be one of the first major post-Cold War international treaties. The GATT can now no longer be described as an institution of the American pole of a bipolar world. The 117 participants and the Single Undertaking have made the Uruguay Round fully multilateral in nature and global in scope. Naturally the Round could only address the problems that were evident when it began. A whole new agenda is now emerging as governments grapple with the challenges of a rapidly changing world economy. There will be future negotiations, although there may not be a future round; GATT's decision rules made periodic rounds of negotiations essential, but the provisions of the WTO, including regular ministerial meetings, may allow the agreement to become self-amending. The Single Undertaking is not carried forward into the WTO, but the integration of all functions under one General Council, the automatic iteration of ministerial involvement, and the new decision rules, should make it possible to construct large packages that would exhibit a dynamic similar to that of the Single Undertaking.[47]

We observed above that globalization involves both new state actors in the international system and a compression of economic space. New rules of the game are thought to be needed both for the game of states and for the game of firms. Of the two, it is probably the new players that are the more significant. Neither the issues nor the fact of increasing interdependence is new. The rules of the game of firms are manifestly sufficient to have allowed an enormous expansion of global commerce. The significant variable affecting calls for harmonization, therefore, is the high and rising number of new players in the world economy who had not been active before.

The trading system reflects these new realities. While many of the Tokyo Round participants did not sign the most stringent of the new disciplines, all participants in the Uruguay Round must accept the entire package as a single undertaking, or accept nothing. It is expected that all participants will sign the package and join the WTO, an indication of the role various groups played in reaching the successful outcome. The need for new rules of the game arises, therefore, because there are a large number of active participants in global commerce who had not been active participants (a distinction that might even include Japan) in the previous processes of elaborating existing rules. These new players must be involved in the consideration of new rules, and they may provide useful allies for Canada, at least for shaping the agenda if not necessarily for negotiating new disciplines. The new WTO, therefore, is an example of the democratization and strengthening of multilateralism envisaged by Keating in chapter 3.

It is sometimes said that globalization erodes sovereignty, but it does no such thing. Sovereignty refers to legitimate authority to act in a certain way in a defined territory.[48] Legitimacy refers to the democratic accountability of the state. Formal state authority is not challenged by globalization. What has been eroded, however, is the effectiveness of policy action, thereby posing a potential challenge to legitimacy, at least to the extent that the state is perceived by its citizens to be unable to regulate in the politically determined national interest. Perhaps the most important implication of the Uruguay Round is that when nothing is agreed until everything is agreed, everybody has a voice, and everybody has to take account of the views of everybody else. This decision rule is neither consensus nor unanimity, both of which are single-shot mechanisms, taking decisions at a fixed point in time. The Single Undertaking, in contrast, proved to be a dynamic, iterative process, allowing elements of agreement to build until a critical mass was reached. The Single Undertaking, by making the WTO fully multilateral, offers a fresh perspective on the meaning of the fundamental norms and principles of the trading system—MFN, national treatment, reciprocity—as we contemplate new international negotiations on domestic policies once outside GATT.

Disengagement from Regionalism

6 Europe after Maastricht

David Long

THE MAASTRICHT TREATY on European Union was finally ratified by all the member states of the European Community and came into force on November 1, 1993. From this time forward, the European Community became the European Union.[1] The sometimes rocky path to ratification began after the signing of the treaty in December 1991 and ended with the decision of the German Constitutional Court that it did not violate the German constitution. Indeed, for certain periods it looked as if the treaty would fail to get the necessary universal assent of the member states.

Following the problems the treaty encountered in 1992 with the Danish referendum defeat of June 2, the arena shifted to the larger states of the Community—Britain, France, and Germany. In Britain and Germany the treaty was challenged in court. The French people narrowly assented in a referendum in the fall of 1992. The British presidency of the EC in the second half of 1992 was marked by a number of disasters, the most significant of which was the crisis concerning the Exchange Rate Mechanism (ERM) of the European Monetary System (EMS). A second Danish referendum backed the treaty by a small margin after the December 1992 Edinburgh meeting of the European Council created extra allowances for the Danes. During the course of 1993 things seemed to go from bad to worse. Speculation against the French franc provoked another crisis in the ERM. At an emergency meeting of finance ministers, the "bands" of the ERM were substantially widened to allow more fluctuations in currency rates. Effectively the ERM had folded. Meanwhile, the attempts by the EC to mediate a resolution to the conflict in the former Yugoslavia palpably failed. The negative impact on the EC's credibility as an actor in international politics was only matched by the clear sense within the EC that the Maastricht formula for a Common Foreign and Security Policy (CFSP) would not be enough. During the ratification process a cloud descended over the Community that recalled the days of Euro-pessimism and seemed worlds away from the heady

---

The author thanks Alan Dabb for valuable and prompt research assistance for this paper.

days of the "1992 Programme" and the euphoria of 1989 to 1991 which followed the fall of communism in Central Europe.

While the failure to ratify the treaty would have been a major setback for the EC and European integration generally, the achievement of full ratification has not removed the doubts about the treaty. The doubts are signalled by the way the final ratification was greeted — that is, with relief and resignation rather than fanfare and exultation. There is little enthusiasm for Maastricht in EU capitals, despite the attempts to go through the motions, for instance, at the special European Council meeting to celebrate Maastricht's ratification on October 29, 1993. Having initially been trumpeted as the largest step forward for the Community since the Treaties of Rome, the goals of the Maastricht Treaty appear distant prospects today: the timetable for monetary union is unlikely to be achieved; the prospect of a coherent, let alone common, foreign and security policy for the EU seems utopian in light of the failure of the Community to stop the fighting in Bosnia and the obvious disagreements over what to do. In comparison to the galvanizing effect of the Single European Act (SEA) and the 1992 Programme, Maastricht is a failure.

This paper will address what went wrong with Maastricht, discuss the key issues facing the member states of the European Union following Maastricht, and examine some implications for Canada. The paper comes to the rather banal conclusion that European affairs are important for Canadians but are relatively little affected by Canadian policy or opinions. Yet there are important implications. These emerge less from the relationship of Canada and the EU as such than from a consideration of the impact of further European integration on the multilateral relations in which Canada engages, and from the common travails of Canadian and European politics.

Why did the Maastricht Treaty Fail?

Despite ratification, Maastricht has failed in the sense that the momentum that led to the Inter-Governmental Conferences that formulated the Maastricht Treaty on European Union has been lost. There has to be renewed effort on the part of member states in order to bring the major items outlined in the treaty into being. What went wrong? Explanations for the problems of Maastricht fall into two categories; one pointing to flaws in the treaty or in the Community itself, the second finding fault beyond the Community in the international political and economic context.

Problems Internal to the Treaty or the Community

The most commonly heard explanation for the failure of Maastricht is that it was too federal to be accepted by the still nationally focused populations of the member states. For anti-Maastricht campaigners such as Lady Thatcher, it was "a treaty too far." According to this argument, the Maastricht Treaty sought to drag the peoples of Europe into a federal union they did not want.[2] Given the chance to express their distrust of the federal vision represented by Maastricht, Europeans gave the treaty a thumbs down, as could be seen in public opinion polls across the Community.[3] It is suggested that political elites simply ran ahead of their publics on European integration. Whatever the euphoria of the period of negotiation leading to Maastricht, it was the hothouse environment of the negotiations that led to decisions that did not reflect the opinions of the populace of Europe. Prime ministers and their ministers are said to have "gone European" far beyond the sentiments of the people they represent.

While Maastricht's aims were said to be too abstract to be attractive to the publics of the member states, the symbols associated with the issues made for a treaty that was hard to defend. Whatever might be the merits of monetary union, most of the arguments regarding, for example, the system of central banks, the European Monetary Institute (EMI) and so on, hardly touch the lives of the average citizen of the European Union. By contrast, the Single European Act was seen as a boon for ordinary people, even if only in the transitional phase when customs duties could be avoided on "duty free" goods. Yet at the same time, the symbolic quality of monetary union rendered it extremely controversial. Monetary union means the supersession of national currencies, just as Union citizenship means the supersession of national citizenship. While in practice EU citizenship amounts to the right of non-national residents to vote in local and European elections, this and monetary union created an impression that national symbols were being bargained away. Germans, in particular, became increasingly antagonistic to the perceived imminent demise of their beloved Deutschmark. The slow adoption of, and controversy surrounding, the European Community passport indicates that popular support for currency union as envisaged in Maastricht will take time to build.

Another criticism of Maastricht suggests that, contrary to the argument that leaders ran ahead of their publics, there was a widespread misplaced enthusiasm for further integration in the lead-up to the negotiations over Maastricht. This zeal was the product partly of the success of the Single European Act, but even more the aftermath of the fall of the Berlin Wall and the end of the Cold War. The two years from the end of 1989 to the end of 1991 were, to be sure, a dramatic period, creating something approaching euphoria in both Eastern and Western Europe. This euphoria is exemplified most clearly in the Charter of Paris of 1990 that institutionalized the Conference on Security and Cooperation in Europe (CSCE). But the EC was far from unaffected. Even war in the Gulf created the sense that the Community must grasp the nettle and *do something*. The result in the Maastricht Treaty was not all the original drafts had aimed for;[4] the compromises and potential opt-outs were larger and the vision of a bigger, better Europe less clear. Nevertheless, the Community saw this as a moment to move forward to meet its destiny as the heart of Europe: Maastricht was to be a first blueprint. The Maastricht Treaty struggled because it was built on sand; the euphoric period came to a close abruptly as the Yugoslav federation fell apart and war in Europe resumed. Optimistic estimates and blueprints rapidly transmogrified into anachronisms.

These criticisms suggest that Maastricht was too bold and too simplistic. A different explanation of the failure of Maastricht is that the treaty was too complex or confusing. One such argument runs that the Treaty on European Union was too confusing for the publics to understand. The document that was finally developed was intricate and arcane. While the Single European Act was also fundamentally dull reading, there was the hook, the 1992 Programme. Europeans in general had little interest in the provisions of the SEA with regard to majority voting in the Council of Ministers or in the marginally improved position of the European Parliament in the decision-making process. But the idea of a deadline in the 1992 Programme by which the European Community would be a single market unfettered from border restrictions and the like caught the public imagination. Maastricht was an attempt to copy the SEA's road to success, adding a timetable for Economic and Monetary Union (EMU) to the design put forward in the earlier Delors Report. The timetable, it was thought, would help this next step in European integration, not just as a plan of the route ahead but as a psychological inducement, as had the idea of "1992." However, EMU was too abstract and too wrapped up in the expectations of financial markets and credibility of member states.

More seriously, it is argued that the treaty was not only confusing in appearance but in essence. It was a messy compromise reflecting no coherent vision of a future Europe. Any attempt to give the treaty a clear message was destroyed in the machinations during the Inter-Governmental Conferences. Despite the hard bargaining, the treaty was not even a consensus decision, relying instead on opt-outs on social policy, foreign policy, and monetary union that ill-disguised the huge divisions between the member states. There were two dates for EMU: 1997 for those who had by then achieved the Maastricht stipulations for economic convergence, and 1999 for the rest, with Britain retaining an opt-out at this point. As is discussed in Alexander Moens's chapter, the provisions on the common foreign and security policy were extremely general and positively tentative on common defence.

Yet specific compromises were not the end of it. The Union created at Maastricht is not a unity but a trinity: the Community itself, suitably restructured to take into account EMU and a strengthened European Parliament; the CFSP; and Justice and Home Affairs—the latter take the form of inter-governmental cooperation between the member states rather than being organized within the Community institutions and being subject to European Court of Justice (ECJ) jurisdiction.[5] The CFSP "pillar" was placed outside Community competence and is therefore conducted inter-governmentally, not greatly different from the current arrangement on foreign policy, European Political Cooperation. The modality for the proposed common defence policy confuses matters still further. The Western European Union (WEU), an organization that has had many roles through its history, is the defence arm of the new European Union. Yet the WEU is both an integral part of the EU and simultaneously a bridge to NATO. To add to the confusion, the Brussels treaty that became the basis of the WEU expires in 1998. Finally, the principle of subsidiarity in the Treaty ended up as a compromise between the maximalists who saw it as a mechanism of federalism and the minimalists who saw it as a way of limiting the powers of the EU.[6]

Buffeted on the Winds of Change

The second set of explanations finds reasons for the failure of Maastricht beyond the control of the Community, in the international political and economic context. There are basically three variants to this argument, focusing in turn on German reunification, global currency volatility, and the changed security environment.

German Reunification[7]

With an increase in population and potential economic power suggesting similar political predominance in Europe, German reunification had already been a stimulus to change within Europe. The parallel Inter-Governmental Conference on Political Union, alongside that on EMU during 1991, was specifically intended to address problems that could be anticipated with the change in Germany's status and power. Yet the ways in which the re-emergence of a united Germany have affected the Community and now affect the Union are varied indeed. The impacts result, on the one hand, from the changed balance of power in Europe but, on the other, from uncertainty associated with the economic and political transition within reunified Germany and with attempts by Germany's partners to accommodate it.

During the Cold War, Germany was somewhat schizophrenic in international relations: it was a huge economic power, including near hegemony in the EC, but having far less than commensurate influence on high politics and security. With reunification, German economic strength remains in the fact that despite transition costs, Germany's economy and especially the D-mark will dominate the EU even more than previously. In addition to the dominance of German finance, the German ideological position in economic, and specifically, monetary policy has won out and this is being reflected in the shape of European Union policies and institutions. The planned European Central Bank is the Bundesbank writ large, economic policy in Europe is set to reflect German priorities more than many others, and Germany will remain the largest contributor to the EC coffers. Furthermore, to the east, Germany is forging new relations with the East-Central European countries and also with

Russia, and is by the far the largest aid donor and investor in these countries.[8]

With reunification and the end of the cold war, Germany has new opportunities in foreign policy but old constraints. It faces a dilemma in the political arena that is summed up in the phrase, "damned if you do, damned if you don't." In political and military strategic terms, Germany is shackled by its past—by the Nazi era and its present constitution. While others in Europe are loathe to admit it, there is a great fear of German reassertion, even if one discounts the history of the Third Reich. Germany's reunification simply changes the relative balance of power in the EU; this has made Germany's partners uneasy.

Changes in the balance of power within the EU have made the coordination of foreign policy both more salient and much harder, as German recognition of Slovenia and Croatia demonstrated.[9] German assertiveness over the former Yugoslavia has created something of a storm over German conduct and passionate denials on the part of the Germans themselves. Similarly, while there was political pressure on Germany to change course on interest rates, this was rebuffed. Though there are no immediate plans for change, there are increased calls for the inclusion of Germany (and Japan) in the UN Security Council, as for the idea of a European Community seat.[10]

But Germany is not just stronger; in the near term, it must pay the price of transition. A motif of the post-reunification period has paradoxically been Germany's economic frailty. German economic performance nosedived after 1990, with the German recession encouraged by the dissonance between the extremely restrictive policies of the Bundesbank and the Kohl government's expansionary policies during the initial reunification period. The lure of initially high wages as a result of the one-to-one exchange rate between the two German currencies created a spending spree that benefited only Western firms. In the longer term, with commitments to bring former East German wage rates into line with their Western counterparts, it led to a substantial lack of competitiveness of the Eastern *Länder*, resulting in a major drain on the German economy. Transition in the eastern *Länder* will, it is clear, take some time, and the effects on the German economy will be similarly long-lasting.

Reunification has important implications for the EU. Incorporation of the new *Länder* into the EC was effectively unilateral by the Germans, and certainly not via the usual route for expanding the Community. Following German demands, voting strength in the European Parliament was revised, with Germany getting eighteen more seats, and France, Britain, and Italy six more.[11] Incorporation of East Germany makes Germany a more agriculturally productive state likely to draw greater benefits than it has traditionally done from the Common Agriculture Policy (CAP).[12] Finally, a less financially strong Germany will find it harder to justify its position as the paymaster of the European Union budget.

In international politics, for all its potential, Germany's power is constrained by its own constitution from sending troops abroad. German influence on European policy in, for instance, Bosnia, is reduced because German forces are not involved in peacekeeping there and arguments for the use of force are not supported by the willingness to use German forces as part of the multilateral effort. Yet German influence is large and growing as the recognition of the Yugoslav republics according to German wishes indicates. In sum, German reunification has had a considerable impact on EMU, on the dynamics of cooperation in Europe, and on Germany's assertiveness outside the EU context. Each of these made Maastricht's road more difficult.

International Currency Volatility

The Maastricht Treaty optimistically projected a single currency within the EU by 1999 at the latest. The success and growth of the EMS partly accounts for this optimism, as does the unifying impetus given in the SEA.[13] It was assumed that both the SEA and the CAP would benefit from monetary integration. After the effective collapse of the ERM in 1993, the timetable for EMU now seems the most pathetic part of Maastricht.

When added to the strains of German reunification and worries over the French referendum on Maastricht, international currency volatility pulled the ERM apart. At the beginning of 1993 the core Franco-German relationship was still intact, despite the crisis of September 1992 that saw the withdrawal of sterling and the lira from the ERM and devaluations of the peseta and the escudo. Nevertheless, despite earlier indications that the French economy was in strong shape, the international money market began speculating heavily against the franc. The reality of the globalization of capital and money markets could hardly have been brought home more starkly than in the vain efforts to fend off currency speculation that was causing pressure on the French franc.

An emergency Council of Finance Ministers meeting on July 31, 1993, widened the ERM bands to plus or minus 15 percent. This figure was little more than a fig-leaf. The bands are so wide as to be non-existent. Nevertheless, the political significance of the continued existence of the ERM bands was large: European leaders could still argue publicly that the EMS was viable and that EMU remained a real prospect, though the Maastricht schedule might have to be reconsidered. There was less acrimony associated with the breakdown than with the 1992 ERM crisis when Anglo-German relations deteriorated significantly over each other's handling of the problems of the Mechanism. While the EMU mantra was still chanted within EC circles, beyond the faithful there was a spirited debate about the cause of the problem with the ERM and how to remedy it.

The Changed Security Environment

Finally, on the external causes of Maastricht's failure, there is what might be described as a meta-cause, the changed bases for international cooperation after the Cold War. The threat to the West from the Soviet Union had been the rationale (or rationalization) of international cooperation in Europe. The collapse of the Soviet threat has led to revaluation of the defence and security policies, especially force levels and postures, of the several European states. The new security environment affects not only security organizations such as NATO, the WEU, and the CSCE, but also poses critical questions for the EU. In times past, the threat from the Soviet Union was enough of a justification for continued European integration. Now there is no such rationale. This leads some to the pessimistic conclusion that the post-Cold War era will be marked by more inter-state conflict and greater likelihood of violent conflict between the nations of Europe.[14] While the pessimistic conclusion may be unwarranted, there are clear indications that the absence of a clear worst-case scenario in Europe is making cooperation more difficult and thus contributed to Maastricht's rocky road. In addition, the removal of the threat from the East blurs the boundaries of integration in the EU. Germany's eastern border is no longer the natural eastern border of the EU.

Weighting the Factors in Maastricht's Failure

There is little doubt that the international context was a significant factor in the failure of Maastricht. The irony of the failure is that it reflects as much the beginnings of hesitancy about the post-cold war world as it does the false optimism of the times. The treaty was a patchwork with some radical measures toward truly federal union with some severe hedging. There was no overall sense that the EC12 agreed what the treaty was supposed to mean. In short, it was a compromised disagreement rather than a compromise agreement. This meant that while Maastricht was not bound to fail, it was hostage to international fortune from the outset because there was already disagreement within the EC about what had been agreed.

After Maastricht: Challenges Ahead

The major challenges ahead for the EU are either the resuscitation of the Maastricht agenda or, alternatively, moving beyond this agenda without too great loss of face. Facing the challenges has been all the harder because Europeans have suffered many of the same political, economic, and social maladies—long-term high levels of unemployment, large and growing government debt, disillusionment with politics—that have been afflicting Canadians, and indeed the advanced industrial world in general in the early 1990s.

The rise in long-term unemployment in the EU has sharpened political debate generally and particularly on some issues, such as immigration. The rise of extreme right-wing parties has been a concomitant of economic and social distress. Greatest attention has been directed somewhat unfairly on Germany, especially in the media sensationalism regarding current events in the context of the history of the country. When the large numbers of refugees there are taken into account and the transformations that are taking place in the Eastern *Länder* are factored in, the relative *lack* of social dislocation is what is more remarkable about contemporary Germany. Regrettably, xenophobia and resurgent right-wing neo-Nazi groups are not restricted to Germany, as the cemetery desecration in Nijmegen and the election of a National Party candidate to a local council in London, England, demonstrate.

Beyond economic hardship and the growth of right-wing agitation, there appears to be a widespread and growing cynicism with traditional politics—both the political process and politicians themselves. This is most clearly evident in Italy, where charges of corruption and influence-peddling against the Mafia and many leading Italian politicians and bureaucrats have been widespread. Local elections in November 1993 saw the demolition of old electoral alliances and the emergence of a right-left split, with the former Communists taking the lion's share. In the process the Socialists and the Christian Democrats were decimated. In the national elections in March 1994, a right-wing coalition was triumphant.

To cap it all, the continuing war in Bosnia and the uncomfortable feeling of unfinished business in other parts of the former Yugoslavia have been a drain on the morale of Europeans and their leaders. The new year of 1994 began with a vote of no confidence in the EC negotiator, Lord Owen, from the European Parliament and a general feeling that EU intervention had not only not settled the conflict but may have prolonged or worsened it.[15]

In the context of this disillusion with politics, despair over economic hardship, fear over possible social and political unrest, and resignation regarding the war in Bosnia, the European Union has been forced onto the defensive. The president of the European Commission, Jacques Delors, presented the Commission's response to the problems of Europe's economies in his white paper, *Growth, Employment and Competitiveness*, put before the December 1993 European Council meeting. Delors' vision was avowedly expansionary, both in terms of governmental intervention in European economies and the Commission's part in directing those interventions, and in making interventions of its own to stimulate the European economy. The reception from the member states was mixed, with the British and the Germans leading the nay-sayers.

Another barometer of change or continued disillusion will be the European parliamentary elections scheduled in 1994. Though it is important not to belittle the EP, the significance of the elections lies as much in their effect on national politics. While the turnout varies across Europe, from the very high in Italy, Belgium, France and Germany, to the dismal in Britain, the elections have an impact akin to a national by-election. In some member states, given the unpopularity of the national governments, this is a cause of worry, if only for its psychological impact. The paradigm here is the EP elections in Britain, where John Major will be under tremendous pressure to resign should the Tories do even worse than their abysmal showing last time.

Economic and Monetary Union

I will consider three of the larger elements of the post-Maastricht agenda: EMU, CFSP, and expansion of the Union.[16] According to the timetable set out in the Maastricht Treaty, the second stage of EMU began on January 1, 1994. It was decided, rather late in the day following all sorts of wrangling about which new institutions of the EU should be housed in which member state, that the European Monetary Institute was to be based in Frankfurt.[17] The EMI will be the forerunner of the European Central Bank should the plan to effect EMU be followed. It is intended to monitor the progress of EU currencies towards the convergence. Whether it will ever perform these duties is a moot point.

The widening of the bands of the ERM undermined the move to EMU as envisaged in Maastricht, though exchange rate convergence was only one of the four convergence criteria in the timetable for EMU in the Maastricht Treaty. According to Maastricht, to qualify under the criteria, a member state's currency had to be in the narrow (plus or minus 2.25 percent) band of the ERM.[18] With the 2.25 percent band no longer in existence, the EU has something of a problem. Or has it? The member states of the EU declare themselves on the way to monetary union. Yet monetary union proposals are not new with Maastricht. The 1970 Werner Report anticipated the completion of monetary union by 1980.[19] This was quietly forgotten in future years. There appears to be no good reason the same could not happen again, although the greater closeness of the EU today compared to the period of the early 1970s suggests a heightened importance for EMU.

The EMU might be forgotten, but it is not gone. With the notable exception of the British, who were in any case latecomers to the ERM, during the latter part of 1993 the economies of the EU states were creeping back towards the bottom of their 2.25 percent bands in the ERM. While some observers are critical of the move back into line with an unnecessarily restrictive monetary policy on the part of the Germans, it seems that there is evidence for the proposition that EMU is a political project associated with European unity as much or more than an economic one.[20] Yet even here there are too many question marks, because exchange rate convergence is only one of the four indicators. Recent figures published by *The Economist* suggest that the EU will have serious problems reaching the targets, especially the fiscal convergence requirements. Germany's situation is critical. Since Germany is the European economic powerhouse, EMU cannot go ahead without it. Indeed, it had always been presumed that if any economy would meet the criteria, Germany would. Reunification has thrown that calculation out of gear. German interest rates are high, inflation is at a level that makes post-war German leaders blanch, unemployment is on the rise, and most significantly of all for monetary union, the German deficit remains large, with little prospect that it will be under the Maastricht criteria by the turn of the century.[21]

In sum, enthusiasm for EMU has apparently waned among the leaders of the key member states, especially Germany where there is a reluctance to give up the D-mark. The very idea that currencies would be merged rankles with European publics. On the other hand, recent actual convergence of currencies among many of the member states should give anyone writing off monetary union pause for thought.

Common Foreign and Security Policy

The CFSP is in part an attempt to give the EU a single voice in international affairs. The Union is hoping to articulate, through the CFSP, collective political power commensurate with its acquired economic power. In addition, the CFSP brings gains in terms of a common identity for the EU; a single voice in international affairs contributes another symbol of the unity of Europe, a federalist aspiration. It does this through setting out procedures in the Treaty on European Union for the defining of a common position (Article J. 2) and the prerequisites for joint action (Article J. 3).

Yet the various difficulties that have led to the weak character of the current format for European foreign policy making, European Political Cooperation (EPC), are repeated in the CFSP and have effectively derailed it, notably in terms of the EU response to the succession of crises in the former Yugoslavia. The problems are the voluntary and declaratory nature of the EPC framework that the CFSP was supposed to address;[22] the extension of the framework into security policy beyond the limits of political and economic aspects as set out in the SEA; and the articulation of the common defence policy, especially the role of the WEU.

The mechanism of EPC has been ruthlessly exposed during the shambles of the response to the rapidly deteriorating situation in Yugoslavia, then Croatia, and finally Bosnia. The EPC, though codified in the SEA, is a political process of consultation and coordination of EU members' foreign policies that takes place outside the EU framework. It is well suited to stating a position and to taking a moral stance. It is less well fitted to active measures to counter actual aggression or de-escalate a war. In the case of war in the former Yugoslavia, observer missions and attempts to mediate an end to the conflict or merely the hostilities have lacked credibility. The reason for this credibility gap was the perceived distance between the major EU actors and the realization that little of substance could or would be agreed, the Union being limited to economic sanctions, public shaming, and coercive diplomacy.[23]

The attempt to deal in CFSP with issues of hard security and defence policy (Treaty on European Union, Article J. 4) draws on a long history of attempts at defence cooperation in Europe that dates back (at least) to the still-born European Defence Community in the 1950s. This may be the wrong tradition to be drawing from. Following David Mitrany's functionalist critique of the development of the European Community,[24] this notion of "hard" security issues is outdated and inappropriate for the foreign policy of the EU as a "civilian power". This argument suggests that the EU is inherently not the type of organization to deal with military issues and that even the limited success of the EPC will be jeopardized by trying to force conformity in foreign, security, and defence policies on the member states. The EU should acknowledge that it is essentially a mechanism for international cooperation and that it is this route to international security to which the EU can contribute.[25]

The problems encountered in Yugoslavia have shown that the CFSP will have to be rethought. The Europeans essentially forswore the right to use force to bring about a settlement and then compromised their legitimacy by recognizing the breakaway republics. Optimists, who argue that if the CFSP had existed there would have been fewer problems, are ignoring the ability of the major players within the EU to go their own way, or at least to drag their feet significantly. Others argue strongly that the mechanism in Maastricht makes for the worst of all worlds, with confusion of institutional responsibility, lack of clarity in the Maastricht formulation, and lack of political will to create the military force necessary to supplement or complement NATO. Several Atlanticists have worried that the attempt to build up a European military capability is fundamentally flawed, both by reasons of inadequate finance and political will to swallow the costs, and by the subversive effect of European defence coordination on cooperation in NATO. It is suggested that the resulting inadequacy of the European arrangements and the confusion over lines of responsibility will severely weaken present security arrangements.[26]

In terms of the articulation of a common defence, the decision at Maastricht to reinvent the Western European Union was the result of a compromise between those (particularly the French) who wanted to see the development of a European security and defence identity, and those who insisted on maintaining the transatlantic connection with the United States (notably Britain and the Netherlands). An inter-governmental conference is scheduled for 1996 to review progress on the Maastricht Treaty and to deal with the CFSP in particular. The relationship of the EU with the WEU will have to be reconsidered before then, as the Brussels Treaty on which the WEU is based expires in 1998.

Expansion of the Union

During the Cold War, the geographical limits of European integration to the East were clear. Now the limits are in flux, and the nations of Central, Eastern, and South-Eastern Europe would like entry into NATO and the EC. The previous reluctance of the neutrals to join western international institutions has waned in the face of likely benefits of membership with lesser costs in terms of alliance discipline. Within the EU there is some sympathy and a lot of hesitation regarding any widening, especially to the East.[27] There are two arenas for expansion, members of the European Free Trade Association (EFTA; members of EFTA are commonly called EFTAns), and applicants from East-Central Europe;[28] these bring particular problems for the EU in terms of increased institutional and decision-making complexity.

The EFTAns

Among other things, Maastricht stipulated that new entrants to the Union would have to accept EMU, CFSP, and all parts of the treaty. While this increases the requirements on the new applicants, they can be assured that EU rules will not change prior to their membership. This, at least, is the scenario for the next enlargement, the inclusion of the EFTAns (Austria, Sweden, Finland, and Norway). Negotiations progressed, though with the anticipated difficulties over fisheries, agriculture, environment, and foreign policy, as well as the rigours of the EU's internal market, such as competition policy rules against monopolies. A step towards inclusion of the EFTA countries into the EU has already been taken de facto with the coming into force on January 1, 1994, of the European Economic Area—a free trade area between the EU and EFTA, which in terms of GNP, is the largest free trade area in the world.

With regard to the institutional and decision-making arrangements, on the other hand, such as number of seats in the EP, votes in the Council of Ministers, commissioners in the European Commission, and so on, the plan was to extrapolate present allocations and arrangements. This will have an impact on policy in the EU as new coalitions, for instance, on environmental policy are created. The increase in numbers and the relatively small size of the new entrants will also make the workings of the Council and Commission more complicated. Yet, the British and the Spanish objected to the dilution of their veto power in the Council of Ministers consequent on enlargement. The blocking minority becomes twenty-seven votes from twenty-three; in the weighted voting system, this means two large countries and two small or three large countries. The compromise was to move to twenty-seven votes as the blocking minority but to try to reach agreement where there are more than 23 votes against. British motivations in this case were to placate anti-EU sentiment at home. Such aims were surely misguided as the final compromise was a climbdown by Britain according to the anti-Europeans. The so-called "Olive Belt" Mediterranean states objected on the grounds of the shift in power to the North in the EU with the inclusion of the EFTAns.

There are, from the point of view of the Nordic applicants, important matters of identity and communication, such as language, to be dealt with in their entry into the EU. Nevertheless, because these applicants are relatively wealthy and thus probably net contributors to the EU, obstacles to their inclusion come from the applicants themselves—for instance, mandated referendums on entry, opposition to the European Economic Area in Switzerland, and lingering doubts and memories of past applications in Norway. By contrast, with the EFTAn applicants willing, opposition within the Union can be bought off. A sticking point in other negotiations, in particular agriculture, is only a problem in the context of the negotiations with the EFTAns because countries such as Norway and Sweden protect their farmers even more than does the EU. The other major problem was getting the negotiations completed in time for accession by the beginning of 1995. While a delay would technically be a small matter, psychologically it would be another blow to the EU, demonstrating that the Union's attractiveness even to outsiders had faded.

East-Central Europe

Here, further enlargement will be much more problematical. Despite initial euphoria, the "return to Europe" of the former Warsaw Pact countries has been more hesitant and strewn with obstacles than expected. The Czech Republic, Hungary, and Poland argue that they, at least, deserve early consideration for inclusion in the important Western institutions in Europe (meaning NATO and the EU). Yet the negotiations leading to the Europe Agreements, the Association agreements for the nations of the former East Bloc, indicate that inclusion into the EU is unlikely to take place until a decade into the next century. Along the way, the bruising process of negotiation has left the East-Central Europeans disillusioned.

Limiting the scope to the most likely candidates in the medium term — the Czech Republic, Hungary, and Poland, with Slovenia an additional possibility — these are states where wage levels are well below the EU average, where there is a skilled work force and significant (though underutilized and inefficient) industrial capacity. Potential gains to these countries from EU membership are high, but this is also the sticking point for present EU members. Areas of particular concern within the EU are agriculture, textiles, and steel. The problem in each case is the admittance into the EU of cheaper goods from the new entrants. France, in particular, has been clear in its determination to protect its benefits in the CAP. Besides the implications for common policies on steel and agriculture, and the impact on the internal market of including more low-cost producers, there is the general question of the EU budget. Given the state of their economies and the necessities of economic transition, applicants from the East would be a net drain on an already strained EU budget. If current arrangements are maintained, regional aid would be applicable to them, as would funds allocated for economic and social cohesion. Besides the narrow question of where the money will come from to aid the new entrants, there is the broader distributional question regarding the impact on the current poor of Europe when funds are redirected away from, say, Greece or Spain to pay for projects in Poland.

Institutional Implications

If we forget for a moment the specifics of the applicants, an EU12 is in principle likely to work differently from an EU16 (with the inclusion of the EFTAns), which (with the inclusion of Central European states) would be different from a EU20. At twenty, the sheer number in the EU would, it has been argued, require revision of the voting in the Council, a change in the criterion for commissioners to avoid the body becoming too large,[29] and a change in the EP to avoid its oversizing.

Including smaller countries in the EC has progressively diluted the influence of the larger players in Europe.[30] Expansion north and east will carry on the trend. This has led to some disquiet among the larger members of the EU, as was evident with Britain's stalling over the admission of the EFTAns in March 1994. Proposals to change voting in the Council aim to restore the large states their position vis-à-vis smaller states, for instance, by giving the large states more votes. Other proposals include double majorities (majorities in both votes on the Council and population in the EU) and super majorities (three-quarters or four-fifths instead of roughly two-thirds). In addition to Council voting changes, there are suggestions that the presidency of the Council should no longer follow alphabetical order for its six-monthly rotation but should be arranged to ensure that at least one large member state is represented on the presidential troika (past, present, and future presidents) that represents the EU to the outside world. This might seem arcane, but an expansion to twenty with the Central Europeans will surely raise these issues anew.

Expansion poses a problem for the EU that up until now it has not dared to face. Expansion is not just a question of increasing numbers or of institutional tinkering; rather it implicates the essential character of the EU as either a closed club or an open society. It has always been discussed in terms of the great success of European integration, which of course it is at one level: the

EU continues to attract applicants who want to share in the EU's economic success and social stability. However, the complacency over EU structures in the face of the changes that are being brought by expansion will no longer do. It is time, as Helen Wallace argues, for the EU to reconsider what it is.[31] Regrettably, there seems to be little vision of *why* the EU should grow in size at all, other than patronizing ad hocery and veiled feelings of guilt.

The central axis of the EU, the French and the Germans, for their different reasons, have recently been supportive of policy deepening for the EU: the French because of their dominance in the EU structures, and the Germans because they want to be fully integrated into Europe, as a way of reassuring their neighbours (and themselves) of their political soundness and because they have the most to gain by an open Europe. Meanwhile, those member states that have opposed deepening, notably Britain but also Denmark, are considered "reluctant Europeans" and are criticized for seeking to weaken the Union by widening it without putting appropriate institutional structures in place to ensure effective decision making.

Identifying widening as being opposed to deepening is a discursive move that disables the articulation of an alternative vision of the EU based on wider membership with or without a tightening of integration.[32] With the inclusion of many of the original EFTAns as well as a move eastward, a new vision of the future of the EU might be possible. The role of Germany is critical. Germany, at the heart of Europe, is as interested in widening as deepening. Since the end of the Cold War, Germany remains the eastern perimeter of the EU but can no longer rely on its border in the face of the influx of refugees and other migrants. Germany's links to the East are being restored rapidly as its aid to the East outruns that of its partners. Yet there are fears of German domination of its weak Eastern neighbours. Routinized relations mediated through the EU is the only way to reconcile the desire of the Germans to stabilize their eastern border and prosper by their geographical location with the requirement that German power be held in check. This does not, however, have to involve membership of the EU. Rather there will be a panoply of arrangements, from the Europe Agreements to the Poland Hungary Aid for Reconstructing Economies (PHARE) program, from extending political dialogue to these countries (in other words, including them in the EPC in some way) to the creation of trans-European networks.[33] This will make for more flexible and varied EU than has been laid out in Maastricht, one that is, in fact, emerging in practice.

THE EU AND CANADA

From the analysis above we can conclude that the EU's halting steps to further integration and wider geographic scope will not necessarily be according to the Maastricht agenda. What are the implications for Canada? Charles Pentland has neatly summarized the Canadian interest in Europe in terms of access and architecture. More recently Evan Potter has identified leverage as the critical question for Canada in its relations with Europe.[34] A more unified Europe appears to suggest less leverage and perhaps less access. The conclusion that follows is that Canada would prefer a slowdown in European integration. Historically this has not been the case. In the past Canada supported European integration as part of the multilateral strategy defending the West. With the threat from the Soviet Union gone, however, the immediacy of Canada's need to be involved in European security decreases (recognized in Canada's closure of its bases in Germany), while deeper and wider European cooperation threatens to render the Canadian-European "transatlantic relationship" almost invisible. Now, on the face of it, the response to this might be "so what?" After all, Canada has very little leverage at present and no God-given right to participate in European affairs. Indeed, reduced influence is probably a normalization of sorts; it was the Cold War period that was extraordinary, uniting the West in the face of a perceived common enemy.

For Canada, the implications of Maastricht, its realization or failure, fall into two broad categories. First, there are changes to the relationship of Canada and the EU and its member states as such. Secondly, any move in world affairs towards regionalism, and particularly the development of a closer, more exclusive union in Europe, slots the Canadians in with the United States as a part of the North American region.

The direct relationship of Canada and the EU itself, with the 1976 Framework Agreement and the 1990 Transatlantic Declaration as its institutional framework, is only one aspect of Canada's relations with Europe.[35] Canadian-EU relations can only be understood in the wider context of Canada's bilateral relations with the member states and the participation of both Canada and the EU and/or its member states in various multilateral forums.

At both the EU and bilateral level, Canada's relationship with Europe is driven by commercial issues, such as fishing off the Grand Banks or the propriety of B.C. lumber practices. For example, Premier Harcourt of British Columbia toured in Europe and particularly Germany as part of an attempt to diffuse the criticism of B.C. lumber practices that had been widely attacked by environmental groups. Harcourt and his entourage, including Native representatives, promoted their case and tried to undercut the supporters of a boycott of B.C. lumber.[36]

The depletion of cod stocks in the North Atlantic has been a source of strain between the EU and Canada as EU states' trawlers continued fishing the northern cod, albeit outside Canada's two hundred mile limit, while Canada imposed a moratorium on its own fisheries industry in order to preserve stocks. Canada managed, to the surprise of many, to convince the Northwest Atlantic Fisheries Organization, the organization that monitors fishing off the Grand Banks and includes among others Canada and the EU, to put in place a one-year moratorium on fishing there.[37]

Beyond direct Canada-EU relations, the impact of Maastricht's progress (or otherwise) will be felt by Canada in the various multilateral forums in which Canada and the EU and/or its members participate, such as NATO and the CSCE, the G-7 and GATT, and in a different way, the Commonwealth and the Francophonie. For instance, restrictions on visitors to Britain from Commonwealth countries will be increased due to the attempt to remove passport controls *within* the EU (which requires controls on those entering from without). Canadians, fortunately, retain their special status for the time being and do not require a visa.[38]

Canada is not immune to the travails of Maastricht. The currency upheavals in Europe associated with the crises in the ERM put downward pressure on the Canadian dollar and money turned to "safe" currencies, the U.S. dollar, the Japanese yen and the D-mark. Further progress to EMU would create a closer economic bloc in Europe, making the EU a stronger player than previously in the range of economic forums such as GATT (or whatever succeeds it) and the G-7. The de facto shrinking of the G-7 to a G-3 of the United States, the EU, and Japan inevitably reduces Canada's already tenuous status in this economic big league.

Similarly, European cooperation on defence, in the Eurocorps and in the WEU, reduces Canadian influence. While the Europeans caucus, as was seen over the decision to threaten the Bosnian Serbs with air strikes, Canada is left isolated. NATO for all intents and purposes becomes a European pillar and an American pillar, the latter subsuming Canada.

One should be careful not to overplay the influence of formal structures such as Maastricht, however. The issue is rather the extent to which the Europeans *in practice* become inward-looking— for instance, bargaining within the EU first, making their trade-offs there, and then emerging with a united front. This ideal is achieved rarely; the various member states retain their autonomy and their divergent interests, as was demonstrated by Greece, which while in the presidency of the EU at the beginning of 1994, decided to close down communications with its northern neighbour, Macedonia, in the face of recognition of the latter by many European nations and the United States. "Fortress Europe" is as unlikely to emerge following Maastricht as with the SEA, as events in Bosnia demonstrate. With expansion to sixteen or more, the EU will be a looser rather than tighter organization.

Moving away from their relationship per se, Canada and the EU are in their different ways confronting the same crisis of state representation. Widespread discontent with politicians is only one superficial marker of this crisis. While Canada is a relatively small, federal state, and the EU is a large proto-federation, many of the challenges of politics at the century's end are the same: multiculturalism, language and other minority rights; regional assistance for depressed regions, calls for direct votes on important issues (e.g., the referendums on Charlottetown and on Maastricht), and questions relating to parliamentary democracy and representation in general.

There were distinct similarities in the problems of selling Maastricht and the débâcle over the Charlottetown Accord. Further, Europeans have been considering some method of controlling the perceived cultural imperialism of the United States in the new information and communications technologies and their impacts, specifically on broadcasting. One reaction is to try to learn from Canadian content rules. While in Canada the debate raged over the Triple-E Senate proposal, the EC was trying to cope with accusations of an increasing "democratic deficit," where the powers of national parliaments are transferred to appointed officials and functionaries in Brussels. Bureaucratic edict from the centre, whether Brussels or Ottawa, is being challenged.

Comparisons can, of course, be overdone, and there are many contrasts also. Nevertheless, we would be foolish to ignore the travails of modern states as they negotiate the terrain of late twentieth-century politics. What is at stake more than anything else are legitimacy and authority in the modern world. It is here that the crisis of the state is most acute: where deficits become political, where centralized power becomes questioned, where large global economic actors become accountable. Problematic questions of sovereignty arise in the threatened secession of Quebec and in the claims to self-government by the Native peoples, just as they do in forging a common EU policy on the environment or foreign affairs and in accommodating the various aspirations to regional autonomy within EU member states.

There are those who argue that Canada and Europe are drifting apart and that, for instance, Canada should look westwards to the Pacific Rim in the future. The common crisis that Canada shares with the rest of the West shows that disengagement will never be that straightforward. Whatever the foreign policy orientation or ethnic make-up of Canada, the political culture has historically been, and will remain for some time to come, essentially European. The shared interest in democracy, rule of law, social progress, and economic prosperity with justice, makes for a bond between Canada and Europe that is deeper than a narrow policy focus would indicate. It is here that the relationship is fundamentally based.

7

A New Security Strategy For Europe

Alexander Moens

> In Europe, everyone is doing what seems right in his own eyes. For every security wagon, you can find a horse behind it. Secretary Baker's December 1989 conception of a new transatlantic framework of security cooperation now sounds like Jimmy who? So far, the so-called security partners have talked about doing complementary things and getting their organizations to interlock. Meanwhile there is a real war going on. All the European acronyms are standing by.[1]

I WILL ARGUE IN THIS CHAPTER that despite three years of post-Cold War reform, the major Western security partners have not found a common understanding on how to respond to potential crises in Europe's eastern rim. Other than economizing on the traditional defence of the alliance's territory, for which no obvious threat exists, progress has been minimal. By this I mean that there is no agreement on strategy, individual or shared commitments, or institutional means to address border and nationalist wars in Central and Eastern Europe.[2] I will summarize first the divergent national interests that have become apparent in the North Atlantic Treaty Organization (NATO), the European Community (EC), the Western European Union (WEU) and the Conference on Security and Cooperation in Europe (CSCE), and secondly, show how these incongruities explain the Western failures in the Yugoslav crisis.[3] Thirdly, I will discuss how these external developments combined with domestic restraints have left Canadian security policy vis-à-vis Europe dangling on a precariously thin thread. I argue for a renewed pragmatism in the form of a joint military capacities approach between the traditional Atlantic alliance and the emerging European Union in order to achieve specific political objectives contained in the so-called Balladur Plan.

I would like to acknowledge the generous support received from the Cooperative Security Competitions Program to conduct a large part of the research for this chapter.

The stagnation in Europe is in large part owing to a lack of definition of an American role, a wavering Russian commitment to democracy, and the absence of a solid political identity for the EC. Meanwhile the European Community and the United States act increasingly as two independent pillars in security and trade.

Canadian security policy toward Europe, as a result, has not displayed a clear sense of direction: we withdrew our NATO troops from Europe, we made a large-scale commitment to the United Nations Protection Force (UNPROFOR) in the former Yugoslavia, and invented cooperative security. But what does it all add up to? Uncertainty in Europe has been exacerbated by severe budget troubles at home and widespread questions as to whether we still have a role to play there.

It is essential that the drift in policy be halted. In a pessimistic scenario where the major Western powers can neither agree on common policy nor on effectively combining military resources, there will be a long period of drift before the new European identity turns into an integrated military force. Meanwhile, the American commitment may dwindle to nuclear deterrence or emergency reinforcement. As a result, Central and Eastern European security will be left completely open-ended. This vacuum will do little to stem the potential for ethnic and border disputes in the area and is likely to increase fears that Russia will reassert its control in the region.

But the end of 1993 gave rise to some optimism. It appears that most Western governments have begun to turn the corner on the institutional rivalry. Practical sense is setting in, sped up by the Bosnian débâcle, falling military capability, and uncertainty in Russia especially in light of the election results of December 1993. I argue that there now exists an opportunity to provide wider European security by tying together a political proposal for border and minority stability, generally known as the Balladur plan, with a pragmatic blending of capacities between NATO and the WEU.

Canada should play a strong diplomatic role to blend the two approaches and commit resources to implement the outcome. But before we address the solutions, we need to understand what went wrong since the end of the Cold War.

Taking Stock Versus Talking Shop

Institutional diplomacy in NATO, the EC/WEU, and the CSCE since the end of the Cold War has been more competitive than complementary. The competition described below is complex and ongoing. It is partly responsible for the failure to find a foundation of a new security arrangement that addresses the sources and solutions of insecurity in Central and Eastern Europe.

The Soviet agreement on full NATO membership for a unified Germany, the Franco-German breakthrough on speeding up European Union in both its economic and political tracks, and the pan-European expectations raised at the Paris CSCE summit created a deceiving sense of momentum towards security reform.

It would not be so easy to change a deeply divided Europe into a united continent. Because of the Soviet departure from Central and Eastern Europe and German unification, NATO's forward defence and force structures had to be adjusted. However, the end of the Cold War did not coincide with the end of the Soviet Union. It was thus necessary to de-emphasize the centrality of the Atlantic alliance but prudent not to do away with it. Secondly, NATO could not be enlarged beyond the Oder-Neisse border while the former Warsaw Pact members sought immediate rapprochement with the West. The CSCE was put forward to accommodate both German unification and the East. But in essence the CSCE was only a political discussion forum. Unless developed quickly, it had no substance to fill the security vacuum in Central and Eastern Europe. Thirdly, German unification triggered a French reaction. Paris attempted to shift weight from its pursuit of nationalistic security and defence policy to an EC identity in security and defence.[4] But that French vocation worried the United States and EC members with a strong Atlantic interest.

Soon after NATO's celebrated London summit of July 1990 that initiated the recent round of reforms, these contradictions and tensions surfaced among the allies as the enormity of defining and organizing new security measures bore down on them. First, the advocates of a rapid European capability in security and defence, led by France, sought an EC track in European security, and eventually defence policy, in cooperation with NATO but not subsumed under NATO. The United States and Britain after Thatcher did not oppose in principle the idea of an European Defence Identity (EDI) but for practical and political reasons did not share France's urgency. Unfortunately for Washington, it did not have an answer to its own future role in Europe and could not slam the debate shut, especially as it was withdrawing many of its troops. The Atlantic-centred position lacked the customary Soviet threat and American commitment while the Europe-centred camp lacked internal cohesion and the military wherewithal to implement its political ideals.

Not surprisingly, a prolonged, complex, and linked series of negotiations followed in NATO, the WEU and the Intergovernmental Conference on Political Union in the EC.[5] Definitions were shuffled, role tasks and mandates jostled, new staffs and offices set up. At times the diplomatic wrangling got nasty. The Americans did not want the integrity of the NATO decision-making process and integrated military command hollowed by a preparatory or concomitant European process. The French did not want NATO to define what the members of the EC could and could not do in their own security and defence. The British, deeply suspicious of Franco-German defence initiatives, tried to push the WEU up the middle to avoid two independent defence mechanisms. The Germans steadfastly adhered to both.

The Rome and Maastricht summits of 1991 harboured compromises on all areas by all parties. NATO was thoroughly streamlined with a British-led Rapid Reaction Corps and maintained as the defence organization of the West, yet it recognized that the EC could set up its own defence mechanism. It established a Cooperation Council (NACC) with the former Warsaw Pact members which in March of 1992 grew to include most republics of the ex-Soviet Union. The EDI was recognized, yet the British succeeded in keeping the wording on defence vague. The paragraph reads as follows: "The common foreign and security policy shall include all questions related to the security of the Union, including the eventual framing of a common defence policy, which might in time lead to a common defence."[6] The French and Germans set up their Eurocorps and the WEU its own planning staff. The European corps never sat well with the Bush administration, which insisted on a NATO connection and got it in 1992 in the form of a Franco-German agreement to put the corps under Supreme Allied Command in Europe (SACEUR) for defence of the NATO area. Yet the corps kept its political independence and its own out of area role for the future. Recently, the Belgians joined. The Spanish might be next.

Meanwhile the CSCE reform process also ran into obstacles. The Bush administration understood the importance of its symbolism to the East but did not seriously consider giving it a real mandate or capability in crisis management or conflict resolution. In terms of concrete cooperation with the East, the United States placed NACC above the CSCE. As a logical extension to its opposition to NATO's dominant role, France was adverse to NACC. It preferred a EC-led liaison with the East.

In the early months of 1992 the CSCE admitted nearly all the republics of the ex-Soviet Union. In so doing, it lost its distinctive European character. The "Old Democracies," as the EC and the United States were called by CSCE activists, fundamentally doubted that the CSCE, with fifty-two members, could prevent or resolve conflicts. In the summer of 1992 both NATO and the CSCE agreed on the principle of a peacekeeping link between the two. But plenty of ambiguity was built in, so that the CSCE could refer such tasks also to the WEU. Of course any member state could veto the connection.

The consensus rule, the distrust of the old democracies, NATO-EC competition, and a lack of implementation machinery hobbled a CSCE conflict-prevention and crisis-management capability. This was clearly illustrated by crises in the Baltics, in Yugoslavia, and in Nagorno-Karabakh. During the Soviet crackdown in Lithuania in January 1991, Moscow blocked consensus to convene a Committee of Senior Officials (CSO) meeting. Almost simultaneous to the Baltic violence, CSCE experts agreed on a dispute settlement mechanism. But it fell short of compulsory third-party arbitration because any party could disallow the mechanism for reasons of sovereignty and territorial integrity. Nothing had changed. Soon after the outbreak of violence in Slovenia on June 27, 1991, the Consultative Committee of the newly formed Conflict Prevention Centre met, followed a few days later by an emergency CSO meeting. Realizing its political paralysis and lack of implementation machinery, the CSCE remitted the Yugoslav crisis to the EC. When the United Nations Security Council rather than the CSCE sanctioned peacekeeping in Bosnia, the latter was technically passed over as Europe's political authority.

It is obvious what we did *not* gain from this round of diplomacy: there was no role for NATO in Central and Eastern Europe despite its new core functions, no real security for the states of Central and Eastern Europe despite a lot of plans for consultation in NACC, and finally a CSCE whose common denominator does not allow more than "low security" consultation. The European defence mechanism seems firmly planted in the Eurocorps and WEU, but like all EC competencies, it needs ample time to develop. Imposing too many tasks may halt its growth, especially in the climate of political uncertainty caused by the public backlash to Maastricht's ambitious designs.

Incremental reform has continued in 1993 and early 1994. Under continuing pressure from Poland and like-minded states for membership, NATO embarked on an American plan called "Partnership For Peace."[7] It builds on NACC and is actually open to all states in the region but falls short of membership. It calls for Central and East European states to negotiate bilateral arrangements with NATO. It capitalizes on what NACC lacks: direct military consultations, joint manoeuvres, training, and peacekeeping.

Given the institutional and political hurdles, CSCE operations began to take on more of a low-level, preventive character, including fact-finding missions, good offices, mediation, monitoring, and arbitration. The Rome CSCE summit in November 1993 did not resolve its institutional weaknesses. Instead it added a festering problem: how to exert some form of CSCE control over Russian "peacekeeping" activities in its so-called "near abroad."

Yugoslavia and the Western Security Stalemate

The Western response to Yugoslavia, to stretch Clausewitz a little, was the continuation of the Rome and Maastricht discord by other means. The crisis exposed the lack of institutional progress for what it really was. Instead of keeping the Western response in one forum, the EC and NATO discussed the same security issues in separate forums. It opened wide the cracks. In their meeting in Germany in October 1993, NATO's defence ministers openly acknowledged that not using NATO's consultative mechanism from the earliest stages of the crisis had fostered policy differences among the allies.[8]

Despite gruesome violence, Western governments at the end of the day did not want to "interpose" their armies to enforce cease-fires or roll back aggression in Bosnia. That said, Western diplomacy during the early stages of the conflict and subsequent inaction was still dismal.[9]

First, the United States and the West European powers agreed in the early summer of 1991 that the former would not get involved and the latter would employ the EC to mediate in the conflict. In so doing, they acted upon the wrong side of the great half-truths of the time: that Europe should be its own soldier and the United States should not be the world's policeman. It defied the logic of the Cold War and of the recent victory in the Gulf. By staying out, the Americans signalled that there would be no Western force. By involving the EC in a hard security issue, the Europeans exposed the infancy of their own EDI. Germany could not play a military role but it could push the EC into early recognition of Croatia. Britain refused to commit force, especially in a WEU setting. Hence France was left as the EC's military instrument but of course could not do it alone.

As in the Gulf War, the EC agreed on applying economic sanctions, but their effect is unclear in bitter ethnic strife and is hampered by practical limitations in a perforated conflict area like Bosnia. The London and Geneva conferences were essential venues to keep the parties talking, but the conveners lacked the means for coercive diplomacy.

With no direct American commitment and no European consensus, the United Nations became the default option in Europe. However, for very practical reasons, the UN mission soon began to look to NATO for help. It is, indeed, an irony to have a tremendously overburdened and under-equipped United Nations running a complex peacekeeping mission on the doorstep of the world's most advanced military organization. It did not seem to make sense. Soon NATO provided a task force in the Adriatic and staff to UNPROFOR's headquarters. In April 1993 the United Nations Security Council authorized a no-fly zone over Bosnia which NATO subsequently agreed to enforce with air power from several of its member states.[10] As the Vance-Owen peace plan neared completion in the spring of 1993, serious talks between NATO and UN staff began. Supreme Headquarters Allied Powers Europe (SHAPE) was planning vigorously. Those advocates who believed that NATO should play an active role by out-of-area peacekeeping now embraced the UN presence as a stepping-stone towards a NATO solution after all. After all the debates about NATO's out-of-area role, it quietly came in through the back door in the form of peacekeeping in partnership with the UN.

Since implementing the Vance-Owen plan could face widespread local opposition, even major breaches, it was generally agreed that more heavily armed peacekeepers than UNPROFOR were needed.[11] Of course, NATO would also be a way to get the Americans committed. While the practical need for NATO grew, the divergent national policies continued to cause wrangling over roles and tasks. The new French government under Prime Minister Balladur took a more practical stand towards NATO. Yet it does not consider peacekeeping as a component of collective defence and therefore sees only limited use for the integrated military command and its associated structures of decision making. Instead, it insisted on handling NATO peacekeeping through the North Atlantic Council of sixteen foreign ministers.

Different commitments produced different interests. America and Germany, with no troops on the ground, prescribed different action to Britain, France, and Canada, which had peacekeeping troops in the area. This brought out the old distinctions about what NATO should do. The dispute filtered into how to keep the safe havens, whether and what targets to bomb, and who should command the Vance-Owen plan implementation forces. Would it be a UN-mandated and politically controlled operation with a special representative of the secretary general alongside a military commander? Or would it be an American or NATO operation with only a UN Security Council resolution to provide initial legitimacy? Would the UN special representative have input into the decisions of the theatre commander?

France, Britain, and Canada wanted to preserve UN primacy, especially as the United States was not committed yet to providing troops of its own. They were worried about the repercussions on their blue helmets from possible unilateral American action. For Canada, it was a matter of principle that the UN have political control. For France, it was also a matter of restraining an independent NATO role out-of-area. Britain was most concerned about not having to send more troops.

Despite the Vance-Owen plan failure, the UN-NATO connection endured. NATO promised to provide UNPROFOR with air cover to protect troops in safe havens and talks continued around the joint action plan throughout the summer of 1993. On August 2 the NATO Council agreed in principle to consider a UN request for implementing a peace agreement in Bosnia under what was now called the Stoltenberg-Owen peace plan.[12] It was estimated that as many as fifty thousand troops would be needed. The United States, it was widely believed, would provide half.[13]

Canadian Policy

Canada's last thorough policy review on Europe was completed in early 1990 and its new objectives were articulated in two speeches by the secretary of state for external affairs, Joe Clark.[14] It concluded that our fundamental security, political, and economic interests in Europe continued but that we had to adjust the means. Canada sought a renewed NATO, a more efficient CSCE, and a consultative link with an open EC.

This three-pillar approach to Europe has formed the backbone to most of our actions. Given the state of flux in 1990, balancing the triangle seemed a sensible holding action. However, this framework rested on the assumption that developments among the pillars would be complementary, not competitive. It also assumed that shuffling weight among them would scarcely affect our standing in any of them. The competitive development among institutions described above, driven home by the Yugoslav crises and combined with an unforeseen UN role on the continent, require a review of this approach.

Naturally, the post-Cold War atmosphere of competition constituted a minefield for Canadian diplomacy. As prudent multilateralists, we did not want to lose ground in any of the institutions, nor did we want to risk offending any of our major allies. In the case of NATO, External Affairs officials insisted that we would not speak out against the European Defence Identity. We emphasized Article 2 of the North Atlantic Treaty briefly because we thought that NATO's political specialty might now flourish.[15] We concentrated on "extending a hand of friendship" to Central and Eastern Europe.[16] Canada proposed associate membership to NATO for stable Visegrad states, i.e., the Czech Republic, Hungary, Poland,

and Slovakia, in the fall of 1991.[17] NACC constituted a German-U.S. compromise, but we were prepared to use it to the fullest. Unfortunately, NACC faced French opposition at every step of its development.

While Canadian diplomats had their hands full keeping our initiatives on the various tables, the Department of Defence, in accordance with the budget cutters, pulled the rug from under our diplomatic standing in NATO. Defence, having been squeezed between ever-aging equipment and never-ending budget cuts and prohibited from closing domestic bases, saw in the new environment an opportunity to withdraw all Canadian troops from Europe and close the two bases in Germany. External Affairs opposed the plan by the Department of National Defence in 1990 arguing quite accurately that Canadian troops in Europe were an important signal of our commitment to European security and were crucial to keeping NATO *North* American.

In 1991 it seemed a compromise on the eleven hundred remaining stationed troops was reached. Certainly, Prime Minister Mulroney's remarks to his German counterpart in September that Canadian troops would remain as long as they were "needed and wanted" looked like a firm commitment. Amazingly, by the spring 1992 federal budget they were already no longer "needed and wanted." Facing allied criticism, Canadian diplomats in the NATO Councils defended their forced position by arguing that we were still committed to NATO and continued to have forces earmarked for NATO operations and to pay substantially into infrastructure costs, that some other members also lacked stationed troops, and that we were not setting a precedent since the Americans did not usually take hints from Ottawa.

Nevertheless, everyone knew that our small forces in Europe were the key symbol of our self-proclaimed Atlantic status.[18] We unilaterally withdrew all troops even though several allies had quietly offered us very substantial help in offsetting costs for base and equipment costs. Canada also turned down several requests by allied partners to join some aspect of the newly formed Allied Command Europe Rapid Reaction Corps (ARRC).

In our purpose to contribute to Europe's new environment, we were particularly keen to make the CSCE the linchpin of its security architecture. The CSCE's comprehensive approach fits our vision of "cooperative security."[19] We wanted a strong Committee of Senior Officials operating as the agent of the CSCE Council that could take on crisis management and enable the Conflict Prevention Centre to implement decisions.

But the Helsinki Follow-Up Meeting in 1992 was not able to produce concrete progress in terms of conflict resolution or crisis management. Our strategy now is to have the CSCE concentrate on first principles, such as democratic development and minority rights as well as transition to market economies. Next, we seek to build up conflict prevention or peacemaking functions,[20] including warning mechanisms. In terms of action, CSCE monitoring missions are more fact-finding than peacemaking or peacekeeping in nature. Finally, we aim to build a more efficient institutional machinery with an office of the secretary general and a single structure in Vienna.

Our consultative link with the EC was enhanced in the form of a Transatlantic Declaration signed in late 1990 that stipulated regular bilateral meetings between the top leadership. The diplomacy leading up to the agreement revealed the difficulty Canada had in getting the attention of Brussels.[21] It did not help that we were involved in bitter trade disputes with the EC, especially on offshore fishing. We got the declaration because the United States got one and because some of our partners in the EC lobbied on our behalf. Canada was reminded of the importance of good bilateral relations with individual EC members but also that an integrating EC is a much more difficult partner.

We were among the first to call for UN peacekeeping in ex-Yugoslavia. Canada made a major commitment in the European arena where it is generally considered a small player. Since the summer of 1991 Canada has committed people to the EC monitoring mission in Yugoslavia and later two battle groups to UNPROFOR. When a connection between NATO and the UN appeared, Canada played a quiet but important facilitatory role in helping along a series of meetings between Brussels and New York staff. Both the liaison person on the Military Committee at NATO and the chief Military liaison in New York happened to be Canadians.[22]

Canada supports UN-NATO cooperation, but we have insisted that the overall integrated command be in the hands of the UN, not NATO. Citing the need for unity of command for the military, civil, and humanitarian aspects of the operation, Ottawa argues that a special representative of the secretary general of the UN should have overall political direction and exercise political control alongside the military commander.

Canadian Interests

Whether we intended it or not, we appear to some allies as having devalued NATO. One can obviously read too much into our weakened position in European councils, but there are tell-tale signs.[23] Our commitment in Yugoslavia deserves full credit, but we should not forget that neither the West Europeans nor the United States wants a revitalized UN to replace European security structures. Do we? Typically, one hears the argument that we showed that our dedication to international security was greater than our membership in any organization. But surely we do not mean that others are less committed nor that we are prepared to be unilateralists when it comes to peacekeeping.

There are at least three opposing views in Canada on our security role in Europe. First, as far as the North American continentalist is concerned, the recent security assertion by the EC as well as the gradual American disengagement, combined with such trade realities as the North American Free Trade Agreement (NAFTA), make Canada's attempt to stay involved in Europe's security look doomed to failure. To them, the double dumb-bell has arrived. The twin pillar operation of NATO leaves little incentive for costly or vigorous Canadian participation. The scenarios that would draw America back to Europe would involve heavy military activity for which we are not prepared. Short of that, the Europeans prefer to develop their own institutions.

A second group, the post-Cold War Atlanticists, argues that the traditional rationale for Canada has not changed. In the worse-case scenario, we want to avoid a deterioration of security in Central Europe, be it intra- or interstate, that would threaten the NATO area itself. Moreover, stable Central European states such as Poland and Hungary, as well as the imminent new EC members, are so closely linked to the West's political and economic interests that their stability affects the stability of NATO and the EC, including Canada. A conflict in Central Europe that spills over and directly pulls in a major West European state will likely draw us back with the United States and will thus be costly. In this logic, we want to do as much as we can to keep the United States directly engaged in Europe, including staying committed ourselves.

There is a third view that has gained respect by virtue of our involvement in Europe via the UN and the general attention given to a revitalized UN after the Cold War. It contends that Canada must deregionalize and concentrate on its first international vocation—the UN. In this view, Europe is just one of many areas for Canadian involvement depending on UN commitments. It favours the development of European institutions as regional implementors of the UN. Thus NATO's next step, it is advocated, is to set up a peacekeeping force. Canada should participate in European councils for the purpose of making them UN-compatible. Apart from our UN obligations, supporters of this view see little independent ground for Canadian policy in Europe.

A problem-solving and interest-based approach for Canada in Europe, in my view, continues to be best pursued by the neo-Atlanticist paradigm. The premise of the continentalist view that a twin pillar structure squeezes Canada's influence is sound, but its conclusion is unhelpful. Quitting European security policy will not advance our North American continental leverage nor enhance our diplomatic and trade status with any of our key allies, nor make our overall security policy more cost-effective. No penny saved there can easily be put to use here to gain more influence. Though the European councils are struggling to get their act together, what do we gain by withdrawing from them? Is there any guarantee that defence money saved in Europe will go to another defence use?

Equally unhelpful in my opinion is a subtle shift toward a hyper-UN strategy that subsumes our European policy. We should not put all our security eggs in the UN basket for the following reasons. First, European security needs are more urgent and demanding than what the UN can offer, including peacekeeping. Secondly, if it is difficult to keep the United States engaged in the European security councils, it will be even more difficult to engage it via the UN.[24] Thirdly, developing NATO into the UN's regional peacekeeping branch leaves NATO's new mandate far too vague and thus risks even more discord.

The danger of a vague UN-NATO design for NATO peacekeeping or crisis management in Central and Eastern Europe is that it may expose the lack of agreement among the major allies.[25] Without a unified objective and agreed commitments, NATO going east might fatally aggravate the differences among its chief members. The so-called indivisibility of security and defence that exists inside the Washington Treaty area becomes very divisible when you go outside. If anything, Bosnia has exposed this divisibility. A dual mandate for NATO — common defence within and peacekeeping without — is not good enough. Without a clear agreement on specific tasks, there is little hope that Germany's status, America's buffet approach, French and British policy differences, and, not least, Russian concern about NATO activity in the area will be resolved. Asmus, Kugler, and Larrabee's catchy dictum that if NATO does not go out of area, it will go out of business begs the question, what business?[26] If crisis management means general fire fighting, NATO is not the vehicle. Extending NATO membership faces serious Russian opposition.[27]

The post-Cold War Atlanticist arguments have suffered near shipwreck amidst the institutional feuding. Canada must base its European policy firmly on the security realities in Europe and our specific interests. If anything were to be gained by withdrawal, then we should do so. You cannot sustain a policy on some naive belief in a third option or for a theological attachment to Atlanticism. Nor can we continue in our recent mode of "peacekeeping for everything" because it is our flagship, or on scattered CSCE monitoring missions because of our political suitability and experience, and because it is cheaper than buying helicopters.

Of course our UN policy and peacekeeping role will remain a vital part of our strategy for international security. But given the type of potential conflicts in Eastern Europe, UN peacekeeping as a form of limiting human suffering is not likely to be more successful than it has been in Bosnia. European stability is not well served by simply concentrating on intensified efforts of peacekeeping. "Eurokeeping" involves the political resolution of immediate sources of insecurity on the one hand, and military enforcement mechanisms to secure these outcomes on the other hand.

Finding a Real Strategy

Towards the end of 1993 most Western governments shared a sense of frustration over the ongoing violence in the former Yugoslavia, "interblocking" institutions, and a lack of will or leadership on what to do with the security vacuum in Central and Eastern Europe. This frustration should be moulded into renewed pragmatism. The immediate question is how to prevent border and ethnic wars in the region. The answer is foremost political and can be found in the Balladur Plan. The next question is how to make the potential political settlements stick. Instead of looking to institutions we must look to an optimal division of military *resources* between the United States and the Western European powers.

Canadian diplomacy can have a genuine sense of direction and purpose and be put to use for the good of Europe's stability, Euro-American relations, and thereby our own political, security, and commercial interests. North America shares with the EC the interest of incorporating a stable Central (and eventually Eastern) Europe into the new European Union. Europe now needs intense diplomacy to tie together these two loose strands: the Balladur Plan and a pragmatic division of military resources between NATO and the WEU.

The Balladur Plan was proposed by the new French prime minister in early 1993. It is not the first French proposal to deal with Eastern Europe's unstable borders and its volatile minorities. It is based, and one can thereby detect the hand of the Elysée, on earlier ideas expressed by President Mitterrand for a confederation of Europe and later a proposal for a pan- European security treaty.[28] The plan calls for a series of conferences, presided over by the EC, to arrive at Europe-wide dispute settlement mechanisms for questions of national minorities and territorial boundaries.[29]

During their June 1993 summit the European Council agreed to consider this proposal within the recently added mandate of "joint action" under the provisions of a Common Foreign and Security Policy.[30] A series of questions from both East and West European countries as well as from Canada, in addition to several rounds of political committee and high-level task force meetings in the EC, have given the plan (now called the Stability Pact) a tough first screening. Some fear that it will undermine the initiatives on minorities and a code of conduct now in discussion in the CSCE. Others wonder who will guarantee the outcome.

The European Council decision of December 10–11, 1993, reveals a much improved plan. The European Union will launch an initial conference in spring 1994 in which roundtables will be set up to accompany the various bilateral talks among states primarily from Central and Eastern Europe that have the prospect of becoming members of the European Union. The aim is to conclude bilateral agreements that cover national minority and border problems. The Stability Pact will then ratify these agreements as well as add "complementary arrangements" that specify the role of the EU, third parties, and organizations. The CSCE will be its final guardian.[31]

Though the plan still faces political and procedural obstacles, it is far more pragmatic now than it was in April 1993. It recognizes that though its geography is flexible, it is really first intended for the most stable Central European states, and that it should build on existing agreements. It is a serious attempt at practical preventive diplomacy. The heart of the plan is more to the point than the mainstream of proposals in NATO or the CSCE. Reduced to its core, its objective is exactly what Europe needs. It has an element of *realpolitik*: Western cooperation on the inviolability of borders in exchange for guarantees from Central and Eastern European governments on the rights of minorities. It excludes, wisely in my view, the Caucasus and Central Asia. European security should stay in Europe. The twelve-odd ethnic conflicts at present raging from Georgia to Tadjikistan are simply beyond its competence.

To prevent it from institutional suffocation, the Stability Pact needs to be even more practical and it needs the support of non-EC members. First, it needs to target states that are within reach of signing a political agreement on minorities and/or borders. It should thus adopt a variable speed approach. The Czech Republic and Poland may be ready. In the case of Poland, there is no need to make a new start—its existing bilateral treaties may be worked into a mutually agreeable overall framework. In this logic, the first cases should provide an incentive for more complex cases such as Hungary to follow suit. Secondly, given the constraints of sovereignty, the objective must be to find sufficient minority protection to avoid Bosnian-like atrocities in exchange for maximum border stability.

The second point requires means to guarantee any such agreement. If such a border and minority rights regime could be negotiated, Europe must have a force ready to back its enforcement and deter its violation. Promises or guarantees by the EC or CSCE are not enough. Nor is the force of a treaty with only an arbitration mechanism sufficient.

The enforcement logic must be understood in the wider context of how to collate long-term EC and NATO membership for Central and East Europe. If you want to join either organization, you cannot have irredentist claims nor forcefully mistreat minorities. Therefore Western assistance to secure such agreements should precede an alliance-based approach to Central and Eastern European security.

If so, the Western allies can begin to concentrate on how optimally to divide labour and tasks.[32] Rather than becoming involved in peacekeeping, the WEU-NATO apparatus must concentrate on deterring violation of the agreement and enforcing its provisions. A treaty between a Central European state and the European Union can already make use of the Maastricht language for enforcement. Under Article J. 4, paragraph two, the Union can request the WEU to elaborate and implement decisions and actions of the Union which have defence applications. The role of NATO is to enable the WEU to do so if the treaty is clearly violated. If the Americans can agree to the framework, the French can agree both to full consultation and to a practical form of military cooperation to enforce the agreement.[33]

In such a joint capacities approach, the present allocation appears as follows: C^3, intelligence, lift, and logistics to the Americans, and manpower and tactical resources to the European armies.[34] The NATO summit of January 1994 agreed to a plan allowing NATO members to combine forces with other European states and use NATO assets while American troops could stay out of the mission.[35]

Canada must be active on the diplomatic front, pointing all noses again in the same direction. Our diplomatic strategy must be clear: politically and institutionally advance the Stability Pact while building a deterrence and military enforcement capability behind it. To do so we must offer concrete Canadian resources (capacities) in the make-up of this force. Canadians and other less heavily armed members should provide their full share in support functions to assure a multilateral approach and to share cost.[36]

This dual-track policy allows us to pursue a genuine post-Cold War policy in Europe, where the Stability Pact forms the political blueprint and a WEU-NATO enforcement capacity the strategic component. Meanwhile membership in NATO *and* the EU/WEU for Central and even Eastern European states should be openly tied together so that rivalries can be avoided and the Stability Pact and a Western enforcement mechanism can be compatible with a slow evolution towards membership for qualifying states in the region.[37]

8

From South to East? Financing the Transition in Central and Eastern Europe

Jeanne Kirk Laux

WITH THE BREAK UP of the Soviet Union, the question of how best to meet the challenge of transition in Central and Eastern Europe moved to the centre of policy debate within and among Western governments. This debate raises in turn the question of how to deal with competing claims from East and South for scarce resources. At the time that the Group of Seven industrial countries (G-7) decided to coordinate Western assistance to the two Central European countries officially committed to reforms (Poland and Hungary) in 1989, no one foresaw the scope these assistance programs would take; nor could they foresee the scale of funding required. Early concern voiced by Third World governments that aid might be "diverted" from South to East could be dismissed. Now however, the assistance offered by the Organization for Economic Cooperation and Development (OECD) member countries (G-24, so-called to distinguish the governments from the OECD as an institution) extends to twelve recipients in Central and Eastern Europe (CEE) including several former Soviet republics (FSU).[1] The scale of funding has dramatically expanded from short-term emergency aid to reach over $70 billion[2] in support of a panoply of programs. Donor governments, including Canada, have had to face the issue of trade-offs between East and South. The resolution of the "aid diversion" debate is crucial to Canadian foreign policy making. It is, after all, a part of the broader process of reorienting institutions and redirecting budgets to support new priorities in the emerging post Cold War world order.

Following a review of the evolution of Western assistance to the post communist transition, we will summarize the debate over the trade-offs between South and East to argue that there is no convincing evidence of *aid diversion* on the narrow basis of financial transfers. The sums are small even by comparison to reduced budgets for aid to developing countries, and the programs offered to the East can scarcely be called aid in the formal sense of what constitutes official development assistance (ODA). Strong objections to assistance for the CEE were provoked in Canada, as we see in the next section of the chapter, because the Conservative government mobilized its new monies for the East while cutting back on aid to the Third World. There is, however, a case to be made for *policy diversion*, as national and international institutions stretch their mandates to encompass the CEE/FSU. The end of the Cold War did not produce the expected shift in policy attention away from European security issues to focus primarily on global issues of equity, environment, and cooperative security relevant to the Third World. Rather, political crises in Russia and protracted war in Bosnia continue to justify new assistance and bolster those promoting a Euro-centred foreign policy against competing regionalisms. Chancellor Kohl of Germany puts it most clearly: "Any setback in reform in the former Warsaw Pact states would demand a high price of us all. Supporting development in these countries is not merely a contribution towards consolidating their stability, but an investment in . . . world peace."[3] To resolve the dilemma of competing regionalisms, the last section of this chapter explains how Western donors, including Canada, are forging a truly global aid policy by promoting convergence between the criteria used to rationalize their assistance programs in both the East and the South.

Western Assistance to the Transition in Central and Eastern Europe

Western assistance to the post communist transition can be demarcated into two phases, divided by the watershed event—the abortive coup in Moscow in 1991 which set off the collapse of the FSU. The extraordinary first phase (1989–91) was characterized by euphoria and assumptions that the transition could be rapid and thus assistance temporary. The second phase (1992–94) was shaped by a sobering re-evaluation of the costs and complexity of transition and resulted in the institutionalization of assistance for the long term. A brief review of the origins of coordinated Western assistance to Central/East Europe and the evolution of who gives what to whom will prepare the way for an analysis of the debate over aid diversion from South to East which these assistance programs provoked.

Phase I (1989–91)

In this first euphoric phase of post-Cold War relations in Europe, a domino effect of democratization toppled communist regimes across Central Europe, the Gorbachev-Bush summit declared the end of the Cold War, the two Germanys moved towards unification, and Western governments' aid initiatives multiplied. The first emergency program, known as PHARE or "Poland and Hungary: Assistance for Restructuring Economies," was initiated by the seven leading industrial countries, among them Canada, and the European Community, at the G-7 Paris Summit in July 1989. The seven reaffirmed their support for "freedom and democracy" and recognized that "the political changes taking place in these countries will be difficult to sustain without economic progress." They pledged to coordinate assistance so as "to sustain the momentum of reform" and "to these ends, we ask the Commission of the European Communities to take the necessary initiatives . . . to associate, besides the Summit participants, all interested countries."[4]

This invitation to coordinate assistance was immediately supported by all twenty-four member states of the OECD whose senior experts met over the summer and fall to put in place the needs assessment and national commitments for the December 1989 ministerial meeting of the G-24. Thereafter the Commission of the European Communities (EC) Directorate-General of External Relations took on the responsibility in Brussels "to provide information on G-24 programmes to . . . donor and beneficiary countries; to strengthen complementarity and coherence of G-24 assistance; and to promote joint actions and new initiatives."[5]

Western governments' immediate support to the fledgling democratic governments in the East was based on a shared belief that assistance could avert their return to authoritarianism and discourage revival of Soviet hegemony. The West Europeans also hoped that emergency aid and financial stabilization programs would discourage mass migrations westward from collapsing planned economies. All Western donors agreed from the outset that G-24 assistance should be conditional on subscribing to Western values of liberalism. More carrot than stick, their statements regarding political conditionality were made under the assumption that the post-communist governments themselves were dedicated to instituting pluralism and markets.

Thus the G-24 quickly considered requests from five other new governments in Central/East Europe anxious to benefit from the battery of programs being offered to Hungary and Poland. In early 1990 the EC launched fact-finding missions to assess whether commitment to reforms justified extending assistance to Czechoslovakia, the German Democratic Republic, Bulgaria, Yugoslavia, and Romania and advised the G-24 foreign ministers to accept all, because "the countries concerned will have put in place the basic legislation needed to move towards democracy and competitive market oriented economic systems."[6] Aid disbursements to Romania were, however, withheld until reports from parliamentary inquiries six months later confirmed that progress had been made toward democratization.

Confirmation of both Western eagerness to support the transition and Eastern readiness to accept conditionality came with the signing of the Articles of Agreement for the new European Bank for Reconstruction and Development (EBRD) in Paris in May 1990. The Bank, which called itself "the first international financial institution of the post Cold War period," included among its founding members the G-24, the six former CEE Comecon countries, Yugoslavia, and the former Soviet Union. All formally subscribed not only to the general principles of liberalism stated in the preamble, but to the stipulation of the EBRD's first article which stated: "The purpose of the Bank shall be to foster the transition towards open market-oriented economies and to promote private and entrepreneurial initiative in the Central and Eastern European countries committed to and applying the principles of multiparty democracy, pluralism and market economies." When G-24 senior officials met in mid-1991 to assess the results of their assistance policies, congratulations were judged to be in order. The volume of bilateral commitments had reached $31 billion and another $10 billion had been committed by the Bretton Woods institutions, not to mention agreements by Paris Club members to write down some of the Polish debt. "For donors and recipients alike the whole G-24 coordination process has developed into a most important instrument of solidarity between the industrialized countries in the West and the emerging democracies in economic transition in the east."[7]

Behind the congratulations, however, a worrisome reality loomed. Over the winter of 1990–91 many had recognized that neither the success of reforms in the East nor Western official commitment to assist them could be taken for granted. The radical drops in industrial output and in national income experienced by the East, even by the model reformer, Poland, created fears about social instability and political regression. The World Bank observed that, "in contrast to the euphoria that existed Eastern and Central Europe a year ago, developments . . . have led to a sobering realization of the difficulties of transition and the short-term cost of reform."[8] In the West, financing fatigue on the part of donor governments, accompanied by doubts about the capacity of the East to "absorb aid," prompted resistance to further appeals by the EC to ante up more funds for assistance programs. And yet in the conditions of uncertainty, expected private capital flows had not materialized, so that the United Nations Economic Commission for Europe found that "inadequate financial support aggravates the economic problems of a number of transition countries."[9]

Such concerns for financing reform in Central and Eastern Europe were eclipsed by the abortive coup in Moscow in August 1991. Major geopolitical interests were at stake with the collapse of a nuclear superpower and as a host of fledging sovereign republics began to clamber for assistance. Suddenly the Bush White House, which had let the Europeans shoulder the main burdens and responsibilities for aid to the CEE, sought to exercise leadership and summoned all potential donors to Washington in January 1992. Then Secretary of State James Baker did not mince words: "the unraveling of the centralized Soviet state confront[s] the West with great opportunities as well as ominous dangers . . . these dangers serve as a call to action. . . . Here is what the West must do . . . we must pursue a diplomacy of collective engagement . . . to crystallize this coalition, the President proposes that we begin by holding a coordinating conference."[10]

This was a pivotal moment for Western policy-making regarding the post-communist transition. As attention focused on the FSU, the future of G-24 assistance to the smaller Central and Eastern European countries was in question. Western governments decided not merely to renew official funding and programs but to expand them. Over 1991–92 the G-24 extended their assistance to new countries—Albania and the three newly sovereign Baltic states—and increased their collective pledges of aid to the CEE countries by 20 percent. Despite the urgent needs of the former

Yugoslav and Soviet republics, the G-24 ministers "confirmed that new challenges to the international community for assistance will not distract the G-24 from support for the economic reconstruction in central and eastern Europe."[11]

Phase II (1992–94)

Since 1991 Western assistance to the CEE has moved from being considered exceptional funding for reforms in a given country to become a set of programs aimed at integrating the post-communist countries into the world political economy over the long term. Canadian foreign policy mission statements, for example, moved the issue up to second position in its rank order of goals, declaring that Canada must "manage the complex questions stemming from the reconstruction of the Soviet Union with the objective of drawing successor economies into the democratic, market-based world with real assistance for real reform *while also* sustaining the transition of Poland, Hungary and the Czech and Slovak Federal Republic to market-based pluralist democracies."[12] To meet the ongoing needs of the smaller CEE recipients, now including Slovenia, not only did the G-24 donors expand their programs, but international institutions' mandates were revised and new mechanisms for program delivery put in place. A summary look at the figures on G-24 bilateral assistance will show just who now gives how much to whom, after which two profiles of multilateral programs—the European Communities and the World Bank—will illustrate how international organizations have reoriented their activities to envelope the post communist countries.

Western assistance, as monitored by the G-24 Coordination Unit, has reached a cumulative figure of over $70 billion pledged by the twenty-four donor countries, the European Communities, and the three international financial institutions (IFIs) to twelve recipient countries in Central/East Europe (not including Russia and the FSU). The IFIs account for $20 billion. This figure of $70 billion covers all programs which are reported by type—e.g., investment projects, technical cooperation, official export credits—as well as by end use—e.g., economic infrastructure, debt reorganization, or food aid. Fundamentally, aid to the CEE is European; the collective commitment of the EC12 and the Communities together account for 61 percent of the cumulative commitments made by the G-24 as such (out of a total of $50 billion). Germany took the lead among bilateral donors early on and still today accounts for 22 percent of all G-24 aid, or fully 58 percent of the European member countries' total bilateral commitments. By contrast the United States accounts for just 15 percent and Japan 7 percent. Canada, with commitments over US$2 billion (or 4.7 percent of the total) contributes a greater share of G-24 assistance than any EFTA member country and indeed is equal to France.

There is as well a disparity among recipients. The first reformers off the mark, Poland and Hungary, continue to receive the largest overall share of G-24 assistance—36 percent and 18 percent respectively—while the Balkans, even countries which have been part of the program almost from the outset, are less favoured; Romania and Bulgaria receive 9 percent and 5 percent of G-24 aid respectively.[13]

More than monies, the EC offers policy assistance through market access and the possibility for some of membership. The Commission has steadily expanded its own assistance program (as distinct from its twelve member countries' contributions). This program, which retains the name PHARE, is funded out of the EC's regular annual budget and the European Council has approved increases from 500 million ECU in 1990 to one billion ECU in 1992 (exchange rate 1 ECU = US$1.25).

The Commission's idea to move to a multi-year budgeting approach to fit in with the funding offered by the international financial institutions was approved and an overall framework for 1993–97 set out with budget guidelines. PHARE programs now extend to twelve countries and others (e.g., the former Yugoslav republic of Macedonia) are under consideration.[14] The EC's banking arm, the European Investment Bank (EIB), has stretched its mandate in order to target more capital to Central and Eastern Europe. EIB's board of governors (one minister from each member state) can, on the basis of unanimity, authorize the Bank to go beyond the EC twelve countries and lend to any country which falls under the EC's external cooperation policy. Before 1989 the EIB's mandate had been stretched from Europe south to the Mediterranean and to those Third World countries party to the Lomé Convention.[15]

When the Commission started the PHARE program, it made Poland and Hungary eligible for project lending by the EIB and added all other CEE countries after 1991. Originally a ceiling of one billion ECU was placed on EIB loans to the transitioning economies, but within two years, lending to just three Eastern countries (Poland, Hungary, and Romania) had surpassed the total EIB lending to all sixty-nine Lomé IV countries. Rather than back away from this growing demand, the EC Council of Ministers decided in September 1993 to guarantee all EIB loans to the East up to a new ceiling of three billion ECU.[16]

The most dramatic institutionalization of EC relations to some of the Central and Eastern European countries goes well beyond assistance. Negotiation of "Europe Agreements" began in 1990 at the time the German Democratic Republic was absorbed into Germany and thus into the EC. Initially, as the Common Framework was worked out over 1990–91 in Brussels for agreements with Hungary, Czechoslovakia, and Poland, these arrangements looked to be a way of buying time for Western Europe to achieve its single-market ambitions by keeping the CEE countries at the gates rather than opening to their stated desire for membership. The framework set by the EC was highly political. It declared the purpose of association to be "political and economic freedoms" and set up ministerial level councils to formalize "political dialogue." Major trade-related provisions were likewise negotiated — trade concessions, liberalized quotas, and timetables to reach a free-trade area within ten years — but they were much criticized for their limited scope and slow timetable. The first three agreements were signed in December 1991 and negotiations begun with Bulgaria and Romania.[17] As it turned out, the EC negotiations set in motion a process which, after the Soviet collapse, evolved to become a fast track to membership for selected CEE countries.

Pushed by the so-called Visegrad countries,[18] the European Commission agreed to re-evaluate the Europe Agreements and in December 1992 recommended that the European Council revise them. The Commission argued that these agreements should become the principal framework for its relations with the CEE countries and that the Council should be clear about their eventual membership in the European Union.[19] This critical change of perspective was made official at the June 1993 EC summit in Copenhagen: "The European Council today agreed that associated countries in Central and Eastern Europe that so desire shall become members of the European Union [and that] the future cooperation with the associated countries shall be geared to the objective of membership which has now been established."[20]

The World Bank has become increasingly involved in the CEE and FSU transitions, stretching funds and its mandate to do so. Once limited to project lending (to public sector borrowers), the Bank already re-interpreted its mandate in 1980 to take on an IMF-like role and offer structural adjustment loans (SALs) in response to the critical needs of debt-ridden Third World countries. One year after the G-24 programs started, the Bank had signed SALs with five CEE countries. Its board of governors — where the preponderance of weighted votes are held by the G-24 countries — voted an extra $5 billion designated for the CEE over a three-year period and most of this was committed by the end of 1991.[21] The extraordinary jump in Bank membership (which comes automatically with acceptance into the IMF) between 1991–93 from the CEE and FSU, justified the creation of a new regional vice-presidency for Europe and Central Asia in addition to the division devoted to "Transition Economies." The break-up of the Soviet Union in particular obliged special funding — for example, a $30 million technical co-operation program. Twelve new field offices have been established in Hungary, Albania, and the FSU to enhance the Bank's ability to supervise projects. The most recent figures show the Bank having committed $3.84 billion to the former planned economies in fiscal 1993, some 16 percent of their total commitments worldwide.[22] Clearly, despite the costs and complexity, all G-24 governments, the EC, and the Bretton Woods organizations reaffirmed their commitment to long-term assistance to the Central and East European countries at a time of great political uncertainty.

The Debate on Aid Diversion

The new funds and new institutional mechanisms put in place to encourage the transition and reintegration of the CEE, especially following the collapse of the Soviet Union, rekindled concern about diversion of aid and policy attention from South to East. Already in 1990 some voices from the Third World sounded the alarm about the impact on financial transfers to the South. The chair of the International Monetary Fund's development committee, a senior minister from Zimbabwe, underscored the need to "study very carefully what is happening in Eastern Europe," because the new demands presented a "danger" of diversion of capital from South to East.[23] Senegal's foreign trade minister attracted much attention for his protest that Poland and Hungary had received ten times more aid per capita than all sixty-eight Third World countries party to the Lomé Convention with the EC.[24] Initially Western donors could forestall serious consideration of the trade-offs in East-South assistance under the presumption that the post-communist transition would be rapid and thus Western assistance programs would be temporary. The G-24 insisted well into 1991 that their cooperation was of an "exceptional character: the assistance is expected to be transitional, with the aim that it can be progressively discontinued."[25] Denial constituted the first line of defence by Western donors, although they did display some empathy for Third World worries. The OECD's Development Assistance Committee (DAC) noted that "there has been continued concern among DAC members and recipient countries alike over potential aid diversion to eastern Europe," but emphasized in a formal statement issued at the June 1991 OECD Council that "their determination to give high priority to their cooperation with developing countries will not be diminished because of their support for central and eastern Europe."[26]

Third World concerns intensified as the full impact of the collapse of the Soviet economy, both as a market and a supplier for major Third World countries, began to be felt.[27] Assistance to the post communist countries, they argued, put the welfare and stability of the South at risk and remedial action should be taken. After the IMF announced a new facility for the FSU, the chair of the caucus of poor and middle-income countries (which meets before the IMF and World Bank annual meetings) put it bluntly: "the fear is that we will be victims of a prodigal son syndrome." There might be a valid case for assistance, and "of course these countries should be aided—as long as we don't have to pay for it."[28] Certainly the mainstream media in Canada picked up the theme to conclude that: "although development officials quickly deny the suggestion that they are shifting funds to Eastern Europe and Moscow, the Third World is clearly losing the competition for new money."[29] A senior policy advisor in the United Nations Development Program (UNDP), Dr. Mahbub ul Haq, concludes that "the Cold War has not been phased out in terms of our global institutions and aid programs," and makes the plea that any aid to the East must take the form of technical assistance or non-concessional lending since, "despite their dire situations, their literacy rates and per capita income are eight times that of Third World countries."[30]

How should the impact on the Third World of Western assistance to the former communist countries be assessed? A full appreciation of the costs to the South of the transition under way in the CEE and the FSU would require taking into account the disruption of East-South aid and trade; the effect of reforms on the former planned economies' competitiveness in Western markets, and changing financial flows, both private and official, which might divert capital from South to East.[31] The aid diversion debate centres more narrowly around the last issue—financial transfers, in particular official transfers—and assumes that the East will require continued assistance. This assumption still holds. Estimates (for example, by the IMF) of CEE needs for official assistance are normally based on the shortfall after other forms of financial transfers, most importantly inflows of private capital, are projected. Although private foreign investment had been expected to move into the region quickly once emergency aid and stabilization programs took effect, economist Carl H. McMillan concludes that, because of instability in the East, "investment flows to the area, in the crucial first years of the transition, have . . . not been of the magnitudes required for FDI to ease domestic resources constraints."[32] Eventually the new stock markets in some CEE countries such as the Czech Republic will draw in more portfolio investment, but to date, "official financing has become the major source of new credits to the eastern countries."[33] It is this continuing reliance on official assistance which generates the debate over East-South trade-offs.

A clear understanding of just what constitutes official development assistance and just which countries qualify to receive it will help to separate the real from the imagined consequences of assistance to the East. ODA as it is now monitored by the OECD's Development Assistance Committee, which regroups the world's major bilateral donors including Canada, is defined as follows: (Category A) Bilateral Official Development Assistance (i.e., grants and grant-like contributions, for example technical assistance); and development lending (i.e., loans or investments made on non-market terms). ODA also includes (Category B) contributions to multilateral institutions—both UN agencies and capital subscriptions to the International Development Agency (IDA) or regional development banks and concessional lending to these organizations. In its broader definition of Official Development Financing (ODF), the DAC calculates other official flows—that is, official export credits and contributions to other multilateral institutions.[34] Only such transfers to those countries placed on the DAC list, reconsidered annually at the high-level group meetings, may qualify as ODA. Therefore *aid diversion* concerns official transfers, other than private or non-governmental organization aid, to developing countries (those on the DAC list) for development purposes (supporting socio-economic changes) made on non-market terms (a certain grant equivalency is calculated). Analysis of diversion focuses on the extent to which such commitments to the transitioning CEE and FSU countries draw from, rather than add to, current or expected levels of ODA.[35]

Three helpful criteria for evaluating aid diversion have been proposed by Ottawa consultant Roger Young: conditionality, concessionality, and additionality.[36] Young asks whether conditions placed on aid to the CEE countries make conditions on new aid to the Third World more stringent. He dismisses this concern by reminding us that "attaching policy conditions to development assistance has a history that predates the recent changes in the East."[37] Are the concessions made to Eastern borrowers—for example, for debt forgiveness—more generous than those offered to the Third World? The terms of debt forgiveness negotiated by Poland were more favourable by far than any granted to the poorest countries in the Third World in Young's view. Other observers, however, point to the Brazil and Mexico cases and note as well that Poland's offer turned out to be an exception not a rule in East/Central Europe. And what of additionality? Young then investigates whether financial transfers to the East are additional to current levels (or expected trend lines) of official development assistance to the Third World and finds that both multilateral and bilateral financial transfers to the East up to 1991 appeared to be additional to ongoing commitments to the Third World. There were, however, some examples of "encroachment" as Holland and Canada, for example, decided to cap Third World aid all the while increasing their commitments to the East. What is the current assessment?

Today the multilateral donors continue to maintain that their commitments to the Central/East Europeans and the FSU are additional to their ongoing programs in the Third World. Official G-24 figures to year-end 1992 show $20 billion in transfers by the main financial institutions (IMF, World Bank, and the EBRD) to the CEE countries and recent commitments made to Russia could double that figure in 1994.[38] The World Bank explains its reallocation of resources in a reassuring manner: "To develop these programs, the Bank has initiated a rapid build-up of the requisite staff, after drawing up rules of redeployment to ensure the continued quality of other Bank programs."[39] The managing director of the IMF, reporting to his board in 1992 on the needs assessment for the FSU, admitted that "exceptional efforts would be required by official creditors, as well as by bilateral and multilateral donors, to address the financing needs of the former states without crowding out financing for Eastern European and developing countries that are implementing appropriate policy adjustments."[40] Yet after the IMF Council set up a new $3 billion "Systemic Transformation Facility" in April 1993 to streamline its disbursements to all post-communist states, his attitude shifted. Asked whether the IMF's preoccupation with Russia might not distract attention from the needs of the developing countries, Mr. Camdessus summarily dismissed this perception as "wrong . . . we are now in this business with 75 countries in the world, and I do not intend to delay our work with 74 countries because we are interested in the historic transformation of an important seventy-fifth one."[41]

It is in truth difficult to posit that these new programs have a direct diversionary impact. The special facilities put in place by the IMF for Central and Eastern Europe are themselves transitional, while the upper limits to lending by these IFIs depend on member countries' quotas. Lending to the CEE by the World Bank is done on the commercial account, and its affiliate, the International Development Agency, which makes concessional loans, does not operate in the CEE or in Russia. Indeed, when the IDA's capitalization was augmented in 1992 by $18 billion to target poverty reduction in the Third World, Poland, Hungary, the Czech Republic, and Russia were among the member countries *contributing* to this replenishment fund.[42]

Looking at the bilateral G-24 programs of assistance to the East, there is no clear case to be made for aid diversion on the basis of financial transfers which would conform to the definition of ODA noted above. The total grant component of the $50 billion committed is 37 percent, but the category of "aid" accounting for most of this is debt reorganization, mainly related to the 1991 restructuring of the Polish debt. The grant component for Hungary and the former Czechoslovakia in 1991 was only 4.4 percent and 6 percent respectively of all assistance after debt reorganization.[43] Technical assistance, which has a large training component, usually takes grant form. As emergency assistance or food aid is phased out in East/Central Europe (now 3 percent of all assistance given), the most prominent category of bilateral assistance is official export credits (27 percent).[44]

Nonetheless, Western donors were still equivocal at year end 1992, as the DAC confessed that "most members have indicated that aid efforts in Eastern Europe and the former Soviet Union have caused rather limited aid diversion from developing countries. Taking a more medium-term view, aid diversion will depend on the extent to which these countries become recipients of major amounts of concessional capital assistance."[45] By entering into the micro debate over aid policy in one donor country, Canada, we will get a sharper picture of the trade-offs between competing regionalisms and the ways chosen to resolve the aid diversion dilemma.

Canada's Assistance Policy and the Aid Diversion Debate

Canada, as one of the G-7 countries to endorse the 1989 Paris Sommet de l'Arche declaration calling for international assistance to support "freedom and democracy" in Central Europe, was quick to mobilize emergency aid. Senior officials took part in the meetings which put together the G-24 consultative process and Ottawa set up a $72 million emergency package of programs for Poland and Hungary. By March 1990 a new mechanism to coordinate bilateral assistance had been invented, the Task Force for Central and Eastern Europe. Under Department of External Affairs and International Trade auspices, the task force had an initial $40 million budget spread over three years. The responsible ministers were clear about the purpose; the task force "brings together public and private resources in Canada in support of what is an irrepressible push towards democracy and private enterprise in Central and Eastern Europe and the Soviet Union."[46]

During the first two years of assistance, a phase which I have called euphoric, Canada's task force found a number of ways to assist the expanding number of economies in transition that did not necessarily require new monies. For example, in Poland a "counterpart fund" was created from the proceeds of food aid (food sold on concessional terms) and the task force was permitted to redirect that local currency to support its projects. Humanitarian aid, such as milk powder for Bulgaria, was donated from surplus stocks by the Department of Agriculture. Canada took part in the debt forgiveness plan for Poland, agreed upon by the Paris Club creditor governments, by foregoing interest on half the debt owed, a gesture worth some $1.6 billion to Poland but not adding to Canada's current deficit. Some new funds had to be found, however, to support multilateral initiatives, as when Parliament approved Canadian membership in the EBRD in December 1990 with its $120 million entry fee. And, where commercial interests could be used for justification, further monies were forthcoming; this is the case for Renaissance Eastern Europe (REE), a program created in 1990 to help Canadian companies find joint venture partners in the post communist countries.[47]

Canada's policy crunch regarding assistance to the East came in July 1991 when the G-7 summit decided to back up reform in the former Soviet Union with what has been called "cheque book diplomacy." Prime Minister Mulroney, an enthusiast for summitry in general and for the transition in Europe in particular, immediately pledged $150 million in food credits and another $25 million in technical assistance. Within weeks his finance minister promised further credits and technical assistance valued at $10 million to the newly sovereign Baltic states. Already, Canadian embassies in the key CEE recipient countries (in Warsaw, Budapest, and Prague) had to bring in extra people in part to handle coordination of assistance programs. It was now clear to the task force that without funding and personnel beyond the three-year sunset clause, it would be impossible to meet both G-7 and G-24 appeals to support an expanding range of programs. The decisions made in Ottawa between 1991–93 clearly committed Canada to long-term support for the transition in Eastern Europe. The means chosen were to routinize program administration by turning the task force into a regular bureau in External (now Foreign) Affairs and to revise the budget allocation process by cutting ODA, all the while ending its protective insulation from other types of assistance.

Canada's intention to stay the course as part of the G-7 and G-24 collective assistance to Central and Eastern Europe was confirmed when cabinet handed the task force an enhanced technical assistance budget ($75 million) in 1992. The ministerial rhetoric backing up this financial commitment connected the projects to foreign policy priorities. "Canadians have come to realize that we all have a direct stake in ensuring the success of democratic and economic reforms in Central and Eastern Europe. Success will result in a more stable, peaceful and prosperous world—failure, the opposite."[48] Subsequently, Prime Minister Mulroney in particular, but followed up by Prime Minister Campbell at the July 1993 Tokyo summit, committed Canada to a multitude of new assistance initiatives, many but not all for Russia and Ukraine. For programs affecting the CEE as well, new funds enhanced the REE fund and a $30 million Canadian Nuclear Safety Initiative was set up in June 1992 to improve nuclear reactor safety. Often new monies are channelled through international organizations; for example, Canada designated $7.5 million of the latter fund to the EBRD's special nuclear safety account and gave $800,000 to the OECD's new Centre for Cooperation with European Economies in Transition.[49]

Approval of a submission to Treasury Board to extend the budget led to the winding up of the task force on March 31, 1993, in favour of a new Bureau of Assistance for Central and Eastern Europe. By choosing to locate this bureau within the Department of Foreign Affairs and International Trade (DFAIT) and therein within its European, rather than trade, division, clearly signalled that assistance was a tool of European policy. Headed by a director general, the bureau has three divisions for the FSU, the CEE, and for Policy, Planning, and Multilateral affairs, with an overall budget of approximately $110 million (including operations technical assistance and the REE program). In addition, the bureau administers the Nuclear Safety Initiative and currently has responsibility for another $37 million which consists of "set asides" or credits for wheat purchases by Russia. Typically, a project officer for a Central European country oversees more than one hundred projects which may initiate within that country, in which case the bureau would find the appropriate Canadian partner by putting the project out to tender. Many projects are initiated by a Canadian company or organization. In these cases the Canadian embassy brings the proposal to the relevant country's ministry to specify needs and priorities before the bureau arranges a contract.

To date, the bureau has helped fund over six hundred technical assistance projects in fourteen countries of CEE and the FSU valued at some $150 million. The bureau successfully applied to Treasury Board in summer 1993 for approval to fund permanent "assistance sections" with new personnel in each Canadian embassy in the CEE to coordinate Canadian assistance.[50]

In the view of the non-governmental organizations (NGOs) engaged in development assistance to the South, "External has created a mini-CIDA (Canadian International Development Agency)."[51] The high-profile summitry, the rapid mobilization of new programs, and the albeit small but new funds worried those concerned about shrinking ODA budgets. Accusations of aid diversion pointed to new budget allocation procedures created to fund assistance to the CEE and FSU. This potential "encroachment" on ODA (to use Roger Young's term) was made in the government's February 1991 budget when an International Assistance Envelope was concocted to define funding limits and expose trade-offs between programs. The envelope includes ODA, contributions to international agencies (from the International Development Research Centre to IBRD) and, for the first time, "assistance to the East" which reappeared as an item in the 1991-92 expenditure Estimates that spring.[52] Any funding to the CEE countries, however, could come only from a sub-envelope or "reserve," initially amounting to $57 million, which three ministers (Finance, External, and CIDA) could draw down. This budgetary innovation set off alarm bells among those dedicated to Third World development issues, particularly when the government placed caps on ODA cash; its growth was limited to 3 percent in the 1991 budget and then effectively pushed downwards to 1.5 percent by applying it to the entire new envelope reserve so that the CEE countries could take half the increase. In the view of the North-South Institute's researchers, "in effect, the money for Eastern Europe has been taken from the ODA budget and, although the amounts involved are not large (some $40 million), it is a most unwelcome precedent."[53]

Such warning about the incipient redirection of official funding to the East might have gone unnoticed had it not coincided with the implementation of major ODA cutbacks by the Mulroney government, including outright elimination of some bilateral programs to the Third World, and with the leak of a DFAIT document suggesting that some officials welcomed aid diversion from South to East. In February 1993 the press leaked a confidential External Affairs memo which asserted that Canada could not afford to maintain current overseas aid programs, even at the reduced levels which had been announced in the mini-budget of December 1992, and that the official objective of reaching the DAC goal of .07 percent of GNP by the year 2000 was illusory. A redirection of scarce funds was counselled to favour the former communist countries because of their market potential and the view that they are "critical to future stability and prosperity of both development and developing countries."[54] With the tabling of the Main Estimates, shock waves hit the NGO development community—not so much because the ODA portion of spending, $2.53 billion, was both a 7.5 percent reduction from actual expenditures the prior year and a 10 percent cut from projected figures (these cuts had been announced), but because bilateral programs to fourteen traditional recipients, including Kenya and Tanzania, were simply eliminated.[55]

Meanwhile, on the other side of the assistance ledger, the small allotment for the CEE countries and FSU increased from $100 million to $147 million. The umbrella group for NGOs, the Canadian Council for International Cooperation, baldly stated that this increase "has been taken from the ODA budget."[56] The Canadian International Development Agency Minister, Monique Vézina, officially "rejected claims that these expenditure-reduction measures were designed to transfer a portion of official development assistance to benefit the countries of eastern Europe and the former Soviet Union. Funds reserved for those countries 'continue to represent only a minor part, about 5 percent, of the Canadian International Assistance Envelope, while the African continent receives 45% of the ODA budget.'"[57] Indeed, the allocation for the CEE countries is a trivial share of the nearly $3 *billion* in overall assistance.

The government's defence of its policy, however, was made less than convincing when a second External Affairs document, dated

March 1993, was leaked to the press. This document argued for new priorities to justify assistance: first the "enhancement of our security and the development of democratic regimes and market economies compatible with our own. And second, on burden-sharing responsibilities as members of G-7 and G-24." Michael Valpy, in a series of *Globe and Mail* columns, adopted the NGO community's critical stance. He saw the Conservative government as wishing "Third World impoverishment be knocked from the traditional No. 1 spot in favour of a strategic focus on rebuilding the economies of the nations of the former Soviet Union and Central and Eastern Europe."[58] Concerted lobbying achieved the promise from External Affairs/CIDA to postpone any major aid policy review until after the federal elections.

Despite the 1993 tempest over aid diversion, there is little to suggest that the Liberal government in Ottawa will undo the broad lines of aid policy defined by the Conservatives, beyond stemming cutbacks to ODA. When in opposition the Liberals constantly called for a more "massive longer-term plan" for assisting the former Soviet Union, arguing that Canada must use economic assistance and make it a priority to "entrench democracy."[59] Upon forming the government, Prime Minister Chrétien streamlined cabinet by taking out ministers of state, including the minister responsible for CIDA. This means effectively that the new minister of DFAIT, André Ouellet, is sole spokesperson in cabinet for assistance policy with responsibility for the International Assistance Envelope (the minister of finance maintains areas of responsibility, such as for the World Bank contributions). Both CIDA and the DFAIT Bureau of Assistance agree that a five-year aid allocation budget is critical to developing their respective programs.

In addition, the very experience of five years of assistance to the East has changed the complexion of domestic lobbies interested in aid policy. The accommodation of some groups worried about aid to the South, the enthusiasm of other groups newly engaged in assistance to the East, and the cooptation of business interests are factors which combine to suggest that the aid diversion debate is dissipating within Canada. At the level of policy evaluation, those chary of the risks of aid diversion, such as the North-South Institute and some branches of CIDA, now consider that the real needs of some of the CEE countries and the FSU indeed justify their becoming recipients of ODA. Greater involvement by traditional development agencies is counselled to bring the expertise they feel is needed to improve program delivery. Many Canadian NGOs involved in the Third World now accept that the CEE countries have a valid claim on scarce funds. Some, the Canadian Bureau for International Education for example, always favoured extending programs to the CEE/FSU. Others, like IDRC, which did not, are now looking for ways around "the ODA constraint" of their mandate so as to source funds by joining in projects co-sponsored by other agencies in Eastern Europe; serious IDRC negotiations are taking place with External Affairs to gain approval for a project in Ukraine, for example.

Canada's ongoing programs to the East have benefited a wide array of consultants, educational institutions, NGOs, and companies and thereby built up a constituency committed to their continuation. The Bureau of Assistance for Central and Eastern Europe works through partnerships, often initiated by Canadians with personal ties to the CEE region. As assistance extends to the FSU, project funding shows a bias in favour of Ukraine and the Baltics in keeping with Canadian political demography. These special ties are said to permit fast, smart, and relevant program delivery, while at the same time building constituencies for further assistance. For example, the Ukrainian Canadian Profession and Business Federation received a bureau contribution of $847,000 toward its internship program which, besides bringing over Ukrainian officials, funds ten Canadians to spend up to two years in Kiev as policy advisors. Across the country, hundreds of groups are engaged in technical assistance programs, from the University of New Brunswick getting monies for sixteen MBA students to study in Poland to the Saskatchewan Wheat Pool receiving $480,000 to send nine Canadian experts to Russia to advise on grain handling.[60]

From the outset of Canada's assistance programs the promotion of Canadian business interests has featured as the third official objective the "increase Canadian trade and investment links with the region." Besides the lines of credit extended to twelve Eastern countries by the Export Development Corporation, the Mulroney government worked to get Canadian companies and business consultants in on European contracts by, for example, committing in 1992 to give $1 million a year to a "Canadian Technical Cooperation Fund" at the EBRD. For direct appeal to business, the bureau's Renaissance Eastern Europe program, managed by the DFAIT European trade division, has succeeded in attracting business support. Enhanced to $10 million (over three years) in 1993, it offers Canadian companies willing to look for joint-venture partners in the East up to $100,000 in "non repayable" matching funds for airfares and per diems. Such sums put scarcely a dent in the accounts of companies like Bombardier, Pratt and Whitney, or Gulf Resources which are now using REE grants, but are more than enough to achieve good press in the *Financial Post*.[61]

Post-Cold War Foreign Aid Policy

In charting a foreign aid policy suited to the post-Cold War world, Canada's Liberal government must manoeuvre within parameters which have been set collectively through the G-7, G-24, World Bank, IMF, and the OECD in particular. Together the advanced industrial countries have renewed their commitment to assist the East and a first effect of these decisions has been to refocus policy attention on Europe. A *Globe and Mail* headline is apt: "From an arms race to an alms race!"[62] In order now to reconcile the claims of competing regionalisms, Western donors are forging convergence between the criteria used to rationalize their assistance programs in both the Third World and Central/Eastern Europe to create a truly global aid policy. Looking from South to East, the criteria used by the OECD to designate resource transfers as official development assistance are now being used to redefine some former communist countries as developing countries. Looking from East to South, the new post-Cold War consensus on liberal values which prevails in the European assistance programs justifies applying stricter political conditionality to Third World aid recipients. By appealing to a single global standard of democracy, good governance, and market economics, donors blur the boundaries of South and East.

The collective redefinition of Official Development Assistance is taking place in the DAC which initiated a far reaching policy review in 1991 to reconsider the list of countries considered to be developing. "Many DAC Members believe that the existing list needs to be reviewed and revised to reflect economic progress in certain countries and to respond to the emergency of newly-independent countries in Eastern Europe and the former Soviet Union." When the lists are completed in 1996 some countries, such as Saudi Arabia, which have moved beyond ODA, will be monitored as a second category, while other countries will come onto the ODA eligible category. The DAC revisions are far-reaching because, although the list was intended as a convenience for statistical data when it was established in the 1960s, it is now used by many donor countries to designate "eligibility for aid allocation, aid procurement, trade preferences and guarantee schemes."[63] Already the DAC has decided, effective January 1, 1993, that five Central Asian FSU republics were eligible for ODA and in 1994 added Georgia, Armenia, and Azerbaijan to the list. This new distinction between "developing" and "transitioning" economies among the FSU adds to the distinctions among the CEE countries between those receiving special trade preferences thanks to their association agreements with the EC and the others. The EBRD implicitly recognized these "have" and "have-not" differences among the transitioning economies when it replaced its sectoral divisions with regional "North" and the "South" divisions within Europe. Moving away from the old first, second, and third world view is part of a pattern of forging global policy convergence of norms and criteria for assistance.

A collective reaffirmation of the purposes of assistance by Western donors involves endorsing conditionality based on norms of liberalism, whether East or South. Certainly since the collapse of the Soviet Union, the celebration of global liberalism has taken on a greater militancy. President Clinton now seeks to be its standard-bearer, having seized upon "enlargement" of democracy as a universal value to orient post-Cold War policy, however contradictory its practice (for example, in the bungled intervention in Haiti). Conditionality—that is, making aid conditional on the recipient country adopting stipulated policies—is an integral part of other Western donors' assistance policy as well. The European Commission continues to emphasize that "assistance [to the CEE] is given conditional upon political stability in the country concerned, and a continuing commitment to democratic ideals and free market principles."[64] Once political conditionality gained a high moral tone with the endorsement of liberal norms by the post-communist regimes, it can more readily be used to justify cut-backs in programs to the South. Together the DAC donors reconfirmed in 1992 that "the issues of democracy and governance remain critical items on the development agenda" and they set out a program to monitor "trends in donor policies and practices; progress in international coordination of good governance . . ."[65] The World Bank insists on its mandate to apply human rights and good governance criteria, and the application of these criteria to rationalize projects is celebrated by some in Canada and denounced by others.[66] When the Canadian government obliged CIDA, in December 1992, to find ways to implement major funding cuts, some branches chose to cut by program and others by region, but in all cases human rights and good governance criteria were among the priorities cited to justify retaining programs.[67]

Conclusion

No sensible post-Cold War assistance policy can be made without a clear recognition that aid diversion in the narrow sense of financial transfers from South to East is fundamentally a myth. The latest United Nations report concludes that "more than four-fifths of the current gross flow of funds is debt-creating. Portfolio and foreign direct investment is negligible, as are official aid and grants."[68] The hard truth is that in a period of recession, Western donor governments, including Canada, chose to cap their assistance to the South and collectively agreed to target programs on the basis of new criteria, in particular "good governance." To counter these trends requires confronting them as such, not waving a diversionary flag to inflate the importance of assistance to the East or to deflate the importance of the real interests at stake in the former communist countries. Policy diversion—that is, an unexpected focus on Europe after the Cold War—is a necessary response to the tragic complexity of a new world disorder. Assistance to the East is not an issue of trade-offs in "cheque book diplomacy," but rather an issue of meeting real human needs as well as geopolitical challenges. Canada is rightly committed to consolidating the historic opportunity in Europe—to reconstruct the institutions of Bretton Woods in order to knit a global economy, to reinsure the security of small states after the setbacks of Balkan conflict, and thereby to set a framework for democratic politics. The narrow debate over aid diversion may soon be academic, should others adopt the stance of Russia's extremist political personality, Zhirinovsky, "We are a rich country; we don't need your aid. Go spend it in Africa!"[69]

9 NAFTA, Uruguay, and Canada-U.S. Relations: Inside Looking Out

Charles F. Doran

WHETHER NORTH AMERICA IS WIDER or deeper in trade and investment terms, and whether trade liberalization is increasingly regionalized or globalized, makes a considerable difference to a great trading state like Canada. The North American Free Trade Agreement (NAFTA) brings Mexico a lot closer than before. This chapter tries to show how and why. It also examines changes in U.S. trade policy and assesses the impact of voluntary export restraints, anti-dumping provisions, and subsidies. It then turns to problems not covered by either NAFTA or the Uruguay Round of the General Agreement on Tariffs and Trade (GATT). Finally, it reflects upon the structure and character of a new North America.

Attitude Toward Regionalism: Bush to Clinton

Bill Clinton inherited regional policy from George Bush. Clinton had a choice. He could either drop the regional initiative while opting for global trade liberalization, or he could emphasize continuity going back to the Canada-U.S. Free Trade Agreement (FTA) and culminating in a successful North American Free Trade Agreement. There were powerful forces in the Democratic Party dragging him in each direction. Ultimately, I believe, President Clinton made the decision to favour continuity in the regional outlook on the basis of what he felt was in his nation's broad interest and in terms of what was best for his presidency. Regional free trade became a test of Clinton's capacity to lead in foreign policy. That, more than anything else, determined the strategy of this president.

Trade today is investment-driven. That is why every country in the world seeks foreign investment. Most foreign trade is intra-industry and intra-firm. Low-end jobs can be retained in the rich countries only as a part of a globalized network of production. This creates new high-end jobs where the skills, technology, and capital permit. Thus a large structural reason existed in favour of NAFTA. Only by using the market forces outside North America, not by trying to exclude them, could the U.S. economy break out of its somnolence. Restructuring is painful. The only way it is likely to happen in a fashion that will keep the North American region competitive with Asia is for the United States and Canada to feel the brunt of low-wage pressure from Mexico in a kind of controlled experiment, preparing North America for the world in the next stage.

A tactical reason for NAFTA bolstered the structural argument. Without NAFTA, North America confronted the possibility of a long slide into protectionism. With NAFTA, Clinton could go to the Asia Pacific Economic Cooperation (APEC) meetings, hopefully with the support of Canada, and obtain at least a symbolic show of support for additional global trade liberalization. He could then go back to Europe and the Uruguay Round of tariff talks with a balance of power composed of North America and Asia at his back, urging the Europeans to make some of the needed concessions on agriculture in order to consummate a global trade deal.

A measure of how the past and present came together in domestic political terms was the outcome of the actual NAFTA vote in Congress. In the president's own party, 156 members of Congress voted against NAFTA, while only a 102 voted for it. Those voting for it often did so under intense duress, or extraordinary incentive, thus indicating the distaste for the agreement in home districts. On the Republican side, 134 members voted for NAFTA, but interestingly, despite the fact that this was a Bush proposal, combined with arm-twisting by the Republican leadership and a letter from Clinton indicating that he would not make trade a partisan issue in the next campaign, some forty-three Republican members of Congress voted against NAFTA as well.

Thus we see that broader economic regionalism was not only quite unpopular with the American electorate, reflected in the voting behaviour particularly of Democrats, but also that this measure was extraordinarily bipartisan. What a contrast to Canadian parliamentary behaviour with its extreme party discipline! In this case the members of the ruling party did not accept the lead of their president, yet the measure passed because of the favourable votes of the opposition party. In the United States partisanship is supposed to stop at the "water's edge." There partisanship so disappeared that opposition party votes were far more numerous than those of the governing Democratic Party on behalf of NAFTA. A Democratic president had passed a Republican initiative on trade and commercial regionalism in North America over the heads of the reluctant members of his own party. Is this the end of political party in the United States?

The answer is no, party is not collapsing in the United States, nor were American voters, nor Democratic members of Congress, very troubled in procedural terms by the outcome, in spite of some disclaimers regarding the "buying of a victory." What was at stake was literally the prestige of the presidency in the conduct of foreign policy. Moreover, the NAFTA vote would determine whether momentum would continue in terms of trade liberalization on the part of the United States, and by extension to some degree throughout the international system. A lot was riding on this vote. No member of the Democratic congressional majority misunderstood this reality.

The answer to the riddle of why a Democratic president passed a Republican trade initiative was that this was probably the only way the initiative could have passed in a period when North America was still slowly climbing out of a recession and when all trade initiatives were looked upon by voters with suspicion. In fact, many Democratic members of Congress quietly voted against NAFTA, and against their president, knowing that in the last analysis the agreement would pass with the polite help from the apparently loyal Republican opposition. In Congress a vote is not always just a vote. One must look behind the vote to comprehend its meaning. So goes policy making in the U.S. House of Representatives.

U.S. View of Trade Liberalization

Americans in the late twentieth century view trade with some unanimity of understanding, despite the split in the NAFTA vote. They tend to see openness of economy in two ways. First they understand something about the *level* or degree of openness. They believe economies can be ranked in terms of this level of openness, encompassing both tariff and non-tariff barriers. They instinctively believe, without any extensive data to back up the belief, that the U.S. economy in the post-1945 period was one of the most open major economies, if not the most open in the world, with respect to both trade and investment.

Secondly, Americans are aware of the *change* in level or degree of openness of each economy. Here there is some pessimism. On the one hand, some of the most closed economies in the system, such as those of Japan, France, and China, have made an effort, usually in the face of considerable outside pressure, to change the level of openness – that is, to open up. But this change has been slow, and in some cases marked by back-sliding. The various rounds of tariff talks have benefited everyone, in the opinion of most Americans, including certainly themselves. But they are quite sceptical about what has been left out of the negotiations. They are also worried about the "new protectionism," which they equate with the problems many of their firms are having in exporting into Japan and other Asian countries and in locating foreign investment in Japan. In short, they see very closed economies, with which they must intensely compete, opening up some, but in an overall sense not nearly to the level of openness of their own economy.

On the other hand, Americans are aware that their economy has slipped in the opposite direction toward greater protectionism. In automobiles, textiles, and steel, for example, they acknowledge the use of trade barriers. The same is true for agricultural goods, including, for example, sugar. In some of these industries, such as automobiles, striking improvements have also occurred, largely because of the beneficial aspects of foreign competition. For instance, 80 percent of the respondents in a recent survey argue that the quality of North American cars has improved.[1] But, despite their own increases in productivity, Americans see a decided loss of share for their own firms in some eight major manufacturing industries.[2] In sum, they know that change in the U.S. economy has been toward greater protectionism. Overall, however, they continue to believe that there is a large gap between the level of openness of their own economy and that of some of their most significant competitors.

How accurate are these American perceptions about their own economy and about those of others? Regarding comparisons across entire economies, including both tariff and non-tariff barriers, empirical analyses are hard to find. Industry-by-industry comparisons are much more common. In agriculture, for instance, the American view is essentially borne out. Although heavily subsidized, like most agricultural sectors in other countries, American farming is less heavily subsidized than that of many countries—including Switzerland, Japan, France, Germany, and Canada—but more subsidized than that of Holland or Denmark. While the United States is the leading exporter of merchandise and commercial services in the world (considering Europe country-by-country), it stands to gain less from the Uruguay Round of tariff talks than the European Union (EU), China, or Japan over the next ten years.[3] But this disparity can be looked at in a couple of different ways.

First, everybody *does* gain from tariff liberalization, including the United States and Canada. That is the most important and self-evident point. Secondly, the fact that others gain more than the United States probably reinforces the point made above (and already believed by Americans) that the United States is the more open economy. Since it is already more open, less is demanded of it in tariff liberalization, but it also obtains somewhat less in terms of benefits. But the really critical point, and the one that escapes most Americans about themselves (as well as most Canadians about themselves), is that the United States has probably gained more in absolute terms since 1945 in terms of economic growth and wealth than have other countries precisely because it has been the most open large economy. That is the argument made by free traders, ignored by "fair" traders, and reinforced by both the size and wealth of the U.S. economy at century's end.

The logic of lowering tariffs for one's own good is fast disappearing from the American mentality. What is now standard is the view that there must be strict reciprocity regardless of the size of an economy, and only slightly qualified in the case of a far less developed economy such as that of Mexico. The sad truth is that this new American "toughness," or perhaps "shortsightedness," is due almost solely to its experience with Japan and with the other Asian economies following the Japanese developmental model. The feeling is that subsidies, predatory pricing, constrained imports, and targeting abetted by governments have created a whole new type of economic competition, neo-mercantilism. The resulting change in attitude toward free trade in the United States is palpable both on the political left and the right. Without the FTA or NAFTA, Canada would surely have been caught in the wake of these new trade perceptions in the United States.

Voluntary Export Restraints, Anti-Dumping and Countervailing Duties

According to I.M. Destler, a curious pattern on trade emerged for the United States in the 1980s.[4] In Congress, it was a period of trade activism, with Super 301 legislation on the books,[5] the provision of anti-dumping and countervailing duty legislation, and much rhetoric. Notwithstanding some Canadian perceptions to the contrary, there is little evidence of direct congressional imposition of trade barriers, according to Destler. However, Hufbauer shows that the percentage of U.S. imports covered by quantitative restraints increased from 12 in 1980 to 21 in 1984.[6] The softwood lumber case was also a watershed in that for the first time Canada alone was targeted within a trade action. Three observations follow from this empirical assessment.

First, most of this increase in restraints on imports occurred in the area of voluntary export restraints (VERs) on automobiles and textiles. The use of anti-dumping duties contributed to the total as well. Most other imports continued to be unaffected by significant trade barriers. Secondly, when translated from VER to tariff-equivalents, the resulting tariffs are high, in the range of 24 percent.[7] Those who think that VERs and other "non-tariff barriers" are trivial in their impact ought to reconsider. Thirdly, NAFTA has turned the automobile and textile quotas into region-wide restrictions, even upping the protectionism involved, and making it equally available to Canada and to Mexico. Canada is not outside this most extensive form (exclusive of agriculture) of protectionism in North America, but rather is a full participant. For example, Canada, like the United States and Mexico, "benefits from" the increase in the domestic content requirement for automobile manufacture from 50 percent to 62.5 percent. As a result Canadians, like others, must pay a lot more for cars.

Although between 1986 and 1990 there was a decided drop in U.S. anti-dumping cases, the trend reversed itself again between 1990 and 1993. Could these numbers be correlated with the business cycle? My rough impression is that such a correlation does exist, operating in opposite ways in the United States and

Canada. Economic nationalism is stronger in the United States in hard times, less so during booms. Economic nationalism is more vigorous in Canada during boom times, less so during recession.

Contentious bilateral issues on both sides of the border are numerous. Softwood lumber, fish, pork, steel, and wheat are only the most familiar. Two generalities are possible. What remains the same is the frequency with which these issues are raised over time and the sameness of their identity. What has changed is that many are included under the dispute resolution panel provisions such that Canadian as well as U.S. nationals are able to evaluate the grounds for the conflicts dispassionately. Success is measured not in the restricted number of such disputes, because few seem to be deterred, but in the manner of their resolution.

The number of U.S. anti-dumping cases is on average higher than for the European Union, or the developing countries as a group. What can be said about this American propensity to rely on anti-dumping duties? Several things. First, anti-dumping can be either a valid or an invalid action. That means that unless it is clear that the actual number of cases of dumping has increased or decreased in a period, little can be determined about the legitimacy of the anti-dumping response. Secondly, the United States *is* an attractive area for dumping in a way that many other countries are not. Why? The American economy is large, rich, and open. In addition, it has become the battleground for market share, particularly between Japanese and U.S. companies. Predatory pricing and dumping are considered prime vehicles for waging this war, especially vis-à-vis weakened industries and poorly financed firms. Thirdly, undoubtedly much anti-dumping action is a response without an authentic stimulus. In other words, the U.S. government is often under domestic pressure to use this form of trade action whether or not there is a severe, verifiable cause in the form of unfair trade practice.

The Problem of Subsidy Definitions

In the aftermath of the NAFTA victory in the U.S. Congress, the special deal cut between the Chrétien government and the Clinton administration to study the matter of subsidies over a two-year period reminds the analyst of the five- to seven-year period set aside by the FTA for the same purpose, with very few results so far.

GATT also is likely to take another look at the problem. A number of aspects of this problem seem ready for timely resolution.

First, everything else being equal, the definition of subsidies is a problem that ought to receive analytic attention by scholars and be laid to rest in policy terms. Lack of agreement here is causing a lot of tension in Canada-U.S. trade relations and elsewhere.

Secondly, the definition of a subsidy is not an easy technical problem to dispense with either in terms of which items to call subsidies, what level of support to equate with subsidy, or how to measure effective damage as the result of an alleged subsidy. The temptation will be for the United States to want to define a few areas, conditions, or levels as free of subsidy, thus leaving the bulk of the trade jurisdiction open to unilateral interpretation — as it is at present. The opposite temptation of many other countries will be to try to define a few subsidies and exclude everything else from the definition. Therefore the approach to definition will require careful planning.

Finally, no one should underestimate the politicization of this topic, especially at a time when (a) the United States feels that it has given up an unprecedented amount of sovereignty in establishing the binational and tri-national trade dispute resolution panels, and (b) GATT has a backlog of cases in which individual countries have refused to adhere to the rulings of GATT panels, thus suggesting a widespread breakdown of authority in the multilateral realm and more incentive for the United States and other countries to seek unilateral trade remedies.

Many free traders feel that subsidies are a kind of gift offered by the country that is providing the subsidy. The judgment is that the real loser is the country that provides the subsidy, not the country whose firms face competition from foreign subsidies. I do not believe that is the way workers and firms facing subsidized competition feel, even though consumers may benefit greatly. Thus the matter of the definition of subsidies is of significance for empirical research and policy analysis and will receive considerable public scrutiny.

Regionalism and Globalism Combined

Regionalism and globalism are becoming intermixed. The FTA and NAFTA launched the region toward partnership in a way not imagined twenty years ago and, indeed, vigorously rejected only ten years ago. If Chile becomes partner to the NAFTA, as seems likely, the Enterprise for the Americas will in effect be very much alive. The North American Accord idea elicited only criticism from Ottawa and Mexico City in 1980. One of the political paradoxes is that a NAFTA would probably have been easier to accept in Canada in 1988 than a trade-investment deal only with the United States. Yet when the Canada-U.S. arrangement was envisaged, NAFTA was barely a gleam in the eye of the Mexican government. How trade perspectives can change in a few brief years!

Likewise, the successful conclusion of the Uruguay Round assures that regionalism will not predominate. Not only will multilateral free trade move forward in a way that all of the leading political parties have preferred, including the governing Liberal party, but the benefits of regionalism and globalism also reinforce each other. Regional groupings are much less likely to become inward-looking. The spontaneity and innovation of the regional initiatives, however (for example, in the area of dispute resolution), tend to carry over to the larger multilateral effort.

What we are seeing in trade liberalization is really a two-track set of achievements. Global and regional free trade is converging. Progress on national treatment for foreign investors and more open trade for all firms promises to accelerate world growth once again after several years of stagnation. How will Canada fare? As a major trading nation, Canada will be at the top of the beneficiaries. Little known in Canada, especially at a time of 11 percent unemployment, is that throughout the 1980s Canada marched at a pace of 4 percent real annual gross domestic product (GDP) growth, among Organization for Economic Cooperation and Development (OECD) countries second only to Japan, its 4.5 percent not much higher. The average for the OECD was about 2.3 percent. Once again with an opening trading system, Canada will prosper, notwithstanding its aggravated debt burden. Access to the U.S. market, now triply guaranteed, is no small part of this export-led prosperity.

Some Problems

Yet, despite all of these attractive trade and investment possibilities, some problems do lurk on the commercial and financial horizon.

Tariff Reduction Matched by Non-Tariff Increases

On one level, world trade has been freed up through multilateral tariff reduction on a grand scale since 1945. This welcome result has fired economic growth in both the industrial and developing worlds. Where economic growth has been fastest, the growth in external trade has been fastest as well. And where the growth of external trade has been most pronounced, economic growth of states has benefited most. Observe this complex causal relationship in Asia today. Not to be "in Asia" in the 1990s is not to participate in the most rapid set of growth opportunities world-wide.

Conversely, this happy co-variance between economic growth and external trade is also offset, or hindered, or potentially reversed in some parts of the world, by an equally potent and much more subtle phenomenon called the rise of the "new protectionism."[8] The new protectionism is in large part composed of non-tariff barriers and governmental actions (when abused), such as the use of voluntary export restraints and anti-dumping policies. While the Uruguay Round, for example, stresses the importance of "transparency"—that is, the conversion of these more subtle trade constraints to measurable and reducible quantities such as tariff-equivalents—the universe of the non-tariff barrier is huge and diabolic indeed.

For purposes of debate, this chapter raises a twofold question. Do we really know on a global basis, for all tradeable goods, services, and commodities, over a sufficiently long time period, whether non-tariff barriers are a serious problem? Not the least of the problem is in defining what constitutes a "non-tariff barrier," and separating it from cultural biases such as an apparently inescapable Japanese prejudice against "foreignness" in products and even in corporate stocks on the Tokyo Stock Exchange. And secondly, has the admitted rise in the use of non-tariff barriers significantly offset the gains to world trade through tariff reduction achieved over the last twenty years? Hidden in this question is whether this offset to trade liberalization is one-sided, occurring systematically against the importation of goods by some countries relative to others, or whether the new protectionism has been pursued as the result of conscious governmental action. Subsidies may be the most pronounced but least harmful instrument here.

Insofar as this problem of a reversal of trade liberalization by the use of non-tariff barriers has validity, the tendencies may be reflected in trends of a decade or more.[9] During the liberalization period tariffs do come down and trade does pick up. When non-tariff barriers are used, obstacles hinder trade movement, and the growth in international trade stagnates.

Clearly, in North America the NAFTA puts the region on the trade-inducing side of this trend line. Tariffs are still coming down. Mexico and its trading partners stand to benefit greatly in terms of the resulting increased volume and value of trade. But beware the second phenomenon. For NAFTA to have a lasting impact on trade patterns, the three countries will need to resist the enticements of the second trend—namely, the rise of the new protectionism. This task may be much tougher than is revealed by the admirable achievement of tariff reduction, liberalized market access in some service areas, and nascent roll-back of subsidies.

Liberalization (Federal) Plus Restriction (State and Provincial)

A similarly troublesome tendency is to negotiate well-meaning and even significant reductions to trade barriers at the federal level in each country, but to encourage, or at least not discourage, barriers at the sub-state level.

A full codification of barriers to interstate trade in the United States has not yet been catalogued, but limited studies are available. The picture is not heartening. Particularly in the ardent pursuit of foreign investment, the sub-units not only try to outbid foreign governments but they also end up struggling to outbid other sub-units in the host economy. The resulting loss of tax revenue and the distortion of investment decisions is large. Canada has belatedly attempted to reduce inter-provincial trade barriers to create the "Canadian Common Market," a phrase that rings with irony. The practices in Quebec in terms of energy subsidies and investment restrictions, for example, make knowledgeable business people wonder how deep the avowed commitment on the part of all Quebec political parties is to pursue North American free trade.[10] Even more interesting is whether trade between Quebec and the other provinces has been in a net sense liberalized or impeded in the last decade. Mexico faces some of the same problems with the Maquiladora industries which, paradoxically, have hurt the growth of foreign investment in other parts of Mexico that, in the absence of the artificiality of the special trade area, would be even more propitious locations for economic development.

In some ways the role of the sub-units in opposing freer movement of goods and capital is the counterpart of the rise of the new protectionism. Each tendency reinforces the other. Trying to reduce barriers to services was once described by a Canadian business person as the "equivalent of nailing jelly to the wall." This homey analogy contains a dual simile. First, services in some cases are as difficult to delineate and to define concretely as jelly is to handle.[11] Secondly, services liberalization is as difficult to facilitate as jelly is to "nail down." Problems of trade liberalization will only be multiplied by allowing more and more impediments to slip under the table, and into units of authority that are able to escape surveillance and enforcement.

A New North America

In some ways, NAFTA can be seen to usher in a new interval of history in North America. In other ways, a new interval of history has ushered in NAFTA. The distinction scarcely matters. At the turn of the twenty-first century, North America is as different in economic and political terms as the world is in security terms after the Cold War. Universal approaches to free trade, and regional approaches, meet in a dual impact.

Political Decentralization and Sub-Federal Economic Development

As the pressures of the arms race and of East-West rivalry seem for the moment to decline (or even to disappear entirely), not to be replaced by any other similarly dangerous threat, the imperatives of economics rise to the surface of policy consciousness. As trade and commerce become relatively more important, a unique structural change is occurring within states everywhere. Political decentralization, accompanied by localized economic development, is happening everywhere at once. These trends are evident in the make-up of modern Germany with many centres of economic power. This pattern is occurring in Europe as a whole, as the centres of prosperity are scattered across the map from Milan to Dusseldorf, and from south of London to north of Paris. The same trend is evident in the United States, as the unchallenged dominance of New York City yields to California, Texas, Chicago, Florida, and even Tennessee. Mexico begins to split its development among Mexico City, the northern states, and the coastal port cities. Canada is not alone in its regionalism, or in its pattern of development in Montreal, Toronto, Calgary, and Vancouver, to name only a few focal points.

The trend as stated is dual-faceted. Political power is drifting downward to the states, provinces, and even cities. The federal governments are more and more tax-gatherers and revenue-distributors. They process cheques. But they do not control the destinies of the nation-state in other than a security sense, which, rightly or wrongly, now gets less attention. Sub-federal units even in a country as federally oriented as the United States, or as politically centralized as Mexico, now can make demands on federal policy and assume power over peoples only imagined earlier in the century.

In the United States it is interesting to see how shared the presidency has been among the different regions of the country. Truman and Eisenhower came from the mid-West but in many ways were a legacy of an earlier America that was more national. Kennedy was the first post-war "regional" president, self-consciously representing Massachusetts and New England. Johnson cannot be separated from Texas. Nixon and Reagan represented the power of California. Carter symbolized the new "Deep South" as much as Ford was a mid-Westerner and Bush a transplanted Easterner to Texas. Clinton is of the newly industrializing upper South, once the centre of poverty and cultural self-abnegation, now the centre of the opposites. Moreover, each president used the region from whence he came to help finance his road to the Oval Office. The region in turn attempted to benefit from the ascendancy of its "native son" to the presidency.

Economics has underpinned political decentralization.[12] Each major country now is composed of multiple growth centres. Recessions can strike one part of each country without hampering others. Booms, whether because of energy, or because of microcomputers, can affect one or more regions without impinging directly on others.

NAFTA once again highlights the regional character of these countries. California and Texas are far more supportive of the agreement, notwithstanding Ross Perot, than Maine or Michigan. Quebec and Alberta like NAFTA a lot more than southern Ontario or Manitoba. Economic fears and hopes explain these politics.

Finally, international trade and commerce are contributing to the decentralization of power and authority throughout the international system. As the formal boundaries to trade and commerce come down, the natural centres of development and comparative advantage become more readily accessible to the firm. External trade also forces urban areas and sub-state actors to compete more vigorously with each other. Linkages between "sister cities," once thought empty examples of civic boosterism, do symbolize the decentralized and globalized character of the modern nation-state.

In North America the nation-state is finding that in many ways it can operate more efficiently in an era of compounding deficits by leaving authority at the local level.[13] Just as elementary school systems are learning to benefit from decentralization and greater autonomy, so entire state economies are recognizing the benefits of deregulation and privatization. Each benefits from decentralization of political authority and contributes to that decentralization. International trade liberalization prospers in a world where deregulation and privatization can occur. Changes in world trade are thus eroding some of the pillars of economic dominance within states, and spreading out wealth and jobs across a wider range of locales than ever before. Trade is truly subverting the centralized dominance of nation-state governments. Democracy thrives.

Investment-driven Trade and Cross-border Growth

Although economic theory has not kept up with international trade reality, a strange thing is occurring in the real world of international goods and services. The multinational corporation is shaping the pathways of international trade more and more. "Managed trade" by democratic governments is made difficult and perhaps unnecessary by the management already provided by the multinational firm.

Given that more and more international trade is intra-industry and intra-firm trade, the distinction between trade and investment is blurring.[14] With this blurring, the question of how economic growth is shaped by trade is less a mystery. Governments now recognize, if the theorists do not, that economic growth requires trade, and significant trade demands investment, both foreign and domestic.

Thus NAFTA becomes a tool of economic growth because it permits a greater amount of cross-border investment, which in turn will lead to forward and backward commercial linkages. That cross-border investment will also speed trade up and down the intra-firm and intra-industry passageways, almost as though the international borders between each pair of countries did not exist, is also self-evident. Not only will North American trade thrive because of greater economies of scale, but this trade will also prosper because of the rapidly expanding cross-border commercial linkages.

The firm will not move its entire operations south or north, creating problems for countries. It will establish facilities and operations in all three countries, spreading its presence according to a specialization of function at the local level. By encompassing widely different areas of comparative advantage within a single, large geographic region, the amount of growth and development that will occur in North America in consequence is much greater than most modellers assume. NAFTA will create within North America a facsimile of the world. As North America decentralizes, the rich complexity of this huge market, led by investment-driven trade, will help translate the cross-border economy into a new type of international regional economy of the twenty-first century.

10

Open Regionalism: East Asia Sets the Pace

Wendy Dobson

UNTIL THE END OF THE COLD WAR, Canadians, like other Westerners, took their standard of living for granted. Competition among Europe, the United States, and the centrally planned economies posed a security, but not an economic, threat. The end of the Cold War in 1990 changed all that. Economic tensions among the "tripolar" economies of the United States, Japan, and Europe began to supersede security issues at the top of their agendas as growing parity in economic clout transformed their economic relations. Increasing interdependence created spillovers of economic policies and performance from one economy to its neighbours. Challenges of interdependence are important to Canadians, but the emergence of significant new sources of competition in Asia, including the emergence of China, are making rapid inroads into future prospects for the Canadian economy. To protect their living standards, Canadians must become innovative and adept at international business — they must be forward- and outward-looking. The recently elected Liberal government must foster a domestic environment conducive to doing international business and should seek to play a leading role in the Pacific, where East Asia is setting the pace.

Today, the dynamism of the East Asian economies[1] and the emergence of China as a major economic power are transforming the shape of the slow-growing world economy. East Asia's economies are growing much faster than the rest of the world. Recent estimates from the United Nations and the International Monetary Fund, using purchasing power parity measures, imply that the world's three largest economies lie in the Pacific. By these measures, China's economy, accounting for 6 percent of world

---

This paper draws on Dobson's recently published *Japan in East Asia: Trading and Investment Strategies*, published by the Institute of Southeast Asian Studies in Singapore. Research support is acknowledged from the Pacific 2000 program of External Affairs and from the Ontario Centre for International Business.

gross domestic product (GDP), is the world's third-largest after the United States and Japan which, respectively, account for 22 and 7.6 percent of world GDP.[2]

These profound shifts in economic relations are creating fluidity and uncertainty about the future of the liberal trading order. Amidst concerns about the shift to a more competitive and possibly more protectionist trading environment, movements in East Asia toward "open regionalism," whereby governments have reduced trade barriers unilaterally to foster the fast growth which is binding these economies together, are providing a powerful offset. This chapter begins with a summary of the patterns of trade and development in the larger Asia Pacific region, which will be termed the "APEC region."[3] It then focuses on four economic developments which are shaping the region and will determine the future of open regionalism. The first factor is the economic integration of the East Asian economies through growing trade and investment ties. United States' economic policy is the second factor, specifically negotiation of the North American Free Trade Agreement (NAFTA) and the evolution of U.S.-Japanese economic relations. In my view, East Asian concerns about NAFTA as a North American trading bloc are overblown. More important will be how Japan and the United States manage bilateral tensions over their continuing savings-investment imbalance and increasing American impatience to open up the Japanese market. The third factor is China's transformation into an economic powerhouse. This development is highly significant because of China's sheer size and the importance of its evolving relations with Japan and the United States and how China will define its global role. The fourth factor, which serves as an important backdrop to these structural developments, is the fact that the rest of the world will be expanding much more slowly. When growth slows down, frictions arise. It is during those times that investments in mechanisms for managing interdependence pay off. Finally, implications of these trends for Canadians are examined.

Patterns of Trade and Investment

As Table 1 illustrates, the value of trade across the Pacific more than doubled between 1980 and 1990. At the same time, the value of intra-East Asian trade has grown faster — from a 27 percent to

Table 1
Intra-Pacific Trade, 1980 and 1990

	1980	1990
1. Intra-Pacific trade		
(billions of US$)	378.0	939.3
2. Intra-North American trade		
Dollar value (billions)	102.0	230.0
Share of (1), percent	27.0	24.5
3. Intra-East Asian trade		
Dollar value (billions)	100.7	286.3
Share of (1), percent	27.0	30.5
4. Trade between North America and East Asia		
Dollar value (billions)	118.6	326.0
Share of (1), percent	31.4	34.7

Source: Hadi Soesastro, "Implications of the Post-Cold War Politico-Security Environment on the Pacific Economy," in C. Fred Bergsten and Marcus Noland, eds., *Pacific Dynamism and the Internatinal Economic System* (Washington, D.C.: Institute for International Economics, 1933), p. 382.

more than a 30 percent share of the total—while the share in the regional total of trade within North America has fallen sharply. But trade between East Asia and North America has also continued to be a major source of dynamism, growing from a 31 percent to a nearly 35 percent share of intra-Pacific trade.

The importance of North America to the East Asian economies (excluding the former socialist economies) is evident in Chart 1, which lays out the destination of exports and origins of imports into those economies. Exports from the newly industrializing economies (NIEs) are particularly dependent on the United States and other industrialized countries because of demand for their increasingly knowledge-intensive products; Association of South East Asian Nations (ASEAN) economies are also dependent on these markets for their more labour-intensive products. Japan, by contrast, has not grown much as an export market for products from the NIEs, and has declined over the decade of the 1980s as a market for ASEAN exports. While the United States has retained its share of imports into the NIEs, Japan's share has sharply declined; the reverse is true in the ASEAN economies.

Chart 1

Direction of Trade, ASEAN and NIEs with U.S., Japan and rest of the World 1980 and 1990 (shares, percent)

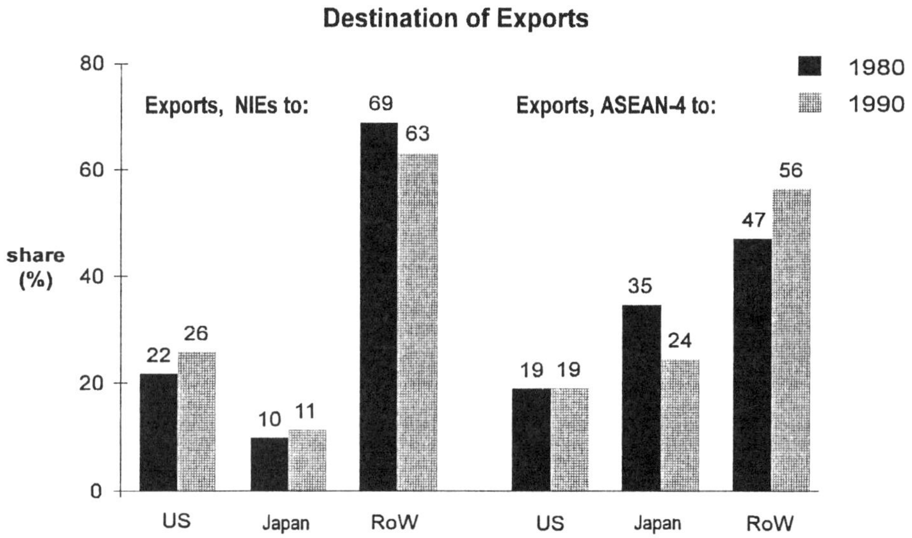

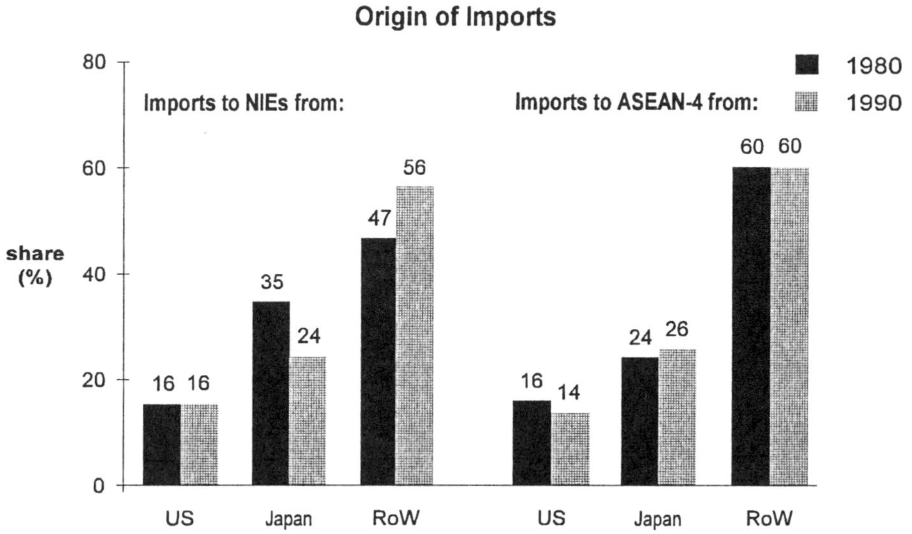

Note: NIEs does not include Taiwan.

Source: IMF, *Direction of Trade Statistics Yearbook* (various years).

Table 2
Stocks of Foreign Direct Investment in APEC Economies
1980 and 1990 (% shares)

Home: / Host:	Year	Canada	North America	Japan	China	NIEs	ASEAN	ANZ	APEC Total
United States[a]	1980	14.6	14.6	5.7	0.0	0.1	0.1	0.5	21.0
	1993	6.9	6.9	20.7	0.0	0.6	0.0	2.1	30.0
Canada[a]	1980	n/a	78.6	1.0	n/a	0.0	n/a	0.1	79.7
	1990	n/a	64.2	3.4	n/a	0.0	n/a	2.2	71.1
Japan[b]	1980	2.6	56.7	n/a	n/a	3.1	n/a	n/a	59.8
	1990	1.8	48.3	n/a	n/a	0.0	n/a	n/a	48.3
Brunei[b]	n/a	n/a	n/a	n/a	n/a	n/a	n/a	n/a	n/a
	n/a	n/a	n/a	n/a	n/a	n/a	n/a	n/a	n/a
China[b]	1984	2.0	25.1	5.8	n/a	52.6	0.4	2.5	86.4
	1987	1.3	17.1	7.2	n/a	58.2	0.7	1.2	84.4
Chinese Taipei[b]	1980	n/a	35.0	18.6	n/a	12.4	15.5	n/a	81.5
	1988	n/a	32.1	27.1	n/a	10.9	13.0	n/a	93.1
Hong Kong[d]	1984	0.3	54.1	21.0	n/a	2.9	3.1	1.6	82.7
	1989	0.7	32.1	29.9	n/a	2.1	2.4	3.7	80.5
Indonesia[b]	1980	0.1	4.4	33.7	n/a	11.6	0.7	2.6	53.0
	1988	n/a	5.8	18.4	3.3	10.8	0.2	1.4	39.9
Malaysia[f]	1981	0.4	6.8	17.6	n/a	36.4	0.2	3.0	64.0
	1987	1.2	7.4	20.1	n/a	35.1	2.2	3.0	67.8
Philippines[c]	1980	3.9	58.5	16.8	n/a	5.5	0.0	2.4	83.2
	1999	1.1	56.8	14.5	n/a	9.4	0.4	1.8	82.9
Republic of Korea[c]	1980	0.0	19.6	60.5	n/a	1.8	n/a	0.0	82.1
	1988	0.0	27.7	52.0	n/a	3.5	n/a	0.0	83.2
Singapore[e]	1980	n/a	29.6	16.8	n/a	n/a	n/a	n/a	46.3
	1989	n/a	33.2	30.7	n/a	n/a	n/a	n/a	63.9
Thailand[c]	1980	−0.3	32.5	29.0	0.0	18.4	1.6	0.6	82.1
	1988	0.3	24.5	36.7	0.4	20.5	0.6	0.6	83.3
Australia[g]	1980	2.5	42.7	6.3	n/a	1.4	n/a	0.8	51.2
	1991	3.0	29.9	16.2	n/a	0.7	n/a	4.5	51.3
New Zealand[c]	1980	20.8	20.8	n/a	n/a	n/a	n/a	28.5	49.3
	1985	13.6	18.6	2.6	n/a	n/a	n/a	37.7	58.9

Data for this entry has been computed:

[a] on a balance of payments basis
[b] using cumulated flows of approved FDI
[c] using cumulated realized flows
[d] using estimates of book value
[e] using gross fixed assets in the secondary industry
[f] using values of net assets of foreign controlled companies
[g] using data on foreign ownership (10% or more)

Source: Derived from United Nations Centre on Transnational Corporations, *World Investment Directory*, vol. I: *Asia and the Pacific*, and vol. III: *Developing Countries*, 1992.

Direct investment patterns in the Asia Pacific Economic Cooperation (APEC) region are summarized in the matrix in Table 2. There are several notable features of these patterns. In the cases of China, the Republic of Korea, Hong Kong, Chinese Taipei (Taiwan), Thailand, and the Philippines, more than 80 percent of their outward foreign direct investment (FDI) is located in the APEC region. A second feature of these patterns is the increasing diversity of sources of FDI in the fast-growing East Asian economies. In the late 1980s stocks of North American FDI exceeded Japanese stocks in Hong Kong, Singapore, Chinese Taipei, the Philippines, and China, while Japanese stocks were higher in Korea, Indonesia, and Malaysia. Available data show that newly industrializing economies, particularly Hong Kong and Taiwan, have become important sources of FDI in China, Malaysia, and Thailand. In the early 1990s Taiwan was the top source of FDI in Malaysia and Indonesia, and the second-most important source in China.[4]

A third notable feature of investment patterns in the APEC region is the asymmetry between Japan's position as a major home country for FDI and its position as a host. In 1992, by United Nations estimates, Japan's stock of inward FDI was one-fifteenth its stock of outward FDI. Various explanations are that Japan has traditionally relied on licensing of technology rather than on inward direct investment; merger and acquisition activities are difficult to implement; and practices of cross-shareholding contribute to difficulties. Nevertheless, UN statistics show that FDI inflows to Japan in the first half of 1992 were double those in the same period in 1991, in part because of the decline in acquisition costs of Japanese firms. Changes in Japanese government practices to boost inward investment are also having a positive effect.[5] To the extent that trade and direct investment are complementary, the limited direct investment in Japan may be a factor in that country's trade surplus.

The rising activity of the East Asian economies as inward and outward investors and related closer economic integration and dynamism are affecting the shape of the APEC region.

Economic Integration in East Asia

It is common to identify two characteristics of East Asian integration: integration is firm-driven; and it occurs spontaneously without formal intergovernmental negotiations to reduce trade barriers. Drysdale and Garnaut use these characteristics to define a Pacific "model" of integration.[6] These are also the characteristics that define open regionalism.

The trade and investment flows that are driving East Asian intra-regional integration are firm-driven; indeed, it is commonly perceived that Japanese production dominates the region. Yet American firms have also been top investors, as, increasingly, have firms from Korea, Taiwan, Hong Kong, Singapore, and Thailand. In the late 1980s, inflows of Japanese investment were very large — much larger than U.S. flows, which were drying up. These flows were adding to a rather small *stock* of investment compared to the existing U.S. stock. By 1990 the distributions of shares of stocks of Japanese and U.S. investment across economies and industries were quite similar (see Charts 2 and 3).[7] The largest shares of these stocks were found in non-manufacturing activities, reflecting resource-seeking investments, and the more recent growth in services investment in Hong Kong and Singapore (reflecting the need to be close to the customer).

While economic integration has occurred without formal intergovernmental negotiations, trade and investment flows have been influenced by public policies. Both home and host government behaviour can be considered to be "strategic" in their impact on the production location decisions of foreign investors. Home government policies are most evident in Japan's Official Development Assistance (ODA) policies insofar as these are used as instruments to reduce the costs to firms of producing abroad. Host government policies, on the other hand, while aimed at capturing the benefits of foreign investment for the host economy, also act as locational incentives. In pursuit of their growth and development goals, governments bid for investment that is already headed for the region, often in economically wasteful ways.

Host governments in the region use two types of policies to influence investment decisions: investment-related trade measures (IRTM), and strategic investment policies.[8] The IRTMs that have been introduced in Malaysia, Thailand, Taiwan, and the Philippines have emphasized export-processing zones (EPZs) and free-trade zones (FTZs), where foreign firms receive duty-free imports and financial incentives if they export all or most of their production. More recently there has been a tendency to link trade

Chart 2
Accumulated Outward FDI from Japan to Eight Asian Economies
1980 and 1990

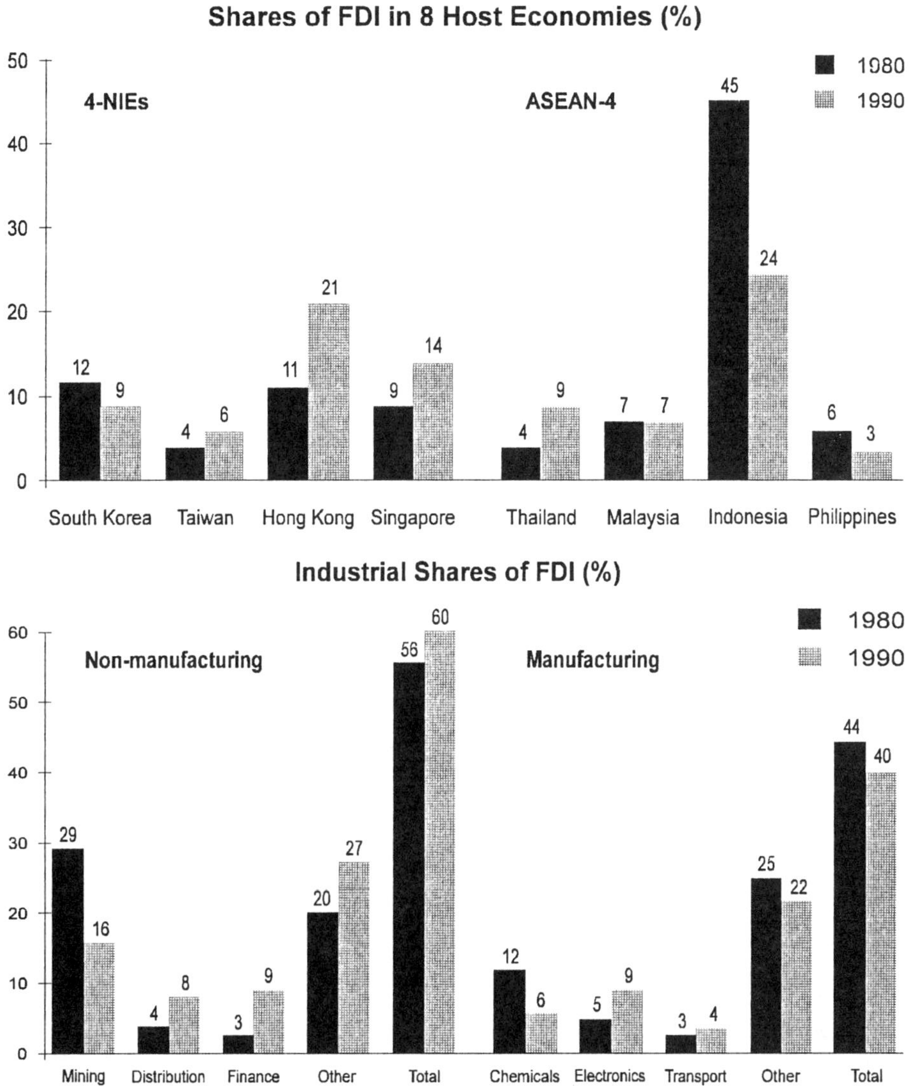

Source: MOF, Japan, "Zaisei Kinyi Tokei Geppo." December 1991: 30, 31, 56 and 57.
Note: Industry shares for total Asia were used because the eight Asian economies were not broken out by industry in "Zaisei Kinyu Tokei Geggo." These shares are close approximations since the eight Asian economies accounted for 98 percent of Japan's FDI to the region in 1980, and 93 percent in 1990.

Chart 3
Stocks of Outward FDI from the United States to Eight Asian Economies
1980 and 1990

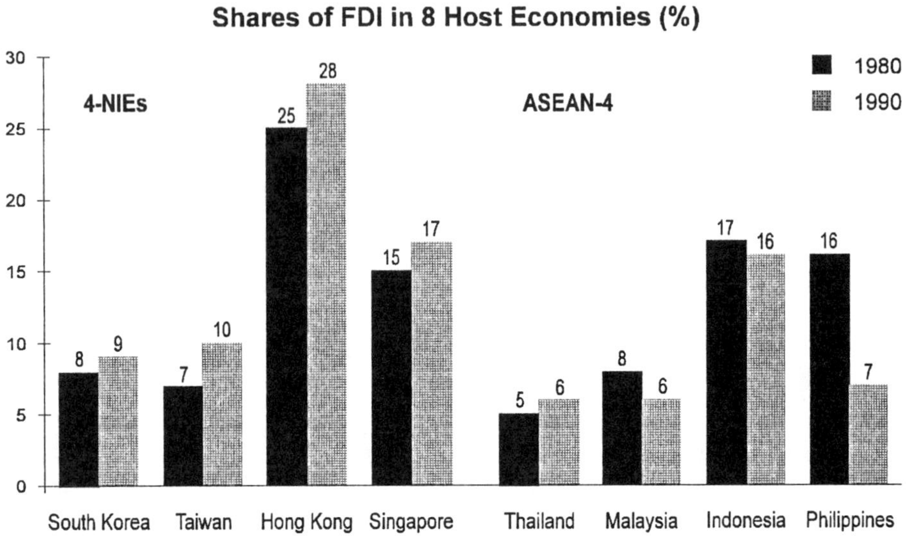

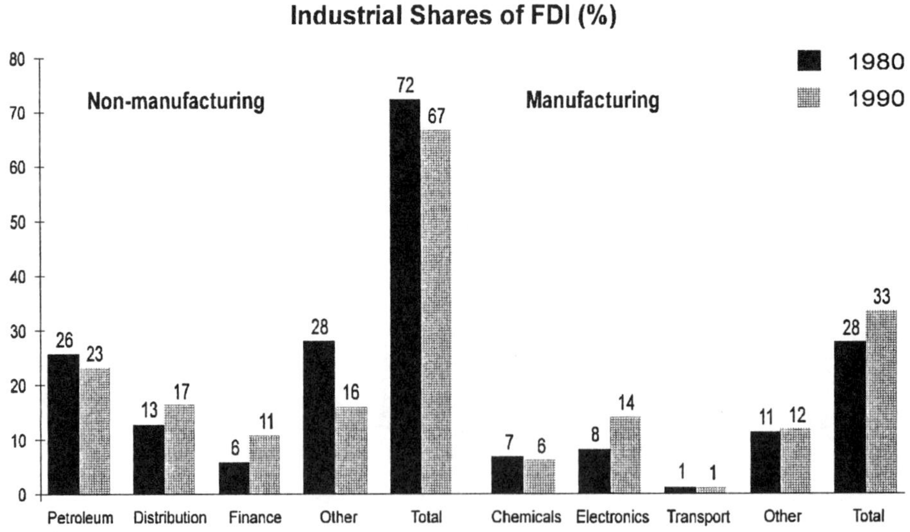

Source: U.S. Dept. of Commerce, Bureau of Economic Analysis, *Survey of Current Business* (Aug. 1981: Table 12, p. 32 and Aug. 1991: Table 11.3, p. 88.

measures and performance requirements in order to achieve certain policy targets.

Strategic investment policies have also been widely used. Foreign investors in Taiwan are eligible for tax breaks if they export most of their production and/or meet local content requirements. Malaysia has targeted such industries as agriculture and forestry and their associated processing industries, chemicals and pharmaceuticals, textiles, electrical parts and components, where trade-offs can be made between local ownership and content requirements and export targets.[9] Singapore uses financial incentives to encourage multinationals to use the island as their regional headquarters for management, information, and R&D activities. Through its Local Industry Upgrading Program (LIUP), Singapore also provides organizational support and financial incentives to encourage the electronics industry to work with local suppliers to upgrade their technological capabilities and product quality. Some ASEAN-wide policies also affect decisions of multinationals, which are enumerated elsewhere.[10]

United States Economic Policy

United States economic policy is the second influence shaping the APEC region. As the world's dominant economic power, the United States provided hegemonic leadership for most of the postwar period. With the rise to parity of Japan and the European Community the United States has lost its pre-eminent position. In addition, the economic successes of the "follower" economies in East Asia have heightened a sense of unease among Americans about imminent economic decline. Both domestic and international economic policies are inward-looking. Yet its economic partners have argued that the international economic position of the United States is largely determined by more than a decade of poor domestic economic management associated with consumption rather than investment in productivity-enhancing human and physical capital.

American trade policy now follows several tracks: multilateral, plurilateral, and bilateral rules-based trade policies, and unilateral "results-oriented" policy. The trade relationship with Japan is being conducted as unilateral trade policy, while NAFTA is an example of a plurilateral arrangement.

The North American Free Trade Agreement

When NAFTA was originally proposed, many Asians regarded it as a threatening trading bloc which would lead to a "Fortress North America" comparable to Fortress Europe. The sense of threat was based on a misunderstanding of the fact that a free trade area involves the reduction of internal barriers only, not the erection of a common external barrier. Indeed, I believe NAFTA should be seen primarily as a Mexican government initiative to improve Mexico's economic prospects by managing its asymmetric economic relationship with the United States.[11] President Salinas sought and achieved assured access to the U.S. market at a time when American fair trade remedies could capriciously disrupt or restrict such access. He also sought to encourage the return of flight capital and to prevent the possible reversal of his liberal economic policies by a future regime by engraving them into an international agreement.

Fears that NAFTA will turn into a trade bloc, which implies adoption of common discriminatory barriers to the rest of the world, are misplaced; NAFTA allows for accession by any country meeting certain economic criteria. Given the asymmetry in their relationships with the United States, neither Mexico nor Canada intends to subject itself to a common commercial policy with the United States. Commercial policies toward Cuba by both countries, for example, differ fundamentally from those of the United States. Indeed, the Mexican government had unilaterally liberalized its trade policies towards the rest of the world even before proposing the U.S. negotiation. Both countries would like to attract investment from outside North America aimed at access to the American market. It is true, however, that particular U.S. interests are imprinted on NAFTA in both autos and textiles, because of the highly restrictive rules of origin that were successfully negotiated in response to the Big Three auto manufacturers and the textile lobby. Both countries are also concerned about the Clinton administration's insistence on side agreements to ensure enforcement of labour and environmental standards, since these agreements threaten intrusion into the domestic policy domain.

These developments should not be misread. They are the outcome of bargaining in an asymmetrical situation. They do not mean that NAFTA is a mechanism which facilitates or promotes automatic NAFTA-country consultation or action in other areas of trade policy or macroeconomic policy. Each NAFTA country pursues its own objectives in the General Agreement on Tariffs and Trade (GATT) independently or in the Cairns Group coalition.[12] Both Canada and Mexico pursue independent policies in many areas, including monetary, fiscal, social, and cultural policies.

United States Relations with Japan

This important relationship is in trouble. Instead of pursuing common goals of global leadership, bilateral relations are increasingly conducted as a if there is a short-term zero-sum game that the United States is determined to win in order to generate employment growth before the next presidential election.

Harmony in the Japanese-U.S. bilateral relationship increasingly is marred by tension and conflict. During the past twenty years Japanese-U.S. relations have been transformed into a form of competitive interdependence.[13] The two sides have come to depend on each other, their national well-being reciprocally intertwined through trade and investment, and by a host of other commercial, technological, educational, and intellectual links. Yet Japan's bilateral trade surplus and the underlying asymmetry in direct investment remain volatile political issues.

The number of stakeholders on both sides of the relationship who are committed to stability and compromise is relatively small. Without symmetry of interests and similar pressure groups on both sides of the relationship, coalitions between Japanese and American stakeholders are difficult to create. The paucity of American businesses in Japan means the community of U.S. interests in Japan and their parent companies in the United States providing political pressures for harmony and stability is weak. Instead, a number of companies in the United States that believe they have grievances arising from difficulties in penetrating the Japanese market apply increasing pressures on Congress to take unilateral action. While the number of Japanese firms with stakes in the American market is much larger, they are unable to defuse tensions by themselves.

At the same time, the complexity of domestic interests in the Japanese political system is such that debate about foreign complaints over trade and investment frictions produces little response in the absence of *gaiatsu*, foreign pressure. Then, in a reactive crisis atmosphere, Japanese consensus emerges on remedial action. Since the response is then perceived largely to be dictated from outside, this mode of decision making contributes increasingly to frustration and resentment of foreign, largely American, pressure.

A harmonious and productive Japanese-U.S. relationship is fundamental to the future of both countries, to the rest of the world, and to smaller countries which are closely integrated with one or both of the protagonists. Despite much-heralded beginnings of a "new economic partnership" in 1993, the old negotiating patterns persist.

China

Japan and the United States are major trading partners for many of the APEC's members; as if tension in that relationship were not already a major source of uncertainty in the external environment, China's emergence has added another source. New estimates of the size of China's economy suggest it is four times as large as when conventionally measured (see endnote 2). Parts of China are growing at rates that put them only a generation behind the leading East Asian economies in per capita incomes and purchasing power. Geopolitical and geo-economic concerns that have been dormant in recent years are fast re-emerging.

For the East Asian economies, explosive growth in China's trade and investment have potentially far-reaching implications. The Asian Development Bank estimates that China's exports and imports in 1993 will be US$80 billion each.[14] Exports of standard-technology labour-intensive products are capturing significant shares of the world market and replacing the exports of some of its neighbours. Import growth, on the other hand, is opening new markets for East Asians and others. Ambitious industrialization plans depend heavily on direct investment from Hong Kong, Taiwan, and an increasing number of countries, including Japan. One of China's advantages in pursuing its market-oriented reforms is its decentralized provincial system which has made it possible to pursue ad hoc reforms to see what works. For the same reason, however, large questions remain about the distribution of growth among the provinces. Internal strains between the booming coastal provinces and a stagnating hinterland could have major implications for China's international economic and security agenda.

It is too early in the life of the Clinton administration to assess the direction of the bilateral relationship with China. Concerns about human rights issues have been linked with trade policies, particularly the renewal of Most Favoured Nation (MFN) status. Yet, as the congressional debate in 1993 showed, U.S. exports (estimated at $7.5 billion in 1993) and rapidly growing business ties are now part of the calculus. Direct investment has expanded beyond production ventures into services, including computer software, accounting, insurance, consulting, and marketing. Removal of MFN status, it has been estimated, could jeopardize 171,000 American jobs if China were to retaliate.[15]

Management of Rising Interdependence

These developments—evolving relationships among the three giants and with the smaller economies—mean that tensions and conflict will not be confined to the main protagonists; everyone in the region will be affected. The U.S.-Japanese relationship will become a larger source of conflict and uncertainty before current tensions ease. The Clinton administration's preference for managed trade in its relationship with Japan is unlikely to stop there or to affect only Japan, because the causes are deeper. As has been pointed out recently, the United States has the largest dollar trade deficit with Japan but, relative to GDP, the countries with the largest deficits are in East Asia. Since they also had superior economic performance—faster growth, faster trade growth, and lower unemployment rates—it is difficult to maintain the American and European Union (EU) arguments that trade imbalances are causes of their structural and recessionary woes.[16]

While American pressure on Japan may yield better access to the Japanese market for these countries, as successful exporting economies they can expect to become objects of future scrutiny. Similarly, areas that are considered to be the domain of domestic policy and beyond outside interference, such as the environment and labour standards, could also become objects of scrutiny and political pressure. Canada and Mexico have recently found this to be so.

China's rapid growth is already spilling over into the region through export competition and through its import demand. The current explosion of credit and related inflationary pressures may cause China a hard landing, the effects of which will no longer be confined just to the mainland and to a few large investors, but will be felt throughout the region.

Continued industrial diversification and to some extent the maintenance of economic growth in East Asia depend on continued inflows of foreign investment. If growth slows down, competitive bidding for foreign flows could become more intense and spill over into political tensions.

These observations lead to a key point. When the external economic environment is a positive one, the rising tide tends to lift all boats; rapid growth allows many objectives to be achieved. Spill-overs tend to be positive ones and easily managed. It is when growth is slow, as it is likely to be in the industrialized world, that frictions arise. It is at those times that investments in institutional mechanisms for managing interdependence pay off.

Clearly, the preferred management mechanism for trade and investment issues is GATT. Yet frustrations and fears about its future have contributed significantly to the proliferation of regional arrangements. Fears that these regional arrangements will undermine the evolution of an open world-trading system as the world splits up into regional (and possibly discriminatory) blocs are, however, overdone. As Professor Robert Lawrence has argued, regional blocs can become building blocks, not stumbling blocks. And some of the issues APEC is tackling would not be dealt with satisfactorily, even with conclusion of the Uruguay Round.[17]

These are some of the reasons why, if APEC did not exist, it would have to be created. Yamazawa makes the intriguing observation about the Asian economies that "there is a strong possibility that the individual countries are framing policies with a clear eye to the policies being adopted by their neighbours. As a result, the effective alignment of trade and investment policies and similar measured approaches to the management of macroeconomic policy by these nations may well be said to have brought with them a certain amount of policy cooperation."[18] The question is, however, how long in this increasingly complex international economy such informality can continue to be successful.

In the area of macroeconomic policy, Yamazawa's point may have validity. The Asian economies have set an example in the prudent management of their economies, and in so doing have created a stable framework for trade and investment activities.

This linkage between macroeconomic policy and trade is an important one, which can work both ways. Bad macro policy can be a stimulus to protectionism. By their success in this area, east Asian economies demonstrate another important point: if governments keep their own houses in order by pursuing prudent domestic policies, there is little need for formal coordination of policies.

In the area of microeconomic policy, however, the potential for conflict is considerable. APEC's great potential lies in the fact that its membership includes the three giant economies whose economic performances and triangular relationships will greatly affect all smaller economies, regardless of any institutional configuration. Its success in managing interdependence will depend on two factors: the extent to which governments identify their own interests with the collectivity; and governments' recognition that the sacrifice of some sovereignty in participating can be offset by the advantages of influencing, through the exercise of peer pressure, the policies and performance of other participants.

The November 1993 meeting in Seattle was a watershed in APEC's development; fourteen leaders met informally for the first time, signifying APEC's importance in their political agendas. Several decisions added to this significance: a second leaders' meeting will be held in Indonesia in 1994; ministers sent a signal to the European Union of the serious intent of the APEC member economies to pursue trade liberalization regardless of the outcome of the Uruguay Round; leaders also decided their finance ministers should meet to begin discussing macroeconomic and monetary issues; and they established a Pacific Business Roundtable, an APEC Education Program, and an APEC Business Volunteer Program.

The willingness of APEC leaders to participate in the informal meeting helped to still some concerns about managing increasing interdependence by creating a process, agreed at highest levels, for addressing them. Yet the diversity of interests and priorities in the economies represented at APEC remain to be bridged and shaped into a consensus about managing the new order. Differing perceptions and expectations, arising from diverse economic characteristics and from divergent economic performance between the dynamic industrializing members and the mature industrial economies, add urgency to the need to build understanding and cooperation. Just how far members will be willing to go toward trading sovereignty for influence in such a forum remains to be seen. Progress will depend on careful consideration of the sensitivities of various economies, and much effort needs to be spent on consultation.

Implications For Canada

These developments have two main implications for Canada: for government policy, and for protecting our standard of living in the face of major competitive challenges. The challenge for government policies is twofold; to play a leading role in APEC's rapid evolution, and to foster a climate for success by Canadian firms in international business.

The key assumption underlying the debate about managing interdependence in the Asia-Pacific region is that the APEC's diversity and open trade policies are crucial to its past and continuing economic success. Intra-regional interdependence is growing, but interdependence with North America is sufficiently important that East Asia cannot afford to look inward, nor should it become an "accessory" to another discriminatory arrangement, as NAFTA is regarded to be. The implication might be drawn that only a Pacific free trade area, which builds on the APEC grouping of countries, makes sense. But such an eventuality is likely to be a long way off.

These observations on managing interdependence have important implications for the foreign economic policy of the Canadian government. APEC participants must find ways to strengthen cooperation and evolve toward the creation of disciplines and benchmarks by which to evaluate each others' policies and performance. Canada has already played, and should continue to play, a leading role in such an evolution. Other smaller APEC economies are unlikely to agree to spearhead a formal initiative of the magnitude of a Pacific Free Trade Area (PAFTA) and would likely be sensitive to such an initiative from one of the big three (as Canada knows well). The dominant countries, while enjoying a period of military peace, are preoccupied with economic competition. They are unlikely to develop consensus on such an initiative.

Of perhaps greater significance for Canada are the implications of East Asian economic dynamism. The NIEs and ASEAN economies are expected to grow at 6 percent annually (after inflation) for at least the next decade. China, which has been growing at 12 percent after inflation during the past year, is expected to average a more stately pace of 9 percent annually during the next decade. At these growth rates, consumer incomes will rise rapidly, creating major business opportunities.

To take advantage of these opportunities, Canadian firms must learn how to do international business — which consists of locating in markets in order to do business there — rather than merely relying on traditional channels of exporting. In order to do business in the Asian economies, Canadians must learn about different business systems, including the Japanese *keiretsu*, the Korean *chaebol*, and the Chinese family firm. These forms of business organization work in groups. We in North America tend to be suspicious of such groups, yet there are good reasons why they exist and even better reasons why they should be understood. Economists understand business groups with explanations that are similar to explanations for the origins of Western multinationals. Just as the explanation for multinationals' existence is that they can be more efficient by controlling production in subsidiaries than exporting on an arm's-length basis to other countries, so the explanation for East Asian business groups tends to be one which emphasizes the superior efficiency of groups in developing economies in which input and output markets tend to be underdeveloped and fragmented. These imperfections can be overcome better within the group than outside it.

This thumbnail sketch helps to underline the important point that to do international business successfully, we have to learn about the rationale for and scope of alternative ways of doing business. This implies the need to make long-term investments in learning the market and in searching for a suitable group of collaborators with whom to undertake strategic alliances or investments.

In addition, Canadian governments need to broaden their knowledge about how well their policies toward trade and outward investment fit with those of "competitor" countries. Ideally, the policy regime for outward foreign investment should be neutral so that a firm's decision is based strictly on business criteria. Yet public policies toward foreign investment tend to be one-sided: toward attracting (or, historically, repelling) investment flowing *into* the country, such as Investment Canada's mandate. This lopsided mandate overlooks potential opportunities for Canadian businesses to penetrate Asian markets. Indeed, when we do think of Asia, we tend to make the assumption that we should focus all effort in the region on the Japanese and the potentially huge Chinese markets; we find it frustrating and extremely expensive, and in some cases, successful. Yet we may be overlooking a much more practical approach; that of linking with East Asian businesses to penetrate both China and Japan.

In conclusion, the main implication of developments in the APEC region for Canadians is that, to protect our standard of living, instead of erecting "protectionist" barriers, we must become more forward- and outward-looking. The East Asian economies are setting the pace of economic and increasingly technical change and it is in these economies that we will find the fastest economic growth during much of our lifetimes. We must trade in these markets, but more importantly, we must know how to invest there and how to engage in alliances and joint ventures with East Asian partners in order to penetrate the key markets of Japan and China that will be so important in the future.

Civil Strife and Efforts to Restore Peace

11 Russia's Monroe Doctrine: Peacekeeping, Peacemaking, or Imperial Outreach?

Teresa Rakowska-Harmstone

NATIONALISM HAS FILLED THE VACUUM left by the collapse of communism in Eastern Europe and the Soviet Union, thus restoring the "normal" historical pattern that had been interrupted, for most of the century, by an effort to build a regional and ultimately global political system on a basis of a supra-national identity. The collapse led to the break-up of the Warsaw Pact regional security system and to the disintegration of multi-ethnic communist states. The demise of the Soviet imperial system was a replay of the earlier disintegration of European dynastic systems (after World War One), and Western colonial empires (after World War Two), thus proving once again that nationalism has been the dominant world force of the twentieth century and promises to remain so on the threshold of the twenty-first.

The break-up of the Soviet Union left a complex legacy of destabilization. All of the successor states still have sizeable minorities, some indigenous and some immigrant. Some twenty-five million Russians now stranded outside Russia form crucial minorities in the new states and look to Moscow for protection.[1] Minority separatism that had been generated in the process of Soviet disintegration continues, while at the same time the successor states are engaged in a vigorous effort of nation-building which on the one hand threatens the national and civil rights of the minorities within, and on the other encourages irredentism among co-nationals outside.

The Russian Federation is very much in the forefront on both counts. Almost 18 percent of its population consists of non-Russians[2] who agitate for greater autonomy, if not outright independence. The Russians, on the other hand, have rediscovered nationalism and push for national integration — a process that includes efforts at internal recentralization, a defence of the rights of their stranded brethren, and a search for an identity on which to build a new Russia. Inevitably the search leads back to imperial

Russia. The imperial component is thus an inextricable part of the new identity. The origins of the Russian identity and of the Russian state are traced directly to medieval Kiev (now the capital of new Ukraine), and to the fifteenth-century conquest of Kazan (now the capital of Tatarstan). Conceptually they transcend, respectively, the Russian ethnic markers and the area of ethnic Russian territorial settlement. The very name of the country, *Rossiia,* denotes a broader identity than that implied by the word *Rus',* referring to the latter, just as an adjective *russkii* describes an ethnic Russian attribute, in contrast to an adjective *rossiiskii,* which applies to a socio-political attribute of the Russian state and society.

The recovery by the Russians of their historic identity has shaped their perceptions of new Russia's role and interests, perceptions which appear to be shared by the whole otherwise fragmented Russian political spectrum. Above all, these perceptions have shaped the policies towards the "near abroad" (*blizhnee zarubezh'e*), a term coined to describe the successor states which used to be an integral part of imperial Russia/Soviet Union, as well as the policies towards East Central Europe, only recently a part of the Soviet security system and traditionally a zone of imperial Russia's westward expansion. Russian perceptions and policies towards the states which formerly were a part of the imperial heritage, and a new policy of peacekeeping designed for their implementation, are the subject of this chapter.

Following an initial period of uncertainty, and a debate over the direction of foreign policy within the newly created Commonwealth of Independent States (CIS), a new "activist" policy emerged on the political, military, and economic fronts. First, the new policy claims "near abroad" as Russia's exclusive sphere of influence by virtue of past imperial heritage and Russia's status as a great power. Second, it legitimizes Russia's interference, by force if necessary, in support of this assumption, specifically focusing on the protection of Russian minorities. Both preclude interference by interested third parties — this has been of particular importance in the case of the Islamic southern crescent but it applies also to the Western periphery and implicitly to East Central Europe — and make the support for the leaders in the periphery contingent on their responsiveness to Russian interests. In practice, the latter requirement has meant support for communist incumbents as against newly emergent nationalist forces and forces for political liberalization. Nationalists and liberals both generate instability and are unwilling to follow Moscow's lead.

Russian spokesmen have compared the policy to the United States' "Monroe Doctrine," and have promoted it in the international arena as "peacekeeping." The former Soviet periphery has been racked by ethnic conflicts, and Russia's preoccupation with the maintenance of stability there has endowed its "peacekeeping" with some legitimacy internationally. This tends to obscure the frankly partisan nature of the exercise, which once again seeks to subordinate the nations of the periphery to Russian hegemony.

The Legacies and Conflict Potential

Many of the conflicts dividing the peoples of the former USSR date to the pre-Soviet period. The non-Russians harbour resentment towards the Russians because of their hegemonial role and colonization policies in the imperial and the Soviet periods, and have themselves been divided for centuries by conflicts engendered by conquests, migrations, economic rivalries, and ethnicity and culture. Each region has had its own historical antagonisms, with the worst case scenario at the southern rim where the ethnic mosaic has been the most complex and the conflicts fed on religious struggle between Islam and Christianity. Tribal warfare and fierce resistance to colonization have been characteristic of the peoples of the North Caucasus; Georgian Muslim minorities have long resisted Georgian efforts at assimilation, and the Armenian struggle with the Turks (represented locally by Azeri Turks of Azerbaijan) has lasted for centuries. In Central Asia the successive invasions by nomadic Turks left residual antagonisms between the nomads and agricultural settlers, especially on the borderline between the Turkish and the Iranian area of settlement, and have metamorphosed in modern times into clan and region-based conflicts.

Historical conflicts were submerged but not eradicated in the Soviet period. Some were aggravated and new ones were added in the wake of Soviet policies. Boundary delimitation of Soviet republics generally conformed to the settlement patterns of their titular groups, each of which was encouraged to develop a "national" (albeit Soviet) identity and culture. But residual minorities remained and new immigrant minorities were added by migration flows encouraged by economic and "internationalization" policies, and as a result of mass-scale deportations of "enemies of the people." The main result was the influx into the periphery of large numbers of Russians. Most cities and industrial centres acquired a multi-ethnic character, but the countryside has retained the indigenous ethnic colouration.

The new states are entangled in the inherited centralized web of public administration, economic management, fiscal institutions and practices, and the economic division of labour, with residual vertical networks converging on Moscow. This has meant lopsided development and economic dependence on Russia, fiscal policies still determined by the centre, and infrastructures dominated by the former cadre with ties to Moscow and loyalties to the old networks. The division of economic assets between Russia, which holds most central assets, and others has been a major problem next to the division of military assets and the negotiations over the return to Russia of strategic nuclear weapons held by Ukraine, Belarus, and Kazakhstan.

Pre-Soviet and Soviet legacies are mixed together in popular attitudes—a mixture that enhances the potential for ethnic and political conflict and contributes little to the future of democracy. Pre-Soviet communal conflicts and ethnic antagonisms have resurfaced, their intensity enhanced by years of official emphasis on "fraternal love" and adulation for the Russian "elder brother." Neither the Soviet nor traditional political cultures have been noted for participatory values and behaviour, and the years of Soviet socialization served to reinforce authoritarian elements of the traditional cultures. Pluralism has emerged, but even in the best of circumstances the prospects for development of working democracies are at best long-range. New democratic institutions are poorly absorbed, and authoritarian models feature prominently in political behaviour.

The focus of conflict and potential destabilization in Soviet successor states has been at the junction of two powerful trends working at cross-purposes: the integrative nation-building by each newly sovereign state starting with Russia, and the self-assertion of the minorities fired by an example of luckier predecessors or, in the case of Russian minorities, incensed over the loss of privileged status. By its very nature, nation-building puts the titular nation in primary position. For the non-Russians the need to emphasize their primacy has been heightened by the years of second-class status; the Russians, on the other hand, glory in the rebirth of their national identity, liberated finally from ideological and Soviet shackles. National integration has been a priority task also in the economic sense because of the need to reduce dependency on the others, especially on Russia. But nation-building and national integration automatically threaten the rights and equal status of the minorities. This situation has acquired explosive dimensions in many successor states because of a lack of tolerance and a violent political culture, hostile stereotypes, and past antagonisms.

The status of Russian minorities in non-Russian states has been the pivot of the minority question in relations between Russia and the "near abroad." In some of the successor states they now form between one-fourth and one-third of the population, as in the cases of Kazakhstan and Kyrgyzstan, and Latvia and Estonia. Most Russian immigrants have no other permanent home; many had been there for generations, and have no place to return to in the Russian Federation. In some regions of the new states, as in northern Kazakhstan, eastern Ukraine, or shore and urban centres of Latvia and Estonia, resident Russians living in compact communities vastly outnumber titular population. Substantial numbers voted for the independence of their countries of residence, but they became disillusioned over the loss of privileged status, economic decline, and alleged mistreatment. Fear of ethnic disturbances, especially in Central Asia and the Caucasus, had driven some of them back to Russia, where no provisions were made for their resettlement, thereby contributing to their militancy. Post-independence problems have driven many towards radical right-wing nationalism, which has been particularly virulent in the Russian communities of Latvia and Estonia.

The minorities problem also affects national communities other than the Russians. Minorities within the Russian Federation have negotiated substantial autonomy; ethnic republics declared sovereignty,[3] and two of them, Chechenya and Tatarstan, declared independence. But since the 1993 April referendum, the October coup, and December elections, Moscow's policy has emphasized recentralization, and conflicts have re-emerged. Some of the "peacekeeping" has been within the Federation, as in the case of the conflict between the Ingush and the Ossetins. Minorities in other successor states have been equally restless, contributing to actual and potential hot spots.

A number of contentious issues have emerged in the relations between Russia and other successor states. One has been the language question. All the new states adopted their titular languages as new official languages. But few Russians and other immigrants in the former republics had bothered to learn local languages; their inability to function in the new official medium has caused hardships and generated hatred and resentment. The language question remains largely unresolved throughout the area.

The issue of citizenship and the exercise of political and civil rights connected with it also remains unresolved. Most successor states granted citizenship to all permanent residents at the time of independence. Latvia and Estonia, the two exceptions, excluded all immigrants who came after 1940, the year of the Soviet invasion. This greatly aggravated communal relations and put both governments under intense pressure from Russia, made easier by the continued presence in both states of Russian forces. Russia is promoting dual citizenship for the Russians in the "near abroad," who were given an option to take the Federation's citizenship within three years. But the host states have been unwilling for the Russians to combine Russian and local citizenship, fearing an incipient fifth column.

Boundaries also represent a problem in the context of divided national communities, of which there were three basic types: contiguous communities (i.e., those cut off from the mother country); the communities divided between two or more states; and enclaves. Drawn arbitrarily in the Stalinist period, the boundaries nonetheless have become "sacred" at independence, and thus inviolable (a phenomenon that has been typical also of the post-colonial Third World), precluding negotiated adjustments in the case of divided communities. It is not accidental, therefore, that all active hot spots which have erupted on the former Soviet periphery, and many more potential ones, have been related in one way or another to the status, treatment, and ambitions of the minorities.

Russia's New Policy

The Commonwealth of Independent States was established in December 1991 by Russia, Ukraine, and Belarus as the Soviet Union collapsed. But the CIS could not get off the ground because of a fundamental disagreement between its two key members, Russia and Ukraine, over the very nature of the organization. Russia, the initiator, wanted to maintain the association in order to safeguard its influence and interests in the former Soviet area. Ukraine was deeply distrustful of Russian motives and accepted the organization only as a framework for an amicable divorce. The built-in imbalance between Russia, which had half of the population and a lion's share of economic and military assets, and the others was at the heart of the disagreement. Simple logic indicated that Russia's weight in the organization could not but lead to a new hegemony.

Four of the former republics, the three Baltic states and Georgia, refused to join. The remainder, a total of ten in addition to Russia, divided along the Russia/Ukraine axis. Six—Belarus, Kazakhstan, Uzbekistan, Kyrgyzstan, Tajikistan, and Armenia—were not ready to stand alone in the period of transition, and were willing to follow Russia for security and economic reasons. The first five were ready to stay in the Union in 1991, while Armenia, battling Azerbaijan over Nagorno-Karabakh, needed Russian support. The other three, Moldova, Azerbaijan, and Turkmenistan, shared Ukraine's viewpoint.

Internal divisions made for little progress either on economic or military fronts in the first year of CIS existence, and the division of assets and contentious issues remained unresolved, except by bilateral agreements. Of hundreds of CIS agreements concluded, few were signed and even fewer were ratified and implemented. Trade and fiscal coordination suffered because of economic crisis. Maintenance of joint forces proved impossible and member states proceeded to build their own national armies.[4]

Russia's decision to create its own national army was a turning point in the country's military thinking and a prelude to enshrining "peacekeeping" as a centrepiece of Russian policy in the "near abroad." Military and political thinking converged by mid-1993 and a consensus emerged on a new policy. The resulting initiatives and the synchronization of the political and military aspects may well lead to a revitalization of the CIS as an instrument of Russia's neo-imperialist policy.

Political Context

The 1992 debate over Russian foreign policy has usually been portrayed as the debate between President Yeltsin's pro-Western "liberals," and the "nationalist right" centred on Parliament (the same Parliament that was forcibly disbanded by the president in October 1993). In retrospect, and in application specifically to the policy towards the "near abroad," it appears that the differences were more apparent than real, and had more to do with the instrumentalities and scope than with the content of the policy.

In the first place, the struggle for power between the president and Parliament led to a polarization of views. But some of the government's most vocal critics came from the democratic side of the spectrum, while some of the outspoken "liberals," such as the foreign minister, Andrei Kozyrev, and the president himself, promoted ideas similar to those advocated by the nationalists. In the second place, the liberal tone in foreign policy seems to have been tailored specifically for Western consumption, or at least with an eye to Western reaction. Once it became clear that the West, in particular the United States, was ready to recognize Russia's great power status and its "legitimate" strategic interests in the former Soviet imperial zone, the liberal camouflage of the "near abroad" policy has been dropped.

A milestone here was Russia's automatic accession to the Soviet Union's permanent seat on the UN Security Council with no questions raised by the Bush administration, as well as Secretary Warren Christopher's November 4, 1993, assurance to the U.S. Congress' Foreign Relations Committee, that the new Russian military doctrine, which explicitly authorizes Russian military intervention in Soviet successor states, does not violate the "crucial principle" of respect for these states' sovereignty and territorial integrity.[5] Another milestone has been the Western governments' acquiescence to Russia's veto of NATO membership for East Central Europe, as well as their blindness to Ukraine's desperate pleas for security guarantees in exchange for giving up nuclear weapons. The message received by Russia was that it has a green light to pursue its imperial interests in the "near abroad" unfettered. By extension the same applies also to East Central Europe.

President Yeltsin's first assessment of Russia's relations with other union republics after the failed August 1991 coup was that they had the right to independence but that Russia's borders may have to be modified to include contiguous Russian population. The border modification demand was muted later, because of the need to keep Ukraine in the proposed commonwealth and because of the general sensitivity of the issue. But the president's attitudes may be gauged by his decision to send troops to stop Chechenya's unilateral declaration of independence (within the Federation) in the fall of 1991. This action was not supported by Russia's Supreme Soviet, which was then in a non-interventionist mood, and the troops were withdrawn, as were the troops (in March 1992) from Nagorno-Karabakh that had been sent there by Gorbachev. The "withdrawal" mood then was reflected also in Yeltsin's March 1992 concessions to the Federation's ethnic republics.

At that stage Russian foreign policy, then identified both with President Yeltsin and Foreign Minister Kozyrev, was based on close cooperation with the West and a strong emphasis on the protection of human rights and the prevention of aggression, with Russia behaving as a "good guy" in the international arena. In relations with the former Soviet republics, the policy proceeded from an assumption of their equal status and stressed negotiations as the means to resolve outstanding issues. The concern over the rights of Russian minorities, for example, was handled by means of "delegations" set up to conduct negotiations in each former republic, and by invoking Western support in cases of alleged abuses, as in the Baltic states. Only in cases of failure could a question of military force be raised "before the international community," according to a deputy minister of foreign affairs interviewed in June 1992.[6]

The largely conservative Russian Parliament became sharply critical of Yeltsin's "West-subservient liberal" policy, which in the eyes of most deputies abandoned Russia's national interests. A document prepared in June 1992 by the then chairman of the parliamentary Joint Committee on International Affairs and Foreign Economic Relations, Yevgeny Ambartsumov, criticized the Foreign Ministry for having no "integral conception of foreign policy" for the "near abroad," and charted an alternative scenario. Its main points are worth quoting, because they actually provide a blueprint for the new policy as it was adopted in 1993–94 by the very officials who were then the targets of criticism (relevant points are italicized).

> As the internationally recognized legal successor to the USSR, the Russian Federation should base its foreign policy on a doctrine *declaring the entire geopolitical space of the former Union to be the sphere of its vital interests* (like the U.S.'s Monroe Doctrine in

> Latin America) and should strive to achieve understanding and recognition from the world community of its special interests in this space. Russia should also strive to achieve from the world community recognition of its role as *political and military guarantor of stability in the entire former space of the USSR*. It should strive to achieve support from the Group of Seven countries for these functions of Russia's, up to and including *foreign currency subsidies for quick-reaction forces (Russian "blue helmets")*. . . .
>
> In subsequent agreements on the CIS and bilateral agreements, it is necessary to . . . (make) . . . special provisions for Russia's *right to defend the lives and dignity of Russians* in the nearby foreign countries. And it is mandatory to *make special stipulation for the status of Russian troops in the CIS countries* . . .[7]

The declaration claims the area of the former Soviet Union as Russia's sphere of influence and claims for Russia the right to act as a gendarme protecting Russian minorities there under a label of peacekeeping. It even includes an idea that the West should pay for such operations. All of these points have now emerged in the mainstream of Russian foreign policy.

Criticism came not only from the Parliament but also from democratic circles. Writing in 1992 Professor Andranik Migranyan, director of the CIS Centre of the Institute of International Economics and Political Research of the Russian Academy of Sciences, strongly endorsed Russia's imperial role, and made policy recommendations which foreshadowed some of the later policies. He not only stressed that "*de jure* and *de facto*" Russia was called upon to play a special role in the entire geopolitical space of the former Soviet Union, but advocated reincorporation of ethno-territorial entities which used to be parts of imperial Russia but were now cut off and asking for Russia's protection, such as Ossetia, Karabakh, the Crimea, and the Dniester region. He also invoked the familiar "hands-off" attitude: no unfriendly alliances by the successor states either with each other or with a third country, and no Western or international interference into Russian geopolitical space, should be tolerated by Russia.

In assessing relations with former republics, Migranyan suggested working for a federal arrangement with Kazakhstan and Belarus, and advocated vigilance in safeguarding Russian interests in Ukraine and a return of, or at the least a special status for, Crimea. In relations with the Baltic states, Russia's access to the Baltic and protection of the rights of the Russians there should be assured. Russia should not and could not withdraw from Transcaucasus, because a vacuum there would lead to incursions by Iran and Turkey, with potentially dangerous consequences for Central Asia and the Turks of the Russian Federation. Migranyan also invoked the Monroe Doctrine to justify the proposed policy in terms understandable to the West.[8]

The conflict between the president and Parliament was not resolved until October 1993 when the Parliament was disbanded and its leaders arrested. Thus the war of words continued until late 1993, although the shape of the new policy which reflected Parliament's main demands began to emerge earlier. Russia's need for "peacekeeping" in its own backyard was raised by President Yeltsin in a speech to the Civic Union in February 1993 in which he stressed Russia's special responsibility for the prevention of conflicts on the territory of the former Soviet Union, and announced that he would seek authorization by the United Nations and other international organizations to grant Russia "special powers as guarantor of peace and security" there.[9]

Shortly thereafter an article appeared by Sergei Stankevich, one of Yeltsin's influential advisors, elaborating the thinking behind the "special relationship." Stankevich talked of the need for Russian foreign policy to have a "mission," and about bridging a gap between Russia's "Atlanticism" and "Eurasianism." "Our state grew strong as a unique historical and cultural amalgam of Slav and Turkic, Orthodox and Muslim components," said Stankevich, but the relations between the two components were "on a brink of a fateful conflict" and an "arc of crisis . . . from the Transcaucasus through North Caucasus toward the Volga region [was] progressively taking shape," with the dominant Near and Middle Eastern powers showing a new interest in Soviet Muslims. Russia's special relationship with the states of the CIS should be strengthened in pursuit of the country's long-term strategic interests; but the policy towards CIS partners should differentiate "between those which use the CIS merely as a means of dividing up the Union inheritance prior to a 'definitive' parting, and those for whom the Commonwealth is a fundamental historical choice." Finally Stankevich pointed out that a given state's attitude towards the Russian heritage and Russian population was "a most important criterion" in the determination of Russian policy, and rejected any charges of "an imperial syndrome," since "such a policy has nothing in common with imperialism. On the contrary, it is for Russia a legitimate and natural aspiration to erase conflict and harmonize relations on the territory of the former USSR. Furthermore, Russia will invariably take the part of the undeservedly insulted and unjustly prosecuted."[10]

A search for international authorization of Russian peacekeeping has been vigorously pursued by Andrei Kozyrev. In March Russia presented a document to the United Nations which pointed out the dangers of regional conflicts for world peace and stability, outlined Russia's peacekeeping operations in the area of the former Soviet Union, and pointed out the utility of regional organizations for peacekeeping purposes, suggesting that the CIS was just the kind of an organization the UN Charter envisaged for the purpose. Vigorous protests by Ukraine, Moldova, and the Baltic states were countered by an assertion that Russia's aims were predominantly humanitarian and that it had no neo-imperialist designs. Parallel to these initiatives, President Yeltsin appealed to CIS leaders to develop joint mechanisms for peacekeeping throughout the commonwealth, stressing Russia's special role but denying any ambitions to resume the leadership.[11]

By September Kozyrev again pressed the Russian peacekeeping case in the UN General Assembly. He defended the right of the states which had vital interests in an area to engage in peacekeeping there, thus departing from the conventional wisdom that peacekeepers should be neutral. He asked for international support for Russia in its efforts to keep peace in the former Soviet periphery, warning that "the threat of ethnic violence today is no less serious than the nuclear threat was yesterday, especially in the former Soviet republics."[12] Russia's vigorous promotion of activist and partisan peacekeeping stood in marked contrast to the position of Western democracies taking a minimalist and neutrality-based approach.

After October 1993 the government's rhetoric became measurably tougher. It stressed Russia's special role in the "near abroad," claimed the imperial heritage, linked Russian peacekeeping operations (as well as the withdrawal of the Russian troops from Latvia and Estonia) to the treatment of Russian minorities and Russian language rights, and denied the right of interference to third parties. Although the CSCE's mediation efforts in Russia's periphery were officially applauded, they were resisted *de facto* either by Russia (we can take care of the problem),[13] or by Russia's clients of the moment.

An invocation of the imperial heritage became standard fare for the "liberal" foreign minister. In an oft-quoted interview with *Izvestiia*, on October 8, 1993, Kozyrev pointed out that Russia's interest in dealing effectively with regional conflicts in the former Soviet Union stemmed from the desire not to lose "geopolitical positions that took centuries to conquer;" and in an interview of November 24 with *Nezavisimaia Gazeta*, he said that by undertaking peacekeeping, and maintaining military bases in conflict zones, Russia had found the best compromise between two impossible options that faced it after the Soviet collapse: trying to keep the USSR together by force, or a total withdrawal. The latter would have been an "unwarranted loss" because "the periphery has been under Russian influence for centuries."[14]

In November it was reported that the Ministry of Foreign Affairs was apparently upgrading its work with former Soviet republics and members of the bloc to accommodate Russia's strengthening commitment to the policy of reasserting its influence in the former Soviet geopolitical space.[15] In January 1994 Kozyrev told a meeting of Russian ambassadors to the "near abroad" that Russian soldiers must remain there to prevent forces hostile to Russia from moving into the existing security vacuum. "We should not withdraw from those regions which have been the sphere of Russian interest for centuries." A report that the statement applied also to the Baltic republics was later denied by the Foreign Ministry.[16]

Addressing the first joint session of the newly elected parliament on February 24, 1994, President Yeltsin strongly reaffirmed the government's commitment to the restoration of a strong Russian state the interests of which transcend the Federation's present borders:

> A strong and powerful Russian state is the most reliable and real guarantor of stability on the entire territory of the former Soviet Union. . . . It is our duty to make the year 1994 the year of close attention to the problems of the people of Russian extraction living in neighboring states. When it comes to violations of the lawful rights of people of Russia, this is not an exclusive internal affair of some country, but also our national affair, an affair of our state.[17]

The message sounded ominous in Ukraine, Moldova, the Baltic states, and other former Soviet republics and caused serious concern in East Central Europe. In the domestic context, however, it seemed moderate, in comparison with the views of Vladimir Zhirinovsky, the leader of the ultra-nationalist Liberal Democratic Party (LDP), the second largest party, after Russia's Choice, in the new Duma, and the largest opposition party. In his electoral campaign Zhirinovsky predicted that successor states will be reintegrated into Russia after "begging on their knees" to be readmitted. His wilder oratory envisages a reincarnated empire extending from Finland and Poland to Alaska, and "a vast drive to Russia's predestined borders on the Indian Ocean and the Mediterranean Sea."[18]

His more sober views, however, are not that far apart from the official policy. He says that he would be satisfied with the "borders of 1990," at least for the time being. At the same time, a presidential spokesman talked of a future political and economic union, once a "few prickly nationalist weeds" are uprooted.[19] In a gesture reflecting the new mood, Russian- language television and radio, heard throughout the former Soviet Union, decided in March 1994 to drop the practice of pronouncing place names according to new official languages, returning instead to the old Russian pronunciation (for example, Belorussia instead of Belarus).[20]

The strength of Zhirinovsky, and hence the danger of his views, lies not in the Duma, which has few powers under the new constitution, but in his constituency, which is broadly based. He capitalizes on the sense of utter humiliation brought about by the Soviet collapse, and on the hardships suffered by the people caught in the chaos of reform. He appeals to the unemployed young, the poverty-stricken seniors, the dispossessed, and the humiliated. The military figure prominently in the latter category. According to President Yeltsin, one-third of the military personnel voted for the LDP in the December elections; but the percentage was reported to have been higher in the elite forces.[21] More militant Russian minorities in the "near abroad" also voted heavily for the LDP: 32 percent in Latvia, and 48 percent in Estonia.[22] Zhirinovsky came third in the presidential elections of 1991, when he was relatively unknown, and he is gearing up to contest the presidency again in the next elections scheduled for 1996.

It was noted earlier that many liberal politicians regretted the break-up of the Soviet federation. This attitude was widely shared by the political centre, and by the communists who made a strong showing, coming in as the second strongest opposition party in the Duma.[23] Individual voices critical of the drive towards a re-assertion of Russia's imperial interests continue to be heard in the press and in academic circles,[24] but it is clear that the policy finds firm support across Russia's entire political spectrum. It is an open question, however, to what extent the support reflects the views of the population at large, apart from Zhirinovsky's militants. Public opinion surveys have shown basic indifference to foreign policy questions.

Military Context

Arguably the military establishment and professional cadre were hit the hardest, in psychological and material sense, by the collapse of the Soviet system. The trauma started with the withdrawal from Afghanistan, and was maximized by subsequent blows to military morale and prestige: Gorbachev's military retrenchment which drastically reduced the resources available to the Soviet armed forces, cut their numbers, and scaled down their mission; the withdrawal from and the "loss" of Eastern Europe; and finally the break-up of the Soviet Union, the break-up of the forces, and partial withdrawal from the "near abroad." Military prestige sunk to the bottom, superpower status was lost, and the conscription base largely disappeared, leaving few Indians and too many chiefs. Living conditions, especially for the troops withdrawn from Eastern Europe, were unsupportable; and jobs, housing, and medical care were not available for the veterans, the retired, and the mustered out.

The shocks generated anger and resentment, nostalgia for the better past, and internal debates between traditionalists and the *Afgantsy* (Afghan veterans), the junior and the senior cadre, the Russians and the non-Russians, over the future shape and mission of the forces. As new national armies were created, most non-Russian officers opted for service in their own countries.[25] The ambiguity of the legal status of Soviet armies stranded in the "near abroad" became a bone of contention between Moscow and new national governments. Of the Russian cadre, some left the service, voluntarily or otherwise; some joined new national armies, largely for economic reasons. Local commanders proceeded to do "their own thing," that is, they built their own fiefdoms, meddled in local politics, and trafficked in arms, contributing to the general chaos.[26]

At the same time, however, the military gained unprecedented political influence. First, political instability made military support the crucial variable in political infighting. Yeltsin won the confrontation of August 1991 because the military supported the new Russia rather than the Soviet status quo; and he won again in the confrontation of October 1993 thanks to (rather reluctant) military support, thus incurring heavy political debts to the generals who backed him. Second, the government has become increasingly dependent on the military-industrial complex reincarnated in an alliance between the "industrialists' lobby" and the military "patriots." Third, the demise of the ruling Communist party broke the civilian fetters constraining top cadre's political ambitions.[27] In the context of Yeltsin's indebtedness to the armed forces, and his dependence on the centre-right constituency, the conversion to a neo-imperial outlook by some of government "liberals" might have been the function of politics rather than inclination.

A new hard-line military policy began to take shape with the decision of May 7, 1992, to create a new Russian Army, and the appointment, on May 18, of General of the Army Pavel Grachev, a paratrooper, an Afghan veteran, and a Yeltsin supporter in 1991 and 1993, to the post of minister of defence. Grachev leap-frogged over several more senior generals, and his appointment definitively ended speculation that a new minister of defence may be a civilian. Shortly, five out of six deputy minister slots were filled by the *Afgantsy*, young and militantly nationalist, including ex-commanders of forces in Afghanistan, Poland, and the Baltic military district.

The new military doctrine, long under discussion, emerged by mid-1993 and was approved in November. It was an activist doctrine designed explicitly to protect Russian nationals and Russian interests in the "near abroad," and implicitly to project Russia's interests regionally and globally, and it was very much the product of the new military establishment.[28] The new main-threat perception was in local wars and regional conflicts. Accordingly, the new doctrine authorized military action in the "near abroad" to defend Russian communities there, to combat insurgencies, and to stop local conflicts—acting, in effect, as peacemakers in Russia's interest. It also authorized domestic military intervention in the specific circumstances of a threat by force to constitutional order, attacks on chemical or nuclear installations, and hostilities by nationalist or separatist groups.[29]

In a global context, the doctrine rejected the "no first use" of nuclear weapons (which at any rate was always largely declaratory, according to Russian spokesmen[30]), authorizing their use against other nuclear powers, or non-nuclear states with nuclear allies. The return to reliance on nuclear arms was justified by the loss of quantitative conventional superiority vis-à-vis NATO, by the development of new conventional technologies demonstrated during Desert Storm, and by the nuclear potential of aspiring members of the "nuclear club." Thus in preparing for war it was assumed that Russia would use nuclear forces, that it might have to use them first, and that it would use tactical nuclear weapons, especially against states with mass land armies, such as China.

Rejecting even a nominal role for the CIS command, in May 1993 Russia claimed exclusive control over the Strategic Rocket Forces (SRF) and insisted on the withdrawal of all nuclear weapons from the three new nuclear states and fellow CIS members, Ukraine, Belarus, and Kazakhstan. War planning was for "one-and-a-half-war," and there was no designated enemy. In a "one war" scenario, China was seen as a principal threat, and NATO would become one if "it extends eastward toward Russia's border." States aspiring to nuclear status represented a potential threat. A "half-war" operations would focus on "peacekeeping," reflecting the doctrine's preoccupation with the "near abroad," and to carry out outside operations under international auspices.

In line with the new mission and reduced capabilities (it was estimated that Russian forces' actual strength was sliding below the projected one and a half million, and that most units were at half-strength[31]), Russian forces were being drastically reduced and restructured, with special emphasis on defence and rapid deployment capabilities needed for the fulfilment of the new mission. Mobility and speed were the primary aim. The reform envisaged three basic force components: Constant Readiness Troops (CRT), mobile Rapid Deployment Forces (RDF), and Strategic Reserves.

The CRT's mission is to react in local conflicts. Most were to be stationed in the North Caucasus Military District, the seat of a newly established army headquarters, and presumably in forward military bases negotiated with interested CIS members.

The preoccupation with Transcaucasus as a "new frontline area" was reflected also in Russia's efforts to raise the limits imposed by the 1990 treaty on conventional forces in Europe (CFE) on the forces stationed there. The RDF were to be more centrally located but highly mobile to reinforce CRT's operations. Strategic Reserves were to be maintained in case of a broader conflict.[32]

Plans for command structure changes envisaged four to six geographic strategic commands replacing the military districts as basic operational divisions, with the districts converted into territorial mobilization units. At the lower level, corps and brigades were to replace divisions and armies as the basic units.[33] New forces were projected to include a much greater share of volunteers, reflecting both new emphasis on professionalism and high rates of draft evasion. More women were admitted. Contract soldiers were assured of better pay and living conditions. Approximately 110,000 volunteers were reported serving in August 1993, with the recruitment of an additional 50,000 planned for 1993, and a further 150,000 for 1994.[34]

A commentary in the Russian press, citing military specialists, expressed alarm over the aggressive nature of the doctrine and new political power acquired by the military. Reflecting on the domestic situation, a retired colonel was quoted as saying that "today no one has any doubts that it is the army which controls the situation in the country . . . what has begun is an era of order which will be brought about by us, the military." In the same vein, an officer of the General Staff noted that "power ministries" (defence and internal security) have never been closer "to the helm of political power." Turning to the "near abroad," a retired major-general commented that the more Russian military bases that are placed there, "the more quickly will the single economic and military union be restored." The same commentator also noted the doctrine's implied warning to the former bloc countries: "Poland, the Czech Republic, Slovakia, Hungary and even Ukraine, dreaming of entering into NATO, must understand that if they do this, it will instantaneously make them targets of Russia's SRF with all the consequences arising therefrom." A retired lieutenant-general opined that the hawks have won in the internal military debate.[35] A journalist quoted General Grachev at an internal briefing stating that "a decision had been made not to pull back to Russia's borders but to maintain old Soviet borders, especially in Central Asia and the Northern Caucasus."[36]

The warnings seem well taken. At the same time the doctrine and its implementation have to be measured against the dimensions of the real situation, namely Russia's social and economic crisis, international constraints (such as they are), and the resistance, open and covert, of the target states.

Peacekeeping in Action: Domestic and the "Near Abroad"[37]

When the CIS was formed it was decided to convert the Soviet armed forces (SAF) into joint military forces under CIS command. But because the organization failed to develop either political control agencies or an apparatus for coordination of the activities of the member states, the one viable channel of political control was the personal relationship between President Yeltsin and Marshal Evgenii Shaposhnikov (another of Yeltsin's August 1991 supporters) the new commander-in-chief of the joint forces. This only reinforced the perception that the forces were in fact run by and for the Russians, and led to Ukraine's decision to establish a national Ukrainian army on the basis of the military forces stationed on Ukrainian territory; Moldova and Azerbaijan followed suit, and eventually the others. The division was formalized at the February 1992 summit, which agreed to divide the SAF into three components: the Strategic Rocket Forces which were to remain under the joint CIS command, General Purpose Forces (also under the joint command), and national armies of member states.

Two fateful decisions were taken in May 1993. The first was to create a national Russian army. The second was to create a regional security system under CIS auspices that would be subordinated to Russia's policy and interests: the Tashkent Collective Security Treaty. Together they changed the character of the CIS. When Russia's national army was established, General Grachev took over the old Soviet Defence Ministry and the General Staff from Marshall Shaposhnikov, while Shaposhnikov and the Joint Command moved to the old and empty Warsaw Pact headquarters, where they remained, a command without an army. Russia's position from the beginning was to oppose the formation of CIS forces in peacetime, and to claim exclusive control over nuclear forces under the Lisbon START I Protocol. The claim was disputed by the three CIS members; Ukraine, Kazakhstan, and Belarus, which inherited 10, 6 and 4 percent of the Strategic Rocket Forces, respectively. The question of the status of the nuclear forces (which included also naval and air components), led to an open conflict between Russia and Ukraine—still unresolved in the spring of 1994—and seriously weakened the organization. Belarus and Kazakhstan agreed to submit their nuclear weapons to Russia, but have been dragging their feet on the implementation.

The May 1993 CIS collective security treaty signed in Tashkent provided an umbrella for the new security arrangements, but only six out of eleven CIS members, all in dire need of Russian support and protection, signed the treaty (Armenia and all Central Asian republics except Turkmenistan). The SRF were excluded from under the CIS jurisdiction, as already noted. The status of the General Purpose Forces was unclear, and was regulated by bilateral treaties. The joint forces were mostly stationed in the conflict zones of Transcaucasus and Central Asia; some were under joint Russian-national command (Turkmenistan); in the four other Central Asian republics they were under national command. There were also Russian forces in the area, under Russian command, such as the notorious 14th Army in Moldova, the 4th and 7th Armies in the Transcaucasus, and the 201st Motor Rifle Division in Tajikistan. These were the forces which were engaged in "peacekeeping." As shall be seen below, some were specifically designated as peacekeeping contingents under UN criteria and were officially, if not necessarily in practice, multinational in composition. Others claimed peacekeeping status but were really engaged in Russia's peacemaking.

In addition to different perceptions of the nature of the strategic and joint forces, differences emerged between the Russian Defence Ministry and the CIS command, supported by CIS members, over a proposed new security system. Shaposhnikov and CIS members favoured a NATO-like structure, while the Russian Defence Ministry pressed for arrangements resembling the Warsaw Pact. By mid-1993, Russian pressure and intransigence intensified, based on a perception in Russian political and military circles that the CIS command was "a fig leaf that Moscow can no longer afford and . . . may not need."[38] At the June 15 Moscow meeting of the CIS defence ministers a decision was taken to abolish the CIS joint military command. Its replacement, on a temporary basis, was the chief of the joint staff for coordinating military cooperation between CIS states, with reduced staff and limited duties. The decision was apparently passed unanimously (shades of recent history!). The details of future arrangements were hazy,[39] probably because Ukraine continued to resist, even though other recalcitrant CIS members were brought back to heel thanks to a year of energetic Russian "peacekeeping," as shall be seen below. A Western observer described the June 15 decision as "the penultimate nail in the CIS's military coffin."[40] Indications were that the future of the organization would be shaped along the lines familiar to the students of the Warsaw Pact.

Peacekeeping was a part of CIS security arrangements under Shaposhnikov. An agreement on peacekeeping (signed by all CIS members except Turkmenistan) was concluded in March 1992. But initially the peacekeeping capacity of the former Soviet forces was limited, and there were differences in the perceptions of the nature and utility of peacekeeping, as well as a reluctance to get involved in the ethnic conflicts of the former periphery, although contingents were sent to Moldova and to South Ossetia and, internationally, to the former Yugoslavia.[41] At the same time there is evidence that from the beginning there were elements in Moscow directly fomenting separatist pro-Moscow movements in the autonomous units of the national republics in order to subvert the latters' drive for independence.[42]

It was only with the change in Russia's military leadership and an emergence of a coordinated Russian foreign and military policy that peacekeeping was adopted as a preferred instrument for the restoration of Russia's hegemony in the "near abroad." By the end of 1993 the Russian army had a peacekeeping division in specialized training, one regiment of which was monitoring a ceasefire in the Dniester republic, while a battalion was peacekeeping in Ossetia.[43] In addition, regular and border forces were deployed for "peacekeeping" in Central Asia and Transcausus.

The new emphasis on peacekeeping, in early 1994, was reflected in the attention paid to it by political and military leaders. The army's holiday was celebrated by President Yeltsin by praising military personnel for their peacekeeping operations in trouble spots, and by Defence Minister Grachev stressing the troops' contribution in preventing further bloodshed in Moldova, Ossetia, Abkhazia, and Tajikistan. Grachev disclosed that some sixteen thousand Russian peacekeepers served in the "near and far abroad." At another occasion the minister of defence described the peacekeeping in the former Soviet space as necessary for the protection of Russian lives there, in the absence of other security safeguards. The chorus of praise would be incomplete without Foreign Minister Kozyrev, who, for his part, emphasized international legitimacy of Russian peacekeeping operations. According to Kozyrev, they were "now traditional" in terms of UN practice because they were "carried out in the territory of neighbouring countries where Russia has serious economic and other interests," a somewhat novel interpretation of UN usages. But Kozyrev diverged somewhat from the general Russian tune by welcoming the presence of UN or CSCE observers—an anathema for the military—and speaking of Russia's desire for "serious help." The invitation was hedged, however, by saying that the "right moment" for foreign observers to come was after a ceasefire, when they could be a "third force" supporting Russian troops.[44]

The instrumental value of a Russian military presence and peacekeeping in 1993–94 for Russian neo-imperial interests is best illustrated by analyzing the sequence of events in the now largely pacified hot spots.

The Caucasus

Enough has been said already about the Caucasus area to underscore its crucial importance to Russia as well as its politically and militarily volatile character. It has had the dubious distinction of harbouring three out of the five hot spots: the Armenian-Azerbaijani war over Nagorno-Karabakh; the conflicts attendant at Georgia's national integration; and separatism and warfare in North Caucasus.

The *Nagorno-Karabakh conflict* was the first to erupt in February 1988, reflecting the desire of the Armenian population of the enclave (the Nagorno-Karabakh Autonomous Province—NKAO) in Azerbaijan to join Armenia, from which it has been divided by a relatively narrow Azeri-populated territory. This extremely complex struggle involved the conflict between Armenia and Azerbaijan, three rounds of fighting and high casualties and "ethnic cleansing" on both sides (with one million displaced Azeris and half a million displaced Armenians, and up to twenty thousand military and civilian casualties),[45] covert and overt Russian military intervention which ran the gamut from a hands-off policy, to support first for Armenia then for Azerbaijan, to an imposition of a Pax Russica, and efforts at mediation by the border states Turkey and Iran, the UN, NATO, and CSCE.[46]

First clashes between Armenia and Azerbaijan came over NKAO's February 1988 declaration of intent to join Armenia, followed by three days of massacre of Armenians in the town of Sumgait near Baku. There are indications that the riots might have been manipulated by the KGB; at any rate, the upshot was the Soviet military occupation of Azerbaijan, as well as Yerevan, the capital of Armenia, and NKAO, which stymied the political momentum of Azeri nationalist Popular Front, and was of assistance to the Armenians.

The second round came after the collapse of the Soviet Union, with a January 1992 Armenian attack (formally from NKAO but aided and abetted by Armenia) to open up a corridor between the enclave and Armenia. Azeri appeal for Russian military assistance was turned down, and Russian troops were in fact withdrawn on February 28 from Nagorno-Karabakh on the orders of Marshal Shaposhnikov. Numerous reports indicated the troops' involvement on the Armenian side, including elements of the 4th and the 7th Russian armies and paratroops. Since the CIS joint command denied any such involvement, it might therefore have been the local commanders' private initiative. Militarily, the result of the action was the opening up of the Lachin corridor between NKAO and Armenia. Politically, the Azeri defeat resulted in a change of government, with the nationalist Popular Front under Abulfaz Elchibey coming to power in March 1992. The new government took Azerbaijan out of the CIS. The Armenian victory was followed by efforts at international mediation and negotiations of numerous ceasefires neither one of which lasted.

The third round came in April 1993, with another Armenian offensive. By August the Armenians opened two new corridors between NKAO and Armenia—in the north (by taking Kelbajar) and in the south (by taking Fizuli), evicting Azeris from the area in between. Again numerous reports indicated Russian military support for Armenia. Rapid Armenian advances, ethnic cleansing, and high human losses caused great international concern, especially in Turkey and Iran (a substantial Azeri minority lives across the border in Iran), both of which issued warnings. The late Turkish president Turgut Ozal accused Russia of interfering.[47] A CSCE meeting in Rome authorized sending a one thousand strong peacekeeping contingent once a ceasefire was arranged.

The Azeri disaster in the third round resulted in the overthrow of Elchibey's nationalist government by a military coup in favour of Haidar Aliev, a former member of the Brezhnev Politbureau who, since the Soviet collapse, was a parliamentary leader of Nakhichevan, an Azeri enclave in Armenia on the border with Iran. With Azerbaijan facing imminent disintegration, Aliev turned to Moscow seeking reconciliation and assistance. A round of Moscow-sponsored negotiations followed. In late October Russia threw its support behind Azerbaijan. On October 25 Russia demanded a stop to the Armenian offensive, and the following day Azerbaijan rejoined the CIS. A rumoured undercover deployment of Russian troops saved the Azeri army from collapse, and prevented further Armenian penetration. On February 18, 1994, a ceasefire was signed in Moscow between Azerbaijan and Armenia, mediated by General Grachev. It allowed the Armenians to keep the Lachin corridor, but not the 1993 gains, and it opened the way for the stationing of Russian troops on the borders with Turkey and Iran and the establishment of Russian military bases in Azerbaijan and Armenia.

In *Georgia* a similar sequence of events took place. Conflicts had been generated there both by separatist aspirations of the Muslim minorities and by the rivalry between factions contending for the leadership of an independent Georgia. Georgia's nationalists spearheaded the drive for independence and, gaining power in the elections of the fall of 1990 under Zviad Gamsakhurdia, refused to join the CIS when it was established. Moscow's response was to foment separatist aspirations of the Abkhazians in the Abkhaz Autonomous Republic and the Ossetins in South Ossetia. In 1989 the Abkhaz demanded a union republic status (even though ethnic Abkhaz constituted only 17 percent of the population) and secession from Georgia. They allied themselves in the next two years with the Muslims of North Caucasus (in the Russian Federation), organized in the Confederation of the Mountain Peoples against Georgia.[48]

An Abkhaz challenge in August 1992 was met by force by the Georgians, led at this point by Eduard Shevardnadze, the former Soviet foreign minister and previously first secretary of Georgia's Communist party. In the resulting struggle the Abkhaz won, forcing the Georgian population, along with Georgian troops, out of Abkhazia. The Georgians and independent observers credit the Abkhaz victory solely to Russian military assistance. "My conviction is that the plan for the occupation of Sukhumi [Abkhaz capital] has been drawn up in Russian headquarters," Shevardnadze was quoted as saying on September 28, 1993.[49] These allegations were vigorously denied by Moscow. With Georgian forces in retreat, Shevardnadze's ousted nationalist rival, Gamsakhurdia, decided to stage a comeback, scoring impressive successes. Pushed to the wall, Shevardnadze appealed to Moscow for help, and in a change of front, Russian troops came to his rescue. But the price was steep and deeply resented in Georgia.

Shevardnadze joined the two other Transcaucasian leaders in Moscow for a round of peace talks in early October, which resulted in a comprehensive peace settlement on Russian terms. On October 8 he signed the statement declaring Georgia's entry into the CIS, followed by the status-of-forces agreement which legitimized the presence of the Russian forces already in the country and authorized the stationing of additional Russian troops and the use of the Poti Black Sea naval base. A Russian-Georgian Friendship Treaty, signed in Tbilisi on February 3, 1994, allows Russia to maintain three military bases in Georgia after 1995, and provides for the Russian military to train and supply the Georgian army, as well as to station troops on the Turkish border.

There was talk also of Georgia coming back into the ruble zone. For his part Shevardnadze has tried to dilute the weight of the Russian presence by negotiating with the West. On a March 1994 visit to Washington, he extracted an American promise of economic help and of a peacekeeping force to be sent to Georgia to "help in the civil war." The latter was hedged by so many conditions that implementation did not seem likely; it was seen by American officials nonetheless as having a potential to go "a long way toward lessening Russia's influence" in the region.[50]

The Muslim peoples of *North Caucasus* regard the Russian change of front as a betrayal, and continue to agitate for greater autonomy. These include the Abkhaz (who asked for a Russian peacekeeping force to be deployed there to defend them from the Georgians), the Ossetins (an officially multi-ethnic but *de facto* Russian peacekeeping contingent has been in South Ossetia since July 1992), Chechenya (which unilaterally declared independence), Ingushetiya (in conflict with the Ossetins over the recovery of their former area of settlement), and Daghestan. Moscow sees the Russian military presence in the region both as a safeguard against Muslim regional powers and against the Muslims of the Caucasus turning against the Russian Federation.[51]

The gain, for Russia, of the 1993 peacemaking in the Caucasus region has been the return to the "family" of two of the stray sheep, however unwillingly, as well as the re-establishment there of a commanding military presence. General Grachev was quoted as saying that "Russia intends to keep three military bases in Georgia and five military bases in the Caucasus as a whole, with a total troop strength of 23,000." Their task, under the CIS security treaty, will be to "protect the region against outside threat."[52] The importance to Russia of the Caucasus region was underscored by Moscow's request of October 1993 to other signatories of the Conventional Forces in Europe (CFE) Treaty for an upward revision of the limits imposed by the treaty on flank deployment of weapons in the region. It is improbable that other CFE signatories will comply with this request.

Central Asia

Central Asia is another frontier which Russia considers vital for several reasons. Strategically it borders on China and the Islamic world. Its Muslim population is vulnerable to the influence both of fundamentalist Islam (of which Iran is the fountainhead) and Pan-Turkic ideas emanating from Turkey, which extends to the Muslim population within the Russian Federation. The region's natural resources are rich and largely unexplored: Kazakh and Turkmen oil and gas are the prime example. In the Soviet period Central Asia was in many ways considered a provincial backwater and an economic burden. This view persisted through the last days of the Soviet Union and new Russia's first year of independence, particularly since Central Asian political leaders, both old and new, felt too dependent on Russia to strike out on their own. But the situation and perceptions had changed on both sides by the end of 1992. The Russians woke up to the dangers of foreign penetration through the soft southern underbelly, and Central Asians took new foreign and economic policy initiatives.

The incumbent Central Asian political leaders recognize their continued dependence on and the need for the Russian security umbrella. Kazakhstan, Kyrgyzstan, Uzbekistan, and Tajikistan joined the CIS as it was created and signed the Tashkent Collective Security Treaty. Turkmenistan made its own security arrangements with Russia. Neither had ambitions to develop national armies and have only now begun to do so under Russian prodding. Central Asians recognize their economic dependence on Russia; at the same time they have all pursued policies to develop economic and political contacts among themselves, with regional powers and with the West. In January 1994 the two largest, Kazakhstan and Uzbekistan, joined by Kyrgyzstan, agreed to create a common market by the year 2000.[53] All but Tajikistan have established their own currency. In 1992 the five Central Asian states plus Azerbaijan and Afghanistan joined the Economic Cooperation Organization, newly established by Turkey, Iran, and Pakistan. Along with other former Soviet republics all five joined the CSCE. Individually each has been developing closer relations with Turkey and Iran, and reaching out to the West — Kazakhstan in particular — on the economic and political front.

The perception in Moscow is that politically and economically Central Asia may be slipping out of Russia's exclusive grasp. The perceived danger to Russian interests represented by the Islamic political forces, secular nationalism, and democratic liberalism has contributed to greater Russian interest, tougher policies in the region, and the concern over Russian minorities living there. In November 1993 Kozyrev made a tour of the area, pressing hard for dual citizenship and closer cooperation.

Central Asia's hot spot has been Tajikistan. With Islamic penetration in the background, the Tajik civil war has involved a range of regional and local issues: internal diversity — ethnic and clan-based — a contest between the old and the new forces, and the ties, by Tajik groups, with elements across the Afghan border. It started when the formation of a national government (built on an alliance between liberal democrats, secular nationalists, and Islamic revivalists) was contested by the ousted communist nomenklatura. Each side had support in specific regions of the country. The communists won because of Russian military help, and have been maintained in power by the Russian troops and Russian border guards, while the opposition fled—the religious elements to Afghanistan, the secular democratic and nationalist intelligentsia to Moscow. By the end of 1993 it was estimated that the losses in the Tajik civil war amounted to some twenty-five thousand casualties with much greater numbers of displaced civilian refugees.

The Russian military presence and operations in Tajikistan have been based on a bilateral treaty concluded under the CIS collective security arrangements and are explicitly designated as peacekeeping, by Russia and the other Central Asian signatories. The Russian contingent (under Russian command) consists of the 201st Motorized Rifles Division (at full strength and consisting entirely of volunteers) and a division of Border Guards stationed on the Tajik-Afghan border, with troops in almost daily combat. According to General Boris Pyankov, commander-in-chief of the peacekeeping forces in Tajikistan speaking on December 22, 1993, the promised Uzbek, Kazakh, and Kyrgyz contingents have yet to materialize, the funding problems have not been resolved, and so far the UN and CSCE have not agreed to designate the forces as a peacekeeping mission, because of the questions raised by the United States of Russian neutrality.[54] By the end of 1993 Tajikistan received 70 percent of its budget from Russia; it was the only one among Central Asian states to join the ruble zone and to subordinate its fiscal policies to Russia in exchange for military assistance, becoming in fact a Russian client state. At the same time new security agreements were signed. Russia and the four states agreed to set up a "coalition" peacekeeping force in Tajikistan, and the signatory states of the CIS Collective Security Treaty signed an agreement to set up a common air defence system and to develop joint forces.[55]

Turkmenia preferred to stay outside the CIS system but, as noted earlier, has concluded separate military arrangements with Russia. An agreement of July 1992 provided for Russia's defence of Turkmenistan (with the costs of the 108,000 Russian troops stationed there to be paid by Turkmenistan), for the joint command over the Russian forces and for Russian officers to build up and train the Turkmen army. Another agreement of military cooperation was signed on September 2, 1993; it allows Russian citizens to carry out their military service in Turkmenistan, and Turkmen officers to be trained in Russia, and provides for Russian military bases in Turkmenistan. A follow-up agreement of December 23 allows for the deployment of Russian border guards along the Turkmen border with Iran and Afghanistan; an accord on dual citizenship for Russians resident in Turkmenistan was signed at the same time.[56] Turkmenistan, so far, is the only former Soviet republic which signed a dual citizenship agreement.

With the conclusion of these agreements the Grachev postulate of stationing Russian troops along the entire southern borders of the former Soviet Union was carried out, and a new joint defence system under the CIS began to take shape.

Moldova's Dniester Republic

The western hot spot, currently quiescent but not resolved, erupted in March 1992, when a region of Moldova, located on the left bank of the Dniester and populated primarily by ethnic Russians, declared independence as the "Dniester republic." The break came over Moldova's professed desire to join Romania. (Moldova is the former Romanian Bessarabia that had been annexed by the Soviet Union during World War Two; the trans-Dniester region, on the other hand, was a part of the USSR in the inter-war period). In the struggle which ensued, the ex-Soviet 14th Army fought with the Dniester rebels against Moldova. The Russian government and military high command disclaimed any knowledge of the action but offered peacekeeping services instead, to be performed by the very same 14th Army. The offer was rejected by Moldova, negotiations proceeded in the CIS, and the fighting continued. By early July CIS members agreed to send a peacekeeping force composed of Russian (not the 14th Army), Moldovan, Ukrainian, Belarussian, Romanian, and Bulgarian contingents. But within a week the last three opted out, while Moldova, frightened by Russian threats, appealed to the CSCE. The UN/CSCE were unable and/or unwilling to act, and in the circumstances Moldova had no choice but to accept Russian peacekeeping. An agreement between the Moldovan and Russian presidents provided for a Russian, Moldovan, and Dniester peacekeeping force, while recognizing the formal autonomy of the Dniester region, thus institutionalizing the partition. The Russian contingent (an additional two thousand troops) arrived by the end of July, but the 14th Army stayed on and an uneasy peace has prevailed since.[57]

Moldova continued its efforts to "internationalize" the dispute and to achieve the withdrawal of Russian forces through 1993, the more so because the Russian Federation openly supported the Dniester republic, and the 14th Army helped in the creation of a Dniester army which, with a strength of eight thousand, doubled the size of the Russian forces there. Bilateral negotiations with Russia over troop withdrawal brought no results, and Russia refused to accept the presence of, or inspection by, a CSCE mission in the disputed territory as requested by the Moldovans. These actions placed Russian demands for a UN peacekeeping mandate in a doubtful light. At the same time strong Russian pressure was brought to bear on Moldova to return to the CIS. Customs duties and excise taxes were imposed on Moldovan agricultural exports to Russia on August 1. The duties priced Moldova out of the Russian market and made payments for the imports of Russian raw materials and fuel impossible. The customs duties were partly rescinded at the end of December when the Moldovan government promised to rejoin CIS economic and political structures after Moldova's 1994 elections.[58]

By the beginning of 1994 it was clear that Moldova, along with the Transcaucasian and Central Asian republics and Belarus[59] had been drawn back into the Russian orbit. The main showdown as the year progressed promised to be with Ukraine, over outstanding issues of territorial claims, division of nuclear and other assets, and Russian minority rights.[60] The relations with the Baltic republics also promised to be tense because of the problem of Russian minorities and the continued, if reduced, presence there of the Russian troops.

International Peacekeeping

Russian participation in international peacekeeping began with two contingents sent to the former Yugoslavia early in 1992. At the time it was a matter of prestige, influence, and commitment to the prevention of aggression. Justifying the action before Parliament, President Yeltsin also mentioned that the experience gained would be helpful in dealing with the Federation's domestic problems.[61] The decision to participate in an international operation, which in the Russian popular mind was designed to stop the Serbs in their efforts to rebuild the Serbian state, did not win popularity contests in Russian nationalist circles. First, it was seen as a betrayal, by the "traitors" Yeltsin and Kozyrev, of the traditions of Russian-Serb friendship and anti-Muslim struggle. Second, it had an uncomfortable domestic relevance — namely, defending the rights of break-away republics.

The two contingents of Russian peacekeepers of approximately twelve hundred men, one stationed in Krajina and the other in Bosnia, were generally welcomed by the local Serbs. But even more welcome were Russian volunteers who came to fight in the Serbian cause. Late in 1992 there were two detachments of such volunteers, one fighting in Bosnia and another in Herzegovina. In addition, individual military specialists served in Serbian units — at least one or two in every unit, according to Serbian commanders interviewed by a Russian paper. With recruiting centres in Moscow and St. Petersburg, there was no evidence of official sponsorship for the volunteers, but strong support for the Serbian cause was noted among recently retired Russian officers.[62]

A new perception of the value of international peacekeeping came with the success of the Russian "peacekeeping" in the "near abroad," coupled with accumulated frustrations of being treated as a junior partner in international forums. The latter was particularly galling in the case of Bosnia — the Balkans have traditionally been Russia's sphere of interest — where the peacekeeping has been run pretty much as a joint NATO-UN operation, which effectively left out the Russians. Matters came to a head over the February 1994 air strikes ultimatum to Bosnia's Serbs over the shelling of Sarajevo; the Russians were opposed, but have had no say in the decision.

In a brilliant tour de force which was a surprise to their Western partners, the Russians at one stroke took the allies off the hook in the matter of enforcing the air strikes, made the Sarajevo ceasefire stick thanks to their influence over the Serbs, and injected themselves back into the policy making as a senior partner. Domestically the move has helped to rehabilitate the image of the government in the eyes of nationalists, with Foreign Minister Kozyrev and particularly the deputy minister, Vitaly Churkin, as the main heroes of the initiative. An additional Russian contingent sent to help in maintaining the ceasefire was greeted by the local Serbs with great enthusiasm, raising some Western doubts of Russian neutrality.[63] But the peace held and probable Western casualties were avoided, so everyone but the Muslims were pleased. The Serbs' face was saved and their territorial gains in Bosnia were secured. Last but not least, by using the traditional Russian-Serbian friendship the Russians turned a liability into an asset and introduced a novel idea into Western peacekeeping—namely, that interested parties not only can but should participate.

The move was an important step also in Russia's new quest for great power status. Acting effectively as one evoked the treatment desired. In the aftermath, the United States agreed to admit Russia to the discussions of the Bosnian problem ("the first time that the United States agreed to include Russia in such discussions"),[64] and agreed to a joint sponsorship of a conference on the crisis. Entering the Bosnian conflict, Russia has taken the first step towards acceptance as an equal partner in a new concert of Europe. Peacemaking may also be the lever to bring Russia back into great powers councils in the Middle East and in East Asia, as it has offered peacekeeping services in the Israeli-Palestinian crisis and, most recently, in offering to defuse the gathering confrontation with North Korea.

Conclusions

"'Peacemaking' has become a central element in Russia's foreign policy," stated Andrei Kozyrev, Russia's foreign minister, at a Geneva conference on the protection of war victims on August 31, 1993.[65] It is not clear whether the substitution of "peacemaking" for "peacekeeping" was intentional; it might have been because he then pointed out that Russian actions in Moldova and Ossetia stopped the bloodshed, while Western efforts in the former Yugoslavia did not. But even if unintentional, the word substitution underscores the difference between the UN and the Russian style of peacekeeping. The UN peacekeeping requires strict neutrality on the part of the participating contingents; it is not undertaken unless a ceasefire is already in place, and is limited to separating the belligerents and maintaining the ceasefire; it precludes active military interference except in self-defence. The Russian peacekeeping has actually served national interests. It allows (requires) military intervention to stop the fighting and/or to achieve peacekeepers' political/strategic objectives; and it allows for the use of force in peace maintenance. United Nations' peacekeeping cannot be undertaken without an international mandate; Russian peacekeeping has been mostly undertaken unilaterally, sometimes coopting partners for greater credibility, and an international mandate has been sought in some, but not all, cases.

In short, Russia's peacekeeping is really peacemaking, and it has been an instrument of national policy in Russia's quest for the restoration of its great power status and the dominant role in its historical geostrategic space. The goals and the perceptions have been clearly articulated by Foreign Minister Kozyrev, in a symbolic gauntlet thrown to the United States on the pages of the New York Times.[66]

"We, Russian democrats," he argues, are engaged in "the transformation of the—volatile post-Communist orbit into a stable, democratic order" (obviously assuming Russia's automatic succession rights to the post-communist orbit), but "have met fierce political—even armed—resistance." Here he refers, presumably, to the efforts of the "near abroad" to maintain independence and to East Central Europe's objections to Russia's exercising its veto power on their behalf. "Sadly," continues Kozyrev, "in these confused days we are neither understood nor adequately supported by our natural friends and allies in the West. Even at this critical moment . . . we hear Western threats to reduce economic cooperation with Russia." These "suggest an almost maniacal desire to see only one leading power—the United States of America." This is "unrealistic," argues Kozyrev, because it would only lead to power exhaustion by the United States, which cannot alone resolve all of the world's problems. "Besides, even at this difficult stage of our transition, Russia remains a superpower," and cannot be treated as a junior partner. What should we do "about the chauvinistic new banners that flap in the Washington wind?" laments Russia's foreign minister, not realizing perhaps that the same question, substituting Moscow for Washington, is increasingly being asked in Western capitals. But, he proceeds, pragmatic politicians on both sides see the "mature" partnership between Russia and the West in terms of *realpolitik*, based on "two premises." First, that "Russia is destined to be a great power"; and second, that "partnerships like ours cannot negate a firm, even aggressive, policy of defending one's own national interests."

If the above genuinely represents the thinking of Russia's leading "liberal democrat," the prospects for future international cooperation, let alone independent democratic development in the Soviet successor states and ex-Soviet bloc countries, are not encouraging. One marvels at the hutzpah of the claims, in one breath, to democracy and imperial expansion, and to a superpower status for a country in economic and political chaos. One marvels even more at the Western tacit approval of Russian imperial pretensions conditioned, no doubt, by the years of Soviet propaganda as much as by the immediate convenience of having Russia take care of the troublesome conflicts at its periphery that otherwise might have required Western intervention. But there is no doubt that the Russian policy, in operation for barely a year, has been successful. The question is whether it can be, or should be, sustained.

In the "near abroad," Russian peacemaking has stopped most of the open conflicts by the judicious use of military power. The price for the new states involved has been the acceptance of the Russian umbrella. The gain for Russia has been the extension, except for the hard-pressed Ukraine and the Baltic states, of its political influence and military control across the former "inner empire." Russia's Monroe Doctrine — that is, its right to the former imperial heritage — has been clearly articulated and has claimed legitimacy, in the eyes of the international community, by its ostensibly humanitarian purpose of peace maintenance and by its very effectiveness.

A similar claim to the former communist East Central Europe has been implied but not explicitly articulated. But all of the arguments based on Russia's traditional geopolitical space, national interest, and great power status are highly elastic and well suited to accommodate the "outer empire," including the Balkans. The first steps in this direction — the veto on the inclusion in NATO of the former Warsaw Pact states and Russia's entry into the Bosnian crisis — have been accepted by the West. Unless Russia again collapses from within, it is only a matter of time before the "outer empire" is also claimed as Russia's rightful heritage.

The policy has succeeded also in the international context. It has revived the concept of Russia as a great power to the applause of the believers in bipolarity and political realists who like to divide the world into spheres of influence. By a fait accompli, Russia established its right to pursue national interests within its own self-proclaimed domain without asking for international approval and excluding international interference and participation. Pax Russica does carry the benefits of stabilization. But stability based on coercion does not offer long-range solution to unresolved conflicts. Nationalism cannot be eradicated and, once tasted, independence can never be forgotten. The age of empires, moreover, has passed, and a second try, at the end of a century, to rebuild an empire which collapsed at its beginning only promises to repeat past disasters, probably on an accelerated timetable.

Russia does have legitimate national interests that have to be accommodated; so do other Soviet successor states, and the states of East Central Europe. Exclusive national claims to geopolitical space carry the seeds of their own destruction, because they mean the suppression of the rights of others who dwell in this space. The road to peace and accommodation of the many issues that divide post-communist states leads through negotiations based on equity and requires mutual compromises. It calls for the development of economic relations and resources based on reciprocity and mutual benefit. Most important, it needs a security umbrella which is not the instrument of a single power and would-be hegemon. Such conditions can be created only in an internationalized environment. As the chapters by David Long and Alexander Moens demonstrate, they already exist and function, however imperfectly, in Western Europe. The beginning of the resolution of the problems of the former East bloc, including Russia, would be to bring the members closer under the European umbrella and to include them within the existing cooperation, conflict resolution, and security mechanisms. Cutting them out opens the way for reincarnation of the imperial Russian system, with all that it implies. In the words of a Russian historian, "Imperial ambition will bring Russia to total ruin. The Soviet empire collapsed because it could not support so many territories, and all attempts to revive that policy are doomed to fail."[67]

12 Le maintien de la paix au Cambodge : La victoire de la diplomatie tranquille

Jocelyn Coulon

> The UN was never meant to create heaven on earth, just to save it from hell. Winston Churchill

LE 14 NOVEMBRE 1993, les Nations Unies mettaient fin, comme prévu, à leur mission au Cambodge. Ce jour-là, les derniers Casques bleus, des soldats français, quittaient le royaume après un séjour tumultueux de 18 mois.[1] Pour certains, ce départ très ordonné était la preuve que les Nations Unies avaient réussi à rétablir la paix dans ce petit pays dévasté par un quart de siècle de guerre. Pour d'autres, au contraire, le retrait des Casques bleus masquait l'échec politique de la mission onusienne. Pourtant, aujourd'hui, force est de constater que les critiques ont eu tort. En effet, pendant le déroulement de la mission, plusieurs — diplomates, militaires, coopérants et journalistes — prédisaient qu'elle aboutirait à un échec complet. Leurs arguments étaient nombreux et ne manquaient pas de poids : les factions violaient leurs engagements sans subir de sanctions; le désarmement des factions n'avait pas lieu tel que prévu; les aspects humanitaires et économiques étaient relégués au second plan; l'ONU cherchait simplement à organiser des élections pour se retirer rapidement. Tout cela était vrai et devant cet état de choses, certains observateurs des opérations de maintien de la paix ont souligné que la mission au Cambodge était un échec. Mais les observateurs les plus pessimistes oubliaient que, même avec la meilleure volonté du monde alliée à un mandat onusien très clair, à un budget important et à des pouvoirs considérables, une mission de maintien de la paix de l'envergure de celle qui a été déployée au Cambodge ne pouvait se dérouler sans quelques problèmes. Après tout, l'ONU s'était engagée dans la plus importante mission de son histoire avec le mandat de reconstruire le Cambodge dans les domaines

---

L'auteur tient à remercier Pierre Lizée, chercheur au York University, Center for International and Strategic Studies, à Toronto, pour ses précieux conseils.

politique, économique, social et humain en moins de deux ans. Une tâche titanesque. Malgré tout, pour une première mission de ce genre — plus complexe encore que celle qui mena la Namibie à l'indépendance en 1989–90 — le résultat obtenu par les Nations Unies n'est pas négligeable et je vais m'appliquer à le démontrer dans les pages qui vont suivre.

L'intervention de l'ONU

Petit pays de la péninsule indochinoise, le Cambodge ne manque pas d'attirer les voyageurs par ses contrastes géographiques saisissants et l'accueil chaleureux de ses habitants. Les rizières du sud-est et du centre du pays, souvent désertées faute d'outils agricoles, s'étendent à perte de vue. L'horizon est parfois troué de temples multicolores et de pics montagneux. Au nord-est, une région peu peuplée mais qui couvre près du tiers du territoire, des montagnes et des collines verdoyantes forment une spectaculaire barrière naturelle face au Laos et au Vietnam voisins. À l'ouest, près de la frontière thaïlandaise, la région n'est pas seulement riche en ressources naturelles — pierres et bois précieux — mais possède un héritage culturel — des temples et des palais de la vieille civilisation khmère du XIIe siècle — qui fait du Cambodge un lieu privilégié du patrimoine mondial de l'humanité. Au centre du pays, s'étend le magnifique lac Tonle Sap, aux eaux calmes et poissonneuses. Enfin, il y a les Cambodgiens, toujours rieurs et aimables même dans la misère la plus abjecte.

Pourtant, sous ce décor paradisiaque agrémenté de sourires bienveillants, se cachent un pays et un peuple qui depuis 1970 ont connu une cascade sans précédent de catastrophes humaines : bombardements américains, guerre civile, génocide, conflit avec le vieil ennemi vietnamien, et guérilla. Le Cambodge a été pris au centre de manoeuvres diplomatiques et militaires des grandes puissances. En deux décennies, le pays aurait perdu le tiers de sa population. Son territoire a été criblé de millions de mines. Ses infrastructures se sont effondrées. Ses élites politiques, profondément divisées, se sont querellées longtemps et obstinément grâce à l'appui qu'elles recevaient des grandes puissances et des acteurs régionaux.[2]

C'est dans ce contexte physique et politique que les Nations Unies ont décidé d'intervenir au Cambodge pour aider au rétablissement de la paix et à la reconstruction du pays.

L'ONU a commencé à s'intéresser au problème cambodgien en 1981 lorsqu'une conférence internationale sur le Cambodge s'est réunie sous son égide à New York le 13 juillet. Cependant, les pays de l'Est et le Vietnam, qui avait envahi le Cambodge et chassé les Khmers rouges du pouvoir en janvier 1979, ont boycotté la réunion, alors que la Chine s'est opposée à l'exclusion des Khmers rouges comme condition préalable à la tenue d'élections au Cambodge. En 1982, le Secrétaire général des Nations Unies a nommé un représentant spécial pour faciliter le dialogue entre les différentes factions politiques.[3] Malheureusement, ces pourparlers ont piétiné pendant plus de cinq ans, la situation politique en Indochine ne permettant pas un rapprochement significatif entre les parties. La Chine, principal soutien des Khmers rouges, était engagée dans une épreuve de force avec le Vietnam qui devait la conduire à des opérations militaires contre ce pays entre 1979 et 1987. Au Cambodge, le gouvernement de Phnom Penh, soutenu par les Vietnamiens, réussissait à repousser les attaques des Khmers rouges et de la résistance cambodgienne sihanoukiste. Enfin, à l'étranger, la coalition de la résistance cambodgienne présidée par l'ancien roi, le prince Norodom Sihanouk, était divisée sur son alliance avec les Khmers rouges et sur l'idée d'entreprendre des négociations avec le gouvernement de Phnom Penh.

Finalement, en 1986, la coalition de la résistance cambodgienne a accepté le principe d'un gouvernement d'union nationale avec le régime de Phnom Penh et a donné au prince Norodom Sihanouk le mandat d'entamer des négociations avec le premier ministre Hun Sen. La première rencontre entre les deux hommes a eu lieu du 2 au 4 décembre 1987 à Fère-en-Tardenois, non loin de Paris. D'autres rencontres ont suivi. Parallèlement, les pays de l'Asie du sud-est ont offert leurs services pour rapprocher les factions cambodgiennes, qui se sont réunies à Djakarta en 1988 et en 1989. Ces démarches diplomatiques ont abouti à l'ouverture de la Conférence de Paris sur le Cambodge, le 30 juillet 1989, qui réunissait 18 pays et les quatre factions cambodgiennes sous la présidence de la France et de l'Indonésie. Cette conférence s'est soldée par un échec mais le dialogue n'a pas été rompu pour autant. L'initiative diplomatique a été reprise par les cinq membres permanents du Conseil de sécurité des Nations Unies qui, au cours de plusieurs réunions tenues en 1990, ont bonifié le plan de règlement global que l'Australie avait mis de l'avant en février 1990, qui préconisait une intervention massive des Nations Unies. Les factions cambodgiennes ont accepté ce plan le 9 septembre 1990. Après de nouvelles rencontres organisées au début de 1991, la Conférence de Paris sur le Cambodge fut rouverte et aboutit, le 23 octobre 1991, à la signature d'un accord international de paix au Cambodge.[4]

L'Accord, signé par les quatre factions cambodgiennes — l'État du Cambodge, les Khmers rouges, les royalistes fidèles à Sihanouk et le FNLPK des républicains de Son Sann — et 18 pays, légitimait la mise en place du Conseil national suprême (CNS), formé en septembre 1990 et présidé par l'ancien roi Norodom Sihanouk, comme gouvernement légal de transition du Cambodge. Par ailleurs, l'Accord autorisait l'installation de l'Autorité provisoire des Nations Unies au Cambodge (APRONUC ou UNTAC en anglais) qui avait pour mandat de conduire ce pays au rétablissement complet de sa souveraineté et de son indépendance grâce, notamment, à l'organisation d'élections générales.

L'Accord de Paris comportait de nombreuses obligations pour les factions cambodgiennes et c'était l'APRONUC qui devait veiller à leur respect. Ainsi, les quatre factions s'engagaient à coopérer avec la mission de l'ONU pour : l'organisation d'élections générales par l'APRONUC; le contrôle par la mission des institutions publiques qui pourraient influer sur le déroulement de ces élections; la libération des prisonniers de guerre et le retour des réfugiés et personnes déplacées; le retrait du territoire cambodgien des forces étrangères et de leurs armes; le maintien d'un cessez-le-feu; enfin, le regroupement et le cantonnement des forces des factions ainsi que le stockage de leurs armes, munitions et équipements. En plus, l'APRONUC devait mettre en place un vaste programme de promotion des droits de la personne et de la démocratie, et faciliter la reconstruction économique et sociale du pays.

Toutes ces dispositions visaient à créer un environnement politique neutre et stable pour assurer le bon déroulement de l'élection des 120 membres de l'Assemblée constituante qui se tiendrait du 23 au 28 mai 1993. Par la suite, le chef de l'APRONUC devait proclamer les résultats seulement si les élections s'étaient déroulées "librement et équitablement." L'Assemblée devrait ensuite approuver une nouvelle constitution, se transformer en assemblée législative et donner son accord à la formation d'un nouveau gouvernement. À ce moment-là, l'APRONUC quitterait le pays.

Pour mener à bien sa mission pendant la période de transition, qui commençait le 23 octobre 1991 et qui ne devait pas excéder 18 mois, l'APRONUC reçut du CNS, "l'organe légitime unique et source de l'Autorité au Cambodge," "tous les pouvoirs nécessaires" pour assurer l'application de l'Accord de Paris. C'est donc dire que pour la première fois dans leur histoire, les Nations Unies prenaient en charge la direction d'un pays. l'APRONUC ne manquerait donc pas de moyens pour faire respecter l'Accord et ses principales dispositions. Ses pouvoirs lui permettaient même de destituer des membres des administrations civiles, qu'elle devait en principe contrôler, ainsi que d'arrêter, d'emprisonner et de poursuivre les individus qui violent les lois du pays ou les ordres de l'APRONUC. On verra par la suite que les dirigeants politiques et militaires de la mission choisiront la voie prudente de la diplomatie tranquille plutôt que celle, semée d'embûches, de la confrontation, quitte à supporter les intimidations, les meurtres et les violations de l'Accord.

Le déploiement de l'APRONUC

Dès la signature de l'Accord de Paris, l'ONU a dépêché des Casques bleus, regroupés au sein de la Mission préparatoire des Nations Unies au Cambodge (MIPRENUC ou UNAMIC en anglais), qui avaient pour tâche de faire observer le cessez-le-feu, de servir d'intermédiaire entre les factions cambodgiennes et de préparer le déploiement de l'APRONUC. Les 300 soldats et employés de la MIPRENUC se sont déployés dès la fin d'octobre 1991 et ont poursuivi leur travail jusqu'à leur absorption par l'APRONUC le 15 mars 1992.[5]

Ce n'est que quatre mois après la signature de l'Accord de Paris que le Conseil de sécurité a autorisé, le 28 février 1992, la création de l'APRONUC dont les effectifs seraient composés de 15 000 Casques bleus armés, de 600 observateurs et de 3600 policiers civils non armés, ainsi que de 1300 employés internationaux et de 700 volontaires pour la supervision des élections.[6] Sur place, l'APRONUC, qui disposait d'un budget d'environ 2 milliards de dollars US, engagera 8000 employés civils pour la durée de la mission et 50 000 Cambodgiens lors des élections de mai 1993.[7] Cette force onusienne était la plus importante mission jamais organisée par l'ONU depuis 1945. Les Nations Unies confièrent la direction de l'APRONUC au Japonais Yasushi Akashi, secondé dans ses fonctions militaires par un Australien, le lieutenant général John Sanderson.

Dans son rapport sur la création de l'APRONUC, le Secrétaire général de l'ONU a divisé les responsabilités de l'Autorité provisoire en sept composantes — droits de l'homme, élections, aspects militaires, administration civile, police, rapatriement et reconstruction — toutes dotées d'un mandat bien précis et requérant des ressources financières, humaines et techniques considérables. Il s'agissait pour l'APRONUC de reconstruire un pays, de sensibiliser la police et les citoyens aux droits humains, de contrôler l'administration civile des factions — particulièrement les activités des affaires étrangères, de la défense, des finances, de la sécurité publique et de l'information — de coordonner le rapatriement de centaines de milliers de réfugiés et, enfin, de gérer un programme de relèvement des services de santé, d'éducation, de logement, de transport et de restauration des installations publiques ainsi que de l'infrastructure de base du pays. De plus, le Secrétaire général a fixé un calendrier précis pour le déploiement des Casques bleus, le cantonnement et le désarmement des forces militaires des factions et la tenue des élections. À chaque phase du processus de paix, le Secrétaire général a prévu la réduction du personnel civil et militaire de l'ONU, et ce, jusqu'à la fin de la mission.[8]

L'intervention des Nations Unies sur le terrain s'est déroulée en deux temps. La première mission, la MIPRENUC, s'est déployée rapidement pour signifier la détermination de la communauté internationale à voir les parties ayant signé l'Accord de Paris respecter leurs engagements. Ainsi, les officiels de cette mission avaient pour tâche d'accueillir les chefs de factions de retour au pays, d'établir le contact avec toutes les forces politiques à travers le Cambodge et de servir d'intermédiaire entre les factions. Toutefois, les effectifs de la MIPRENUC n'étaient pas suffisants pour la tâche et n'ont pu, par exemple, empêcher une violente attaque contre le leader des Khmers rouges, Khieu Samphan, lors de son retour à Phnom Penh le 27 novembre 1991. La faible représentation de l'ONU sur place n'a pas dissuadé les factions d'agir et elles se sont livrées à des assassinats politiques.

La deuxième mission, celle de l'APRONUC, n'a entrepris son déploiement officiel que le 15 mars avec l'arrivée du chef de la mission, Yasushi Akashi, et des bataillons indonésien, malais, thaïlandais, ainsi que d'une unité de communications australienne. La plupart des bataillons de Casques bleus — néerlandais, français, bangladeshi, pakistanais, uruguayen, indien, bulgare, ghanéen, tunisien, chinois et japonais ainsi que les unités médicales, aériennes, navales, de déminage et de logistique — n'arrivèrent sur le terrain qu'à partir du début de juin et se déployèrent jusqu'en novembre. Ce retard dans le déploiement des effectifs de l'APRONUC aura des conséquences militaires et politiques importantes dans l'application du mandat de la mission.

En effet, dans le souci de faciliter un déploiement rapide des bataillons d'infanterie dans les neuf secteurs délimités par l'ONU sur l'ensemble du territoire cambodgien, le plan du Secrétaire général prévoyait l'envoi d'unités d'ingénieurs, de démineurs et de logisticiens pour réparer et déminer les routes et pour mettre sur pied un système de transport. Malheureusement, c'est la séquence inverse qui s'est déroulée. Voulant établir une présence immédiate et importante au moment de l'arrivée de son représentant spécial, M. Akashi, l'ONU a autorisé certains bataillons d'infanterie à se déployer aussi rapidement que possible. Plusieurs de ces bataillons — le néerlandais et le pakistanais en particulier — ont été incapables d'atteindre le secteur qu'on leur avait désigné et de s'y déployer à cause de l'état des infrastructures, de la présence de mines sur les routes et de l'obstruction des Khmers rouges.[9] Le déploiement des autres contingents s'est fait de façon chaotique. Ainsi, le bataillon uruguayen n'a pas été en mesure de s'installer dans le secteur 4 à la date fixée par l'ONU, ce qui a obligé les Français à couvrir tout ce secteur pendant plusieurs mois. La plupart des bataillons ont commencé à se déployer en pleine saison des pluies — qui commence en mai — alors que le plan initial prévoyait le déploiement final de la composante militaire avant la fin de mai. La présence de tous les bataillons sur l'ensemble du territoire cambodgien à cette date était importante, car le 13 juin 1992 commençait une phase clé de l'application de l'Accord de Paris, soit la démobilisation des forces armées des quatre factions.

Une des réussites essentielles au bon déroulement du processus électoral et à l'instauration d'un environnement politique neutre avait trait au nettoyage du paysage militaire. Au programme : cantonnement et désarmement de 200 000 soldats et démobilisation de 70 % d'entre eux, désarmement de 250 000 miliciens, stockage des armes et du matériel des forcesmilitaires cantonnées et démobilisées ainsi que localisation et confiscation des caches d'armes et des fournitures militaires dans l'ensemble du pays. Le processus de cantonnement et de démobilisation devait être terminé à la fin de septembre 1992.[10] Pour que ce processus soit mené à bien et simultanément pour les quatre factions, les Casques bleus devaient être installés dans leur secteur et avoir accès aux territoires que contrôlaient les factions. Or, en juin, plusieurs contingents commençaient à peine à se déployer, alors que les Khmers rouges interdisaient l'accès aux territoires qu'ils contrôlaient. Signataires de l'Accord de Paris, les Khmers rouges ont commencé à s'opposer aux Nations Unies avant même le déploiement de l'APRONUC. Ainsi, en février 1992, ils ont profité de l'absence des troupes de l'ONU pour étendre leurs bases et se sont mis à refuser systématiquement l'accès de leurs territoires aux représentants de l'ONU qui devaient faire des tournées d'inspection.[11]

Dans son rapport du 1er mai au Conseil de sécurité, le Secrétaire général de l'ONU, qui affichait toujours son optimisme, soulignait que les Khmers rouges avaient levé certaines restrictions sur l'accès à leurs territoires.[12] Mais le 30 mai, ce fut la confrontation avec les dirigeants de l'APRONUC. Yasushi Akashi et le général John Sanderson se sont vu refuser l'entrée dans la zone de Pailin, contrôlée par les Khmers rouges.[13] Ils ont rebroussé chemin. Le 8 juillet, lors d'une réunion du Conseil national suprême, les Khmers rouges ont réitéré leur refus d'appliquer l'Accord de Paris et ont demandé une enquête sur la présence des Vietnamiens au Cambodge et sur le contrôle, par l'APRONUC, de l'administration civile du gouvernement de Phnom Penh, ainsi qu'un renforcement des pouvoirs du CNS. L'ONU, après avoir critiqué les Khmers rouges, a cédé et a tenté d'apporter des correctifs à sa politique pour les satisfaire.[14] Mais les Khmers rouges ont rejeté les ouvertures des Nations Unies. Le 13 octobre, le Conseil de sécurité leur a donné un mois pour réintégrer le processus de paix.[15] Le 15 novembre, constatant le refus de coopérer des Khmers rouges et malgré le fait que les trois autres factions avaient commencé à regrouper leurs forces et à rendre certaines armes, l'ONU a suspendu le processus de cantonnement et de démobilisation et a porté ses efforts sur le processus électoral.[16] Le 30 novembre, le Conseil de sécurité a adopté des sanctions contre les Khmers rouges.[17] À partir de ce moment, ceux-ci se sont mis à s'attaquer systématiquement aux forces militaires et civiles de l'APRONUC, et ce jusqu'à la veille des élections de mai 1993.

Le travail sur le terrain

L'évolution de la situation politique et la modification des responsabilités de la composante militaire de l'APRONUC ont eu des incidences sur le travail quotidien des Casques bleus sur le terrain. La saison des pluies, les infrastructures routières inadéquates, le danger lié aux mines et les difficultés d'approvisionnement ont ralenti l'arrivée des contingents et surtout leur déploiement dans leur secteur. Malgré les directives onusiennes spécifiant que tous les bataillons devaient apporter du matériel militaire pour effectuer leurs missions et des provisions pour tenir 60 jours sans réapprovisionnement, de nombreuses unités sont arrivées sur place sans ce minimum.[18] À l'instar de ce qui s'est passé pour d'autres missions onusiennes à travers le monde, des Casques bleus ont passé tellement de temps à s'installer et à tenter de vivre au jour le jour qu'ils n'ont pu exécuter immédiatement leur mandat. Certains contingents ne sont devenus opérationnels que vers la fin de 1992. Ainsi, à cause de problèmes de politique intérieure au Japon, le bataillon d'ingénieurs japonais chargé de réparer routes et ponts ne s'est installé dans la région de Takéo qu'en novembre.

Selon de nombreux employés civils et militaires de l'APRONUC, la force ou la faiblesse d'un contingent dans son secteur était due à une multitude de facteurs : entraînement, présence sur le terrain, contacts avec les factions, interprétation du mandat de l'APRONUC, comportement avec la population locale, directives politiques du pays d'origine.[19] Selon le commandant adjoint de l'APRONUC, le brigadier général Robert Rideau, la mission militaire était divisée en deux : les bataillons actifs — ceux qui étaient très présents sur le terrain et souvent très agressifs dans l'exécution de leur mandat — et les bataillons passifs — ceux qui faisaient le minimum et qui se dérobaient rapidement devant leurs responsabilités. Voyons quelques exemples.

Lorsque les Nations Unies ont suspendu le processus de cantonnement et de démobilisation en novembre 1992, elles n'ont pas, comme cela était prévu, réduit le nombre de bataillons sur place. Dans le plan initial, l'APRONUC avait envisagé que la phase de cantonnement et de démobilisation exigerait la présence de 12 bataillons sur l'ensemble du territoire. Ce nombre devait être réduit à six pendant la phase électorale (décembre 1992 à avril 1993) et à trois pendant la phase postélectorale. Devant la dégradation de la situation politique, l'ONU a décidé de maintenir sur place les 12 bataillons. À ce moment-là, les Casques bleus ont reçu comme instructions d'accentuer leur travail de patrouille des secteurs et de protection du personnel de l'ONU — policiers civils, superviseurs électoraux, observateurs militaires — et des permanences des partis politiques. Pour exécuter cette tâche, les militaires onusiens devaient connaître parfaitement le secteur dans lequel ils étaient déployés. Chaque commandant de bataillon avait donc procédé au déploiement de petites unités dans l'ensemble de son secteur. Tous les contingents ont disséminé leurs soldats sur des sites dont le nombre variait entre 8 et 14, sauf le contingent français, qui occupait la région 6, dans le sud du Cambodge, qui a étiré ses forces sur 22 sites.

Ce type de déploiement, qu'on retrouve dans la plupart des missions de l'ONU, comporte plusieurs avantages. Il permet à chaque contingent de Casques bleus d'être plus visible auprès de la population locale du secteur, d'avoir un effet dissuasif auprès d'éventuels trouble-fête, d'assurer des patrouilles régulières sur les routes et dans de nombreuses localités et de réagir rapidement en cas de crise dans le secteur. Sans contredit, les Français connaissaient très bien leur secteur qui devait rester un des plus calmes de tout le Cambodge pendant toute la période de présence des Casques bleus. Les légionnaires français ont effectué des patrouilles sur l'ensemble de leur territoire et ont offert une aide médicale ainsi qu'un soutien à la reconstruction des infrastructures, souvent à leurs frais.[20] Au nord-ouest et dans le centre du pays, la situation était différente. À la frontière thaïlandaise, là où les activités des Khmers rouges étaient plus intenses, cinq bataillons étaient déployés et avaient installé environ le même nombre de sites (entre 12 et 14). Le bataillon néerlandais, tout aussi actif dans son secteur que les Français dans le leur, n'a subi que des attaques mineures et aucune perte humaine, alors que les bataillons pakistanais, bangladeshi et malais étaient régulièrement harcelés. À l'intérieur du pays, dans les secteurs indonésien et bulgare, les pertes humaines furent nombreuses et les incidents, avec les forces des Khmers rouges et même de l'armée gouvernementale, réguliers.[21]

Dans la plupart des missions de maintien de la paix, l'utilisation de la force doit s'exercer uniquement en cas de légitime défense. Il faut que les militaires onusiens aient été l'objet d'une attaque directe et intentionnelle pour qu'ils puissent répliquer. Le manuel de procédures des Nations Unies indique que l'utilisation de la force doit se faire par séquences mais qu'ultimement c'est le commandant sur le terrain qui doit en juger.[22] Au Cambodge, chaque contingent a interprété à sa manière cette directive de l'ONU. Ainsi, les membres du bataillon d'ingénieurs japonais, qui ne patrouillaient aucun secteur et étaient tous regroupés dans leur quartier général de Takéo, avaient reçu comme directive que le recours aux armes devait se faire en dernière extrémité dans le but de "persuader l'attaquant de se replier en tirant en l'air."[23] Les autres contingents suivaient le même genre de directives. Chez les Français, les légionnaires avaient reçu l'ordre de ne pas attendre d'être attaqués directement pour répliquer.[24] La politique musclée du contingent français était de faire savoir aux factions, surtout aux Khmers rouges, que les Casques bleus français qui se sentiraient menacés pouvaient utiliser leurs armes pour dissuader ou même neutraliser un adversaire. Les Néerlandais appliquaient la même politique.

La fermeté des contingents européens s'explique par le fait que les Français avaient dépêché, en deuxième rotation, une unité de la Légion étrangère alors que les Néerlandais avaient déployé des Marines, deux corps d'élite particulièrement coriaces et bien entraînés. Du côté bulgare, les Casques bleus étaient des conscrits fraîchement entrés dans l'armée, mal entraînés et qui ne recevaient pas de salaire.[25] Paradoxalement, la Malaisie, l'Indonésie et le Bangladesh avaient aussi envoyé des soldats aguerris à la lutte anti-guérilla, mais cela n'a pas empêché les attaques contre eux.

Les relations entre les Casques bleus et la population locale variaient d'un contingent à l'autre. Ainsi, les soldats indonésiens étaient nombreux à maîtriser la langue khmère et les contingents français et thaïlandais comptaient dans leurs rangs des soldats d'origine cambodgienne, ce qui facilitait les contacts avec la population et les leaders politiques locaux. Pour leur part, les soldats du contingent bangladeshi ont été accusés de trop fréquenter les prostituées vietnamiennes et de ne pas effectuer leur travail le jour pendant le Ramadan.[26] Les membres du contingent bulgare se sont acquis une réputation désastreuse. Les officiers ne comprenaient ni le français ni l'anglais et plusieurs soldats se livraient à la contrebande. Selon de nombreux témoignages, les Casques bleus bulgares, même s'ils entretenaient des relations amicales avec les factions, ne quittaient que rarement leurs campements pour effectuer des patrouilles et prendre contact avec la population. Ils étaient si turbulents et indisciplinés qu'un jour, alors qu'il s'adressait à ses soldats, le commandant du contingent a dû tirer un coup de feu en l'air pour rétablir l'ordre et se faire écouter.[27]

Enfin, les dirigeants de l'APRONUC étaient aux prises avec deux problèmes récurrents dans toutes les missions de maintien de la paix : d'une part, le commandement et le contrôle des contingents militaires et, d'autre part, l'intervention des États contributeurs dans le déroulement de la mission.[28] Le commandant militaire d'une mission a théoriquement la main haute sur l'ensemble des activités militaires de la mission. Il peut même ordonner à un contingent de Casques bleus de changer de secteur ou de quitter la mission. Dans les faits, son contrôle s'arrête à l'entrée des camps des différents contingents. Il est de notoriété publique que les commandants militaires des contingents prennent leurs ordres les plus importants de leurs gouvernements respectifs. Si un ordre donné par le commandant de la mission à un contingent ne coïncide pas avec les intérêts du pays contributeur, le commandant du contingent peut l'ignorer sans subir la moindre sanction.

Les comportements différents de divers contingents de Casques bleus et leur approche contradictoire sur l'utilisation de la force allaient être testés sur le terrain tant par les Khmers rouges que par l'armée gouvernementale. Dans le secteur du bataillon bulgare, le contingent le plus indiscipliné et le plus passif, 10 Casques bleus ont été tués ou blessés à la suite d'attaques. Dans la province de Siem Reap, patrouillée par des soldats bangladeshis, les attaques ou les incidents impliquant des Casques bleus ont été nombreux. Plus la date des élections approchait, plus les attaques dans les secteurs bangladeshi, bulgare, indonésien et tunisien se multipliaient.

L'ancien commandant adjoint de la composante militaire au Cambodge, le brigadier général français Michel Loridon, a fourni une explication des différences entre contingents et des problèmes rencontrés par la composante militaire dans l'application de son mandat et dans son travail quotidien. Sous forme de questions, il critique durement l'organisation de la mission :[29]

> Quel exemple et quelle sécurité peuvent apporter à des populations martyrisées et cependant pleines d'espoir dans l'ONU, des Casques bleus peu instruits, mal formés, mal commandés, pas payés qui sont les premiers, pour survivre, à organiser des rackets, des combines et des commerces illicites d'armes, de carburant, de vivres ou de matériel? Quelle crédibilité accorder à une troupe qui débarque dans un pays difficile, alors que les appelés viennent d'apprendre au poser de l'avion que leur séjour sera de dix-huit mois, sans permission et sans argent? Est-il possible de travailler correctement avec des unités dont les chefs ont reçu des instructions pour favoriser telle ou telle faction et surtout essayer de torpiller les actions d'un autre bataillon de Casques bleus, suspecté de nuire à ses intérêts nationaux?

Sans jamais nommer personne, le général Loridon porte des accusations sérieuses, crédibles et pleines d'enseignement pour les futures missions de l'ONU.

La diplomatie tranquille

Un des facteurs qui ont miné, aux yeux de beaucoup d'observateurs, la crédibilité de la mission de l'ONU au Cambodge jusqu'aux élections générales de mai 1993 a été l'adoption, par le leadership civil et militaire de l'APRONUC, d'une approche prudente envers ceux qui violaient l'Accord de Paris et qui rendait le mandat de la mission difficile à exécuter. Paradoxalement, cette "diplomatie tranquille" de M. Akashi et du général Sanderson, fermement appuyé par le Secrétaire général Boutros Boutros-Ghali, a contribué à son succès.

Lorsque M. Akashi et le général Sanderson sont arrivés au Cambodge en mars 1992, les Khmers rouges avaient déjà commencé leur travail de sape. Ils avaient consolidé leurs positions dans certaines régions et interdisaient aux observateurs de l'ONU de se rendre dans les territoires qu'ils contrôlaient. L'ONU réagit en reculant. Ainsi, dès juillet 1992, dans un rapport spécial, le Secrétaire général, constatant le refus de coopérer des Khmers rouges, suggérait au Conseil de sécurité deux options : suspendre le processus jusqu'à ce que toutes les parties respectent l'Accord de Paris ou poursuivre le processus même sans la collaboration de l'une des parties. Le Secrétaire général favorisait la seconde option.[30] Le Conseil de sécurité lui donna raison. Cette souplesse — certains diront cette capitulation — allait demeurer la marque de l'ONU durant toutes les étapes menant aux élections de mai 1993. Encouragés par le manque de réaction de l'ONU, les Khmers rouges se sentirent suffisamment sûrs d'eux pour interdire à Akashi et à Sanderson l'accès à leur quartier général de Pailin; ils ne subirent pas la moindre sanction. Ces confrontations quotidiennes devaient culminer à l'automne 1992 par le refus des Khmers rouges d'appliquer formellement l'Accord de Paris.

Dans un premier temps, les dirigeants de l'APRONUC étaient divisés sur la stratégie à suivre face aux Khmers rouges. L'adjoint du général Sanderson, le brigadier général Michel Loridon, était partisan de la manière forte. Les Khmers rouges sont signataires de l'Accord, plaidait-il, ils doivent le respecter. Selon le général, si les Khmers rouges résistaient, les Casques bleus devaient envahir leurs zones et saisir leurs armes. Cette opinion n'était pas partagée par le général Sanderson qui subissait de fortes pressions pour éviter toute confrontation. D'une part, le gouvernement australien avait clairement fait savoir que son contingent quitterait le Cambodge si un seul de ses soldats était tué. D'autre part, le gouvernement japonais, qui partageait la même opinion, désirait que cette opération, dont il assumait une part considérable de l'effort financier en plus d'en fournir le chef, se déroule le plus calmement possible. C'était la première fois que le Japon participait politiquement et militairement à une opération internationale de cette envergure et ses dirigeants ne voulaient pas rater ce test. Loridon persistait dans ses opinions et étalait dans la presse ses divergences avec ses supérieurs. À la fin de son séjour, en août 1992, son mandat ne fut pas renouvelé. Akashi et Sanderson avaient pris la décision d'éviter une effusion de sang dans le seul but de faire respecter les engagements d'une faction "qui ne représente qu'une petite minorité."[31]

Les reculades de l'ONU eurent pourtant des effets sur le terrain. Si les Khmers rouges pouvaient humilier les dirigeants de l'APRONUC sans aucun risque, ils pouvaient aussi intimider les contingents de Casques bleus. Dès novembre 1992, les actes de violence et d'intimidation envers le personnel de l'ONU ont augmenté; en avril et mai 1993, ils ont atteint un rythme presque quotidien. M. Akashi, qui pendant longtemps avait espéré voir les Khmers rouges réintégrer le processus de paix, se disait, à la veille des élections, exaspéré par leur attitude mais confiant dans le processus électoral.[32] À la fin, la panique s'était emparée de certains membres des différentes composantes de l'APRONUC. Ainsi, après le meurtre de deux Japonais — un volontaire électoral et un policier — en avril 1993, des volontaires de plusieurs pays ont quitté leur secteur alors que le gouvernement japonais a ordonné le retrait de ses policiers civils.[33] Cette décision a été vivement condamnée par l'ONU qui a souligné qu'elle minait la chaîne de commandement de l'APRONUC. Selon des rapports non publiés, le tiers des 75 policiers japonais ont quitté leur poste, certains allant même se réfugier en Thaïlande.[34]

C'est donc dans une atmosphère de peur que le scrutin s'est ouvert le dimanche 23 mai 1993. Il s'est poursuivi, sans incidents sérieux, jusqu'au vendredi 28 mai. Quelque 4,2 millions de Cambodgiens, sur 4,7 millions d'inscrits, se sont présentés aux 1400 sites fixes et aux 200 équipes mobiles pour exercer leur droit de vote. Contre toute attente, 46 % des électeurs avaient voté le premier jour des élections, et ce, malgré des pluies diluviennes qui tombaient sur l'ensemble du pays. À la fin de la semaine, près de 90 % des Cambodgiens, dont des centaines de Khmers rouges, avaient voté et le 29 mai, le représentant spécial, M. Akashi, proclamait, au nom des Nations Unies, que "les élections s'étaient déroulées librement et équitablement."[35] Cette déclaration, qui fut reprise le 10 juin devant les membres du Conseil national suprême, mettait fin à toute contestation légale du scrutin. La balle était maintenant dans le camp cambodgien. Après quelques semaines de tension entre le gouvernement de Phnom Penn, dont le parti PPC avait obtenu 38 % des voix et 51 sièges, et le vainqueur, le parti royaliste FUNCINPEC, qui avait obtenu 45 % des voix et 58 sièges, le prince Norodom Sihanouk, président du Conseil national suprême, a réussi à convaincre les deux partis de former un gouvernement d'union nationale. Le 21 septembre 1993, l'Assemblée constituante a adopté une nouvelle constitution qui fait du Cambodge une monarchie constitutionnelle avec, comme roi, Norodom Sihanouk qui fut intronisé le 24 septembre.[36] Le mandat de l'APRONUC se terminait et les derniers Casques bleus quittèrent le pays le 14 novembre.

Observations

Comme je le soulignais au début de ce chapitre, les Nations Unies avaient entrepris de rebâtir le Cambodge en un peu plus de 18 mois. Le mandat de l'APRONUC était ambitieux et sans doute irréalisable dans sa totalité. Et il n'est pas certain que si l'ONU avait investi plus d'argent, maintenu sa mission sur place plus longtemps et utilisé la force armée, ses relations avec les factions et le sort des Cambodgiens auraient été améliorés. Il suffit de penser aux exemples somalien et bosniaque où ni la force ni la durée ne peuvent rien contre des factions qui décident de ne pas collaborer. Je pense qu'il faut juger l'intervention de l'ONU au Cambodge non pas sur le seul critère du respect complet de son mandat, mais en fonction de ce qui a été accompli. Comme le souligne le chercheur William J. Durch, "success and failure in peacekeeping are not readily definable in black and white terms."[37]

Tout au long du processus de rétablissement de la paix (de septembre 1991 à septembre 1993), l'APRONUC a bénéficié de plusieurs atouts qui ont joué en sa faveur et qui sont décrits par Durch comme les éléments essentiels au succès d'une mission : l'appui des grandes puissances, des factions impliquées et de la population locale ainsi que l'impartialité de la mission.[38] Dans le cas du Cambodge, les cinq éléments suivants ont, à mon sens, permis le succès de la mission :

- La signature d'un accord de paix international par les quatre factions et 18 pays;
- L'appui des cinq Grands du Conseil de sécurité de l'ONU et des puissances régionales asiatiques durant le processus de paix;
- Le contrôle de 80 % du territoire par une des factions — le gouvernement de Phnom Penh — prête à jouer le jeu des élections;
- L'acceptation par trois des quatre factions du résultat des élections et la constitution d'un gouvernement d'union nationale sous la direction du roi Norodom Sihanouk;

- Enfin, le déploiement massif d'une force des Nations Unies dirigée par des personnalités dont la flexibilité politique a préservé une paix relative au Cambodge pendant la période de transition de 18 mois.

Les cinq membres permanents du Conseil de sécurité ont appuyé unanimement toutes les interventions des Nations Unies dans le processus de paix et ont garanti l'accord de paix signé à Paris en octobre 1991. Même la Chine, longtemps alliée des Khmers rouges, n'a pas ménagé ses efforts pour que la mission de l'APRONUC se déroule comme prévu. Sur le terrain, seule la faction des Khmers rouges a refusé de collaborer avec l'ONU et de respecter tous ses engagements. Or, même si les Khmers rouges représentaient un élément perturbateur, leurs forces armées — bien plus minuscules que certains voulaient le faire croire avant les élections — n'ont jamais menacé réellement le pouvoir en place ou les forces de l'ONU.[39] De plus, l'APRONUC a compté sur l'entière collaboration des trois autres factions qui n'ont jamais sérieusement remis en cause le processus de paix et ont accepté le résultat des élections. L'appui de la population locale n'a jamais fait défaut malgré une certaine insécurité dans plusieurs régions particulièrement visées par les activités des Khmers rouges. Enfin, si l'impartialité de la mission a été mise à rude épreuve par son laxisme envers les Khmers rouges et son apparente impossibilité à réellement contrôler l'administration civile et la police du régime de Phnom Penh, il semble bien que cette attitude n'ait pas joué contre la mission.[40] M. Akashi était conscient de tout cela lorsqu'il a décidé, de concert avec les membres du Conseil de sécurité, de poursuivre le processus de paix malgré la rupture avec les Khmers rouges et son incapacité à remplir toutes les conditions de son mandat. Son objectif était d'organiser des élections où 90 % des Cambodgiens pourraient voter librement pour la première fois de leur histoire. Il voyait la tenue des élections comme un catalyseur qui permettrait au Cambodge de reprendre sa place sur la scène internationale et de se doter d'un système démocratique, aussi imparfait put-il être.[41]

Reste que les critiques ont raison sur un point : la capacité des Nations Unies de mettre sur pied une mission, de la déployer et de la faire fonctionner convenablement fait cruellement défaut. Il semble certain que si la mission s'était déployée dans les jours qui ont suivi la signature de l'Accord de Paris le 23 octobre 1991, les

Khmers rouges, en particulier, n'auraient peut-être pas eu le choix de respecter leurs engagements. On peut également se poser des questions sur la qualité des Casques bleus envoyés au Cambodge et sur le caractère multinational de la mission. Lorsque le général Loridon pose la question de l'honnêteté de certains chefs de contingents vis-à-vis des factions cambodgiennes ou même des autres contingents, il est évident qu'il parle du rôle ambigu des contingents japonais, thaïlandais, indonésien, chinois et australien sur place. Certains de ces contingents avaient leurs propres buts politiques et intérêts économiques à défendre au Cambodge. Ainsi, les Thaïlandais entretenaient un bataillon d'ingénieurs à la frontière khméro-thaïlandaise, là même où les Khmers rouges se livraient à un lucratif commerce de pierres et de bois précieux avec des militaires thaïlandais. Les Japonais et les Australiens entendaient bien voir leurs hommes d'affaires obtenir des contrats importants pour la reconstruction du pays. Quant aux Français, leur présence pouvait aussi donner lieu à bien des spéculations. Après tout, la France avait colonisé ce pays pendant un siècle et son retour ne la mettait pas au-dessus de tout soupçon.

La mission de l'ONU au Cambodge a été une réussite dans la mesure où la collaboration entre les acteurs — sauf les Khmers rouges — a prévalu jusqu'à la fin. Il faut bien reconnaître qu'il s'agit là d'un cas rare qui n'est sans doute pas susceptible de faire école ailleurs. Toutefois, sur le terrain, l'ONU a certainement acquis une expérience exceptionnelle dans la gestion d'une pareille mission et tiré quelques leçons du travail en commun de contingents venant des quatre coins de la planète. Il faut espérer que les observations recueillies serviront à mieux planifier les futures missions de maintien de la paix.

13

Beyond Peacekeeping: Somalia, the United Nations and the Canadian Experience

Nancy Gordon

THE WORLD'S ATTENTION TURNED to the beaches outside Mogadishu on December 9, 1992, when American forces — dressed, camouflaged, and armed for battle — waded ashore to be greeted not by an opposing army, but by an array of television cameras, lights, and reporters. They were witnessing another chapter in the tragic and bizarre story of Somalia — a drama which continued to unfold throughout 1993 and into 1994.

What had led to this peaceful invasion? What had aroused the attention of the world's media? What was the role of the UN? Of Canada? Was this peacekeeping or some new form of UN intervention?

Background

Somalia achieved independence in 1960, when the former Somaliland colonies of Britain in the north and Italy in the south opted to merge into an independent unitary state. While the merger was difficult and Somalia faced many of the same types of problems as other newly independent states, the country enjoyed nine years of relative domestic stability. External, rather than internal forces, initially caused difficulty. Large Somali minorities in Ethiopia and Kenya were either the cause or the excuse for Somalia to engage in aggressive behaviour toward its neighbours, and for the government to neglect domestic development and problems. The Somalis engaged in futile wars with Ethiopia over the Ogaden region in 1964 and again in 1977. In 1969 internal unrest over both the deteriorating domestic situation and the failure to assert control over Ethiopian territory ended when Siad Barre seized power in a coup d'état. He disbanded the National Assembly, suspended the constitution, and personally ran the country for the next twenty-one years.

Throughout the years of the Cold War, Somalia had been a classic pawn, allied first with the Soviet Union and then with the United States. In the mid-1960s Somali leaders developed close ties with the Soviets. Somalia's port of Berbera was thought to be strategically important, and in return for access to it the Soviet Union provided aid and vast amounts of arms to assist in the war in the Ogaden.

In 1977 a shift in superpower policies in the area caused a realignment. The United States became increasingly disillusioned with the Marxist regime which had overthrown Haile Selassie in Ethiopia and began to distance itself from it. The Cubans and the Soviets moved into Ethiopia, with the result that the Americans began to bid for the friendship of Siad Barre. The United States provided military equipment, training and support, and in turn received access to Berbera.

Somalia is a nomadic, clan-based society, poor by any of the standard international indicators.[1] The severe drought which affected Horn of Africa states during 1990, 1991, and 1992 created extremely difficult conditions in Somalia, especially in 1991 and early 1992. The country is made up of large sections of shifting desert, and the drought expanded those areas.

Although official 1991 figures put the population at seven million, most observers estimated the actual population between four and a half and six million. Ethnically, the people of Somalia are made up of a single unit, but "in reality, they are a collection of complex nomadic and tribal societies whose members are loyal to their clan, not their country."[2]

There are two main tribes, Samal and Sab. The Samals are the most numerous and include four major clans or families — the Dire, Darod, Hawiye, and Isaq. The Sab are located in southern Somalia and include two major families or clans; the Digil and Rahanwein. The latter tend to be more sedentary farmers.

Clan divisions dictate political allegiance, and those clans and divisions are roughly as follows:

- United Somali Congress: Hawiye clan but split into two rival factions, one led by Mohammed Farrah Aidid and the other by Ali Mahdi Mohammed;
- Somali National Front: Marehan sub-clan of the Darod clan of the former president, Siad Barre;

- Somali Patriotic Front: Ogaden sub-clan of the Darod clan, allied to Aidid;
- Somali Salvation Democratic Front: Majertian sub-clan of Darod, a close ally of the National Front;
- Somali Democratic Association: Dir clan, largely in the north-west;
- Somali National Movement: Isaq clan, largely in the north-west.[3]

Siad Barre was the president of Somalia until 1991. During his tenure the seeds of the breakdown of civil and political society were sown. He first proclaimed "scientific socialism" as an organizing principle for the economy. Following another ill-judged and badly executed war against Ethiopia over the Ogaden in 1977, he embraced capitalism and the American connection. While he had initially begun to run the government, civil service, and army on the merit principle rather than on the division of spoils between clans, he had replaced that attempt by a "blatant manipulation of the clan system that was worse than anything under the old civilian government."[4]

By the end of the 1980s the two major political players were Ali Mahdi and General Aidid, both founding members of the United Somali Congress in 1989. They come from different sub-clans of the Hawiye. Civil war erupted during 1990; Barre fled Mogadishu in January 1991 after mutinies in his army and an uprising by the inhabitants. Ali Mahdi seized his chance and declared himself interim president. General Aidid and his backers felt betrayed, and the country was soon carved up amongst various factions.

When Barre's regime collapsed, the country did not revert to the old rivalry between clans which had always marked Somali society, but to what Martin Wollacott refers to as a

> new kind of social violence, still clan-based, but with vicious differences. First, the main actors were not traditional "big men" from the clans, but upstart leaders without the same responsibilities or background. Second, the fighting was mechanized: armed vehicles replaced camels, machine guns replaced rifles. Third, traditional institutions which had mitigated and mediated clan rivalries, like the blood price system, had withered away. Fourth, the violence was now commercially sustained by a complex trade in which drugs, mainly the local favourite qat, and food,including aid shipments, are traded off for the fuel,

ammunition, and other supplies necessary to maintain armies and patronage structures of warlords.[5]

With the fall of Barre, all forms of government and public order collapsed in Somalia. The combination of war and drought created intolerable conditions; many Somalis fled to refugee camps in northern Kenya, Ethiopia, Djibouti, or Yemen. According to United Nations estimates, some one million Somalis fled the country and hundreds of thousands died in the war-induced famine.[6] The depth and scope of the tragedy prompted a broad international response.

The International Response

The United Nations and Its Agencies: UNOSOM I

International humanitarian relief organizations had been working in Somalia for a number of years, but throughout 1991 and early 1992 widespread violence and chaos made the distribution of relief supplies within the country extremely dangerous and difficult. Many agencies, including those of the UN itself, left the country. In December 1991 then Secretary General Pérez de Cuéllar designated a special envoy whose role was to bring about a cessation of hostilities. In March 1992 a ceasefire agreement between the two principal adversaries, General Aidid and Ali Mahdi, was reached in New York through the mediation of the UN. But the agreement excluded smaller and potentially neutral Somali groups—an oversight that was to haunt the UN, as the warlords became virtually the only power brokers dealing with the international community.

At the same time, acting on a UN study which reported that 1.5 million people were on the verge of starvation and 3 million in desperate need, the Security Council passed Resolution 751, establishing the United Nations Operation in Somalia (UNOSOM). Originally consisting of 550 soldiers and 79 civilians, UNOSOM was deployed to safeguard UN personnel, supplies, and equipment in and around the port and airport of Mogadishu.

The situation in the country improved only slightly; widespread banditry, looting, and civil disorder continued unabated. Humanitarian relief agencies such as CARE, whose job it was to transport food from the port to the interior of the country where it was desperately needed, had to hire armed guards or "technicals" to protect their shipments and personnel. Even then, transporting supplies depended on the whim of whichever local political warlord seemed to be in charge.

In July 1992 the Security Council adopted Resolution 767, calling for accelerated efforts to prevent mass starvation, to end hostilities, and to stabilize the situation in Somalia. In August, Security Council Resolution 775 authorized the establishment of a country-wide UN military presence to secure the delivery of humanitarian assistance. Four additional UN security units, each with a strength of up to 750, were to be deployed in four operational zones of the country. The Security Council resolution called for a consolidated UN effort to carry out relief and recovery programs in each zone, to monitor the ceasefire and contain potential hostilities, to oversee security, demobilization, and disarmament, and encourage a peace process through conciliation, mediation, and good offices.[7] In October, thirty-nine countries met in Geneva for a UN donor conference on Somalia. The meeting called for a one-hundred-day accelerated plan to expedite and better coordinate international relief efforts.

In May of 1992, the UN secretary general had named Mohammed Sahnoun, an Algerian diplomat, as his special representative to Somalia. As the first secretary general from Africa in the history of the UN, Boutros-Ghali had a strong personal interest in getting the organization to respond to the crisis in Somalia at a time when world interest tended to concentrate on the conflicts in the former Yugoslavia. Although it is not clear that Sahnoun's negotiations would have produced a breakthrough, he did win widespread Somali respect for expanding his rounds of consultations beyond the warlords to include clan elders, intellectuals, women, and professionals. In addition, he called attention to the inconsistent UN actions in Somalia during 1992, pointing out for instance that the UN had not taken advantage of its own ceasefire. Repeated requests from private relief agencies for medical supplies largely went unheeded. The United Nations Development Programme (UNDP) did not use the $68 million which was budgeted for Somalia for nine months "for lack of a signature from the non-existent Somali government. A four-month dispute between the UN High Commissioner for Refugees and the World Food Programme delayed delivery of food to Somali refugee camps in Ethiopia."[8] The UN Department of Humanitarian Affairs, formed in early 1992 to coordinate the organization's humanitarian response, was largely unengaged in Somalia until Jan Eliasson, its under secretary general visited Somalia in September 1992. Sahnoun was forced to resign in October and was replaced by Ismat Kittani, a senior UN bureaucrat who had to begin the mediation and negotiation process almost from the beginning.

The various UN resolutions had authorized the deployment of up to 4,219 peacekeeping troops during the fall of 1992. However, even that small number was not deployed, and indeed, until the major deployment of American and other forces in December, the UN force never grew beyond the initial 550 Pakistani troops. The latter could not be deployed outside Mogadishu since various factions of Somali authorities refused to concur, and conditions were such that the dispatch of lightly armed soldiers, as the UN peacekeepers were, would have been unacceptably dangerous.

The major humanitarian effort essentially came to a halt during November 1992. Conditions in Mogadishu were bad, and outside the capital they were horrendous. Death rates at relief camps in Baidoa and Bardere, for instance, rose from about ten per day to 350 a day. Lack of security meant relief convoys could not reach those in desperate need. Anarchy, lawlessness, and brutality predominated. There was no political order, none of the usual government services, no government.

The Media and the Public

By the end of August 1992 the media had begun to highlight the Somalia story. Television crews and reporters seemed almost to outnumber relief personnel in Mogadishu from September through December. Images of starving and dying people made a profound and unsettling impression on publics in the Western world, and the response was a demand "that someone do something," particularly when it was clear that the amount of relief supplies available in the country was adequate; the problem was the inability of the UN and the relief agencies to deliver the food and medicines because of the lack of security.

The Creation of the Unified Task Force (UNITAF)

The government of the United States, influenced by the graphic and horrible media reports of famine and violence in Somalia, as well as by entreaties from some of the relief organizations trying unsuccessfully to work there,[9] notified the secretary general on November 25, 1992, that "if the Security Council were to decide to authorize Member States to use forceful means to ensure the delivery of relief supplies to the people of Somalia, the United States would be ready to take the lead in organizing and commanding such an operation."[10]

On November 29, the secretary general wrote to the Security Council indicating that the basic premise of UNOSOM required serious review. Boutros Boutros-Ghali asked, "What can the United Nations legitimately undertake to stop an intra-state conflict or major humanitarian catastrophe when traditional peacekeeping is not enough?"[11] He put five options to the Council. The first three would not have altered the basic nature of UN intervention: a larger peacekeeping force; a withdrawal of military personnel, leaving the humanitarian agencies to negotiate as best they could with the various factions; a show of force by UNOSOM in Mogadishu. The secretary general urged the Security Council to consider enforcement action under Chapter VII of the UN Charter and to this end he offered options four and five: a country-wide enforcement action undertaken by a group of member states authorized to do so by the Security Council; or a country-wide enforcement operation under direct United Nations command and control. While the secretary general indicated his preference for option five, he also admitted that the UN did not have the capability to command and control an operation of the size and urgency required, particularly at a time when the organization's resources were stretched by the operations in ex-Yugoslavia and Cambodia. Thus member states which contributed to the operation would have to provide not only troops for the field but also personnel for the headquarters, and both of these groups would have to take their orders from the United Nations, not from their national governments.

If instead the Security Council chose the fourth option — that is, an enforcement action undertaken by a group of member states authorized to do so by the Security Council — Boutros-Ghali suggested various means of linking the operation to the United Nations, such as the submission of regular reports from the participating states to the Security Council. In addition, the Security Council could set out the purpose of the operation and ensure that as soon as the purpose was accomplished the forces would be replaced by a peacekeeping operation.

On December 3, 1992, the Security Council decided in favour of an enforcement action along the lines of option four by unanimously adopting Resolution 794, which welcomed the United States' offer and authorized member states to cooperate "in implementation of the offer . . . to use all necessary means to establish as soon as possible a secure environment for humanitarian relief operations in Somalia." The resolution also authorized "the Secretary General and the member states concerned to make the necessary arrangements for the unified command and control of the forces involved which will reflect the offer referred to above [the American offer]." Resolution 794 led to the creation of the Unified Task Force (UNITAF), a coalition led by the United States and made up of more than thirty thousand troops from twenty-three countries, whose mandate was to use all necessary means, including force, to secure the distribution of humanitarian supplies. Thus it was, on December 9, that American troops landed on the shores off Mogadishu.

UNITAF Deploys

As early as December 4, when it became obvious that the UN was about to take more action, the situation in Mogadishu began to stabilize and become more secure. As the Americans, followed by a small contingent of French troops, came ashore and took up positions in the city, the "technicals" as well as some of the heavier guns moved out. Indeed, UNITAF was welcomed by the Somali population in Mogadishu, and almost immediately humanitarian supplies were allowed to leave the port and reach much-needed destinations in and around the city. To the dismay of relief agencies, there was some delay in the force's ability to secure the routes inland to Baidoa and Bardere, and death rates continued to rise in those areas until the routes could be secured. But as soon as the convoys resumed and food and medicine began to reach the people, the relief operations began to take hold.

While political stability continued to elude Somalia during the early months of 1993, the humanitarian situation improved immeasurably. The rains throughout 1993 were good, and those farmers who were able to plant, reaped a good harvest. By midwinter most relief agencies had begun to distribute seeds and tools, as opposed to emergency relief, throughout central and southern Somalia. In Mogadishu itself, however, security remained a major problem, and little or no progress was made in solving the political problems of the country.

The Canadian Response

Political and Military

The Canadian government agreed to participate in UNOSOM, and to that end had decided to contribute 750 troops to the peacekeeping force. The Canadians were to go to Bassasso in the north, an assignment which puzzled most observers since the area was secure and not suffering the effects either of civil disorder or famine. Just prior to the departure of the main body of troops for Somalia in December 1992, the UN created UNITAF and changed the operation. On December 4, Barbara McDougall, the secretary of state for external affairs, announced that following requests from the secretary general of the UN and the president of the United States, the Canadian government had decided to participate in the multilateral force with up to nine hundred personnel. She also announced that Canada would participate in the enforcement action only; we do not plan to participate in any subsequent peacekeeping operation. Other countries will be called up to play their full part in this international humanitarian operation.

The Canadian contingent of approximately thirteen hundred military personnel was in the field by the first week of January 1993. The main body of Canadians comprised nine hundred soldiers from the Canadian Airborne Regiment Battle Group based at Petawawa, Ontario. The battalion was assigned to Belet Heun, Somalia, and its mandate was to protect humanitarian operations in the surrounding territory. The unit was supported by armoured vehicles, a signal platoon, engineers, and support staff. The HMCS *Preserver*, a Canadian Forces supply ship, was stationed off Mogadishu to provide reconnaissance and logistic support. Eighteen air crews and a number of aircraft delivered equipment, vehicles, and supplies from Canada for the troops in Somalia.

The Canadian troops fulfilled their mandate with little or no military opposition, and the region in and around Belet Huen was made safe for humanitarian relief. However, the reputation of the Canadians was seriously marred by an incident in Somalia in

March when a young Somali, Shidane Abukar Aroune, who had been arrested and was held in custody by the Canadian forces for attempting to break into the Canadian compound, was found dead in his cell. The reporting of the incident to the Canadian public was delayed, one of the Canadian troops attempted suicide, and the headquarters staff of the Department of National Defence found itself under severe scrutiny for its handling of the incident. The minister of national defence, Kim Campbell, was a candidate for the leadership of the Progressive Conservative party, the campaign for which was going on at the time, with the result that the issue received wide public attention.

Eight members of the Canadian Airborne Regiment, including the commander of the force, were subsequently charged in connection with the Somali's death. The charges and subsequent courts martial highlighted for Canadians the difficult situation in which the troops were operating, as well as the difference between usual peacekeeping operations and the enforcement mandate in Somalia. In addition, it was clear that when troops were to undertake a mission with a mandate such as that in Somalia, military training had to be supplemented with cultural sensitivity and knowledge of the local situation. A number of humanitarian agencies had been working in Somalia for years and most had continued through the civil disruptions; while consultation and briefing may not have prevented subsequent difficulties, the military would have been wise to contact those who had local knowledge.

In July 1993 the Canadian service personnel handed over responsibilities to a component of the United Nations Operation in Somalia II (UNOSOM II), which succeeded the UNITAF operation, and returned home. Seven Canadians continued to serve at UNOSOM headquarters in Mogadishu, and for 1993 Canada's assessed share of the UNOSOM II general budget was approximately US$50 million.

Humanitarian Assistance

Canada was one of thirty-nine countries at a UN donor conference in Somalia which was held in Geneva in October 1992. Canadian non-governmental organizations (NGOs), such as CARE, Oxfam-Quebec, Médecins sans frontières, and the Unitarian Service Committee, were operational in Somalia; the Canadian government also supported international NGOs such as the International Committee of the Red Cross and several UN agencies such as the World Food Program and UNICEF.

A Canadian Forces airlift operation began on September 12, 1992, and ran until February 28, 1993, in response to the UN appeal for emergency assistance to Somalia. The Canadian Forces had three Hercules C-130 planes and Canadian military personnel in Nairobi, Kenya, to support humanitarina relief efforts. Five hundred and fifty Canadian military relief flights delivered 7.44 million kilograms of food aid from Kenya to over twenty locations in Somalia. As UNITAF secured the roads, the need for airlifts lessened, allowing the humanitarian agencies to deliver food by road, which is a much more efficient and effective means of delivery than airlift.

Subsequent Developments

In January 1993 the United Nations initiated discussions with Somali factional leaders in Addis Ababa, Ethiopia, on a peaceful resolution to the conflict in Somalia. Agreement was reached on an immediate ceasefire, the surrender of heavy weapons to the UN, and the encampment of factional militias at fixed sites by March 1, 1993. It was also agreed that UN humanitarian assistance and national reconciliation conferences would take place in Addis Ababa in March. At the March meeting, Somali representatives agreed to a ceasefire, to disarm, and to establish a transitional national council as well as district and regional councils.

These were paper agreements, honoured "more in the breach than in the observance." The humanitarian situation in the country had improved, but there was little or no progress in disarming the populace, or in establishing a political order. "The closely related tasks of weakening the warlords and militiamen, restoring security and starting a genuine process of political reconciliation and economic rehabilitation have so far defied both the U.S. military leaders and the UN commanders."[12]

From UNITAF to UNOSOM II

In March 1993 Boutros-Ghali reported to the Security Council that there remained a need for sustained international action on humanitarian assistance, public order, and political reconciliation.

He also said that the UN, again acting under Chapter VII of the Charter, should be mandated to take aggressive action as required to maintain security for the safe delivery of assistance. On March 26, 1993, the Security Council approved a plan for another phase of the operation in Somalia. Resolution 814 proposed a transition from UNITAF to an UNOSOM II force of twenty-eight thousand personnel on May 1, 1993. This second phase of UNOSOM was to be deployed throughout Somalia to establish a secure environment, to provide humanitarian relief, and to promote political settlement and national reconciliation.

In May, when the overall situation appeared to have stabilized, American forces handed over command of the intervention in Somalia to the United Nations. While the majority of U.S. forces returned home to be replaced by troops from other countries, four thousand American military personnel, including an eleven-hundred person rapid-response team, remained in Somalia under UN command. The overall leader of the UN in Somalia was Jonathan Howe, a retired U.S. Navy admiral and national security aide in the Bush administration. UNOSOM II was commanded by Lieutenant-General Cevik Bir from Turkey; his deputy commander was an American, Major-General Thomas Montgomery. The Security Council gave UNOSOM II a mandate to move throughout the country disarming the Somali factions. However a shortage of troops and money delayed this work, and banditry as well as armed factionalism continued to be a major problem.

On June 5, 1993, General Aidid struck a major blow. Gunmen loyal to him ambushed UN peacekeepers in Mogadishu, killing twenty-three and wounding sixty in a bloody outbreak of fighting. Some two hundred Somalis were killed or wounded in subsequent fighting. It was the highest casualty toll inflicted on a UN peacekeeping operation in three decades, and caused an evacuation of hundreds of civilians working for the UN and private relief agencies.

The Security Council responded with a resolution calling for the arrest, prosecution, and trial of the killers of the UN peacekeepers, a resolution which caused observers to wonder under what rules or mandate the UN would undertake such action. There followed an unsuccessful series of raids by UN forces attempting to capture Aidid—a strategy which not only failed but did nothing to enhance the reputation of the UN.

In October sixteen Americans were killed in another unsuccessful attempt to capture Aidid, the body of a dead U.S. helicopter pilot was dragged through the streets of Mogadishu, and an injured helicopter crewman was captured and questioned by Somalis in front of television cameras. Approximately three hundred Somalis were killed and seven hundred wounded during clashes with the Americans. As Aidid had undoubtedly intended, the American public was outraged by these events, and Somalia was once again in the headlines. What was the United States doing in Somalia? How did an intervention to feed starving people turn into a deadly battle against hate-filled Somalis? What interest did the United States have in Somalia that could conceivably justify the suffering and humiliation of American soldiers?

In light of these developments, U.S. policy changed dramatically. On October 14 President Clinton announced a deadline of March 31, 1994, for the pull-out of American troops, along with an immediate increase of seventeen hundred troops for Somalia. He ordered more armoured personnel carriers and helicopters, and announced the stationing of thirty-six hundred more Marines offshore in case they were needed. To indicate its displeasure with the UN's handling of the situation, the additional troops were put under American, not UN command, and Robert Oakley, a former American ambassador, was sent to Somalia as the president's senior representative.

These decisions calmed American public opinion, especially the decision for a March 31, 1994, withdrawal which was carried out on schedule. A ceasefire was arranged between the Americans and Aidid's forces, the overt hunt for Aidid was quietly called off, and not long after these events, in another bizarre twist, Aidid was given transportation to a peace conference in Addis Ababa by a U.S. plane.

Explanations for what went wrong during the fall of 1993 are incomplete, but centre around the difficulty of brokering a political settlement in a society where values and experience differ considerably from the Western tradition. In the countryside, the UN had managed to organize three dozen councils of elders and other community representatives, and outside Mogadishu crops were growing and rehabilitation was beginning. But within the capital, where General Aidid still controlled most of the south, political discussions had been almost non-existent, and had not included him. His show of force in June and again in October reinforced and emphasized his importance to the process.

In mid-November the Security Council suspended its arrest warrant for General Aidid and established an international commission of jurists to investigate the fighting between UN forces and Somali militias. Led by Zambian Chief Justice Matthew Ngulube, the commission began its work in early December 1993 and proposed to examine all relevant incidents in the undeclared war between the UN and General Aidid's Somali National Alliance.

Yet another reconciliation conference amongst Somali leaders in early December made tentative progress. However, because it was sponsored by the UN, General Aidid did not attend. The same group met the next day under the auspices of the Ethiopian government, and this time General Aidid participated. Subsequent meetings under sponsorship of members of the Organization of African Unity produced the March 1994 Nairobi accord between the clans controlled by General Aidid and Ali Mahdi.

Conclusions

Conditions in Somalia are much better in January 1994 than they were in January 1993. People are no longer dying of starvation, crops are growing, the rains have been adequate, and some refugees have returned to their homelands. However, the magnitude of the need for development has not declined; Somalia was a severely underdeveloped state prior to 1990, and the ravages of war and famine have only increased the need for internal economic renewal and external assistance. There is still no government, there is no lasting peace, and security remains inconsistent at best, especially in the south and central sections of the country. In Mogadishu itself, especially in southern Mogadishu, there is a very fragile peace, and outbreaks of violence are common.

It should be noted that northern Somalia has remained a relatively calm area, struggling to rebuild under its leader Mohamed Egal who has kept open all communications channels with his people.

The Somali experience is instructive on a number of counts for the United Nations. In the first instance, as James Sutterlin points out, it provides a very important precedent.[13] The preamble of Resolution 794 states: "determining that the magnitude of the human tragedy caused by the conflict in Somalia, further exacerbated by the obstacles being created for the quick distribution of humanitarian assistance, *constitutes a threat to international peace and security*."[14] This was the first time that an internal humanitarian crisis had been defined as a threat to international peace and security, justifying enforcement measures. The Council acted for a different purpose than it had in Korea or the Persian Gulf. Sutterlin goes on to list the important precedents which the Somali emergency established:

> 1. A severe humanitarian emergency within a country can constitute a threat to international peace and security and thus warrant enforcement action.
> 2. Military troops can be used to enforce an end to violence as necessary to permit the safe delivery of humanitarian assistance. The enforcement action is without prejudice to the political position of any party and thus can be considered a provisional measure under Chapter VII of the UN Charter.
> 3. The troops that are used for enforcement do not need to be provided on the basis of a formal agreement between the contributing countries and the Security Council, as foreseen in Article 43 of the Charter.[15]

Somalia may have been a unique situation in that there was no government with which the UN could negotiate or seek permission to intervene, but there was little serious objection to UN action on the grounds of domestic sovereignty. While member states continue to pay homage to the principle that the UN will not interfere with issues which are determined to be within the domestic jurisdiction of states — as described in Article 2(7) of the Charter — prominence was not given to that issue during the debates on intervention in Somalia. Indeed, the opposite was the case; the principle of humanitarian intervention was elevated over claims of sovereignty.

Absent from most of the discussion, at least at the beginning of the discussion, was the Organization of African Unity. According to Julian Ozanne, "a fundamental re-examination of the OAU Charter is an urgent priority." He goes on to assert that a new charter should enshrine the humanitarian principle of the right to life and liberty and allow for intervention to override claims to sovereignty. "Under this new charter, the OAU could play a more active and dynamic role in the resolution of disputes and become a credible spokesman for Africa in the international arena. The OAU's negligence of Somalia allowed the country's fate to be decided in Washington. Such a scenario should not be repeated."[16] It is interesting to note that in the most recent peace talks the governments of Ethiopia and other African states are playing a larger role, and that they are having much more success in brokering agreements than did the UN.

Operationally, the Somali experience was not positive for the UN. Initially, neither the mandate nor the size of the force was adequate. Resolution 794 establishing the Unified Task Force provided both a stronger mandate and the forces to carry it out. However, the troops were not under UN command, and there were only sporadic attempts at disarming the thousands of Somali militia and others who brandished the weapons which had so generously been supplied in previous decades by both superpowers. When UNOSOM II was created and deployed, political reconciliation did not accompany its work, and the integration of the military and humanitarian operations was incomplete at best. UNOSOM II commanders were accused by other states which were contributing troops, as well as by Somalis, of becoming caught up in a personalized vendetta against General Aidid, which, in the end, only increased his power and prestige amongst Somalis. "The UN has simply become another clan, fighting for supremacy," said a relief worker recently, with bitter irony.

Dialogue amongst all the clans, factions, and parties is an absolute necessity if there is to be a political solution. And a political solution is an absolute requirement if Somalia is to develop economically, to repatriate and resettle the thousands of refugees living outside its borders, and to free itself from dependence on outside agencies for emergency relief. That process showed signs of promise as 1994 began.

For Canada, the Somali experience provided a number of sobering lessons. Incoming military need to become familiar not only with the geographic terrain but also with the cultural and sociological make-up of their destination. Canadian soldiers know more about peacekeeping than any others in the world—Canada not only invented the concept, but also honed the craft with vast experience over the past forty years. But the function is changing as the types of disputes change. Intra-state conflict as well as humanitarian interventions are more likely to dominate the international agenda, and Canadians, along with the UN, must prepare appropriate responses for these future developments.

14 Bosnia and Other Balkan Powder Kegs

John M. Fraser

THE CHALLENGES POSED FOR THE WORLD by the disintegration of Yugoslavia are easy to set down, if hard to meet. How can the bloodshed in Bosnia be brought to an end, renewed war in Croatia prevented, and the explosive deterioration of the situations in Kosovo and Macedonia be avoided? How can the people in these tumultuous and grudge-bearing areas be brought to live together again in peace? How can Serbia, the most populous and powerful of the countries in the region, be persuaded to play a more positive role in the search for peace and the implementation of whatever settlement may eventually be reached? Is the frustrating and, as yet, mostly unsuccessful process of pushing all sides to compromise and arranging seemingly endless negotiations to this end the best way? Is it, perhaps, the only way? Is there any way, or are some crises beyond the capacity of the world community to solve?

As an early advocate for and continuing participant in the international peacekeeping effort, Canada is obviously involved. As the crisis drags on, proposals may again be made for various kinds of military action; Canada will have to decide how to respond. Whether or not there is any such escalation, Canada will have to decide with each renewal of a United Nations peacekeeping mandate whether or not we are still prepared to take part and on what scale. A related diplomatic and political issue for Canada will continue to be appropriate participation in conferences and other initiatives for a diplomatic solution to the problem. We have not always been included in the past, despite our major part in the peacekeeping effort.

We will also be presented, at some stage, with the need to decide on our participation in international efforts to rebuild the shattered economies of the various Yugoslav successor states. Substantial assistance will undoubtedly be needed if there is to be any kind of stable peace, but our own resources, like those of all potential contributors, will not be unlimited.

Having withdrawn our ambassador from Belgrade, in company with the European Community and the United States, we will have to decide at some point what our relations with the Federal Republic of Yugoslavia (Serbia and Montenegro) are going to be, and what conditions are realistic to insist upon before lifting this and other sanctions. Rightly or wrongly, the international community has placed the major blame for the continuing intransigence of Bosnian Serbs, and hence the continuing war, on Serbia. This is the rationale for sanctions, which are beginning to have a devastating effect on the daily life of the Serbian and Montenegrin people. Is it still a fair assessment? Serbia's leaders certainly bear a heavy responsibility for fanning the fires of nationalism that produced the present conflagration in Bosnia, but it is a good deal less certain that Belgrade exercises effective control over its Bosnian compatriots; obeying orders is not the supreme national virtue, and history shows that the peoples of this tormented region are extraordinarily stubborn and single-minded.

Historical Roots

As everyone who reads a newspaper must know by now, the horrors attendant on the disintegration of Yugoslavia are rooted in history. This is not to say that history offers a complete explanation, much less a justification for the extraordinary atrocities that have been committed by all sides. These cannot be minimized by reflecting that similar atrocities were committed by the same groups in much the same areas during World War Two, or that the history of the Balkans has been replete with bloodshed.

History does, however, shed some light on the myths, hatreds, ambitions, and fears that led to the destruction of the Yugoslav federation and made it certain there could be no "velvet divorce." The conflicting nationalisms within Yugoslavia are the product of historical and cultural/religious differences, not of ethnic divisions. Serbs, Croats, and Bosnian Moslems are of the same ethnic stock, speaking essentially the same Slavic language. Although the term is often used, this is not an ethnic conflict ("communal" might be a more accurate term); nor is it a religious war. Religion is a category — often the only way to distinguish one group from another — not a *casus belli*.

The Serbs, of course, are Orthodox, and the Serbian Orthodox Church has always been a central pillar of Serbian nationalism. Another pillar is the folk-memory (bolstered by epic poetry and heroic legend) of the medieval empire of Serbia, the succeeding centuries of Turkish occupation, and, not least, Serbia's success in freeing itself from Turkish rule with little outside help.

Serbian independence was eventually recognized and ratified by the Great Powers of Europe, although not until 1878 and without any great enthusiasm. It was a continuing aim of Austrian policy to keep Serbia in its place—and a minor place at that. At various times Austria led the Great Powers in blocking territorial changes that would have given Serbia and Montenegro a common border or given Serbia access to the sea. Austria also did its best to force Serbia into a position of economic dependency. In 1914 those in Austria-Hungary who wanted war sooner rather than later believed it urgent to bring Serbia to heel once and for all. They feared the attraction of an independent South Slav kingdom for their own South Slavs, and considered Serbian expansionist ambitions a threat not only to their ambitions for hegemony in southeastern Europe, but to the integrity of the Austro-Hungarian Empire itself.

The Serbs have drawn several lessons from this period of their history, not entirely without reason. They believe that Germany and Austria do not wish them well (in 1991 people in Vienna were saying that the Serbs deserved everything they might have to suffer for their complicity in the assassination of Archduke Franz Ferdinand in Sarajevo in 1914), that no one else cares very much, and that in the end, they can rely only on themselves.

The Croats, on the other hand, are Roman Catholic, were part of the Austro-Hungarian Empire (within which they cherished certain vestigial and largely formal institutions of independent statehood), and have always considered themselves to be part of mainstream Europe. They probably thought of the Serbs, when they thought of them at all, as unsophisticated or even barbarian heretics. Certainly the Croatian intellectuals who conceived and promoted the idea of a union of South Slavs ("Yugoslavia") must have assumed that Croatia would be the dominant partner, for all their belief that Serbs and Croats were really one nation.

That is not how things turned out when the Kingdom of Serbs, Croats, and Slovenes was created in 1919, with the King of Serbia to be its ruler. The Slovenes (who had nowhere much else to go) and the Croatian political elite joined willingly enough, as did Montenegro, although all of them would have preferred a more decentralized and federal state. It had not been thought necessary to seek popular ratification for the union, and any proposal to join a unitary state under the Serbian crown would probably have been rejected had it been put to a referendum in Croatia. Disaffection, which was evident there from the very beginning, was kept alive and intensified by the fact that the new state was run almost entirely by Serbs as if it were Greater Serbia. In a sense, the whole point of Yugoslavia for the Serbs was to bring all of them within one country, but "Serbian hegemony," or the threat of it, has been a Croatian grievance from the first to the last days of Yugoslavia.

Bosnia, then as now, was more complicated. The Serbs had always considered Bosnians, whether Serbian or Moslem, to be their countrymen and Bosnia to be a part of historic Serbia. To the fury of Belgrade, however, it was Austria-Hungary that took it over from the Turks in 1878 and formally annexed it in 1908. The Croats, who had always considered the Bosnians to be Croatian and Bosnia to be part of Croatia's historic territory, were outraged that it was kept separate within the Austro-Hungarian Empire and administered directly by Vienna, whereas Croatia was ruled from Budapest.

The Bosnian Moslems are all descendants of Slavs who converted to Islam at the time of the Turkish occupation. They came to identify themselves with their Turkish rulers and tended to be the landowning class in Bosnia, neither of which attributes endeared them to their tenant farmers (sometimes hardly more than serfs). Since Austria did little to disturb the status quo, the Bosnian Moslems had little difficulty in transferring their allegiance to the new rulers. Relations between Bosnian Moslems and Bosnian Serbs were usually bad and occasionally bloody, as witness the "Sarajevo frenzy of hate" — anti-Serb riots that followed the assassination of the Archduke Franz Ferdinand by a Bosnian Serb.

Yugoslavia between the two world wars was plagued with political instability and problems of economic development. There was a recurring threat of Croatian separatism, egged on by Mussolini, who had ambitions to "restore" most of the Dalmatian coast to Italy. The most extreme group of Croatian separatists, calling themselves Ustase (which means uprising), lived mostly in exile in Italy. A compromise, worked out between the Prince Regent and the leader of the Croatian Peasant Party and declared in 1939, provided for an autonomous Croatia within Yugoslavia. This was attacked by Serbs as going too far and by Croats as inadequate, but World War Two intervened before it could be implemented. In Macedonia, taken over by Serbia in the Balkan Wars of 1912 and 1913 and one of Europe's poorest areas, a terrorist group (the Internal Macedonian Revolutionary Organization or IMRO) sought to take the region out of Yugoslavia to become part of Bulgaria.

World War Two and After

For Yugoslavia World War Two was primarily a civil war. More Yugoslavs were killed by other Yugoslavs than by the enemy. The German forces swept through Yugoslavia within two weeks, and in Croatia, the Ustase leader, Ante Pavelic, was installed at the head of an "Independent State of Croatia" (including Bosnia) under the nominal rule of a minor Italian prince. Crowned under the name of Tomislav II, he prudently avoided setting foot in his new realm, which was run on Nazi principles and in a manner which even some of the Germans found excessively zealous. The chief targets for persecution, and frequently annihilation, were Jews, gypsies, and Serbs. The Serbs have never forgotten the atrocities of those years, and the present nationalist leaders in Serbia have made very sure that the memory stays alive. The Ustase, of course, were not the only ones committing atrocities. As in any civil war, then and now, it was a game that any number could play.

The other Yugoslav protagonists were the Cetniks and Tito's Partisans. The Cetniks were the first resistance movement in conquered Yugoslavia, organized by Colonel (later General) Draza Mihajlović of the Royal Yugoslav Army. It was based mainly in Serbia and consisted almost entirely of Serbs. Its aims were to restore the pre-war Kingdom of Yugoslavia. The Partisans were led by Josip Broz Tito and the Communist Party of Yugoslavia. Once Hitler had invaded the Soviet Union and Communist parties were no longer inhibited by the Molotov-Ribbentrop Pact, Tito was able to form what came to be the most effective anti-German resistance movement in Yugoslavia. Unlike the Cetniks, the Partisans were not deterred from attacking German targets by fear of reprisals against the civilian population; the Partisan theory was that such reprisals would drive more people to the resistance.

As well as fighting Germans (or, in some cases, instead of fighting the Germans and Italians) the two resistance groups fought each other. Each, from time to time, made local accommodations with the occupying forces so as to concentrate on their Yugoslav antagonists. The British having determined to their own satisfaction that the Partisans were, in Churchill's phrase, "killing more Germans," redirected the flow of military assistance accordingly. This, predictably, ensured that the Partisans, with the Yugoslav Communist Party at their core, would determine the political future of Yugoslavia. There was a bloody settling of scores at the end of the war with those who had fought against them, including the execution of Draza Mihajlovic and the massacre of Croats who had fled to Austria, surrendered to British forces there, and been returned to Yugoslavia for Tito's summary "justice." No one who had worked with the Germans in Yugoslavia or elsewhere, for whatever reason, got much sympathy from the Allies in disputes with compatriots who had fought on the Allied side.

The nature and role of the Ustase regime in the war earned Croatians the enduring suspicion of Tito and the Communist leadership, exacerbated by Croatia's steadfast Catholicism. Archbishop (later Cardinal) Stepinac of Zagreb, a fervent anti-Communist, was tried for collaboration with the Ustase after he refused to encourage his flock to cooperate with Tito's regime, convicted, and imprisoned. He has been a hero to Croats ever since.

Another wartime legacy stemmed from the annexation of Kosovo to Albania under Italian occupation. For the Serbs, Kosovo had (and has) an almost mystic significance as the heart of Serbia's medieval empire and the site of the doomed but heroic battle of Kosovo Polje, when the flower of Serbian chivalry was defeated by the Turks in 1389. The recovery of Kosovo in the First Balkan War was the fulfilment of a Serbian dream. In the meantime, unfortunately for the Serbs, it had been largely populated with Albanians. Had they been given a choice in 1945 (or in 1919, for that matter) the Albanians, both in Kosovo and in Albania itself, would probably have opted for Kosovo's union with Albania. Instead Kosovars were "deemed" to have chosen voluntarily to be part of

Serbia and Yugoslavia, albeit with a slightly enhanced status as an Autonomous Region within Serbia.

Kosovo's autonomy, nebulous as it was, neither pleased the Serbs (it was, indeed, part of Tito's policy of cutting Serbia down to size) nor satisfied the Kosovo Albanians, whose nationalist feelings endured through both periods of repression and those of genuine autonomy. Their population continued to increase, at the fastest rate in Europe.

Tito's new Yugoslavia almost had to be a federation—if only to lay to rest the spectre of the old, Serb-dominated Kingdom of Yugoslavia. Serbia was deprived of Macedonia, which became a separate founding republic, and its authority was diluted in Kosovo and in the Autonomous Region of Vojvodina. For most of Tito's reign it did not much matter whether Yugoslavia was a federation or not. The dominance of the Communist party (later rechristened the League of Communists of Yugoslavia), the dictates of democratic centralism, and the power of Tito's own personality all worked against any real diffusion of power. Memories of World War Two also led the regime to deny its citizens the freedom to express regional or national animosities. Even under Yugoslavia's last and most decentralized constitution it was a criminal offence to affront the sensitivities of a "nation or nationality."

Stirrings of Nationalism

If he had ever forgotten, Tito was reminded of the threat posed by regional nationalism when the Croatian government and party responded sympathetically to nationalist pressures in 1971 during the so-called "Croatian Spring." The Serbs in Croatia reacted by preparing for self-defence, as they were to do in 1991.[1] Tito's solution was to purge the Croatian leadership (and, later, leaders in Belgrade sympathetic to Serbian nationalism) and press ahead with constitutional revisions which made Yugoslavia a very decentralized federation, almost a confederation. The theory was that national cohesion would be assured by a united and disciplined League of Communists (LCY). In the event, perhaps not too surprisingly, the LCY also fragmented along regional lines.

Worst of all, from the Serbian point of view, constitutional evolution had enhanced the status of Kosovo and Vojvodina (now called Autonomous Provinces) to make them independent parts of the federation, equal in all practical respects to Serbia. Even this was not enough for the Albanian nationalists in Kosovo. In 1981 demonstrations which developed into riots broke out urging full republic status for Kosovo, carrying with it the recognition of Albanians as a "nation" of Yugoslavia (rather than a "nationality" or "national minority") with the right of secession. Both Serbian and federal authorities saw such a demand as a first step towards the separation of Kosovo from Yugoslavia and its union with Albania (an unlikely goal, one might think, in the days of Enver Hoxha).

For the Serbs, in any case, the separation of Kosovo from Serbia, even within Yugoslavia, was unthinkable. Its autonomous status, which effectively guaranteed predominance for Albanians and their language, was bad enough. Serbian nationalists urged that Serbia had the right to be "a republic like the others" with "control over all its territory." Such arguments were beginning to come more or less into the open in 1986, along with a more general complaint, not entirely unfounded, that Serbia had suffered systematic diminution and discrimination from the start in Tito's new Yugoslavia. The plight of Serbs in Kosovo (supposedly the victims of "Albanian genocide") was exploited by Slobodan Milosevic to harness the rising tide of Serbian nationalism in his pursuit of power.

Once having achieved power in Serbia at the end of 1987, Milosevic proceeded to eliminate any real autonomy for Kosovo and Vojvodina and asserted Serbia's claim to greater weight within the federation as a whole. In the first objective he was successful, unilaterally amending the constitution of Serbia and bullying the other republics and the federal government and party not to meddle in this "internal" Serbian affair. In so doing, however, he triggered apprehensions of Serbian hegemonism that had never entirely died away in the other republics, in particular in Croatia and Slovenia. As to his second objective, greater weight for Serbia within the federation was precisely what the others would not accept.

Slovenia had for some years been testing the limits of Yugoslav orthodoxy. Slovenian youth organizations and publications had shown particular zeal and ingenuity in tweaking the tail of the Yugoslav establishment, and the Slovenian authorities seemed in no hurry to stop them. This was not so much an expression of

Slovenian nationalism—although the Slovenes had always felt themselves to be somewhat apart from the rest of Yugoslavia—as agitation for a more liberal, more democratic, more Western society. One senior official greeted an ambassador making his first visit with the rather surprising words: "Welcome to our little Alpine country on the wrong side of Switzerland!"

Slovenes also resented the drain on their more efficient economy by demands for investment and support in the poorer regions in the south, from which they also feared an influx of job-seekers (unlike the rest of the country Slovenia had a labour shortage) as a threat to their distinct language and small but unique society. To begin with, at any rate, Slovenians wanted not so much to be an independent country as to be left alone by Belgrade to run their own affairs. In both Slovenia and Croatia the collapse of Communist regimes in Eastern Europe generated increasing pressure for fundamental changes in how Yugoslavia was governed. In Slovenia, where organized political groups outside the party had come into being in 1988 and 1989 and multi-party elections were held in April 1990, the Communists lost the elections for the Assembly to a coalition of six parties jointly known as the Democratic United Opposition of Slovenia (DEMOS), but won the presidency.[2]

In Croatia the Communist leadership had yielded to popular demand in December 1989 and agreed that other political parties should be permitted to run in free elections. When they did, in elections held one week after those in Slovenia, the clear winners were the Croatian Democratic Alliance (HDZ) led by a former Partisan General, Franjo Tudjman, who had broken with the Communists to support Croatian nationalist causes, and had been involved in the nationalist upheavals in 1971. The expression of Croatian nationalism had become respectable—not least in reaction to the upsurge of Serb nationalist rhetoric under Milosevic. In his election campaign Tudjman called for the restructuring of Yugoslavia as a loose confederation in which Croatia would have virtually total freedom of action. To begin with, he also called for the new Croatia to incorporate all of its "historic territory"—in other words, Bosnia. Serbs in Croatia quickly made it clear that they wanted nothing to do with an independent Croatian state, which Tudjman envisaged as the homeland of the Croatian people. Minorities would have rights, but could never really be part of this homeland.

Breaking Up

By the end of the year both Croatia and Slovenia were asserting sovereignty. In June 1991 they declared their independence, Croatia suddenly doing so the day before Slovenia and thereby rather undermining the loosely co-ordinated approach they had been trying to pursue. Negotiations for a confederation of sovereign Yugoslav states broke down on Serbia's insistence that either the Yugoslav federation be preserved with real powers for the central government, or, if it were to break up, Serbs in other republics be able to exercise their right of self-determination by opting out, with frontiers to be adjusted accordingly. While the borders between Serbia and both Croatia and Bosnia within Yugoslavia (often denigrated as "Tito's borders") corresponded roughly with the pre-1914 frontiers (except that Vojvodina was never part of the Kingdom of Serbia), they would leave a large number of Serbs living in a foreign country if they became international borders.

Macedonia and Bosnia-Herzegovina, both grindingly poor, were not comfortable with the idea of independence and attempted to negotiate a confederation or asymmetrical federation. Failing this, they preferred independence to membership in a Serb-dominated federation of what was left of Yugoslavia.

Except for the Yugoslav National Army (JNA), federal institutions were falling apart. As early as January 1990 the League of Communists of Yugoslavia virtually disintegrated in the course of its Fourteenth Extraordinary Congress, when the Slovenian delegation walked out and the Croatians refused to participate without them. Ironically, the federal government, under the leadership of the dynamic and effective prime minister, Ante Markovic, was having some success in bringing Yugoslavia's hyper-inflation under control. His economic reform plan offered some hope of an end to the ten years of unrelieved and accelerating economic deterioration which had been a sour back-drop and exacerbation to the political conflict.

The ambitions of the most important republics, together with the autonomy they already enjoyed, made the implementation of a coherent federal economic program almost impossible, and the federal government was virtually excluded from discussions on reshaping Yugoslavia. Nor was political reform feasible at the federal level. While all the republics were having multi-party elections, it would require a constitutional amendment to permit multi-party federal elections. Since this might confer greater legitimacy on the federal government, the major republics were opposed to any such change, and the federal Assembly and government only continued in office by decree when their legal term expired. This made dubious the constitutionality of some of the federal government's subsequent actions.

Towards the end of 1990 multi-party elections were held in Bosnia-Herzegovina. Eighty-four percent of the votes were split, more or less in proportion to their share of the population, among the three "ethnic" parties—Moslem, Serb, and Croat. Pan-ethnic parties, including the former Communists, fared poorly. Within the Moslems' Party of Democratic Action the majority, led by Alija Izetbegovic, were religious militants who stressed the need for a new Bosnia to reflect its Islamic character.[3] This, combined with a tendency on the part of the Moslems to ally themselves with the Bosnian Croats rather than the Serbs and growing fears about the future of Yugoslavia, made the Bosnian Serbs profoundly uneasy. As with the Croatian Serbs, their fears and sense of being threatened were hardly assuaged by the stream of nationalist propaganda coming out of Belgrade. If Serbs in Croatia looked upon Croatian independence as a return of the Ustase, it is not a very great exaggeration to say that their Bosnian compatriots were encouraged to feel that an independent Bosnia in which the Moslems were predominant amounted to a return of the Turkish occupation.

Elections were also held in Macedonia, where the party winning the largest number of seats was the reborn and nationalist Internal Macedonian Revolutionary Organization; Slobodan Milosevic and his renamed Communist allies triumphed in Serbia and Montenegro. The major Serbian opposition parties were then even more nationalist than Milosevic; prospects for a compromise which could keep Yugoslavia together in some form seemed to be fading rapidly. No one wanted civil war in Yugoslavia, but few were prepared to make the concessions that might have prevented it.

Having voted overwhelmingly in favour of independence in their December 1990 referendum, the Slovenes moved gradually to "disassociate" themselves from Yugoslavia. Failing agreement on a confederation, Slovenia declared independence on June 25, 1991, whereupon the Yugoslav National Army, which had always been dedicated to preserving the integrity of Yugoslavia, sought to restore federal control over border posts the Slovenian government had put under its own authority. Their action seemed to go well beyond decisions made by the federal government. The war to hold Slovenia was brief, casualties were relatively few, and the Slovene Territorial Defence forces were totally successful. The army had not really taken them seriously, expecting that they would yield to merely a show of force, while conscripts in the JNA (particularly the non-Serbs) were reluctant to shoot at what they still saw as fellow Yugoslavs with whom they had no quarrel.

In Croatia, where the fighting was much bloodier and more protracted, the JNA was not so much trying to keep that republic within Yugoslavia as to protect and support Croatia's Serb minority and its claims to independence (no doubt to be followed, where feasible, by union with Serbia). By this time the army was shedding its non-Serbian members, many of whom deserted rather than take part in a civil war; before long it became de facto a Serbian and Montenegrin force.

International Involvement

It is often said that the international community, and, in particular, the European Community and the United States, have simply ignored the crisis in Yugoslavia. They certainly did not solve the problem—nor could they have done—but they have not been inactive. They first tried to avert the disintegration of Yugoslavia, not simply from Cold War force of habit, but because they saw the dangers of fragmentation and instability in what was once called the powder-keg of Europe. Foreign observers also believed that it was in the best interests of all concerned, particularly the Yugoslavs, that the country stay together in some form. Many Yugoslavs shared that opinion.

The governments which might have become involved sooner were also anxious to avoid precipitating a break-up by talking or acting as if it were inevitable. Virtually on the eve of Slovenian and Croatian declarations of independence both the Community and the United States urged them not to separate and said that their independence would not be recognized if declared. When the Yugoslav National Army tried to reverse Slovenian secession and their effort turned out to be a military fiasco, the European Community was able to arrange negotiations for its withdrawal.

The Brioni Accord also provided for a three-month moratorium on the implementation of Slovenian and Croatian independence, and for negotiations under Community auspices (the Hague Conference or the Peace Conference on Yugoslavia, chaired by the former British foreign secretary and secretary general of the NATO, Lord Carrington). The European Community Monitor Mission, in which Canadian officers participated, was set up to supervise the withdrawal and later to monitor, but not to enforce, various ceasefires in Croatia.

The Community, which had hoped to use the Yugoslav crisis as a shining example of a common foreign policy, was badly split on the question of recognizing the new states. The Federal Republic of Germany, euphoric at the accomplishment of German unification and under considerable pressure from German public opinion, pressed for quick recognition. Other members of the Community were more cautious, and those involved in mediation took the view that such a move would make it more difficult to obtain the concessions needed to reach a negotiated settlement. President Izetbegovic of Bosnia-Herzegovina also urged delay, fearing serious repercussions that would threaten the unity of Bosnia-Herzegovina. The UN secretary general argued against premature recognition, while the United States, at the other end of the spectrum from Germany, was also opposed and did not itself take this step until some months after the Community had done so.

By the end of 1991 Germany forced the hands of its Community partners by declaring that it would go ahead, alone if necessary. Having secured rather grudging agreement to move together on January 15, 1992, the Germans jumped the gun by extending recognition four weeks earlier.[4] Membership in the United Nations, however, did not come until May 1992. Canada extended recognition at the same time as the Community, but did not establish diplomatic relations until early 1993. The role of Germany in pushing for international recognition of Croatian and Slovenian independence was given the most sinister interpretation possible by the Serbs, most of whom saw the German role as reflecting centuries of anti-Serb hatred and some of whom went so far as to accuse the Federal Republic of Germany, with Austria (also an enthusiast for early recognition), of seeking to create a "Fourth Reich."

A more general view was that the German zeal for extending recognition had been unhelpful. Croatia had achieved a major goal—international recognition—without really having to address seriously the question of its Serbian minority, the resolution of which is a prerequisite to any stable peace.

Bosnia-Herzegovina embarked on the road to independence when President Izetbegovic applied to the European Community in December 1991, over the protests of the Bosnian Serbs, for recognition as an independent state. In February 1992 a referendum on Bosnian independence was announced; the Bosnian Serbs made it clear they would boycott the referendum and ignore its results. When Bosnian Moslems and Croats voted massively (99.7 percent of the 64.4 percent of those eligible who voted) for independence on February 29 and March 1, Bosnian Serbs began to prepare for war.[5]

The European Community, urged on by the United States and possibly believing that it had been a mistake to delay recognition of Croatia and Slovenia and that recognition, when it came, had been a factor in ending the fighting in Croatia, decided that quick recognition of Bosnia-Herzegovina would have a stabilizing effect (a quixotic notion as it turned out). They moved to recognition despite the explicit urgings of both Lord Carrington and the UN secretary general that to do so would seriously damage the prospects for a negotiated settlement. To ignore the fierce objections to independence by Bosnian Serbs, constituting 31.4 percent of the population, almost guaranteed that they would fight, while it would at the same time encourage Moslems and Croats in Bosnia to resist compromise.

The Bosnian government, for its part, saw recognition and membership in the UN as committing the world community, under the Charter, to defend the territorial integrity of the new state, by military force if necessary. That integrity had been under threat even before Bosnia-Herzegovina declared its independence. Not only had Bosnian Serbs made clear, at every stage, their opposition and unwillingness to co-operate, but talks were almost certainly going on between the leaders of Serbia and Croatia on splitting Bosnia between them as part of an overall settlement. What stood in the way of such an agreement was Croatian insistence, on one hand, that every inch of Croatian soil within its borders as part of the Yugoslav federation must be under the control of the new government, and the Serbian position, on the other, that Croatian Serbs must have the right to remain in Yugoslavia (that is, be part of Serbia) or be independent if they so chose. The conflicting claims of territorial integrity and national self-determination have been at the heart of the conflict, both in Bosnia and Croatia, ever since. The idea that such a deal would leave a significant number of Serbs under "alien" rule was greeted with severe criticism in Belgrade, not least by the Serbian Orthodox bishops, who were otherwise condemning the bloodshed.

United Nations involvement had been suggested by Prime Minister Mulroney, among others, in August 1991, and the UN Security Council adopted Resolution 713 on September 25, in which it commended efforts by the European Community and the Conference on Security and Co-operation in Europe (CSCE), appealed to all parties to settle their disputes peacefully, and, under Chapter VII of the Charter, imposed "a general and complete embargo on all deliveries of weapons and military equipment to Yugoslavia." (Comprehensive sanctions were imposed by Security Council Resolution 757 of May 30, 1992.) There was no reference to peacekeeping, but Canada had already indicated a willingness to participate in a peacekeeping operation.

A ceasefire agreement was worked out under the mediation of the UN secretary general's special representative, Cyrus Vance, and signed on January 3, 1992. It provided for the withdrawal of Yugoslav National Army forces from Croatia, disarming Croatian Serb irregular forces, and impounding their heavy weapons. On February 21, Security Council Resolution 743 called for a UN force in Croatia to monitor implementation of the ceasefire. The force was deployed at the end of March, with a Canadian contingent of approximately eleven hundred out of fourteen thousand. Although the agreement has only been partially implemented (all JNA forces were withdrawn and weapons were turned over to the UN force in some areas) and the Croatian government periodically threatens not to renew its acceptance of a peacekeeping force unless its terms are carried out in full, the ceasefire has generally held (up to early 1994).

What makes it fragile, and the resumption of conflict likely, is that Serbian and Croatian perspectives and aims remain diametrically opposed. The government of Croatia sees the function of the UN force as to bring the Serb-dominated areas under its control. The Croatian Serbs see it as to protect them from the exercise of Zagreb's authority, and, in particular, from the deployment of Croatian soldiers or police in "their" areas. While the government in Zagreb offered guarantees of minority rights (about which Croatian Serbs were highly sceptical) and may have been willing to concede some form of local administrative or cultural autonomy, they rejected any real *political* autonomy or self-rule until President Tudjman moved in this direction with his proposals late in 1993. It was not entirely clear how far he was prepared to go. It seems unlikely that Croatian Serbs and their patrons in Belgrade would ever settle for anything less, and if Croatia eventually absorbs the Croatian areas in Bosnia-Herzegovina, the Serbs in the Krajina enclave will be almost encircled and even less inclined than they are now to trust the government in Zagreb.

The Bosnian Cauldron

At least in Croatia there is a ceasefire, however fragile. In Bosnia there have been dozens of ceasefire agreements, but rarely as much as an hour when the firing has actually ceased. The repugnant process of ethnic cleansing, engaged in by each of the three parties, continues with atrocities such as have not been seen in Europe since World War Two. There have been three almost successful comprehensive peace plans since Bosnia-Herzegovina declared its independence. In the first, worked out before Bosnia had received international recognition, the Bosnian Serbs were persuaded to agree to preserve Bosnian integrity. In return, the Moslem-dominated Bosnian government agreed to the creation of three ethnically-based "cantons" which would enjoy considerable autonomy. This agreement was short-lived; President Izetbegovic decided to concentrate on winning international recognition and support in the hope of involving the world community to defend and preserve Bosnia-Herzegovina as a unitary state.

The second plan, known as the Vance-Owen Peace Plan after the two chairmen of the London Conference (or International Conference on the former Yugoslavia, set up jointly by the UN and EC and taking over from the Hague Conference), proposed ten "provinces" within Bosnia, set up only partly along ethnic lines. Bosnian Serbs would have had to withdraw from much of the territory acquired in a year of savagery and bloodshed. Radovan

Karadzic, the leader of the Bosnian Serbs, was persuaded to sign the agreement in Athens on May 2, 1993 under heavy pressure from all sides, including President Milosevic of Serbia who threatened to join in sanctions against Bosnian Serbs if they did not accept it. Karadzic did insist that it be ratified by the Bosnian Serb "parliament," which, in the end, turned it down. The Americans gave little support for the plan, which involved a large military force (estimates ran from forty to seventy thousand, much of which would have had to come from the United States) to implement it. Probably for that reason, no real attempt was made to salvage it.

The third near miss came a few months later, when another tripartite division of Bosnia-Herzegovina was worked out, tentatively agreed to, and rejected by one of the parties—this time the Moslems, who considered that they had been allocated too little territory. Unless Bosnia-Herzegovina simply splits into three separate states, some loosely confederal partition still seems the only basis for an agreement. In either case, borders will be constantly disputed and a secure peace still remote.

United Nations peacekeeping activity in Bosnia is strictly limited to humanitarian purposes—something not always understood and often resented by Bosnian Moslems, who expected active military support, not merely a UN presence. The first troops in Sarajevo formed the headquarters of the peacekeeping force in Croatia (in the hope that even a small UN presence would prevent conflict from spilling over into Bosnia-Herzegovina). It had no mandate of any kind in Bosnia.[6] A contingent (initially Canadian) was later sent (under Security Council Resolution 761 of June 29, 1992) to hold Sarajevo airport to keep it open for humanitarian supply flights.

The UN force mandate also included assisting the UN high commissioner for refugees (UNHCR) with the negotiation of safe passage for aid convoys, providing protective support if necessary. The secretary general's report of September 10, 1992, noted that the normal peacekeeping rules of engagement would apply, including the use of force in self-defence. "In this context," the report went on, "self-defence is deemed to include situations in which armed persons attempt by force to prevent United Nations troops from carrying out their mandate."[7] When the Security Council declared six towns as "safe areas" (Resolution 824 of May 6, 1993), the UN force was to monitor the humanitarian situation in these towns;

their terms of engagement again included the right to use force to defend themselves and those under their protection. The first safe area, Srebrenica, was protected by a Canadian unit up to the beginning of 1994. While the rules of engagement are fairly broad in defining "self-defence," and the Security Council has authorized "all necessary means" to carry out its resolutions, peacekeepers and the governments providing them have been very cautious about using force. There has been little willingness in practice to countenance a more aggressive role, or to provide the resources that would make it possible.

Many suggestions have been made for the UN force to be given the means and the task of escorting aid convoys in armoured columns able to fight their way through, or for member states to enforce the Security Council's "no fly" zone imposed by Security Council Resolution 781 of November 5, 1992. (Five months later, Resolution 816 of March 31, 1993 authorized member states or their regional organizations—i.e., NATO—to "ensure compliance with the ban.") It has also been proposed, in particular by the Clinton administration, that air strikes on Bosnian Serb artillery positions beseiging Sarajevo, or even on targets in Serbia itself, might have a salutary effect, and that the arms embargo should be lifted for Bosnian Moslems. No government has seriously suggested that the UN, the European Community, or anyone else should consider imposing peace in Bosnia by force of arms.

This would be an enormous effort, costly in resources, probably in casualties, and indefinite in duration. When could the victorious armies withdraw without conflict breaking out again as soon as they had left? Tito, or so everyone thought, had brought peace, reasonable prosperity, and a cooling of ethnic frictions to the area for over forty years, not hesitating to use repressive means when it seemed necessary. His achievement turned out to be unexpectedly fragile.

Less comprehensive military operations would certainly be less costly, but there is good reason to wonder how effective they would be—and what action would follow if they were not. Many NATO members, including Canada, have looked at such ideas with caution, not least because of the very real danger that any United Nations or NATO military engagement, however justified, would invite retaliation against their peacekeepers. As for lifting the arms embargo for Bosnian Moslems, it is fair to ask whether adding to the number or sophistication of weapons in the area would really be a contribution to peace. In any case, a shortage of weapons or munitions does not seem to be an inhibiting factor for any of the warriors in Bosnia, although the Moslems are short of heavy weapons. Some arms have been getting through, one way or another, and there was a fairly impressive supply to begin with.

Other Powder Kegs

If Bosnia's future continues to look bleak, it is not the only powder keg in the Balkan peninsula. Croatia could blow up again, at any time. Then there is the situation in Kosovo, which has only been kept under control by a heavy Yugoslav/Serbian military and police presence. Almost the only means of expression available to Kosovo Albanians (who declared their independence in 1992) has been repeated boycotts of Serbian elections, most recently in December 1993. Repression may serve to prevent Albanians in Kosovo from precipitating an explosion, but there is always a danger of Serbian over-reaction to some incident, thereby provoking a spontaneous uprising which might not be quickly controllable. Albania would not stand idly by, however little it could do militarily. There would also be destabilizing ripples in Macedonia with its large (probably about 25 to 30 percent) and discontented Albanian minority.

The threat of a wider war should Macedonia collapse persuaded the UN secretary general to send a contingent of peacekeepers (180 Canadians at first) to monitor Macedonia's borders with Serbia and Montenegro as a form of "preventative diplomacy." Roughly one thousand Nordic and American troops are now deployed. Canada has also participated in small CSCE monitoring missions in Kosovo and the Sanjak of Novi Pazar to investigate incidents and prevent them from escalating. These missions played a useful if probably minor role, but the government of Yugoslavia (Serbia and Montenegro) withdrew its consent for their presence on Serbian territory at the end of June 1993. Canadians are also part of a group monitoring Macedonian enforcement of sanctions, and of the NATO/Western European Union (WEU) naval force patrolling the Adriatic coast.

The threat to Macedonia is not really invasion by Serbia. Yugoslav forces withdrew quietly and without incident after the declaration of independence following a plebescite on September 8, 1991 (boycotted by the Albanians). Rabid Serbian nationalists exaggerate the size and plight of the Serbian minority there—or still think that all "Macedonians" are really South Serbs (and their region "Old Serbia"), as they were designated from 1913 until 1945, but this cause has little resonance with most Serbs. A Macedonian sense of distinct identity, with its own literature and even (to the fury of the Serbian church) its own Orthodox church, was one of Tito's more successful nation-building efforts. Between the two world wars there had been constant mutual terrorism amounting to a minor civil war between those who thought of themselves as Serbs and those who identified with Bulgaria and thought Macedonia should be (re)joined to it. As nearly as an outsider can tell, Macedonians of the Slavic majority are now confident in their identity as Macedonians. The Albanian minority complains that this identity excludes them; Bulgaria and Greece assert that there is no such thing, with the Greeks going further to argue that even calling the new state "Macedonia" amounts to an implicit territorial claim on the Greek province of the same name.

No government now asserts a claim to the territory of "The Former Yugoslav Republic of Macedonia," as it was named for the purpose of United Nations membership (sitting between Thailand and Togo). All neighbouring states would probably pursue claims if Macedonia were to crumble. The reasons that it may not be viable as an independent state are internal: the restiveness of its Albanian minority, and the wretched state of its economy, made worse by United Nations sanctions against Serbia and Montenegro (and frequent closings of the frontier with Greece). The prolonged delay in its acceptance by the world community has not helped, and the closing of the Greek port of Salonika to Macedonia threatens its economic viability.

Future Choices

Assuming that there will continue to be great reluctance to use military force on the scale necessary to reverse the changes that have taken place, in this case, the international community may have to reassess its insistence that territory cannot be acquired by force, there being no reason to suppose that Bosnian Serbs or Croats will just give up territory they fought to acquire. We shall also have to decide when and under what conditions we are prepared to relax or terminate the sanctions against Serbia; it is unlikely that we will be in the happy position of seeing all the objectives met for which they were imposed. We would be accepting a less than satisfactory situation. Can we do so without sending the message that we accept and condone the horrors that created it?

A more far-reaching challenge is to learn from the Yugoslav experience, since there are almost certain to be more countries facing disintegration as a result of ethnic and nationalist tensions. Could we have done anything to avert the Yugoslav wars of succession? Did we raise unrealistic expectations of decisive action, perhaps chilling the prospects for compromise and encouraging aggressors thereby? What is the proper balance between the claims of history and territorial integrity and those of self-determination? What criteria are there, or ought there to be, for the recognition of newly independent countries that have torn themselves apart from an existing state? How can outsiders promote or ensure orderly "disassociation" (which is how Slovenia and Croatia first described what they were doing)? How can generations of hatred, fear, and suspicion be overcome and present grievances (not all of them rational) dealt with peacefully?

The Canadian dilemma will no doubt continue. On one hand, there have been intense feelings that "something must be done" to end the horrors, leading to instinctive support for such initiatives as the American call for air strikes. On the other hand, we rightly fear the consequent dangers to our own peacekeepers on the ground. Nor can we be sure that such action would really contribute to a solution to the problem.

Endnotes

Chapter One:

1 Joseph Nye, Jr., *Peace in Parts: Integration and Conflict in Regional Organizations* (Boston: Little Brown, 1971).
2 John Gaddis, "The Long Peace: Elements of Stability in the Postwar International System," *International Security* 10, no. 4 (Spring 1986), pp. 99–142.
3 For the concept of reassurance in deterrence, see Richard Lebow and Janice Stein, "Beyond Deterrence," *Journal of Social Issues* 43, no. 4 (1987), pp. 40–63.
4 Max Singer and Aaron Wildavsky, *The Real World Order: Zones of Peace/Zones of Turmoil* (Chatham, N.J.: Chatham House Publishers, 1993).
5 Kal Holsti, "A 'Zone of Civility' in European Diplomatic Relations? The CSCE and Conflict Resolution," a paper presented at the annual meeting, International Studies Association, Atlanta, March 31–April 4, 1992.
6 Singer and Wildavsky, *The Real World Order*, p. 12.
7 Zbigniew Brzezinski, *Out of Control* (New York: Charles Scribner's Sons, 1993).
8 Ibid., p. 51.
9 Kal Holsti, "A 'Zone of Civility'," p. 2. One might dispute Holsti's claim that these rules reaffirmed the Westphalian principles. They correspond more closely to the operating principles of the post-Vienna Concert of Europe which enhanced cooperative norms and practices far beyond the original Westphalian practices.
10 Stephen Van Evera, "Primed for Peace: Europe after the Cold War," *International Security* 15, no. 3 (Winter 1990/91), pp. 48–49.
11 John Mearsheimer, "Back to the Future: Instability in Europe after the Cold War," *International Security* 15, no. 1 (Summer 1990), pp. 5–56; see also Mearsheimer, "The Case for a Ukrainian Nuclear Deterrent," *Foreign Affairs* 72, no. 3 (Summer 1993), pp. 50–80.
12 Friedrich Kratochwil, "The Embarrassment of Changes: Neo-Realism as the Science of Realpolitik without Politics," *Review of International Studies* 19 (1993), p. 79.
13 Charles Glaser, "Why NATO Is Still the Best: Future Security Arrangements for Europe," *International Security* 18, no. 1 (Summer 1993), pp. 5–50.
14 Holsti, "A 'Zone of Civility'," p. 15.
15 Kratochwil, "The Embarrassment of Changes," p. 70.

16 Robert Keohane, "Multilateralism: an agenda for research," *International Journal* 45, no. 4 (Autumn 1990), p. 761.
17 Robert Cox, "Multilateralism and World Order," *Review of International Studies* 18 (1992), p. 164.
18 Liberal Party of Canada, *Creating Opportunity: The Liberal Plan for Canada* (Ottawa, 1993), p. 108.
19 Ibid., p. 109.
20 Hon. David Collenette, "National Defence: Budget Impact" (Ottawa: Department of National Defence, February 1994).
21 Canada 21, *Canada and Common Security in the Twenty-First Century* (Toronto: Centre for International Studies, University of Toronto, 1994).
22 Liberal Party of Canada, *Creating Opportunity*, p. 108.
23 Government of Canada, Department of External Affairs, *Competitiveness and Security: Directions for Canada's International Relations* (Ottawa: Minister of Supply and Services, 1985). For a critical assessment of this green paper, see Maureen Appel Molot and Brian W. Tomlin, "The Conservative Agenda" in Maureen Appel Molot and Brian W. Tomlin, eds., *Canada Among Nations 1985: The Conservative Agenda* (Toronto: James Lorimer and Company, 1986).

Chapter Two:

1 Super 301 actions refer to provisions that were added to the Omnibus Trade and Competitiveness Act of 1988. These provisions made it mandatory for the United States Trade Representative's Office (USTR) to identify trade policy priorities with respect to implementation of sections 301 through 310. The provisions required the USTR on schedule to prepare an inventory of foreign trade barriers, establish a priority list of countries and their unreasonable practices, and then set deadlines for their removal. The provision expired after 1990.
2 Governor Bill Clinton and Senator Al Gore, *Putting People First: How We Can All Change America* (New York: Times Books, 1992), p. 13.
3 Jagdish Bhagwati of Columbia University, the former economic policy advisor to the secretary general of GATT, has used this phrase to describe the U.S. reaction to the rise of competing states in the global economy. He compared it to the reaction of Britain in the late nineteenth century to the rise of new industrial states such as Imperial Germany and the United States. See Jagdish Bhagwati, *The World Trading System at Risk* (Princeton, N.J.: Princeton University Press, 1991) for a good description of this analysis. For an updating of

Bhagwati's views, see Bhagwati, "The Diminished Giant Syndrome," *Foreign Affairs* 72, no. 2 (Spring 1993), pp. 22–26.

4 The most celebrated declinist analysis is that of Paul Kennedy, *The Rise and Fall of the Great Powers: Economic Change and Military Conflict from 1500 to 2000* (New York: Random House, 1987). It was in this volume that Kennedy described what he called imperial overstretch, which led inevitably to the decline of such great powers as Spain, Holland, and Great Britain. But the decline of American power had been discussed much earlier though without the same broad popularity. See Richard Rosecrance, ed., *America as an Ordinary Country: U.S. Foreign Policy and the Future* (Ithaca, N.Y.: Cornell University Press, 1976). In the 1980s decline became linked to the American economic competitiveness.

5 For a discussion of the Uruguay Round, see chapter 5 by Curtis and Wolfe.

6 Again, this a phrase that has been popularized by Jagdish Bhagwati (see *The World Trading System at Risk*).

7 Section 301 of the Trade and Tariff Act, 1974 directs the USTR to enforce U.S. rights under international trade agreements and to take other actions necessary to remove unfair foreign trade practices.

8 Sylvia Nasar, "The Risky Allure of Strategic Trade," *New York Times*, February 28, 1993, p. E1.

9 *Wall Street Journal*, February 8, 1994, p. A12.

10 Many analyses have examined the course and consequences of the negotiations between the United States and Japan over semiconductors. Some of the best include: Clyde V. Prestowitz, Jr., *Trading Places: How We Allowed Japan to Take the Lead* (New York: Basic Books, Inc., Publishers, 1988); Laura D'Andrea Tyson and David B. Yoffie, "Semiconductors: From Manipulated to Managed Trade," pp. 29–78 in David B. Yoffie, ed., *Beyond Free Trade: Firms, Governments, and Global Competition* (Boston: Harvard Business School Press, 1993); and Laura D'Andrea Tyson, *Who's Bashing Whom? Trade Conflict in High-Technology Industries* (Washington, D.C.: Institute for International Economics, 1992), pp. 85–154.

11 Trade Negotiations Committee, *Final Act Embodying the Results of the Uruguay Round of Multilateral Trade Negotiations* (Geneva: GATT Secretariat, December 15, 1993, Special Distribution [UR-93-0246]).

12 *World Economy Trade Outlook*, May 1993, Annex IV "Revised Weights for the World Economic Outlook," pp. 116–19.

13 Report of the Royal Commission on the Economic Union and Development Prospects for Canada, *Volume One* (Ottawa: Supply and Services, 1985), p. 229.

14 Committee on the Competitiveness of the Resource Industries, Report of the National Advisory Board on Science and Technology,

Competitiveness in the Canadian Mining and Forestry Industries (May 1993), p. 1.

15 A presentation by Industry Canada to the Canadian Council for International Business, January 13, 1994, "Canada's Competitiveness Challenge," p. 14.

16 Scott Haggert, "Canada's World Trade Up," *Financial Post*, September 25, 1993, p. 21.

17 Presentation by Industry Canada, "Canada's Competitiveness Challenge," p. 11.

18 Sylvia Ostry, *Governments and Corporations in a Shrinking World* (New York: Council on Foreign Relations Press, 1990), p. 1.

19 Lynn K. Mytelka, "Strategic Alliances" in Fen Osler Hampson and Christopher J. Maule, eds., *Canada Among Nations, 1993–94: Global Jeopardy* (Ottawa: Carleton University Press, 1993), p. 129.

20 Hon. Jean Chrétien, "Closing Remarks," delivered at the Aylmer Conference, Château Cartier Sheraton Hotel, Aylmer, November 24, 1991.

21 Roy MacLaren, quoted in Peter Morton, "Liberals Back off from Vow to Block NAFTA," *Financial Post*, September 30, 1993, p. 13.

22 Roy MacLaren, "Beyond Continentalism: In Search of an Independent, Global Trade Policy for Canada," a preliminary trade discussion paper prepared for the Economic Committee of the Liberal Caucus, June 1991, pp. 4, 1.

23 Ibid., p. 8.

24 *Creating Opportunity: The Liberal Plan for Canada* (Ottawa: The Liberal Party of Canada, 1993), p. 25.

25 Hon. Roy MacLaren, quoted in Barrie McKenna and Jeff Sallot, "Canada Seeks Trade Deal in Asia," *Globe and Mail*, November 27, 1993, p. B1.

26 Robert Keatley, "Commerce Department Changes Tune, Trumpets Investing in 'Top 10' Nations," *Wall Street Journal*, February 11, 1994, p. A6.

27 The Liberal Party of Canada, *Creating Opportunity*, pp. 24–25.

28 Ibid., p. 44.

29 Ibid., p. 53.

Chapter Three:

1 John Gerard Ruggie, "Multilateralism: The Anatomy of Institution," in John Gerard Ruggie, ed., *Multilateralism Matters* (New York: Columbia University Press, 1993), p. 14.

2 Ibid., p. 11.

3 Ibid., p. 14.

4 David Cox, testimony before the House of Commons Standing Committee on National Defence and Veterans Affairs, February 23, 1992, no. 34, p. 23.
5 Paul Lewis, "U.S. Nearing $1 Billion in Arrears at the U.N.," *New York Times*, October 22, 1993, p. A4.
6 Thomas L. Friedman, "Theory vs. Practice," *New York Times*, October 1, 1993, p. A2.
7 Ibid.
8 Joseph T. Jockel and Joel J. Sokolsky, "Dandurand Revisited: Rethinking Canada's Defence Policy in an Unstable World," *International Journal* 48, no. 2 (Spring 1993), pp. 392–400.
9 Paul Lewis, "Boutros Backs NATO Role," *New York Times*, September 20, 1993, p. A6.
10 Thomas Friedman, "Clinton, at U.N., Lists Stiff Terms for Sending U.S. Force to Bosnia," *New York Times*, September 28, 1993, p. A4.
11 William J. Durch, "Building on Sand: UN Peacekeeping in the Western Sahara," *International Security* 17, no. 4 (Spring 1993), p. 151.
12 Stephen S. Rosenfeld, "Passing hot potatoes to the UN," *Manchester Guardian Weekly*, March 7, 1993, p. 17.
13 Some suggestions for reform are presented in Jonathan Clarke, "Replacing NATO," *Foreign Policy* 43 (Winter 1993–94), pp. 34–40.
14 Simon Tisdall, "Clinton criticizes 'selfish' Europe," *Manchester Guardian Weekly*, October 24, 1993, p. 1.
15 David Plummer, Project Ploughshares, before House of Commons Standing Committee on National Defence and Veterans Affairs, April 1, 1993, no. 43, p. 4.
16 Adam Roberts, "The United Nations and international security," *Survival* 35, no. 2 (Summer 1993), p. 26–27.
17 Yaroslav Trofimov, "Canada urges reform of UN," *Edmonton Journal*, November 25, 1993, p. A11.
18 Hon. Michael Wilson, address at the OECD Meeting of Council at the Ministerial Level, Paris, June 3, 1993, *Speeches and Statements*, 93/44.
19 Miles Kahler, "Multilateralism with Small and Large Numbers," in Ruggie, ed. *Multilateralism Matters*, pp. 295–326.
20 Government of Canada, Department of Foreign Affairs and International Trade, "Ouellet to pay official visit to the United Nations," November 9, 1993, no. 209.
21 Andrew F. Cooper, Richard A. Higgott, and Kim Richard Nossal, *Relocating Middle Powers: Australia and Canada in a Changing World Order* (Vancouver: University of British Columbia Press, 1993), p. 173.

Chapter Four:

1 See Paul Collins, "The Administrative reform process in international development organizations: special issues," *Public Administrations and Development* 7 (April/June 1987); K.P. Saksena, *Reforming the United Nations: The Challenge of Relevance* (New Delhi: Sage Publications, 1993); Shijuro Ogata and Paul Volcker (co-chairmen), *Financing an Effective United Nations: A Report of the Independent Advisory Group on U.N. Financing* (New York: The Ford Foundation, 1993); and Final Report of the United States Commission on Improving the Effectiveness of the United Nations, *Defining Purpose: The U.N. and the Health of Nations* (Washington: September 1993).

2 This point is made by Caporaso, in James Caporaso, "International Relations Theory and Multilateralism: The Search for Foundations," *International Organization* 46, no. 3 (Summer 1992), p. 630. This problem is being redressed by a number of scholars. One recent attempt is a research project on multilateralism conceived by Robert Cox. See his "Multiculturalism and World Order," *Review of International Studies* 18, no. 2 (April 1992).

3 I use "world order" here similarly to Robert Cox—that is, world order "designates an historically specific configuration of power of whatever kind." In this usage, "world order" is "neutral as regards the nature of the entities that constitute power" in global relations. See Cox, "Multilateralism and World Order," p. 161.

4 See Robert Cox, *Programme on Multilateralism and the United Nations System, 1990–1995* (Japan: United Nations University, 1993) for a slightly different explanation of competing approaches to multilateralism.

5 In 205 substantive issues raised in the Security Council between 1946 and 1987, the Soviet Union cast 121 vetoes, the United States 58, the United Kingdom 27, China 22, and France 16. See W. Andy Knight and Mari Yamashita, "The United Nations' Contribution to the Maintenance of International Peace and Security," in David Dewitt, David Haglund, and John Kirton, *Building a New Global Order: Emerging Trends in International Security* (Toronto: Oxford University Press, 1993).

6 United Nations, General Assembly Resolution 377 (V), November 3, 1950. See also Adam Roberts and Benedict Kingsbury, *United Nations, Divided World: The UN's Roles in International Relations* (Oxford: Clarendon Press, 1988), p. 34. For a good discussion of the Uniting for Peace proposals, see G. Goodwin, *Britain and the United Nations* (New York: Manhattan Publishing Co., 1957), pp. 245–55.

7 For example, the Atomic Energy Commission (AEC) in 1946, the International Atomic Energy Agency (IAEA) in 1957, the drafting of

a Non-Proliferation Treaty (NPT) in 1968 (signed by 136 states as of May 1990), the UN Scientific Committee on the Effects of Atomic Radiation (UNSCEAR), and the ad hoc Committee on the Indian Ocean.

8 For example, the 1959 Antarctic Treaty, the 1967 Treaty of Tlatelolco, the 1985 Treaty of Rarotonga, the Partial Test-Ban Treaty of 1963, the 1967 outer space treaty, the 1972 Convention on the Prohibition of the Development, Production and Stockpiling of Bacteriological (Biological) and Toxin Weapons and on Their Destruction (the Biological Weapons Convention), a Convention on the Prohibition of Military or Any Other Hostile Use of Environmental Modification Techniques (the ENMOD Convention) that came into effect in 1977, the 1981 Prohibitions or Restrictions on the Use of Certain Conventional Weapons Which May Be Deemed to Be Excessively Injurious or to Have Indiscriminate Effects (Inhumane Weapons Convention).

9 Since the peacekeeping function was not anticipated by the UN founding fathers, Dag Hammarskjöld once joked that this invention could really be considered as falling under "Chapter six and a half" of the UN Charter, i.e., representing that "grey zone" between the two means given to the UN for maintaining international peace and security — pacific settlement and collective enforcement. Also see Ramesh Thakur, "International Peacekeeping, UN Authority, and US Power," *Alternatives* 12 (1987), p. 461.

Peacekeeping initially conceived as the deployment, under UN auspices, of lightly armed military or para-military personnel or forces in an area of political conflict, with the aim of separating and disengaging disputing parties long enough to allow them to engage in negotiations for pacific settlement of their disputes.

10 Dag Hammarskjöld, *Introduction to the Annual Report of the Secretary General on the Work of the Organization*, June 16, 1960. General Assembly, 15th Session, supplement no.1A (A/4390/Add. 1).

11 This was aided by the establishment of a new committee, the Committee on Information from Non-Self-Governing Territories.

12 See Brian Urquhart, "The Management of Change: The Role of the UN," *Canada and the United Nations in a Changing World*, report of a UNA Canada Conference held in Winnipeg, Manitoba (May 12–14, 1977), p. 44.

13 See Edmund P. Wellenstein, "The North-South Dialogue: Another Confrontation or a Basis for a New International Economic Order?," in Jan A. Van Lith, ed., *Change and the New International Economic Order* (London: Martinus Nijhoff Publishing, 1979), pp. 150–64.

14 For example, the United Nations Development Programme (UNDP), the Commission on Transnational Corporations (CTC), the Advisory

Committee for the Application of Science and Technology for Development (ACASTD), the Committees on Natural Resources (CNR) and development planning, the Office for Secretariat Services for Economic and Social Matters (OSSECS), the Departments of International Economic and Social Affairs (DIESA), Technical Cooperation for Development (DTCD) and a number of Regional Economic Commissions.

15 Examples of this include: laws to regulate the activities of transnational corporations; the UN Convention on the Law of the Sea (UNCLOS); a number of other conventions, including the International Convention on the Elimination of All Forms of Racial Discrimination (January 4, 1969), the International Covenant on Economic, Social, and Cultural Rights (adopted December 16, 1966), the International Convention on Civil and Political Rights (March 23, 1976).

16 The General Agreement on Tariffs and Trade (GATT), the International Monetary Fund (IMF), the International Development Agency (IDA), and the World Bank — the International Bank for Reconstruction and Development (IBRD).

17 By international human rights law, I refer to that compilation of norms in the Declaration of Human Rights, the twin covenants, and other declarations and covenants drafted under the aegis of the United Nations; also that body of rights listed under international legal authorities such as the International Labour Organization, international refugee law, and international humanitarian norms; and the provisions of the Geneva Conventions of 1949 and Protocols of 1977.

18 John S. Gibson, "International Human Rights Law: Progression of Sources, Agencies and Law," *Suffolk Transnational Law Journal* 14, no. 1 (Fall 1990).

19 See Barbara Ward and Rene Dubos, *Only One Earth: The Care and Maintenance of a Small Planet* (Harmondsworth: Penguin, 1972).

20 See United Nations General Assembly resolution 2997 (XXVII) of 1972. Among UNEP's goals were the promotion of international cooperation in the environmental field; the promotion of general policy guidance for the direction and coordination of environmental programs within the UN system; the implementation of environmental programs drawn up by the UN system; monitoring the global environmental situation; reviewing the impact of national and international environmental policies; and facilitating the exchange of knowledge concerning the environment.

21 An international surveillance and early warning network with i) a Global Environmental Monitoring System (GEMS); ii) INFOTERRA — a computerized referral service which provides environmental information and expertise to 20,000 sources in over one hundred countries; iii) the International Register of Potentially Toxic Chemicals (IRPTC) — which provides scientific and regulatory information on chemicals that may be dangerous to health and to the environment.

22 Adopted by the UN Conference on Desertification (Nairobi, 1977).

23 Begun as a pilot project in the Mediterranean, but now includes an anti-marine pollution program in the Kuwaiti region, the Red Sea, the Gulf of Aden, the Caribbean Sea, East, West, and Central Africa, the East Asian Seas, and the South Pacific.

24 Out of that conference came five major instruments signed by participating world leaders: the Rio Declaration (a statement of principles); Agenda 21 (a large document which identifies global environmental priority actions and guideline towards their achievement, including the creation of a new Commission for sustainable development); a Framework Convention on Climate Change; a Framework Convention on Biological Diversity; and a Statement of Principles on Forests. See Shanna Halpern, *The United Nations Conference on Environment and Development: Process and Documentation Reports and Papers*, no. 2 (Providence, RI: The Academic Council on the United Nations System, 1993).

25 Many of them were Canadians. Note for instance the contributions of John Humphrey, William Barton, Escott Reid, Stephen Lewis, and Maurice Strong.

26 Patrick Connor and Linda Lake, *Managing Organizational Change* (New York: Praeger, 1988), p. 4.

27 The entire managed change process is usually conceived as having at least five main stages: problem recognition and diagnosis; initiation; implementation; routinization; and evaluation or feedback.

28 Reform is generally accepted to mean purposive changes in structures, practices, policies, bureaucratic arrangements, etc., that would lead to greater efficiency and effectiveness within the organization.

29 For a good description of these strategies, see James Quinn, Henry Mintzberg and Robert James, *The Strategy Process: Concepts, Contexts, and Cases* (Englewood Cliffs, New Jersey: Prentice Hall, 1988) and Stephen Michael, et al., *Techniques of Organizational Change* (New York: McGraw-Hill, 1981).

30 For a substantial discussion on this issue, see Yves Beigbeder, *Management Problems in the United Nations Organizations: Reform or Decline?* (London: Frances Pinter, 1987), pp. 45–47.

31 This system was initially modelled on the U.S. federal administration system; see Joachim Müller, *Reform of the United Nations*, vol. 1 (New York: Oceana Publications, Inc., 1992), p. 16.

32 Secretariat members are compensated for agreeing to take certain "hardship" posts or for living in areas with high cost of living.

33 The Noblemaire principle is named after Mr. G. Noblemaire who was the rapporteur for the Fourth Committee of the League of Nations in 1921. This committee recommended that the level of salaries for international civil servants should be determined by three basic principles: that remuneration of international civil servants be such as to attract and retain the most competent and efficient citizens of any member-state of the League; that the expatriation factor be taken into account; and that the level of international civil servants' salaries should not be subject to ebb and flow of public criticism. For more detail on this, see Alexander S. Efimov and Nasser Kaddour, *Staff Costs and Some Aspects of Utilization of Human and Financial Resources in the United Nations Secretariat* (Geneva: Joint Inspection Unit, 1984), JIU/REP/84/12, pp. 4–18.

34 See United Nations, General Assembly Resolutions 3042 (XXVII) in 1972 and 3357 (XXIX) in 1974. Note that the ICSC is responsible for making recommendations to the Assembly for the regulation and coordination of conditions of service within the UN, specialized agencies, and other international organizations which participate in the UN common system.

35 This was a consequence of the undue emphasis placed on the geographical distribution principle.

36 Another expert body, the Negotiating Committee on the Financial Emergency of the United Nations, was established. See United Nations, General Assembly Resolution 3538 (XXX) (1975).

37 One temporary solution recommended by this committee to the recurring financial problem within the UN was to increase, in 1981, the organization's Working Capital Fund (WCF) from $50 million to $100 million.

38 Some of them, including the Soviet Union and France, refused to make the necessary contributions to the UN regular budget that were required to cover the annual peacekeeping payments.

39 For example, note the refusal of the Soviet bloc and several Arab states to contribute to UNEF. At other times, Belgium, China, Egypt, France, Israel and the United Kingdom, among others, failed to pay for UN peacekeeping operations citing several different reasons. See A. Leroy Bennett, *International Organizations: Principles and Issues*, 5th ed. (New Jersey: Prentice-Hall, 1991), p. 92.

40 For a detailed explanation of this formula, see Ogata and Volcker, *Financing an Effective United Nations*, pp. 13–14.

41 Special attention in this case was paid to the categories of posts that were subject to geographical distribution as well as the criteria for determining the range of posts for each member state.

42 The troika would represent the three main groups of UN member states, that is, the socialists, the neutrals, and the members of the Western military bloc. For criticism of this proposal, see Interview with UN official from the Joint Inspection Unit, Geneva (1990).

43 See Müller, *Reform of the United Nations*, pp. 21–22.

44 At its seventh session in 1982, the special committee finalized the Manila Declaration on the Peaceful Settlement of International Disputes which was adopted by the General Assembly in Resolution 37/10 (1982). At its ninth session the committee finalized its conclusions of the rationalization of existing UN procedures, and these were approved by the General Assembly in Resolution 39/88B (1984).

45 Gangadhar Gadgil, "The Proliferation of International Bureaucracy," in Arvind A. Deshpande, ed., *Accountability in Development, National and International* (New Delhi: Vikas Publishing House, 1982). For a greater elaboration of these problems, see Hari Mohan Mathur, "Experts of the United Nations in Third World Development: A View from Asia," in David Pitt and Thomas Weiss, eds., *The Nature of United Nations Bureaucracies* (Colorado: Westview Press, 1986), pp. 165–86.

46 There were other proposals for inter-agency coordination which were not even tried. Examples include the proposal to develop a system-wide computerized information system for development activities, the initiation of a combined UN Development Service, and the harmonization of development policy through the ACC Development Resources Panel under the UNDP. See Douglas Williams, *The Specialized Agencies and the United Nations: The System in Crisis* (New York: St. Martin's Press, 1987), pp. 47–49.

47 See Robert Ramsay, "UNCTAD Failures: The Rich get Richer," *International Organization* 38, no. 2 (1984), and K.P. Saksena, *Reforming the United Nations*, p. 35.

48 See David Nicol and John Renninger, "The Restructuring of the United Nations Economic and Social System: Background and Analysis," *Third World Quarterly* IV, no. 1 (1982), pp. 74–92.

49 The representatives of the Soviet Union and the other countries with centrally planned economies did not particularly like the report either.

50 United Nations, Report of the Group of Experts on the Structure of the United Nations System, *A United Nations Structure for Global Economic Cooperation*, E/AC.62/9 (New York: United Nations, 1975).

51 In the end, General Assembly Resolution 32/197 was passed unanimously, but it reflected much compromise.

52 The seven major industrialized countries that formed the G-7 were Canada, France, Germany, Italy, Japan, the United Kingdom, and the United States.
53 Saksena, *Reforming the United Nations*, pp. 39, 43.
54 Evan Luard, *The United Nations: How it Works and What it Does* (New York: St. Martin's Press, 1979), p. 124.
55 Mr. Abe, the Japanese foreign minister and the catalyst for this effort, urged the 40th Session of the Assembly to establish "a group of eminent persons" to examine ways in which the UN could function more efficiently.
56 See the *Report of the High-level Intergovernmental Experts to Review the Efficiency of Administrative and Financial Functioning of the United Nations*, A/41/40 (1986) (hereinafter referred to as the Group of 18 Report). See also United Nations Document A/40/PV.7 (1985).
57 See Tapio Kanninen, "Organizational Retrenchment and Reorganization: The Case of the United Nations' Response to the Financial Crisis of the Mid-1980s," Ph.D. dissertation, City University of New York, 1990.
58 This suspension was not intended to apply to temporary recruitment of personnel who serve on missions, or to replacement of staff members who were assigned mission duties, or to temporary assistance appointments for conferences and meetings. UN, Secretariat, "Temporary Suspension of Recruitment," *Secretary-General's Bulletin* ST/SGB/247 (February 6, 1992), also *Personnel Manual*, Index No. 4087.
59 These offices/departments were: Office of the Director General for Development and International Economic Cooperation (DIEC); Office for Political and General Assembly Affairs and Secretariat Services; Office for Research and Collection of Information (ORCI); Office for Ocean Affairs and the Law of the Sea (OOALS); Department of Political and Security Council Affairs (DPSCA); Department for Special Political Questions, Regional Cooperation, Decolonization and Trusteeship; Department for Disarmament Affairs (DDA); Department of International Economic and Social Affairs (DIESA); Department of Technical Cooperation for Development (DTCD); Centre for Science and Technology for Development (CSTD); United Nations Centre on Transnational Corporations (CTC); Department of Conference Services (DCS).
60 UN Department of Public Information, "Secretary-General Announces Changes in Secretariat," *Press Release* SG/A/479 DPI, New York (February 7, 1992); UN, *Secretariat News* (March 1992), p. 7; UN, DPI, "Secretary-General appoints Dick Thorburgh to Head Administration and Management, Jan Eliasson as Emergency Relief Coordinator," SG/A/484 (February 13, 1992).

61 See Final Report of the United States Commission on Improving the Effectiveness of the United Nations, *Defining Purpose: The U.N. and the Health of Nations*, especially pp. 46–48.
62 See Shirley Hazzard, "Why the UN Is Like a Blind Man in a Dark Room," *The Australian* (September 24, 1992); editorial, "The UN Needs Work," *Washington Post* (September 24, 1992).
63 For instance, the International Decade for Natural Disaster Reduction is now in its second decade. Its Secretariat has been accused of waste, mismanagement, and lack of productivity. In 1991 the organizers took more than $2 million in pledges and spent 50 percent on salaries and travel.
64 William Branigin, "Once Created, Agencies Refuse to Just Fade Away: Many Offices Hang on Despite Seeming Obsolescence," *Washington Post* (September 20, 1992).
65 William Branigin, "Costly Publications Raise Concerns About Red Ink: Documents Criticized as Out of Date, too Esoteric," *Washington Post* (September 20, 1992).
66 Ogata and Volcker, *Financing an Effective United Nations*, pp. 1–2.
67 Paul Taylor, "The United Nations system under stress: financial pressures and their consequences," *Review of International Studies* 17, no. 4 (October 1991), p. 365.
68 Although since 1990 the United States has been paying its UN assessed contribution almost in full and gradually clearing its past arrears, it still owes $240 million to the regular budget. At one stage the outstanding figure amounted to 80 percent of the UN's total internal indebtedness. Today that figure is close to 50 percent. The United States also withholds funds from programs of which it does not approve, e.g., the Office of Ocean Affairs and the Law of the Sea, and the Division for Palestinian Rights — a total of about $10 million annually (this could change under Clinton).
69 See UN Secretariat, *Status of Contributions as at 30 June 1992*, ST/ADM/SER.B/384 (July 6, 1992).
70 See Frederick Lister, *Fairness and Accountability in UN Financial Decision-Making* (New York: United Nations Association of the United States of America, 1986), p. 4.
71 Maurice Bertrand, *The UN in Profile: How its Resources Are Distributed* (New York: UNA-USA, 1986), p. 41.
72 John Mackinlay and Jarat Chopra, *A Draft Concept of Second Generation Multinational Operations* (Providence, RI: Thomas J. Watson Jr. Institute for International Studies, Brown University, 1993).
73 See U.S. Congress, *UN Security Council Resolutions on Iraq: Compliance and Implementation*. Report prepared for the Sub-Committee on Europe and the Middle East of the Committee on Foreign Affairs, U.S.

House of Representatives (Washington: CRS, Library of Congress, March 1992), 102nd Congress, 2nd session.

74 Robert Cox, "The Crisis of World Order and the Problem of International Organization in the 1980s," *International Journal* 35, no. 2 (Spring 1980), p. 395.

75 Some recent studies are addressing this problem. See David Dewitt, David Haglund and John Kirton, eds., *Building a New Global Order: Emerging Trends in International Security* (Oxford: Oxford University Press, 1993).

76 Some preliminary assessments are being attempted in the academic community. See James N. Rosenau, *The United Nations in a Turbulent World* (Boulder: Lynne Rienner Publishers, 1992), and Gene M. Lyons and Michael Mastanduno, *Beyond Westphalia? International Intervention, State Sovereignty, and the Future of International Society*, summary of a conference held at Dartmouth College, Hanover, New Hampshire, May 18–20, 1992.

Chapter Five:

1 On the failure of the International Trade Organisation (ITO), which would have been the third Bretton Woods institution, see Richard N. Gardner, *Sterling-Dollar Diplomacy: The Origins and the Prospects of Our International Economic Order, New Expanded Edition* (New York: McGraw-Hill, 1969).

2 The views expressed in this paper should not be taken to represent the policy of the Government of Canada.

3 *News of the Uruguay Round*, NUR 066, 27 September 1993. Similar statements were made in the fall by the International Chamber of Commerce, and by consumer organizations.

4 James A. Caporaso, "International Relations Theory and Multilateralism: The Search for Foundations," in John Gerard Ruggie, ed., *Multilateralism Matters: The Theory and Praxis of an Institutional Form* (New York: Columbia University Press, 1993), pp. 74–77. See also John S. Odell, "Understanding International Trade Policies: An Emerging Synthesis," *World Politics* 43, no. 1 (October 1990), pp. 139–67.

5 The Uruguay Round is situated in the long history of international trade agreements in Gilbert R. Winham, *The Evolution of International Trade Agreements* (Toronto: University of Toronto Press, 1992). "International regimes" are defined as the norms, principles, rules, and decision-making procedures around which actor expectations converge in a given issue-area by Stephen D. Krasner, "Structural causes and regime consequences: regimes as intervening variables," in Stephen D. Krasner, ed., *International Regimes* (Ithaca: Cornell

University Press, 1983), p. 2. See also Jock A. Finlayson and Mark W. Zacher, "The GATT and the regulation of trade barriers: regime dynamics and functions," in Krasner, *International Regimes*, pp. 273–314.

6 Jock A. Finlayson and Mark W. Zacher, "International trade institutions and the North/South dialogue," *International Journal* 36, no. 4 (Autumn 1981), pp. 732–65.

7 The best survey of the changing involvement of developing countries is to be found in John Whalley, ed., *The Uruguay Round and Beyond: The Final Report from the Ford Foundation Supported Project on Developing Countries and the Global Trading System* (London: Macmillan, 1989). See also Diana Tussie and David Glover, eds., *The Developing Countries in World Trade: Policies and Bargaining Strategies* (Boulder, Colo.: Lynne Rienner Publishers with the International Development Research Centre, Ottawa, 1993).

8 Thomas J. Biersteker, "The 'triumph' of neo-classical economics in the developing world: policy convergence and the bases of governance in the international economic order," in James N. Rosenau and Ernst-Otto Czempiel, eds., *Governance Without Government: Order and Change in World Politics* (Cambridge: Cambridge University Press, 1992), pp. 102–31.

9 The Quadrilateral Group of Trade Ministers (Quad) was established at the Ottawa Economic Summit in 1981. See Robert D. Putnam and Nicholas Bayne, *Hanging Together: Cooperation and Discord in the Seven-Power Summits* (Cambridge, Mass.: Harvard University Press, 1987), p. 131. The Quad meets regularly to discuss multilateral trade issues. The four European Union states that are members of the G-7 Finance Ministers, established at the Tokyo Summit of 1986, are not in the Quad because the European Commission has responsibility for commercial policy.

10 Sylvia Ostry, *Interdependence: Vulnerability and Opportunity* (Washington, D.C.: The Per Jacobsson Foundation, 1987).

11 The first meeting was hosted by Bill Brock in Washington in May 1984, but the group was often called the Rio Group after a larger meeting held in Brazil in September 1984. Subsequent meetings were held, inter alia, in Sweden, Republic of Korea, New Zealand, and Pakistan.

12 This discussion draws heavily on Richard A. Higgott and Andrew Fenton Cooper, "Middle power leadership and coalition building: Australia, the Cairns Group and the Uruguay Round of trade negotiations," *International Organization* 44, no. 4 (Autumn 1990), pp. 589–632.

13 Colleen Hamilton and John Whalley, "Coalitions in the Uruguay Round," *Weltwirtschaftliches Archiv* 125, no. 3 (Winter 1989), pp. 547–62; Winham, "GATT and the international trade régime."

14 For example, the same group of countries had used the 1978 Bonn summit to bring the Tokyo Round to a conclusion, but not because of a discussion among leaders. The four decided months beforehand that they would force the pace in Geneva by requiring officials to present a report to leaders in Bonn. As the deadline for preparing the report approached in the days before the summit, negotiators were being called in to the drafters, and some difficult issues were being crunched on the spot. The impending report to the summit was a useful device for forcing officials in Geneva to settle political matters. See Gilbert R. Winham, *International Trade and the Tokyo Round Negotiation* (Princeton: Princeton University Press, 1986), pp. 205ff.

15 "France wants GATT to leave farm issues," *Financial Times* October 12, 1993 p. 5.

16 For a description, see "The Final Act of the Uruguay Round: Press Summary," *News of the Uruguay Round*, NUR 080, 14 December 1993; and "MacLaren Hails World Trade Breakthrough," Government of Canada news release, December 15, 1993, with attachments.

17 The idea of global free trade, or "zero for zero" as the Americans termed it, was an interesting aspect of the Tokyo Quad package. The agreement was based on a reciprocal exchange of "concessions," but it resulted, in some sectors, in an elimination of barriers. Canada could afford to offer zero because it was in our interest to do so in resource sectors, and it could be used to pull others along.

18 For a discussion of the issues at stake, see Carl B. Hamilton, ed., *Textiles Trade and the Developing Countries: Eliminating the Multi-Fibre Arrangement in the 1990s* (Washington: The World Bank, 1990).

19 The literature on agriculture is enormous. For a quick overview of the sector, see Edward Carr, "The New Corn Laws: A Survey of Agriculture," *The Economist*, December 12, 1992. See also Fred H. Sanderson, ed., *Agricultural Protectionism in the Industrialized World* (Baltimore: Johns Hopkins University Press for Resources for the Future, Washington, D.C., 1990).

20 A similar but not identical idea is used in the agreement on industrial subsidies.

21 The agreement will provide the mechanism under which the United States will make its Section 337 provisions GATT-consistent, while the establishment of an international system of dispute settlement will help discipline American unilateral trade sanctions under Section 301. Section 337 refers to a provision of American trade law that has been used primarily to allow U.S. courts to decide whether foreign practices have violated American intellectual property law.

The Super 301 provision of the Omnibus Trade Bill of 1988 was used to justify unilateral attacks on foreign intellectual property practices deemed inadequate by the United States. See Jagdish Bhagwati and Hugh T. Patrick, eds., *Aggressive Unilateralism: America's 301 Trade Policy and the World Trading System* (Ann Arbor: University of Michigan Press, 1990).

22 See David Dessler, "What's at stake in the agent-structure debate?," *International Organization* 43, no. 3 (Summer 1989), p. 455.

23 The rationale is described in Richard Blackhurst, "Strengthening GATT Surveillance of Trade-Related Policies," in Meinhard Hilf and Ernst-Ulrich Petersmann, eds., *The New GATT Round of Multilateral Trade Negotiations: Legal and Economic Aspects* (Deventer: Kluwer Law and Taxation Publishers, 1988), pp. 123–55. There is a brief description in Victoria Curzon Price, "GATT's New Trade Policy Review Mechanism," *The World Economy* 14, no. 2 (June 1991), pp. 121–37.

24 GATT, *Trade Policies for a Better Future* (Geneva: General Agreement on Tariffs and Trade, 1985), pp. 35–37, 42. The Leutwiler group advised the Director General of GATT on problems facing the trading system.

25 OECD, Report by the Economic Policy Committee, *Surveillance of Structural Policies* (Paris: Organisation for Economic Co-operation and Development, 1989), p. 26.

26 Sylvia Ostry, "Changing Multilateral Institutions: A Role for Canada," in A. Claire Cutler and Mark W. Zacher, eds., *Canadian Foreign Policy and International Economic Regimes* (Vancouver: University of British Columbia Press, 1992), pp. 337–44. Canada's proposal was supported by the EU and Mexico.

27 John H. Jackson, *Restructuring the GATT System* (New York: Council on Foreign Relations Press for the Royal Institute of International Affairs, 1990).

28 For an assessment of the nearly final package, see "GATT Background Paper Looks at Value of Possible Round Results, Especially to Developing Countries," *News of the Uruguay Round*, NUR 078, December 1, 1993.

29 GATT, "Trade, the Uruguay Round and the Consumer," *Focus—GATT Newsletter*, no. 101 (August-September 1993), pp. 4-7. In this chapter we accept the general *economic* benefits of trade liberalization by assumption. These merits of a successful GATT Round are well described in Jagdish Bhagwati, *Protectionism* (Cambridge, Mass.: MIT Press, 1988). See also Paul R. Krugman, "What Do Undergraduates Need to Know about Trade?," and "The Narrow and Broad Arguments for Free Trade," *American Economic Review* 83, no. 2 (May

1993), pp. 23–27 and 362–65; and Michael Mussa, "Making the Practical Case for Freer Trade," *American Economic Review* 83, no. 2 (May 1993), pp. 372–76.

30 For a comparison of this and other econometric models of the outcome, and a general review of the results, see OECD, *Assessing the Effects of the Uruguay Round*, Trade Policy Issues 2 (Paris: Organisation for Economic Co-operation and Development, 1993).

31 Kym Anderson and Richard Blackhurst, eds., *The Greening of World Trade Issues* (London: Harvester Wheatsheaf, 1992); J. Owen Saunders, "Trade and environment: the fine line between environmental protection and environmental protectionism," *International Journal* 47, no. 4 (Autumn 1992), pp. 723–50; Candice Stevens, "The Environmental Effects of Trade," *The World Economy* 16, no. 4 (July 1993), pp. 439–51.

32 In response to a 1990 "Green Plan" commitment, the Canadian government conducted a thorough environmental review of NAFTA in parallel to the negotiations. The review received kind press treatment when it was released in 1992, and seemed to be well received by environmental groups, but opponents of free trade were not convinced. Opposition critics were not impressed with the review either, observing that it was conducted by the same people who negotiated the deal and that it did not consider the likelihood of companies migrating to pollution havens.

33 Richard G. Harris, "Globalization, trade, and income," *Canadian Journal of Economics* 26, no. 4 (November 1993), pp. 755–76.

34 Sylvia Ostry, "Beyond the Border: The New International Policy Arena," *Strategic Industries in a Global Economy: Policy Issues for the 1990s* (Paris: Organisation for Economic Co-operation and Development, 1991), p. 83.

35 Geza Feketekuty, *The New Trade Agenda* (Washington: Group of Thirty, 1992).

36 There are other issues to consider, however, including the potential incompatibility both between regional agreements (the EC and NAFTA are based on quite different principles, for example) and between regional agreements and the GATT. For a review of the evidence, see Kym Anderson and Richard Blackhurst (eds.), *Regional Integration and the Global Trading System* (London: Harvester Wheatsheaf, 1993).

37 William J. Drake and Kalypso Nicoloaïdis, "Ideas, interests, and institutionalization: 'trade in services' and the Uruguay Round," *International Organization* 46, no. 1 (Winter 1992), p. 69.

38 John H. Jackson, *The World Trading System: Law and Policy of International Economic Relations* (Cambridge, Mass.: MIT Press, 1989), pp. 49–52. On how decisions are taken in GATT, see also Stephen

Zamora, "Voting in International Economic Organizations," *American Journal of International Law* 74 (1980), p. 579.

39 Caporaso, "International Relations Theory and Multilateralism," p. 53.

40 Ibid., p. 54. See also Robert O. Keohane, "Reciprocity in International Relations," reprinted in Robert O. Keohane, ed., *International Institutions and State Power: Essays in International Relations Theory* (Boulder: Westview Press, 1989), p. 146.

41 Keohane, "Reciprocity in International Relations," p. 150.

42 Winham, *International Trade and the Tokyo Round Negotiation*, p. 364.

43 Jacob Viner, "Conflicts of Principle in Drafting a Trade Charter," *Foreign Affairs* 25 (July 1947); reprinted in *International Economics*, Studies by Jacob Viner (Glencoe, Illinois: The Free Press, 1951), p. 356.

44 *Goldfarb Report*, August 1993.

45 Canada, Department of External Affairs "Speaking Notes for Hon. Pat Carney, Minister for International Trade, to the 43rd Session of Contracting Parties of the GATT," Geneva, December 1, 1987 (Statement 87/69).

46 We have a less pessimistic view of the future possibilities of rules-based multilateralism than John Whalley, though he would probably agree that the Final Act is well worth having. See John Whalley, "The Uruguay Round and the GATT: Whither the Global System?," in C. Fred Bergsten and Marcus Noland, eds., *Pacific Dynamism and the International Economic System* (Washington, D.C.: The Institute for International Economics, 1993), pp. 65–109.

47 Articles IX and X provide for amendment and interpretation of the multilateral trade agreements under the WTO by combinations of consensus, two-thirds, and three-quarters majorities. There are also provisions for the members to allow waivers, and in effect to expel members who do not choose to accept new agreements. The WTO, therefore, will evolve through the agreement of its members, but the rules seem to allow the members to maintain the coherence of the WTO as they extend its coverage to new areas.

48 David Held, "Democracy, the Nation-State and the Global System," in David Held, ed., *Political Theory Today* (Stanford, Calif.: Stanford University Press, 1991), pp. 196–235.

Chapter Six:

1 In this paper I shall be referring to the European Union (EU) for the current period and the European Community (EC) in the past.

2 A variant of this type of argument in the academic literature claims that the Community has progressed and been successful when it has followed the path of negative integration, that is, the removal

of barriers to inter-state trade and other forms of non-governmental, largely business transactions. The classic instance of this is, of course, the SEA itself. On the other hand, so the argument goes, the Community has failed when positive attempts to build up structures of a European super-state, whether of defence policy or redistributive social and regional policies. For these and other anti-EC arguments, see Patrick Minford, ed., *The Cost of Europe* (Manchester: Manchester University Press, 1992).

3 For instance, reports on polls in Germany, France and Britain in *Globe and Mail* (Toronto), November 9, 1993; *Financial Post* (Toronto), November 4, 1993; *The Times* (London), November 2, 1993.

4 For a discussion of the various draft treaties on European Union, see Richard Corbett, "The Intergovernmental Conference on Political Union," *Journal of Common Market Studies* 30, no. 3 (September 1992), pp. 271–98.

5 The institutions of the EU have thus reacted to the name change in different ways: the Council of Ministers is now the Council of Ministers of the European Union; the Commission remains the European Commission; and the ECJ maintains the name Court of Justice of the European Communities. See "A Guide to Institutions After Maastricht," *ECSA Newsletter* 7, no. 1 (Winter 1994), p. 26.

6 Anthony L. Teasdale, "Subsidiarity in Post-Maastricht Europe," *Political Quarterly* 64, no. 3 (April-June 1993), p. 187ff.

7 The impact of German reunification is considered as a cause external to the EU because, on the one hand, it is a member state's problem at its narrowest; yet, on the other hand, it is much wider than a European issue, as Germany is a microcosm of the changes in the world system following the end of the Cold War.

8 Stephan Haggard and Andrew Moravcik, "The Political Economy of Financial Assistance to Eastern Europe, 1989–1991," in Robert O. Keohane, Joseph Nye, Jr., and Stanley Hoffmann, eds., *After the Cold War: International Institutions and State Strategies in Europe, 1989–1991* (Cambridge, Mass.: Harvard University Press, 1993), pp. 246–85.

9 Beverley Crawford, "United Germany, Divided Yugoslavia, Weak Europe? The Decision to Recognize Croatia," paper presented to the European Community Studies Association Biennial Conference, Washington, D.C., May 1993.

10 "Facts on Germany," release by Embassy of the Federal Republic of Germany (Ottawa), September 15, 1993.

11 As of January 1, 1994, Germany's seat allocation in the EP increased from eighty-one to ninety-nine; Italy, Britain, and France each increased their allocation from eighty-one to eighty-seven.

12 Gisela Hendricks, "Germany and the CAP: National Interests and the European Community," *International Affairs* 65, no. 4 (Winter 1988–89), pp. 75–87; T.K. Warley, "Europe's Agricultural Policy in Transition," *International Journal* 47, no. 1 (Winter 1991–92), pp. 112–35.

13 Richard Pomfret, "What is the Secret of the EMS's Longevity?", *Journal of Common Market Studies* 29, no. 6 (December 1991), pp. 623–33.

14 Particularly John J. Mearsheimer, "Back to the Future," *International Security* 15, no. 1 (December 1990), pp. 5–56. See also the responses in "Letters to the Editor," in ibid., no. 2 (Fall 1990), pp. 191–99, and no. 3 (Winter 1990–91), pp. 216–22.

15 *Manchester Guardian Weekly* (January 30, 1994), p. 1.

16 I realize that this leaves out a number of important issues, notably efforts in various policy areas and especially the matter of the so-called Democratic Deficit. On this last matter, see Shirley Williams, "Sovereignty and Accountability in the European Community," in Robert O. Keohane and Stanley Hoffmann, eds., *The New European Community* (Boulder: Westview Press, 1991), pp. 155–76.

17 Frankfurt apparently won out over Bonn. There had been thoughts that locating European institutions in the former capital would ameliorate the impact of any shift of the German government to Berlin.

18 Micheal Artis, "The Maastricht Road to Monetary Union," *Journal of Common Market Studies* 30, no. 3 (September 1992), pp. 299–309.

19 Loukas Tsoukalis, *The New European Economy*, 2nd. ed. (Oxford: Oxford University Press, 1993), pp. 176–82.

20 For the creeping convergence of EU currencies, see *The Economist*, January 15, 1994, pp. 75–81. For the political and wider economic aspects of the EMU project, see Pomfret, "EMS's Longevity."

21 *The Economist*, January 15, 1994, p. 76.

22 Christopher Hill, "European Foreign Policy: Power Bloc, Civilian Model — or Flop?", in R. Rummel, ed., *The Evolution of an International Actor* (Boulder, CO: Westview, 1990), pp. 31–55.

23 Jacques Delors, "European Integration and Security," *Survival* 33, no. 2 (March-April 1991), pp. 99–109; "Questions Concerning European Security," speech to the International Institute of Strategic Studies Conference, September 10, 1993. For a critique of EC procedure in dealing with Yugoslavia, see James Goodby, "Peacekeeping in the New Europe," *Washington Quarterly* 15, no. 2 (Spring 1992), pp. 153–69.

24 David Mitrany, "The Prospect of European Integration: Federal or Functional?", *A Working Peace System* (New York: Quadrangle Books, 1996), pp. 174–213.

25 I have developed this argument in "The EC, Security and Peaceful Change in Europe," paper presented at the Second Biennial Conference of the European Community Studies Association, Washington, D.C., May 1993.

26 Fred Chernoff, "Can NATO Outlive the USSR?", *International Relations* 11, no. 1 (April 1992), pp. 1–16; Philip Zelikow, "The New Concert of Europe," *Survival* 34, no. 2 (Summer 1992), pp. 12–30.

27 As was clearly evident in the January 1994 NATO summit, where the limited "Partnership for Peace" was agreed.

28 I am "forgetting" the so-called Forgotten Europeans, those countries that have applied for membership but whose application has been turned down or deferred — most notably, Malta, Cyprus, and Turkey.

29 Nevertheless, there is an argument that says that the Commission is still smaller than the cabinets of most countries in the Western world and should not be accused of being oversized.

30 Madeleine Hosli, "Voting Powers in the EC Council of Ministers after an Adhesion of EFTA States," paper presented at the International Studies Association annual meeting, Atlanta, Georgia, April 1992.

31 Helen Wallace, "The Europe that Came in from the Cold," *International Affairs* 67, no. 4 (Winter 1991), pp. 647–63; Anna Michalski and Helen Wallace, *The European Community and the Challenge of Enlargement* (London: Royal Institute of International Affairs, 1993).

32 John Major's recent article in *The Economist* (September 25, 1993) demonstrates the inability of the British prime minister to move beyond a "reluctant European" stance.

33 "Towards a Closer Association with the Countries of Central and Eastern Europe," report by the Commission to the European Council, Edinburgh, December 1992.

34 Charles Pentland, "Europe 1992 and the Canadian Response," in Fen Osler Hampson and Christopher Maule, eds., *Canada Among Nations 1990–91: After the Cold War* (Ottawa: Carleton University Press, 1990), pp. 125–44; Evan Potter, "Editor's Note," *Canadian Foreign Policy* 1, no. 2 (Spring 1993), pp. i–iii; and Alexander Moens and Evan Potter, "Canada-European Community Relations in the 1990s: Adjustment versus Radical Change," unpublished manuscript, 1993.

35 Discussed in Pentland, "Europe 1992 and Canada's Response."

36 "Harcourt Challenges Greenpeace," *Globe and Mail* (Toronto), February 2, 1994, p. B1, B16.

37 Fisheries Minister Brian Tobin was reputed to have threatened to use the Canadian navy to prevent overfishing. This implausible threat was most likely part of a strategy to convince the EU and other North Atlantic Fisheries Organization (NAFO) members how seriously Canada viewed this issue. Unfortunately, the moratorium did not cover ships flying flags of convenience of non-NAFO states.

See "Canada finally secures breeding space for cod," *Ottawa Citizen*, February 18, 1994, p. A4.

38 See "Europe to Force Visa Law on UK," *Manchester Guardian Weekly* January 16, 1994, p. 1.

Chapter Seven:

1 Canadian diplomat, November 1993.

2 I do not mean collective security which is even more difficult to achieve. See, for example, the three preconditions laid out by Charles A. Kupchan and Clifford A. Kupchan, "Concerts, Collective Security, and the Future of Europe," *International Security* 16, no. 1 (Summer 1991), p. 124. See also Richard K. Betts, "Systems for Peace or Causes of War?" *International Security* 17, no. 1 (Summer 1992). Obviously, the southern rim of the NATO area is also a potential trouble spot for which even less consensus exists. However, migration problems or other contingencies are even less likely handled in a forum like NATO.

3 Given the depth and extent of the member states' involvement and expression of their national policies especially in the EC and NATO, an institutional focus provides a good indicator of state responses. See Robert O. Keohane, J.S. Nye, and S. Hoffmann, eds., *After the Cold War* (Cambridge, Mass.: Harvard University Press, 1993), p. 381. In the fall of 1993 the member states of the European Community officially adopted the Maastricht Treaty amendments. As a result they are now called the European Union (EU). However, as the above analyis concentrates on the developments just prior to the EU, I will employ the term EC.

4 David S. Yost, "France and West European Defence Identity," *Survival* (July/August 1991), pp. 327–51.

5 Several accounts exist that analyze these processes. See Anand Menon, Anthony Forster, and William Wallace, "A Common European Defence?," *Survival* (Autumn 1992), pp. 98–118; Catherine McArdle Kelleher, "A New Security Order: The United States and the European Community in the 1990's," Occasional Paper by the European Community Studies Association, June 1993; Alexander Moens, "Behind Complementarity and Transparency: The Politics of the European Security and Defence Identity," *Journal of European Integration* 16, no. 1 (Autumn 1992), pp. 29–48.

6 Treaty on European Union, Title V, Article J4.1, Maastricht, February 7, 1992. In the following three paragraphs the Union received the mandate to request the WEU "to elaborate and implement the decisions of the Union which have defence applications." At the same

time, however, defence issues were exempted from the joint action procedure under the Common Foreign and Security Policy which includes qualified majority voting (J4.3) and the Union is to respect the obligations of certain member states under the NATO (J4.4).

7 *Atlantic News*, No. 2565 (October 27, 1993); NATO Communiqué. *Ministerial Meeting of the North Atlantic Council*, Brussels, December 2, 1993.

8 *Atlantic News*, No. 2564 (October 22, 1993). Notice also that NATO's four core security functions — agreed to as early as the North Atlantic Council meeting of June 6 and 7, 1991, in Copenhagen — included among the purposes for NATO the provision of a stable security environment in Europe based in part on the peaceful resolution of disputes. Technically, NATO could have been the principal forum for the Yugoslav crises.

9 Of course, alternative explanations exist. A careful reconstruction of events can be found in Michel Fortman, "L'epreuve du feu: organisations et acteurs internationaux dans la crise yougoslave," *Project Report for the Directorate of Strategic Analysis*, Department of National Defence, June 1993. He argues with great care that given their inexperience in real crises, and the need not to fall too far out of line with Russia, the institutions acted with initiative and coordination as far as their mandates permitted. Richard L. Rubenstein, in "Silent Partners in Ethnic Cleansing: the UN, the EC, and NATO," *In Depth* (Spring 1993), pp. 35–57, provides an outrageous and unsupported thesis that Christian Western Europe quietly condoned the elimination of a viable Muslim political entity in Europe. Edward Luttwak summarizes the Western failure in terms of the well armed (West) watching the moderately armed (Serbs) kill the unarmed (Bosnian Muslims) and blames the Weinberger-Powell military intervention doctrine as being far too restrictive. Edward N. Luttwak, "If Bosnians Were Dolphins . . . ," *Commentary* 96 (October 1993), pp. 27–32.

10 *Atlantic News*, No. 2514 (April 7, 1993). NATO AWAC monitoring had begun already in the fall of 1992. See Fortmann, "L'epreuve du fue," p. 86.

11 Paul Lewis, "UN Is Developing Control Center to Coordinate Growing Peacekeeping Role," *New York Times*, March 28, 1993.

12 The former Norwegian foreign minister, Thorvald Stoltenberg, replaced Cyrus Vance as the special representative of the secretary general of the United Nations.

13 *Atlantic News*, No. 2554 (September 17, 1993).

14 Speeches by Secretary of State for External Affairs Joe Clark, delivered at McGill University, Montreal, February 5, and Humber College, Toronto, May 26, 1990.

15 Joe Clark, "Canada's Stake in European Security," *NATO Review* 5 (1990), p. 3. In fact Article 2 application within the West was the first casualty of the end of the Cold War.

16 The NATO Declaration of Turnberry, Scotland, May 1990, added this phrase as a result of a German-Canadian initiative.

17 Prime Minister Mulroney seemed to refer to this diplomatic initiative in his Stanford speech on September 29, 1991.

18 Kim Richard Nossal, "A European Nation? The Life and Times of Atlanticism in Canada," in John English and Norman Hillmer, eds., *Making a Difference? Canada's Foreign Policy in a Changing World Order* (Toronto: Lester Publishing, 1992), pp. 79–102.

19 For a definition of this maxim, see Christopher Anstis, "CSCE Mark II: Back to Helsinki from Paris via Berlin and Prague," *NATO Review* 2 (April 1992), pp. 20–21. See also Department of External Affairs and International Trade, "Foreign Policy Themes and Priorities 1991–1992 Update," *Policy Planning Staff Paper* (Ottawa: Supply and Services, December 1991), p. 11.

20 I am using here the definitions laid out in Boutros Boutros-Ghali, *An Agenda For Peace* (New York: United Nations, 1992), p. 11.

21 See Evan H. Potter, "Canadian Foreign Policy-Making and the European Community-Canada Transatlantic Declaration: Leadership or Followership?," *Policy Planning Staff Paper*, No. 92/6 (Ottawa: External Affairs and International Trade Canada, April 1992)

22 Interview with External Affairs Official, October 1993.

23 Notice that in think pieces and speeches on transatlantic security even friendly interlocutors leave out Canada. For example, the EC's new foreign affairs minister Hans van den Broek, in his June 1993 address to the Royal Institute of International Affairs, called for a renewed United States-EC partnership but completely forgot to mention Canada. Ronald Asmus, Richard L. Kugler, and F. Stephen Larrabee, in "Building a New NATO," *Foreign Affairs* (September/October 1993), pp. 28–40, do not mention Canada. See also a recent report from the Netherlands Atlantic Commission titled "Transatlantic Relations and the Management of Disorder," February 1993.

24 In autumn 1993 the Clinton administration securely tightened its "multilateralist" rhetoric by means of a series of speeches culminating in Clinton's September 27 address to the UN General Assembly. Despite a campaign emphasis on multilateralism, the Clinton administration made it clear that American interests determine American involvement and that the U.S. involvement in UN operations will be strictly judged by such criteria as congressional approval, exit strategy, and threat to U.S. interests. See Anthony Lake, "Address

to Johns Hopkins University School of Advanced International Studies," Washington, D.C., September 21, 1993; Madeleine Albright, "Address to the National War College," Washington, D.C., September 23, 1993.

25 Many call for a NATO role in the region without specifying what actions it should take. For example see Andrew Cohen, "Security and NATO," in Fen Osler Hampson and Christopher J. Maule, eds., *Canada Among Nations 1993–1994: Global Jeopardy* (Ottawa: Carleton University Press, 1993), pp. 258–65.

26 Asmus, Kugler, and Larrabee, "Building a New NATO," p. 31.

27 Moreover, as long as the NATO-WEU rivalry remains unsolved, France is likely to oppose membership expansion.

28 For the European confederation idea, see Daniel Vernet, "The Dilemma of French Foreign Policy," *International Affairs* (October 1992), pp. 655–64.

29 *Projet de Pacte sur la stabilité en Europe*, Aide-mémoire, Ambassade de France au Canada, 15 juin 1993.

30 European Council, *Presidency Conclusions* (Copenhagen: June 21–22, 1993), pp. 16–17.

31 *Atlantic News*, No. 2580 (December 15, 1993).

32 I agree with Bracken and Johnson that a threat-based framework is a dead-end political road for NATO. Instead, as they advocate, the allies should seek a complementary capacities approach. What the authors do not provide is a political framework in which to pursue such a capacities approach in the European area. I think the Stability Pact offers exactly such a framework. See Paul Bracken and Stuart E. Johnson, "Beyond NATO: Complementary Militaries," *Orbis* (Spring 1993), pp. 205–21.

33 The Stability Pact can also address Russian interests in the Baltic republics. Obviously it would need a different enforcement mechanism.

34 Bracken and Johnson, "Beyond NATO," p. 216.

35 Steven Greenhouse, "NATO Clears Way for Approving All-European Task Forces," *New York Times* (January 6, 1994), p.5.

36 An excellent way for the Liberal government to raise funds for this purpose is to close unnecessary domestic military bases early in its term.

37 In terms of ascension to NATO-WEU, Jeffrey Simon's arguments on NATO membership are still useful. He identifies a gradual process (ten years) via NACC and associate membership depending on a series of political, economic, and military criteria to be met by the candidate. Jeffrey Simon, "Does Eastern Europe Belong in NATO?", *Orbis* (January 1993), pp. 21–35.

Chapter Eight:

1 The term FSU (former Soviet Union) used in this chapter is common. Some international organizations use NIS (New Independent States).
2 All figures are in U.S. dollars except those relating to Canadian donations (which are in Canadian dollars).
3 Interview with *The European,* November 12–18, 1993, p. 1.
4 G-7 summit in Paris, "Declaration on East-West Relations," July 15, 1989.
5 Commission of the European Communities, Directorate-General, External Relations, "G-24 Coordination Unit," Brussels, March 12, 1991. The EC set up a task force to oversee both G-24 and EC assistance, creating a G-24 Co-ordination Unit therein; five experts seconded from the twelve non-EC member countries (e.g., Canada) work within the G-24 unit.
6 Frans Andriessen, vice-president of the commission, "Report on G-24 Coordinated Assistance," speaking notes, G-24 ministerial meeting, Brussels, July 4, 1990.
7 Commission of the European Communities, Directorate-General, External Relations, "G-24 Coordinated Economic Assistance, an initial stocktaking," prepared for the meeting of the G-24 at senior officials level, Brussels, June 13, 1991, p. 2.
8 International Bank for Reconstruction and Development (IBRD), *World Bank Annual Report 1991,* p. 42.
9 United Nations, Economic Commission for Europe, *Economic Survey of Europe in 1992–1993* (New York, 1993), p. 250.
10 "America and the Collapse of the Soviet Empire: What Has to Be Done," Secretary Baker, address at Princeton University, December 12, 1991, *U.S. Department of State Dispatch,* December 16, 1991, p. 883.
11 Commission of the European Communities, Directorate-General, External Relations, "Conclusions of the Group of 24 on coordinated assistance to central and eastern European countries," Brussels, April 8, 1992, p. 1. Neither Russia nor the CIS member states have ever been included in the G-24 programs, although the Baltic states have since been brought under this umbrella.
12 External Affairs and International Trade Canada, *1992–93 Estimates,* Part III, Expenditure Plan "Departmental Overview: Priorities," pp. 1–5 (emphasis added).
13 Commission of the European Communities, Directorate-General, External Relations, G-24 Coordination Unit, "Scoreboard of G-24 Assistance" (1993). These tables give data to year-end 1992.
14 Commission of the European Communities, Directorate-General, External Relations, PHARE 1992 (Brussels, 1993) and EC Bulletin of the European Communities (Commission), vol. 26, no. 7/8 1993, p. 71.

The EC has a separate program for the FSU and Mongolia called TACIS with a 1993 budget for technical assistance of 510 million ECU. See ibid., p. 74.

15 The Lomé Conventions are an evolving series of cooperation agreements between the European Community and the sixty-nine African, Caribbean and Pacific countries which deal with trade, aid and some social/cultural relations. The latest Lomé IV agreement runs from 1990 for ten years.

16 European Investment Bank, *Loans to Build the European Community* (October 1990); Commission of the European Communities, Directorate-General, External Relations, G-24 Coordination Unit, *G-24 Update* (May 1993), p. 2 and (August/September 1993), p. 2.

17 These two agreements were finalized in 1993 along with a new agreement for Slovakia. Although no Europe agreements are as yet ratified by all the parties, their trade provisions are being implemented on an interim basis and regular political consultations are also under way.

18 The Polish, Hungarian, and the Czechoslovakian governments signed a cooperation agreement in February 1991 to coordinate their oftimes arduous negotiations with Brussels so as to ensure each achieved the same benefits. Now they, plus Slovakia, are known as the Visegrad 4, after the town in Yugoslavia where this meeting took place.

19 Commission of the European Communities, "Towards a New Partnership with Central and Eastern Europe," Report by the Commission to the European Council, Sec. (92) 2301, Edinburgh, December 11–12, 1992, p. 2.

20 European Council, "Conclusions of the Presidency," SN 180/93 Copenhagen, June 21–22, 1993, p. 13. The Copenhagen summit also reduced customs duties, accelerated the timetable for liberalizing quotas, and created a special fund within the overall PHARE assistance program to provide investment capital for major infrastructure projects.

21 IBRD, "The World Bank Group's Support for Economic Transformation in Central and Eastern Europe," June 5, 1991 (document submitted to the EC, G-24). The Bank's move from project-lending to program-lending, with attendant policy conditions, is detailed in Paul Mosely, Jane Harrigan, and John Toye, *Aid and Power, the World Bank and Policy-based Lending* (London: Routlege, 1991).

22 The World Bank, *Annual Report 1992*, p. 135; *Transition, the newsletter about reforming economies*, vol. 4, no. 7 (September 1993), p. 14. *Transition* is a publication of the World Bank's Policy Research Department. Stephan Haggard and Andrew Moravcsik analyse the new role of the Bretton Woods organizations in "The Political Economy of Financial Assistance to Eastern Europe, 1989–1991," in Robert O. Keohane, Joseph S. Nye, and Stanley Hoffmann, eds., *After the Cold*

War: International Institutions and State Strategies in Europe, 1989–1991 (Cambridge, Mass.: Harvard University Press, 1993), pp. 362–64.

23 Lawrence Malkin, "Third World Fears Funding Competition," *International Herald Tribune*, May 7, 1990, p. 1.

24 Jenny Pryke, "Diverting Aid from the Developing World: Fighting over the Pie," *Ploughshares Monitor* (September 1990), p. 12.

25 EC, "G-24 Coordinated Economic Assistance, an initial stocktaking," p. 3.

26 OECD, *Development Co-operation* (Paris: OECD, 1991), p. 17.

27 There has been a diversion of CEE/FSU funds from the South back to domestic economies; the OECD calculated that "flows from Eastern Europe and the former Soviet Union have continued to drop from $4 billion in 1988 to an estimated total of about $1 billion in 1991." OECD, *Development Co-operation* (Paris: OECD, 1992), p. 22.

28 John Stackhouse, "Soviet aid seen as a big bite," *Globe and Mail*, October 14, 1991, p. B2.

29 John Stackhouse, "Third World pays for Soviet collapse," *Globe and Mail*, February 5, 1992, p. A1.

30 Speech to the seminar on the Future of North South Relations, Ottawa, February 2, 1993, cited in *Au courant* (Canadian Council for International Co-operation) vol. 3, no. 6 (March 1993). pp. 1, 3.

31 These criteria and tentative assessments are provided by Jozef m. van Brabant, "Overview of the Implications of Western Assistance to the East for Developing Countries," *Journal of Development Planning* 23 (1992), pp. 45–70 summarizing the papers in this special issue on "Revolutions in the East and their Implications for Developing Countries," which is the best single source for the topic.

32 Carl H. McMillan, "The Role of Foreign Direct Investment in the Transition from Planned to Market Economies," paper to be published in *Transnational Corporations*, p.32.

33 United Nations, Economic Commission for Europe, *Economic Survey of Europe 1992–1993* (New York, 1993), pp. 237–38.

34 See the statistical tables for any OECD annual report for these categories: (e.g., *Development Co-operation* (Paris: OECD, 1992). The EC is also a DAC member.

35 For a comparison between DAC categories and the types of assistance provided to the East, see Institute for East West Studies, European Studies Center "Moving Beyond Assistance," Final Report of the IEWS Task Force on Western Assistance to Transition in the Czech and Slovak Federal Republic, Hungary and Poland (New York: IEWS, 1992), and its appendix 1 on grant equivalence calculations.

36 Roger Young, "Official Financing for Development: The Implications of Reforms in Eastern Europe," *Journal of Development Planning* 23 (1992), pp. 355–75.

37 Ibid., p. 368.
38 EC, "Scoreboard of G-24 Assistance," and *IMF Survey*, July 12, 1993, p. 215.
39 World Bank, *Annual Report 1992*, p. 16. To create its new transition economics unit the Bank management allows each department to transfer no more than two officers and brought in new staff to make up the balance needed.
40 As reported in IMF, *Annual Report 1992*, p. 29.
41 *IMF Survey*, "IMF Board Approves Russian Loan," July 12, 1993, p. 214. The new facility can be drawn on by Cambodia and Vietnam as well as the CEE/FSU.
42 World Bank, *Annual Report 1993*, p. 58.
43 Institute for East-West Studies, "Moving Beyond Assistance," p. 29. Western assistance is frequently the target of criticism in the CEE for slow disbursement, bias toward Western consultants, lack of strategy, and low grant component. See, for example, András Inotai, "Western Economic Support for Central and Eastern Europe: A Hungarian View," Institute for World Economics, Hungarian Academy of Sciences, Working Paper no. 25 (Budapest, September 1993), pp. 12–18. (Inotai is director of the Institute.)
44 Calculated from EC, "Scoreboard of G-24 Assistance." The EC centres its PHARE program on technical assistance, most of which is given as non-reimbursable grants.
45 OECD, *Development Co-operation* (OECD: Paris, 1992), p. 94.
46 External Affairs and International Trade Canada, Joe Clark and John Crosbie, "Joint Message on the Task Force on Central and Eastern Europe" (1990). Of this $40 million, $10 million was carried over from the initial pledge.
47 Canada, House of Commons, Minutes of Proceedings and Evidence of the Legislative Committee on Bill C-88, An Act to provide for the membership of Canada in the European Bank for Reconstruction and Development, Issues no. 1 and 2 (December 12 and 13, 1990). The EBRD capitalization was spread over five years. For the REE program, see *Canada Export*, December 3, 1990.
48 External Affairs and International Trade Canada, Task Force on Central and Eastern Europe, "Joint Message by Barbara McDougall and Michael Wilson" (Summer 1992), p. 1.
49 A major package of new assistance for Russia was announced just prior to the Vancouver summit (Clinton-Yeltsin). See Canada, Office of the Prime Minister, Release (April 2, 1993) where the components of "a $200 million increase in Canadian bilateral assistance to Russia" are detailed. Other information provided by Bureau for Assistance for Central and Eastern Europe, Department of Foreign Affairs and International Trade Canada.

50 Information provided by Bureau for Assistance for Central and Eastern Europe, Department of Foreign Affairs and International Trade Canada.
51 Canadian Council for International Co-operation (CCIC), "Political Scene" (April 1993), p. 6.
52 Young, "Official Financing," p. 367; Maureen O'Neill and Andrew Clark, "Canada and International Development: New Agendas," in Fen Osler Hampson and Christopher J. Maule, eds., *Canada Among Nations 1992–93: A New World Order?* (Ottawa: Carleton University Press), 1992," pp. 221–22.
53 Andrew Clark, "Paradox: ODA cash up but ODA levels fall," *Review* (Newsletter of the North-South Institute) (Summer 1992), p. 2.
54 Dave Todd, "Canada plans deeper cuts to foreign aid, confidential memo says commitments may be broken," *Ottawa Citizen*, February 3, 1993, p. 1.
55 Louise Crosby, "Canada cuts aid to several nations," *Ottawa Citizen*, March 2, 1993, p. A5.
56 CCIC, "The Political Scene" (March 1993), p.5.
57 Minister for External Relations and International Development, Communiqué (April 21, 1993).
58 Michael Valpy, " Agenda for Peace," *Globe and Mail*, March 18, 1993, p. A2; memo citations from Valpy, "The aid that Canada will not be giving," ibid., March 4, 1993, p. A2. Only a few CCIC member organizations, like Canadian University Service Overseas (CUSO), were adamant that the CEE countries were not developing countries and any aid directed to them was to the detriment of the Third World. Most Canadian NGOs were concerned mainly that funds not be withdrawn from the scarce ODA budget. Information based on the survey of members conducted for the CCIC, Summer 1993.
59 House of Commons, Communiqué, Hon. Lloyd Axworthy, opposition critic for External Affairs, January 23, 1992 p. 1; and "Liberal Statement: Canadian Policy Re: Aid to the Commonwealth of Independent States" (January 1992), p. 1.
60 See Department of External Affairs and International Trade Canada, Bureau of Assistance for Central and Eastern Europe, "Canadian Technical Assistance to Ukraine" (September 20, 1993), p. 17; DFAIT, Bureau, "Technical Assistance Projects: Poland," November 15, 1993, p. 7, and other country project listings.
61 Neville Nakivell, "Canadian bureau a catalyst in European reform," *Financial Post*, January 29–31, 1994, p. S2. Companies receiving REE funds are named in the DFAIT, Bureau, "Canadian Technical Assistance to Russia — Project Listing" (June 1993) and other country

listings. Another attraction for business is the government's $1 million annual contribution to the World Bank earmarked for Canadian consultants and advisors engaged on projects in the CEE/FSU.

62 Headline from *Globe and Mail* for Murray Campbell's article on the Clinton-Yeltsin summit, April 1, 1993, p. A5.

63 OECD, *Development Co-operation* (OECD: Paris, 1992), p. 21–22. The UN Development Planning Committee has, until now, set the criteria for considering countries to be among the "least developed" and thus eligible for trade preferences. At its final meeting in early 1994, just before UN reforms dissolved it, the committee recommended that whatever new body supersedes it examine the basic data for all of the CEE and FSU.

64 EC, *PHARE 1992*, p. 2.

65 OECD, *Development Co-operation* (OECD: Paris, 1992), p. 607.

66 David Gillies sees this as a progressive trend in "Human Rights, Democracy, and 'Good Governance': Stretching the World Bank's Policy Frontiers" (Montreal: International Centre for Human Rights and Democratic Development, 1993), while Gerald J. Schmitz shows how democratization can serve as an ideological mask for programs which effectively marginalize the disadvantaged in "Human Rights, Democratization, and International Conflict," in Fen Osler Hampson and Christopher J. Maule, eds., *Canada Among Nations 1992–93: A New World Order?* (Ottawa: Carleton University Press, 1992), pp. 235–55.

67 Documents provided by CIDA Public Inquiries Service, dated March 12, 1993. The direct connection between human rights and aid conditionality was first made in Prime Minister Mulroney's statement at the 1991 Commonwealth heads of government meeting. See Ross Howard, "PM links aid giving to policies on rights," *Globe and Mail*, October 15, 1991, p. A1.

68 The World Bank, *Transition* 4, no. 9 (December 1993), p. 15, using prepublication excerpts from UN ECE reports. In 1992, they found, some CEE countries had net outflows of capital due to servicing debts incurred by the pre-transition governments.

69 Press Conference, transmitted by CBC Radio National News, January 14, 1994.

Chapter Nine:

1 Time/CNN poll of five hundred respondents taken on December 2, 1993, by Yankelovich Partners, Inc. Sampling error of ±4.5 percent. *Time*, December 13, 1993, p. 64.

2 Michael L. Dertouzos, Richard K. Lester, and Robert M. Solow, eds., *Made in America: Regaining the Productive Edge* (Cambridge, Mass.: MIT Press, 1989).
3 *The Economist*, December 4–10, 1993, p. 24.
4 I.M. Destler, "U.S. Trade Policy-making in the 1980s," in Alberto Alesina and Geoffrey Carliner, eds., *Politics and Economics in the Eighties* (Chicago, Ill.: University of Chicago Press, 1991), pp. 276–77.
5 Super 301 is the section of the 1988 Trade Act which empowers the U.S. administration to establish a hit list of countries deemed to be erecting trade barriers to U.S. exports. In early 1994 President Clinton decided to revive Super 301 which had expired.
6 Gary Clyde Hufbauer, Diane T. Berliner, and Kimberly Ann Elliott, *Trade Protection in the United States: 31 Case Studies* (Washington, D.C.: Institute for International Economics, 1986).
7 Patrick Low, *Trading Free: the GATT and U.S. Trade Policy* (New York: Twentieth Century Fund Press, 1993), p. 25.
8 Lawrence R. Klein, Peter H. Pauly, and Christian E. Petersen, "Empirical Aspects of Protectionism: Results from Project LINK," in Dominick Salvatore, ed., *The New Protectionist Threat to World Welfare* (New York: North-Holland, 1987), pp. 69–94.
9 Destler, "U.S. Trade Policy-making in the 1980s," pp. 276–77.
10 Robert J. Grenier, "Theoretical and Real Investment Restrictions and Incentives in the Province of Quebec," in Earl Fry and Lee Radebaugh, eds., *Regulation of Foreign Direct Investment in Canada and the United States* (Provo, Utah: Brigham Young University, 1983), pp. 63–68.
11 Helena Stalson, *U.S. Service Exports and Foreign Barriers: An Agenda for Negotiations* (Washington, D.C.: National Planning Association, 1985), p. 9.
12 Leonard A. Rapping, *International Reorganization and American Economic Policy* (New York: New York University Press, 1988), p. 163.
13 Jonathan D. Aronson and Paul R. Krugman, "The Linkage between International Trade and Financial Policy," in John N. Yochelson, ed., *The United States and the World Economy: Policy Alternatives for New Realities* (Boulder, Colo.: Westview Press, 1985), p. 42.
14 The crisis in international trade theory is never more evident than in the applications to the NAFTA debate. The elegance of the Hecksher-Ohlin theorem is nowhere to be found in the more recent necessity of integrating the reality of intra-industry and intra-firm trade with investment-driven characteristics into the modern understanding of comparative advantage, in which all is dynamic, including the movement of factors and even the creation of new factors of production. A very genuine explanatory gap thus emerges in both the policy and empirical literature. Who will be the losers and winners from the

liberalization of trade in a world in which the multinational firm is the principal vehicle for trade expansion and growth? The older understanding is not very convincing when capital-intensive U.S. agriculture displaces labour-intensive Mexican maize farmers, on the one hand, and when comparatively low-paid Mexican workers displace much higher-paid American workers in a high-tech computer chip firm that moves from California to Mexico, on the other. Two models that attempt to come to grips with the new reality of intra-industry and intra-firm trade are W.M. Corden, *Protection, Growth and Trade* (Oxford: Blackwell, 1985), and John Dunning, "Trade, Location and Economic Activity of the Multinational Enterprise: A Search for an Eclectic Approach," in B. Ohlin, ed., *The International Allocation of Economic Activity* (London: Macmillan, 1977).

Chapter Ten:

1 East Asia includes Japan, mainland China, the NIEs (Hong Kong, Taiwan, the Republic of Korea, and Singapore) and the ASEAN-4 (Indonesia, Malaysia, the Philippines, and Thailand).

2 International Monetary Fund, *World Economic Outlook*, May 1993, Annex IV; pp. 116–19. Aggregate output growth estimates are calculated using weights based on an individual country's GDP as a share of aggregate GDP. Weights based on conversion of national GDP into a common currency, such as U.S. dollars, commonly use market exchange rates. Such exchange rates can deviate significantly from their purchasing power parity equivalents for a variety of reasons, such as speculative bubbles, exchange market intervention, or macroeconomic shocks. When such deviations occur, aggregates calculated using market exchange rates can be misleading. The alternative is to use purchasing power parity-based weights. These weights value the goods and services a country's currency can buy, compared with the purchasing power of other countries' currencies.

3 APEC here refers to the Asia Pacific Economic Cooperation forum which is a grouping of the following fifteen economies: Australia, Brunei, Canada, China, Chinese Taipei (Taiwan), Hong Kong, Indonesia, Japan, Malaysia, New Zealand, the Republic of Korea, the Philippines, Singapore, Thailand, and the United States. Mexico and Papua New Guinea joined in late 1993. Chile will join in 1994.

4 United States International Trade Commission, *East Asia: Regional Economic Integration and Implications for the United States* (Washington, D.C.: USITC Publication 2621, 1993), p. 45.

5 United Nations Centre for Transnational Corporations, *World Investment Report: Transnational Corporations and Integrated International Production* (New York: United Nations, 1993), p. 43.
6 Peter Drysdale and Ross Garnaut, "The Pacific: An Application of a General Theory of Economic Integration," in C. Fred Bergsten and Marcus Noland, eds. *Pacific Dynamism and the International Economic System* (Washington, D.C.: Institute for International Economics, 1993), p. 189.
7 The data on which these charts are based exclude mainland China. They are taken from Wendy Dobson, *Japan in East Asia: Trading and Investment Strategies* (Singapore: Institute of Southeast Asia Studies, 1993).
8 United Nations Centre for Transnational Corporations. 1992. *World Investment Report 1992* (New York: United Nations, 1992).
9 Linda Y.C. Lim and Eng Fong Pang, *Foreign Direct Investment and Industrialization in Malaysia, Taiwan and Thailand* (Paris: OECD Development Centre, 1991).
10 Wendy Dobson, *Japan in East Asia: Trading and Investment Strategies* (Singapore: Institute of Southeast Asia Studies, 1993), p. 23.
11 Wendy Dobson, "Economic Integration in North America" in *The Future of the World Economy* (OECD: Paris 1992).
12 For a discussion of the Cairns Group see chapter 5 by Curtis and Wolfe.
13 Robert O. Keohane and Joseph S. Nye, *Power and Interdependence: World Politics in Transition* (Boston: Little Brown and Co., 1977).
14 Alexander Nicoll, "China's unique path towards the free market," *Financial Times of London*, May 21, 1993.
15 Nancy Dunne, "Clinton's $7bn. dilemma on China," *Financial Times of London*, May 20 1993.
16 Edward Balls, *Financial Times of London*, July 19, 1993.
17 Robert Z. Lawrence, "Regional Trading Arrangements: Stumbling Blocks or Building Blocs?", *Finance and the International Economy: The Amex Bank Review Prize Essays* (London: Oxford University Press, 1991). For detailed discussion of the conclusion of the Uruguay Round, see chapter 5 by Curtis and Wolfe in this volume.
18 Ippei Yamazawa, "Economic Integration in the Asia-Pacific Region and the Options for Japan" (Tokyo Group on Asia-Pacific Economic Integration towards the 21st Century, 1993), p. 33.

Chapter Eleven:

1 Twenty-five million ethnic Russians lived outside the Russian Federation at the time of the last population census in 1989. Gosudarstvennyi Komitet SSSR po Statistike, *Narodnoe Khoziaistvo SSSR v 1990 g. Statisticheskii Iezhegodnik* (Moscow: "Finansy i Statistika," 1991), p. 81. By 1994 the number was undoubtedly reduced, but not substantially. Moreover, as applied by Moscow, the definition varied: it meant, variously, ethnic Russians, and/or Russian speakers and culturally Russified communities.

2 Ibid.

3 In the Soviet and post-Soviet context the term "sovereignty" implied control over resources and policies, and the primacy of national over federal laws, but did not call for a separation.

4 See Ann Sheehy, "The CIS: A Progress Report," *RFE/RL Research Report* 1, no. 28 (September 25, 1992), pp. 1–6.

5 "Christopher Spells out New Priorities," *New York Times*, November 5, 1993, p. A8.

6 F. Shelov-Kovedyayev, interviewed by *Izvestia*, June 26, 1992, p. 6. Translated in the *Current Digest of the Post-Soviet Press* XLIV, no. 26 (1992), pp. 20–21.

7 Cited by Konstantin Eggert, "Russia in the Role of 'Eurasian Gendarme'?," *Izvestia*, August 7, 1992, p. 6, translated in ibid., no. 32 (1992), pp. 4–5.

8 "Real and Illusory Guidelines in Foreign Policy," *Rossiiskaya Gazeta*, August 4, 1992, p.7, translated in ibid., pp. 1–4. In 1994, Migranyan was a member of Yeltsin's presidential council.

9 Cited in Susanne Crow, "Russia Asserts Its Strategic Agenda," *RFE/RL Research Report* 2, no. 50 (December 17, 1993), pp. 1–8.

10 Sergei Stankevich, "Russia in Search of Itself," *The National Interest* (Summer 1992), p. 50 and passim. This is an abbreviated version of an article from *Nezavisimaya Gazeta*, (March 28, 1992). Stankevich was dismissed by the president after the December 1993 elections.

11 Crow, "Russia Asserts, pp. 2–4.

12 Paul Lewis in the *New York Times*, September 29, 1993, p. A11.

13 In a conversation with the Swedish foreign minister, for example, October 19 in Moscow, Kozyrev stressed Russia's readiness to take care of the conflicts on its periphery. Expressing satisfaction with the CSCE willingness to mediate in the Caucasus, he nonetheless insisted that Russia will itself deal with Georgia's problems. Suzanne Crow in *RFE/RL News Briefs* October 18–22, 1993, October 20, p. 4.

14 Suzanne Crow in ibid., October 4–8, 1993, October 8, p.7, ibid., November 22–26, and, November 12, p. 9.

15 Ibid., November 27, 1993.

16 *Ukrainian Weekly*, January 23, 1994, "Newsbriefs," p. 2.
17 Celestine Bohlen, "Yeltsin Urges Foes to Join in New Amity," *New York Times*, February 25, 1994.
18 Serge Schmeman, "Muscovite with Bravado," ibid., December 14, 1993, pp. A1 and A16 and passim.
19 Vyacheslav Kostikov, September 1993, quoted in Elizabeth Teague, "The CIS: An Unpredictable Future," *RFE/RL Research Report* 3, no. 1 (1994), p. 10.
20 *Ottawa Citizen*, March 15, 1994, p. A9.
21 Such as the Strategic Rocket Forces, the two Guards divisions stationed in Moscow and in the Moscow military districts. The figures were not considered to be reliable, however. See John Leppingwell in *RFE/RL News Briefs*, December 11–24, 1993, December 23, pp. 7–8.
22 Saulius Girnius in ibid. December 14, p. 14.
23 See Alexander Rahr, "The Implications of Russia's Parliamentary Elections," pp. 32–37, *RFE/RL Research Report* 3, no. 1 (January 7, 1994).
24 Yuri N. Afanasyev, a historian and rector of the Russian State University for the Humanities, condemns the new "great power ideology" and warns that "Imperial ambitions will bring Russia to total ruin." See "Russia's Vicious Circle," *New York Times*, February 28, 1994, Op-Ed page, and his forthcoming article in *Foreign Affairs*. Melor Sturua, a political columnist for *Izvestiia*, called Russia's claim to historical geopolitical space "nothing less than an abbreviated version of the Brezhnev Doctrine." Ibid., October 27, 1993, p. A23.
25 The effect was not as drastic as might have been expected, considering that approximately 80 percent of the officer cadre was ethnic Russian. New armies, on the other hand, suffered from a shortage of officers and NCOs, and hired many Russians to fill the jobs.
26 For an overall assessment as of mid-1992, see chapters on Russia in "Post-Soviet Armies," Special Issue, Post-Soviet Armies, *RFE/RL Research Report* 2, no. 25 (June 18, 1993), especially John W.R. Leppingwell, "Is the Military Disintegrating from Within?," pp. 9–16.
27 See Stephen Foye, "Post-Soviet Russia: Politics and the New Russian Army," ibid., 1, no. 33 (August 21, 1992), pp. 5–12.
28 This and the following four paragraphs analyzing the doctrine are largely based on two seminar reports by the Center For Naval Analyses (CNA) in Alexandria, Virginia. *Seminar Report* (July 1993) was based on discussion with Colonel General Vladimir Dworkin, head of the (formerly secret) Main Institute of the Armed Forces of the Russian Ministry of Defence dealing with Strategic Rocket Forces, and Dr. Alexei Arbatov, head of the Centre for Geopolitical and Military Forecasting; *CNA Seminar Report* (November 1993), was based on the in-house discussion of Dworkin-Arbatov presentations.

29 Reported in *New York Times*, November 3, 1993.
30 The discussion with General Dworkin and Alexei Arbatov revealed that real control of nuclear weapons always was and still is "with the central command of the Strategic Forces and the General Staff," and not with the politicians, as assumed in the West. See *CNA Seminar Report* (July 1993).
31 Michael R. Gordon, "As Its World View Narrows," *New York Times*, November 28, 1993, pp. A1 and A10.
32 This and the paragraph above are based on "Russia," *The Military Balance 1993–1994* (London: Brassey's Ltd., 1993), p. 95.
33 John W.R. Leppingwell, "Restructuring the Russian Military," Special Issue: Post-Soviet Armies, *RFE/RL Research Report*, (June 18, 1993), pp. 17–32.
34 Stephen Foye in *RFE/RL News Briefs*, August 30–September 3, 1993, September 1, p. 4.
35 Alexander Zhilin, "Military policy and a war of politicians," *Moscow News*, no. 48 (November 26, 1993), p. 3.
36 Pavel Felgengauer, correspondent for *Sevodnya*, as reported in Steven Erlanger, "Troops in Ex-Soviet Lands," *New York Times*, November 30, 1993, pp. Al and A12.
37 This section is based largely on two articles by Stephen Foye, "The Soviet Legacy," *RFE/RL Research Report*, Special Issue: Post-Soviet Armies 2, no. 25 (June 18, 1993), pp. 1–9, and "The Armed Forces of the CIS," ibid. 3, no. 1 (January 7, 1994), pp. 18–21; Dmitry Trenin, "'Blue Helmets' for the CIS," *New Times International* (May 1993) pp. 14–17; *The Military Balance 1993–1994*; and *RFE/RL News Briefs*, 1994, passim.
38 Foye, "The Soviet Legacy," p. 7.
39 Alexander Zhilin, "The CIS Army Starts from Scratch," *Moscow News*, no. 36, September 3, 1993, p. 3.
40 *The Military Balance 1993–1994*, p. 93.
41 See Suzanne Crow, "The Theory and Practice of Peacekeeping in the Former USSR," pp. 31–36, and "Russian Peacekeeping: Defense, Diplomacy, or Imperialism?," pp. 37–40, *RFE/RL Research Report* 11, no. 37 (September 18, 1992).
42 The KGB was instrumental in organizing the drive for autonomy in Abkhazia and South Ossetia in order first to prevent and then to subvert Georgia's independence. See Svetlana Chervonnaya, "The Technology of the Abkhazian War," *Moscow News*, no. 24, October 15, 1993, pp. 1–4. See also *Military Balance 1993–1994*, p. 93.
43 Leppingwell, "Restructuring the Russian Military," p.20.
44 Suzanne Crow and Stephen Foye, in *RFE/RL Daily Report*, no. 38, February 24, 1994.

45 Estimated by UN sources. "Caucasus City Falls to Armenian Forces," *New York Times*, August 24, 1993, p. A7, and passim.
46 Coverage in the NKAO section is based on the reports in *New York Times, Ottawa Citizen, RFE/RL Research Reports* and *News Briefs* and Robert V. Barylski, "The Caucasus, Central Asia and Near Abroad Syndrome," Conclusion, *Central Asia Monitor*, 5 (1993), pp. 21–28.
47 "Turk says Russia is Tangled in Caucasus War," *New York Times*, April 15, 1993, p. A9.
48 Chervonnaya, "Technology of the Abkhazian War."
49 "Georgian Leader Charges Atrocity," *New York Times*, September 29, 1993, p. A9.
50 Steven Greenhouse, "Georgian Asks U.S. to Back Peace Force," *New York Times*, March 8, 1994, p. A10.
51 Barylski, "Caucasus," Part I, *Central Asia Monitor* 4 (1993), pp. 31–37; and Ludmila Leontyeva, "Where Do Russia's Southern Borders Pass?," *Moscow News*, no. 46, November 12, 1993, p. 12. Except for the Abkhaz and South Ossetia, the others (including North Ossetia) are located in the Russian Federation. The Chechen and the Ingush were deported to Central Asia in World War Two, and were allowed to return only after Stalin's death. In the meantime the Ossetins took over Ingush property and have been unwilling to give it back. This has led to fighting and eventually Russian peacekeeping.
52 Celestine Bohlen, "Russia and Georgia Sign Military Cooperation Treaty," *New York Times*, February 4, 1994. Other sources used in this section were Raymond Bonner, "Pact with Russia Bedevils Georgian," ibid., December 9, 1993; Barylski, "The Caucasus," Part I, pp. 35–37; Akaki Mikadze, "CIS Worse than Slavery?," *Moscow News*, no. 42, October 15, 1993, p. 4.
53 "News and Comments," *Central Asia Monitor* 1 (1994), p. 2.
54 *RFE/RL News Briefs*, December 11–24, 1993, esp. Suzanne Crow, December 23, p. 12.
55 Barylski, "Caucasus . . . ," Conclusions, pp. 24–27; Steven Erlanger, "Troops in Ex-Soviet Lands," *New York Times*, November 30, 1993, pp. A1 and A12; "News and Comments," *Central Asia Monitor* 5 (1993), pp. 1–2 and 7.
56 Barylski, "Caucasus . . . ," Conclusions, p. 35; "News and Comments," *Central Asia Monitor* 5 (1993), p. 3, and "Russia Agrees to Patrol Turkmenistan Borders," *New York Times*, December 24, 1993.
57 Suzanne Crow, "The Theory and Practice of Peacekeeping in the Former USSR," *RFE/RL Research Report* 1, no. 37 (September 18, 1992), pp. 31–36.
58 Vladimir Socor, "Moldova: Democracy Advances, Independence at Risk," *RFE/RL Research Report* 3, no. 1 (January 7, 1994), pp. 47–50.

59 Belarus joined the military and economic union under the CIS in December and the reform pro-independence president, Stanislav Shushkevich, was ousted by Parliament in January. The leader of the opposition described the removal as "a creeping communist coup aimed at eliminating Belarussian statehood," while his deputy said: "Now the last stage of the reconstitution of the Russian empire will begin." Steven Erlanger, "Belarus Says Aide's Ouster Won't Stop Reform," *New York Times*, January 28, 1994.
60 In the candid opinion of two military specialists (General Dworkin and Dr. Alexei Arbatov), a showdown with Ukraine is coming, with or without a nuclear dimension. *CNA Seminar Report* (July 9, 1993).
61 Crow, "Russian Peacekeeping," pp. 39–40.
62 Lyudmila Telen, "Yugoslavia: the Russians Have Come," and Igor Nekrasov, "As Told by Yuri Belyayev," *Moscow News Weekly*, no. 49, 1992, p. 12.
63 *New York Times*, February 16–22, 1994, passim.
64 Douglas Jake, "Serbs Compliance Cheers US Aids," ibid., February 21, 1994, p. A6.
65 *RFE/RL News Briefs*, August 30–September 3, 1993; and Suzanne Crow, September 1, 1993, p. 4.
66 Andrei Kozyrev, "Don't Threaten Us," *New York Times*, March 18, 1994, p. A29.
67 Afanasyev, "Russia's Vicious Circle."

Chapter Twelve:

1 Dépêche de l'Agence France-Presse, 14 novembre 1993.
2 Pour une description de la situation au Cambodge entre 1970 et 1991, voir Ricolas Regaud, *Le Cambodge dans la tourmente*. Paris : Éditions L'Harmattan-FEDN, 1992.
3 Jarat Chopra, John MacKinlay et Larry Minear, *Report on the Cambodian Peace Process*. Oslo : The Norwegian Institute for International Affairs, 1993, p. 15.
4 Jean-Claude Pomonti, "L'accord de Paris sur le Cambodge met fin à plus de vingt ans de conflits," *Le Monde*, 24 octobre 1991, p. 1. Patrice de Beer, "La plus importante opération de l'histoire des Nations Unies," *Le Monde*, 24 octobre 1991, p. 8.
5 Nations Unies, résolution 717, 16 octobre 1991.
6 La participation canadienne à cette mission de paix était minuscule. Le Canada a dépêché un contingent de 215 personnes qui était formé de membres du génie, d'une unité de transport, de personnel pour le quartier général de l'APRONUC et d'observateurs militaires navals. Dans ce dernier cas, c'était la première fois que du personnel de la

Marine canadienne participait à une opération de paix. Trente militaires canadiens ont eu pour tâche de patrouiller les eaux territoriales cambodgiennes ainsi que les fleuves du pays. Enfin, le commandant du contingent canadien, le colonel George Focsaneanu, était responsable de l'Unité d'entraînement pour le déminage.

7 Nations Unies, résolution 745, 28 février 1992 et communiqué de presse de l'APRONUC, 26 février 1993.

8 Nations Unies, document numéro S/23613, 19 février 1992.

9 Chopra, Mackinlay et Minear, *Report on the Cambodian Peace Process*, p. 20.

10 Nations Unies, document numéro S/23613, pp. 12 à 16.

11 Patrice de Beer, "L'ONU au chevet du Cambodge," *Le Monde*, 3 mars 1992.

12 Nations Unies, document numéro S/23870, 1er mai 1992, p. 5.

13 Jean-Claude Pomonti, "Les Khmers rouges multiplient les violations de l'accord de paix," *Le Monde*, 2 juin 1992.

14 Nations Unies, documents numéros S/24286, 14 juillet 1992, et S/24578, 21 septembre 1992.

15 Nations Unies, résolution 783, 13 octobre 1992.

16 Nations Unies, document numéro S/24800, 15 novembre 1992, p. 2.

17 Nations Unies, résolution 792, 30 novembre 1992.

18 Nations Unies, *Requirements for United Nations Peacekeeping*, document numéro A/45/217, 8 mai 1990.

19 Entretiens avec le commandant adjoint de la composante militaire, le brigadier général Robert Rideau, 10 avril 1993; le commandant des forces canadiennes, le lieutenant-colonel George Focsaneanu, 23 avril 1993; le diplomate Jean-Marc Parent du Quai d'Orsay, 8 novembre 1993; et de nombreux Casques bleus au Cambodge entre le 9 et le 23 avril 1993.

20 Entretien avec le chef du contingent français au Cambodge, le colonel Yves de Kermabon, 12 avril 1993.

21 UNTAC, Detention of UNTAC Personnel, 4 mars 1993. UNTAC, Fatalities of civilian and military personnel while serving with UNTAC, 15 avril 1993.

22 *Guideline Standard Operating Procedures for Peace-keeping Operations*, UN Restricted, document numéro 91-15137. Pas de date de publication.

23 Le Cambodge ou la paix enlisée, Québec, Centre québécois des relations internationales, Bulletin numéro 4, avril 1993, p. 4.

24 Entrevues avec des légionnaires français au Cambodge du 12 au 15 avril 1993.

25 Transcription de la présentation du lieutenant-colonel S. H. Ayling, dans Chief of the General Staff Exercise, Canungra, Australie, du 21 au 25 juin 1993, p. 186.

26 Rémi Favret, "Cambodge : la peur à l'ombre d'Anghor," *Le Figaro*, 12 mars 1993.
27 Entretiens avec des Casques bleus au Cambodge, du 9 au 23 avril 1993.
28 William J. Durch, "Running the Show : Planning and Implementation," dans William J. Durch, dir., *The Evolution of UN Peacekeeping*. New York : St. Martin's Press, 1993, pp. 64–65.
29 Michel Loridon, "Le rôle des Casques bleus," *Le Casoar*, juillet 1993, p. 30.
30 Nations Unies, document numéro S/24286, 14 juillet 1992, p. 4.
31 Entretien avec Yasushi Akashi au Cambodge, 21 avril 1993.
32 Ibid.
33 Philip Shenon, "Khmer Rouge Reported to Attack Chinese and Polish Peacekeepers," *The New York Times*, 6 mai 1993.
34 Philip Shenon, "Actions of Japan Peacekeepers in Cambodia Raise Questions and Criticism," *The New York Times*, 24 octobre 1993, p. 8.
35 Nations Unies, document numéro S/25913, 10 juin 1993.
36 Nations Unies, document numéro S/26529, 5 octobre 1993.
37 William J. Durch, "Introduction," dans William J. Durch, dir., *The Evolution of UN Peacekeeping*. New York: St. Martin's Press, 1993, p. 12.
38 William J. Durch, "Getting Involved : The Political-Military Context," dans William J. Durch, dir., *The Evolution of UN Peacekeeping*. St. Martin's Press, 1993, pp. 16–38.
39 René Backmann, "Le nouveau défi de Pol Pot." *Le Nouvel Observateur*, 26 mars 1993, pp. 34–36. Jean-Claude Chapon, "Les principales forces en présence," dépêche de l'Agence France-Presse, 16 mai 1993.
40 Entretien avec Jarat Chopra, chercheur au Thomas J. Watson Jr. Institute for International Studies, Brown University, qui a passé plusieurs semaines au Cambodge, 23 novembre 1993. Dans son entretien du 21 avril, M. Akashi affirme que "le contrôle des cinq ministères fonctionne bien. Nous surveillons les activités du gouvernement de Phnom Penh."
41 Entretien avec Yasushi Akashi, 21 avril 1993.

Chapter Thirteen:

1 In the Human Development Report of 1991, for instance, Somalia is ranked at 149 of 160; the 1993 report lists it at 166 of 173. *Human Development Report, 1991 and 1993* (Oxford and New York: Oxford University Press, 1991 and 1993).
2 Hassan Hirave, "The Intricate Bonds of the Somali Clans,"*Globe and Mail* (Toronto), September 3, 1993.

3 Bernard Bennell, "How a Saviour became a Warlord," *Globe and Mail*, September 3, 1993.
4 Martin Wollacott, "Why Rambo's Boot has no Place on Somalia's Door," *The Guardian* (London), December 6, 1992.
5 Ibid.
6 Department of External Affairs and International Trade, Communications Division, "Canada's Response to the Crisis in Somalia," November 1993, p. 1.
7 James Sutterlin, "Military Force in the Service of Peace," *Aurora Papers* 18 (Ottawa: Canadian Centre for Global Security, June 1993), p. 24.
8 Jeffrey Clark, "Chronology of a Catastrophe," *The Humanitarian Monitor: Quarterly Review of Humanitarian Issues in the Horn of Africa* (June 1993), p. 6.
9 Malcolm Fraser, president of CARE International, for instance, wrote to President Bush in November, setting out the case for American involvement in order to provide a secure environment for the delivery of humanitarian aid. Officials from CARE later met with high-level State Department officers to discuss their ideas in more detail.
10 UN Document S/24868, November 29, 1992, quoted in Sutterlin, "Military Force," p. 24.
11 Ibid.
12 Keith B. Richburg, "The U.S. and Somalia: Passing the Torch," *Humanitarian Monitor* (June 1993), p. 6.
13 James Sutterlin, "Military Force," p. 26.
14 UN Security Council Resolution 794, December 3, 1992 (emphasis added).
15 James Sutterlin, "Military Force," p. 26.
16 Julian Ozanne, "After the Somali Intervention: A Challenge for Africa," *Humanitarian Monitor* (June 1993), p. 13.

Chapter Fourteen:

1 Duncan Wilson, *Tito's Yugoslavia* (Cambridge: Cambridge University Press, 1979), p. 202.
2 For more detailed election results, see Lenard J. Cohen, *Broken Bonds* (Boulder: Westview Press, 1993), pp. 88–90.
3 Ibid.
4 John Zametica, "The Yugoslav Conflict," *Adelphi Paper* 270 (Summer 1992), pp. 64–65.
5 Cohen, *Broken Bonds*, p. 237.
6 Major-General Lewis MacKenzie, *Peacekeeper: The Road to Sarajevo* (Vancouver and Toronto: Douglas and McIntyre, 1993), p. 106.
7 UN Security Council Document S/24540, September 10, 1992, para. 9.